T0192142

Communications in Computer and Information Science 1693

More information about this series at https://link.springer.com/bookseries/7899

Zhiping Cai · Yijia Chen · Jialin Zhang (Eds.)

Theoretical Computer Science

40th National Conference, NCTCS 2022 Changchun, China, July 29–31, 2022 Revised Selected Papers

Editors
Zhiping Cai
National University of Defense Technology
Changsha, China

Yijia Chen
Shanghai Jiao Tong University
Shanghai, China

Jialin Zhang
Chinese Academy of Sciences
Beijing, China

ISSN 1865-0929 ISSN 1865-0937 (electronic)
Communications in Computer and Information Science
ISBN 978-981-19-8151-7 ISBN 978-981-19-8152-4 (eBook)
https://doi.org/10.1007/978-981-19-8152-4

This Springer imprint is published by the registered company Springer Nature Singapore Pte Ltd.
The registered company address is: 152 Beach Road, #21-01/04 Gateway East, Singapore 189721, Singapore

Preface

The National Conference of Theoretical Computer Science (NCTCS) has become one of the most important academic platforms for theoretical computer science in China. So far, NCTCS has been successfully held in more than 20 regions of China, providing a place for exchange and cooperation for researchers in theoretical computer science and related fields.

NCTCS 2022 was hosted by the China Computer Federation (CCF) and organized by the Theoretical Computer Science Committee of the China Computer Society along with the School of Information Science and Technology of Northeast Normal University. It was held from July 29 to July 31, 2022 in Changchun, Jilin. This conference invited famous scholars in the field of theoretical computer science to give presentations, and carried out a wide range of academic activities and showed the latest research results. In total, 221 people registered for NCTCS 2022, and 353 authors submitted 108 papers between them (43 papers were finally accepted). We invited 97 reviewers from colleges and universities for peer review (single blind), where the average number of papers assigned to each reviewer was three and average number of reviews per paper was also three. All papers were managed through the Online Submission System (CCF Consys), and more details can be found on the website: https://conf.ccf.org.cn/TCS2022.

This volume contains 19 of the accepted papers for NCTCS 2022, included under four topical headings: Computational Theory and Model (four papers), Approximation Algorithms (three papers), Artificial Intelligence (seven papers), and System and Resource Scheduling (five papers). These papers cover the spectrum of theoretical computer science and were selected for the quality of presentation and technical content.

The proceedings editors wish to thank the dedicated Program Committee members and external reviewers for their hard work in reviewing and selecting papers. We also thank Springer for their trust and for publishing the proceedings of NCTCS 2022.

September 2022

Zhiping Cai
Yijia Chen
Jialin Zhang

Organization

General Chairs

Xiaoming Sun	Chinese Academy of Sciences, China
Haiyang Xu	Northeast Normal University, China

Program Committee Chairs

Zhiping Cai	National University of Defense Technology, China
Yijia Chen	Shanghai Jiao Tong University, China
Jialin Zhang	Chinese Academy of Sciences, China

Steering Committee

Xiaoming Sun	Chinese Academy of Sciences, China
Jianping Yin	Dongguan University of Technology, China
Lian Li	Hefei University of Technology, China
En Zhu	National University of Defense Technology, China
Kun He	Huazhong University of Science and Technology, China

Area Chairs

Kerong Ben	Naval University of Engineering, China
Kun He	Huazhong University of Science and Technology, China
En Zhu	National University of Defense Technology, China
Yitong Yin	Nanjing University, China
Mingyu Xiao	University of Electronic Science and Technology, China
Lvzhou Li	Sun Yat-sen University, China

Program Committee

Jigang Wu	Guangdong University of Technology, China
Lei Luo	National University of Defense Technology, China
Zhaoming Huang	Guangxi Medical University, China
Zhiyi Huang	University of Hong Kong, China
Xin Han	Dalian University of Technology, China
Zhigang Chen	Central South University, China
Juan Chen	National University of Defense Technology, China
Jun Long	Jide Technology Company, China
Cheng Zhong	Guangxi University, China
Zhanyou Ma	North Minzu University, China
Huanlai Xing	Southwest Jiaotong University, China
Kerong Ben	Naval University of Engineering, China
Yicheng Xu	Shenzhen Institute of Advanced Technology, CAS, China
Mengting Yuan	Wuhan University, China
Jinyun Xue	Jiangxi Normal University, China
Zhiping Cai	National University of Defense Technology, China
Naijie Gu	University of Science and Technology of China, China
Meihua Xiao	East China Jiaotong University, China
Biaoshuai Tao	Shanghai Jiao Tong University, China
Jiaohua Qin	Central South University of Forestry and Technology, China
En Zhu	National University of Defense Technology, China
Feng Shi	Central South University, China
Guojing Tian	Institute of Computing Technology, CAS, China
Changjing Wang	Jiangxi Normal University, China
Gang Wang	Nankai University, China
Haiyu Pan	Guilin University of Electronic Technology, China
Hong Zheng	East China University of Science and Technology, China
Dantong Ouyang	Jilin University, China
Shenggen Zheng	Pengcheng Laboratory, China
Yu Yang	Pingdingshan University, China
Ming Zhao	Central South University, China
Yan Yang	Southwest Jiaotong University, China
Yuncheng Jiang	South China Normal University, China

Qian Li	Shenzhen Institute of Computing Sciences, China
Dongjing Miao	Harbin Institute of Technology, China
Yongzhi Cao	Peking University, China
Zhengwei Qi	Shanghai Jiao Tong University, China
Qi Fu Hunan	University of Science and Technology, China
Peng Zhang	Shandong University, China
Chihao Zhang	Shanghai Jiao Tong University, China
Yong Zhang	Shenzhen Institute of Advanced Technology, CAS, China
Yong Gan	Zhengzhou University of Light Industry, China
Zhao Zhang	Zhejiang Normal University, China
Jialin Zhang	Institute of Computing Technology, CAS, China
Hao Liao	Shenzhen University, China
Zhengkang Zuo	Jiangxi Normal University, China
Yitong Yin	Nanjing University, China
Penghui Yao	Nanjing University, China
Feng Qin	Jiangxi Normal University, China
Zhihao Tang	Shanghai University of Finance and Economics, China
Mengji Xia	Institute of Software, Chinese Academy of Sciences, China
Chang Tang	China University of Geosciences, China
Nan Wu	Nanjing University, China
Shuai Lu	Jilin University, China
Liwei Wang	Wuhan University, China
Wenjun Li	Changsha University of Science and Technology, China
Zhanshan Li	Jilin University, China
Zhendong Liu	Shandong Jianzhu University, China
Jin Wang	Changsha University of Science and Technology, China
Xiaofeng Wang	North Minzu University, China
Qiang Liu	National University of Defense Technology, China
Zhen You	Jiangxi Normal University, China
Aiguo Wang	Foshan University, China
Jiaoyun Yang	Hefei University of Technology, China
Qilong Feng	Central South University, China
Kun He	Huazhong University of Science and Technology, China
Kun He	Institute of Computing Technology, CAS, China
Hengfu Yang	Hunan First Normal University, China
Min-ming Li	City University of Hong Kong, China

Yongming Li	Shaanxi Normal University, China
Tongyang Li	Peking University, China
Jian Li	Tsinghua University, China
Kuan Li	Dongguan University of Technology, China
Bo Li	The Hong Kong Polytechnic University, China
Daming Zhu	Shandong University, China
Liming Zhang	Jilin University, China
Yuhao Zhang	Shanghai Jiao Tong University, China
Lei Zhuang	Zhengzhou University, China
Zhengjun Xi	Shaanxi Normal University, China
ShaofengJiang	Peking University, China
Xiaoyan Kui	Central South University, China
Xiaoyong Tang	Changsha University of Science and Technology, China
Qingyang Zhou	National University of Defense Technology, China
Yi Zhou	University of Electronic Science and Technology of China, China
Rigui Zhou	Shanghai Maritime University, China
Jinzhao Wu	Guangxi Minzu University, China
Yuxin Ye	Jilin University, China
Panyu Liu	National University of Defense Technology, China
Yuling Liu	Hunan University, China
Xinwang Liu	National University of Defense Technology, China
Peiqiang Liu	Shandong Technology and Business University, China
Shengxin Liu	Harbin Institute of Technology, Shenzhen, China
Huawen Liu	Zhejiang Normal University, China
Zhenyan Ji	Beijing Jiaotong University, China
Cai Dai	Shaanxi Normal University, China
Hai Wan	Sun Yat-sen University, China
Chau Vincent	Southeast University, China

Contents

Computational Theory and Model

General-Nondeterministic Fuzzy Pushdown Automata and Their Languages

Fangping Zhou and Chao Yang(✉)

College of Information Engineering, Yangzhou University, Yangzhou 225127, China
yangzzfp@163.com, yangch12@yzu.edu.cn

Abstract. Inspired by nondeterministic fuzzy finite automata theory proposed by Cao and Ezawa [1], we define general-nondeterministic fuzzy pushdown automata (GN-FPDAs). For a GN-FPDA, the fuzzy transition function in a state may have more than one transitions labeled by the same input symbol and stack symbol, which apparently reflects nondeterminism. Here, it is also shown that the set of fuzzy languages accepted by GN-FPDAs by final states is coincide with that accepted by GN-FPDAs by empty stack. Amazingly, with help of the Pumping lemma of fuzzy context-free languages, we elaborate that GN-FPDAs accept more kinds of languages than common fuzzy pushdown automata. Furthermore, we introduce general-nondeterministic fuzzy context-free grammars (GN-FCFGs) and investigate the relationship between GN-FPDAs and GN-FCFGs. In addition, taking advantage of GN-FCFGs, the closure properties of operations, such as union, intersection, concatenation and Kleene closure, on the set of fuzzy languages accepted by GN-FPDAs are discussed in detail.

Keywords: Fuzzy language · General-nondeterministic fuzzy pushdown automaton · General-nondeterministic fuzzy context-free grammar · Closure property

1 Introduction

To bridge the gap between the accuracy of formal languages and the vagueness of natural languages in our real life, fuzzy automata theory and fuzzy languages have been paid much attention by a host of scholars. So far, applications of fuzzy automata in a wealth of areas including model checking, word-based computational model, pattern recognition, and automata theory can be found in [2–7]. Initially, Wee [8] was the first to propose the concept of fuzzy automata which may go from the current state to another state equipping with a certain possibility degree. In the sequel, fuzzy automata can represent nondeterminism appearing in state transitions of fuzzy systems [9–11]. Lee and Zadeh [12] put forward the concept of fuzzy languages and studied their properties. Besides, some algebraic properties of fuzzy languages were discussed in [13,14]. However, fuzzy automata have shortcomings in dealing with the problem of language recognition. Therefore, Bucurescu and Pascu [15] introduced the concept

Z. Cai et al. (Eds.): NCTCS 2022, CCIS 1693, pp. 3–25, 2022.
https://doi.org/10.1007/978-981-19-8152-4_1

of fuzzy pushdown automata which are regarded as another kind of satisfactory mathematical models. Here, we enumerate some works on them for readers of interest [16–23]. In order to improve the processing ability of fuzzy pushdown automata, several variants of fuzzy pushdown automata have been investigated. Xing [24] introduced the concept of fuzzy pushdown automata based on lattice-ordered structure and studied their behaviors. Also, Xing et al. [25] established fuzzy pushdown automata in the framework of complete residuated lattice-valued logic and proved that the sets of languages accepted by final states and by empty stack in them are the same. Furthermore, Han and Li [26] showed that orthomodular lattice-valued pushdown automata can be constructed from orthomodular lattice-valued context-free grammars and vice versa.

It is worth noting that the nondeterminism in common nondeterministic fuzzy automata is not a real sense of nondeterminism. As its consequence, Cao and Ezawa [1] introduced fuzzy automata with nondeterminism to establish more computational models and give a mathematical representation of nondeterministic fuzzy systems [27]. At the same time, they verified that the nondeterministic fuzzy automata they defined have the same recognition ability as original nondeterministic fuzzy automata. Based on this, we will extend ideas of nondeterminism proposed by Cao and Ezawa to fuzzy pushdown automata. Meanwhile, in order to distinguish the common nondeterministic fuzzy pushdown automata, we will name the new model we defined in this paper as general-nondeterministic fuzzy pushdown automaton (GN-FPDA). Additionally, we introduce the concept of general-nondeterministic fuzzy context-free grammars (GN-FCFGs) and call languages generated by them general-nondeterministic fuzzy context-free languages (GN-FCFLs).

A crucial theoretical problem here to consider is whether common fuzzy pushdown automata are equivalent to GN-FPDAs, that is, they accept the same fuzzy languages. Whereafter, we find a fuzzy language accepted by a GN-FPDA which does not satisfy the Pumping lemma of fuzzy context-free languages as shown in Lemma 5. As a result, we have that the set of fuzzy languages accepted by GN-FPDAs strictly contains that accepted by common fuzzy pushdown automata. Moreover, we show that GN-FPDAs are equivalent to GN-FCFGs (see Theorem 18 and Theorem 19). And then, utilizing GN-FCFGs, we conclude that the set of GN-FCFLs is closed under the operations of union, concatenation and Kleene closure. Finally, we show that the intersection of GN-FCFL and fuzzy regular language is recognizable by a GN-FPDA. The most important contribution of our work is that we give an hierarchy of the sets of fuzzy languages accepted by some kinds of fuzzy pushdown automata (see Corollary 12). The advantage of the study of GN-FPDAs is that we can apply them to model fuzzy discrete event systems with nondeterminism. The achievements of this paper can also be used in web application [28], model checking [29], and in other fields.

The paper is organized in the following ways. Section 2 reviews some basic notions. Section 3 introduces GN-FPDAs and deliberates on the inclusion relation between the set of fuzzy languages accepted by common fuzzy pushdown automata and that accepted by GN-FPDAs. Section 4 introduces GN-FCFGs and studies the relationship between GN-FCFGs and GN-FPDAs. In addition, the closure properties of some operations on the set of GN-FCFLs are discussed.

2 Preliminaries

At first, we give some basic notions to which be referred in the following. For any $a, b \in [0, 1]$, we write $\vee$ and $\wedge$ for the maximum operation and the minimum operation of $\{a, b\}$, respectively. The symbols "$\bigvee$" and "$\bigwedge$" are interpreted as the supremum and the infimum of real numbers contained in [0, 1], respectively. Meanwhile, J is used to denote the index set.

Let A and A' be classic sets. Then $A \subseteq A'$ represents that A' contains A (or A is contained in A'), and $A \subset A'$ represents that A' strictly contains A (or A is strictly contained in A'). $|A|$ stands for the number of elements in A. If $|A| = 0$, then we say that A is a null set, denoted by $\emptyset$.

Let Σ be a finite alphabet and Σ^* is the set of all finite strings over Σ. We use ε to denote the empty string. $l(\theta)$ means the length of θ for any $\theta \in \Sigma^*$. For any natural number i, $\theta^i = \underbrace{\theta\theta\cdots\theta}_{i}$ and $\theta^0 = \varepsilon$.

Let A be a nonempty set. A fuzzy subset of A is a mapping $f : A \to [0, 1]$. We use $\mathcal{F}(A)$ to denote the set of all fuzzy subsets of A, namely, $\mathcal{F}(A) = \{f \mid f : A \to [0, 1]\}$. If $f(a) \in \{0, 1\}$ for any $a \in A$, then the fuzzy subset f degrades into the crisp one. The support set of a fuzzy subset f is a crisp set, defined as follows:

$$supp(f) = \{a \in A | f(a) > 0\}. \tag{1}$$

Note that a fuzzy subset is empty when its support set is empty. We write Φ the empty fuzzy subset. We say $supp(f) = \{a_1, a_2, \cdots, a_n\}$ whenever $supp(f)$ is finite and we can write f in Zadeh's notation as

$$f = \frac{f(a_1)}{a_1} + \frac{f(a_2)}{a_2} + \cdots + \frac{f(a_n)}{a_n}. \tag{2}$$

2.1 Fuzzy Languages and Fuzzy Pushdown Automata

We firstly recall the concept of fuzzy languages. As shown in [30], a fuzzy language f over Σ is a fuzzy subset of Σ^*. Let f_1 and f_2 be fuzzy languages over Σ. The equality of f_1 and f_2 is defined as: $f_1 = f_2$ if and only if $f_1(\theta) = f_2(\theta)$, for any $\theta \in \Sigma^*$. By the above definition of fuzzy languages, we use $\mathcal{FL}(\Sigma^*) = \{f \mid f : \Sigma^* \to [0, 1]\}$ to denote the set of all these languages.

We now recall some operations on $\mathcal{FL}(\Sigma^*)$ (see [10,30]) such as union, intersection, concatenation, and Kleene closure.

Let f, f_1, $f_2 \in \mathcal{FL}(\Sigma^*)$. The union $f_1 \cup f_2$, the intersection $f_1 \cap f_2$, the concatenation $f_1 f_2$ and the Kleene closure f^* induced by $\vee$ and $\wedge$, are defined for any $\theta \in \Sigma^*$ by

$$(f_1 \cup f_2)(\theta) = f_1(\theta) \vee f_2(\theta), \tag{3}$$

$$(f_1 \cap f_2)(\theta) = f_1(\theta) \wedge f_2(\theta), \tag{4}$$

$$(f_1 f_2)(\theta) = \bigvee_{\theta_1\theta_2=\theta} [f_1(\theta_1) \wedge f_2(\theta_2)], \tag{5}$$

$$(f^*)(\theta) = f_\Lambda \cup f \cup ff \cup \cdots \cup f^n \cup \cdots, \tag{6}$$

where

$$f_\Lambda(\theta) = \begin{cases} 1, & \theta = \varepsilon, \\ 0, & \theta \neq \varepsilon. \end{cases}, \ f^n = f^{n-1}f.$$

We next recall the concept of fuzzy pushdown automata (FPDAs).

Definition 1 *(See [31]). A FPDA $\mathcal{M}$ is a seven-tuple $(Q, \Sigma, \Gamma, \delta, q_0, Z_0, F)$, where*

(i) Q is a finite nonempty set of states,
(ii) Σ is a finite input alphabet,
(iii) Γ is a finite stack alphabet,
(iv) $\delta : Q \times (\Sigma \cup \{\varepsilon\}) \times \Gamma \to \mathcal{F}(Q \times \Gamma^*)$, called the fuzzy transition function,
(v) $q_0 \in Q$ is the initial state,
(vi) $Z_0 \in \Gamma$ is a start stack symbol,
(vii) $F : Q \to [0, 1]$ is a fuzzy subset of Q, called the fuzzy subset of final states.

For each $q \in Q$, $F(q)$ is used to denote the possibility degree of q being a final state. The fuzzy transition function δ takes a state in Q, an input symbol in $(\Sigma \cup \{\varepsilon\})$ and a stack symbol in Γ as arguments and returns a possibility distribution on $Q \times \Gamma^*$. Concretely, for any $q, p \in Q$, $\sigma \in (\Sigma \cup \{\varepsilon\})$, $Z \in \Gamma$, and $\gamma \in \Gamma^*$, $\delta(q, \sigma, Z)(p, \gamma)$ means the possibility degree that the FPDA in state q and the top stack symbol Z, with input symbol σ, may enter next state p and replace Z with γ.

Formally, in order to describe a FPDA's configuration, we define $(q, w, \gamma) \in Q \times \Sigma^* \times \Gamma^*$ as an instantaneous description (ID) which records that the FPDA is in the current state q, and has remaining input string w and the contents of stack γ.

Let $\alpha, \beta \in \Gamma^*$. If there exists $\gamma \in \Gamma^*$ such that $\alpha = \gamma\beta$, then we call that β is the tail of α (i.e., $\beta = tail(\alpha)$), denoted by $\beta \leq \alpha$ and $\gamma = \alpha \backslash \beta$. We use $head(\beta)$ to denote the first symbol of β. For any $(p, w, \beta), (q, v, \alpha) \in Q \times \Sigma^* \times \Gamma^*$, the extension of δ, denoted by ∇, is as follows:

$$\nabla((p, w, \beta), (q, v, \alpha)) =$$
$$\begin{cases} \delta(p, \varepsilon, head(\beta))(q, \alpha \backslash tail(\beta)), & \text{if } v = w, tail(\beta) \leq \alpha, \\ \delta(p, head(w), head(\beta))(q, \alpha \backslash tail(\beta)), & \text{if } v = tail(w), tail(\beta) \leq \alpha, \\ 0 & \text{otherwise.} \end{cases}$$

Note that ∇^* is the reflexive and transitive closure of ∇. Based on this, there are two ways to define the fuzzy language accepted by $\mathcal{M}$.

(i) The fuzzy language $L_{\mathcal{P}}(\mathcal{M}) \in \mathcal{FL}(\Sigma^*)$ accepted by $\mathcal{M}$ by final states is defined for any $\theta \in \Sigma^*$ by:

$$L_{\mathcal{P}}(\mathcal{M})(\theta) = \bigvee_{q\in Q,\gamma\in\Gamma^*} [\nabla^*((q_0,\theta,Z_0),(q,\varepsilon,\gamma)) \wedge F(q)]. \tag{7}$$

(ii) The fuzzy language $N_{\mathcal{P}}(\mathcal{M}) \in \mathcal{FL}(\Sigma^*)$ accepted by $\mathcal{M}$ by empty stack is defined for any $\theta \in \Sigma^*$ by:

$$N_{\mathcal{P}}(\mathcal{M})(\theta) = \bigvee_{q\in Q} \nabla^*((q_0,\theta,Z_0),(q,\varepsilon,\varepsilon)). \tag{8}$$

Theorem 2 *(See [31]). For any FPDA $\mathcal{M}$, there exists a FPDA $\mathcal{M}'$ such that $N_{\mathcal{P}}(\mathcal{M}') = L_{\mathcal{P}}(\mathcal{M})$ and vice versa.*

We use $\mathcal{F}_{\mathcal{P}}(\Sigma^*)$ to denote the set of all fuzzy languages over Σ accepted by FPDAs.

Finally, we turn to the concept of deterministic fuzzy pushdown automata (DFPDAs).

Given a FPDA $\mathcal{M} = (Q,\Sigma,\Gamma,\delta,q_0,Z_0,F)$. If the fuzzy transition function δ is deterministic and crisp, i.e., δ is a function from $Q\times(\Sigma\cup\{\varepsilon\})\times\Gamma$ to $Q\times\Gamma^*$ and F is a fuzzy subset of $Q\times\Gamma^*$, then $\mathcal{M}$ is called a DFPDA. For any $(p,w,\beta),(q,v,\alpha)\in Q\times\Sigma^*\times\Gamma^*$, we write ∇ the extension of transition function δ, i.e.,

$$\nabla((p,w,\beta),(q,v,\alpha)) = \begin{cases} \delta(p,\varepsilon,head(\beta)), & \text{if } v=w, tail(\beta)\le\alpha,\\ \delta(p,head(w),head(\beta)), & \text{if } v=tail(w), tail(\beta)\le\alpha,\\ 0 & \text{otherwise,}\end{cases}$$

where $\delta(p,\varepsilon,head(\beta)) = \delta(p,head(w),head(\beta)) = (q,\alpha\backslash tail(\beta))$. Meanwhile, ∇^* is also used to represent the reflexive and transitive closure of ∇.

Analogously, a fuzzy language accepted by DFPDA $\mathcal{M}$ is defined in two distinct ways. One is by final states

$$L_{\mathcal{D}}(\mathcal{M})(\theta) = F[\nabla^*((q_0,\theta,Z_0),(q,\varepsilon,\gamma))], \tag{9}$$

where q is a final state, and the other is by empty stack

$$N_{\mathcal{D}}(\mathcal{M})(\theta) = F[\nabla^*((q_0,\theta,Z_0),(q,\varepsilon,\varepsilon)], \tag{10}$$

for any $\theta\in\Sigma^*$.

We use $\mathcal{F}_{\mathcal{D}}(\Sigma^*)$ to denote the set of all fuzzy languages over Σ accepted by DFPDAs. Then, we have that $\mathcal{F}_{\mathcal{D}}(\Sigma^*)\subset\mathcal{F}_{\mathcal{P}}(\Sigma^*)$.

2.2 Fuzzy Context-Free Grammars and Their Languages

Firstly, we recall the concept of fuzzy context-free grammars (FCFGs).

Definition 3 *(See [31]). A FCFG $\mathcal{G}$ is a quadruple (V, T, P, S), where*

(i) V is the set of variables,
(ii) T is the set of terminals, and $V \cap T = \emptyset$,
(iii) $S \in V$ is the start symbol,
(iv) P is a finite set of fuzzy productions of the form $u \xrightarrow{\rho} v$, where $u \in V, v \in (V \cup T)^*$, $|u| \leq |v|$, and $\rho \in [0,1]$ stands for the possibility degree of u producing v.

Formally, in order to define the fuzzy language generated by FCFG $\mathcal{G}$, we firstly define two fuzzy relations $\underset{\mathcal{G}}{\overset{\rho}{\Rightarrow}}$ and $\underset{\mathcal{G}^*}{\overset{\rho}{\Rightarrow}}$ on $(V \cup T)^* \times (V \cup T)^*$, with possibility degree ρ, respectively. For simplicity, if no confusion occurs, then we use $\overset{\rho}{\Rightarrow}$ and $\underset{*}{\overset{\rho}{\Rightarrow}}$ instead of $\underset{\mathcal{G}}{\overset{\rho}{\Rightarrow}}$ and $\underset{\mathcal{G}^*}{\overset{\rho}{\Rightarrow}}$, respectively. Furthermore, for $\alpha, \beta \in (V \cup T)^*$, $\alpha u \beta \overset{\rho}{\Rightarrow} \alpha v \beta$ denotes that $\alpha u \beta$ directly derives $\alpha v \beta$ by applying the production $u \xrightarrow{\rho} v \in P$. Note that $\underset{*}{\overset{\rho}{\Rightarrow}}$ indicates the reflexive and transitive closure of $\overset{\rho}{\Rightarrow}$. For $u_i \in (V \cup T)^* (1 \leq i \leq n)$, if $u_1 \overset{\rho_1}{\Rightarrow} u_2 \overset{\rho_2}{\Rightarrow} \cdots \overset{\rho_{n-1}}{\Rightarrow} u_n$, then we say that u_1 derives u_n, denoted by $u_1 \underset{*}{\overset{\rho}{\Rightarrow}} u_n$ where $\rho = \rho_1 \wedge \rho_2 \wedge \cdots \wedge \rho_{n-1}$.

The fuzzy language $f_{\mathcal{G}}$ generated by $\mathcal{G}$ is a fuzzy subset of T^*, defined by

$$f_{\mathcal{G}}(w) = \bigvee \{\rho | S \underset{*}{\overset{\rho}{\Rightarrow}} w\}, \tag{11}$$

for any $w \in T^*$.

If $f \in \mathcal{FL}(\Sigma^*)$ and there exists a FCFG $\mathcal{G} = (V, \Sigma, P, S)$ such that $f = f_{\mathcal{G}}$, then we say that $\mathcal{G}$ generates f (or f is generated by $\mathcal{G}$) and call f a fuzzy context-free language over Σ. We use $\mathcal{FCFL}(\Sigma^*)$ to denote the set of all fuzzy context-free languages over Σ. Evidently, $\mathcal{FCFL}(\Sigma^*) \subseteq \mathcal{FL}(\Sigma^*)$. We also have that some operations we mentioned above are closed in $\mathcal{FCFL}(\Sigma^*)$, in other words, if $f_1, f_2 \in \mathcal{FCFL}(\Sigma^*)$, then $f_1 \cup f_2$, $f_1 f_2$, $f_1^* \in \mathcal{FCFL}(\Sigma^*)$. The complete proofs can be seen in [31].

Theorem 4 *(See [22]). For any FPDA $\mathcal{M}$, there exists a FCFG $\mathcal{G}$ such that $f_{\mathcal{G}} = N_{\mathcal{P}}(\mathcal{M})$ and vice versa.*

Combining Theorem 2 and Theorem 4, we conclude that if $f \in \mathcal{FL}(\Sigma^*)$, then f accepted by a FPDA is a fuzzy context-free language.

As an application of Theorem 4, we recall the Pumping lemma of fuzzy context-free languages.

Lemma 5 *(See [10, 31]). Let $f \in \mathcal{FCFL}(\Sigma^*)$. There exists a positive integer N, and for any $\theta \in \Sigma^*$, if $l(\theta) \geq N$, then there exist $u, v, w, x, y \in \Sigma^*$ such that*

(i) $\theta = uvwxy$,
(ii) $l(vwx) \leq N$,
(iii) $l(vx) \geq 1$,
(iv) for any nonnegative integer i, $f(uv^iwx^iy) = f(\theta)$.

3 General-Nondeterministic Fuzzy Pushdown Automata

In this section, we are ready to define general-nondeterministic fuzzy pushdown automata (GN-FPDAs). Also, we show that two ways of accepting fuzzy languages in GN-FPDAs have the same recognition ability. Eventually, the relationship between FPDAs and GN-FPDAs is studied.

Definition 6. *A GN-FPDA $\mathcal{M}$ is a seven-tuple $(Q, \Sigma, \Gamma, \delta, q_0, Z_0, F)$ where the components $Q, \Sigma, \Gamma, q_0, Z_0, F$ are the same as those in Definition 1. The fuzzy transition function is defined by δ: $Q \times (\Sigma \cup \varepsilon) \times \Gamma \to 2^{\mathcal{F}(Q\times\Gamma^*)}$.*

For any $q \in Q$, $\sigma \in (\Sigma \cup \{\varepsilon\})$, and $Z \in \Gamma$, $\delta(q, \sigma, Z) = \{\mu_j | j \in J\}$ refers to as the set of possibility distributions on $Q \times \Gamma^*$, and for any $\mu \in \delta(q, \sigma, Z)$, $q \overset{\sigma,Z}{\to} \mu$ denotes a transition. The transition $q \overset{\sigma,Z}{\to} \mu \in \delta(q, \sigma, Z)$ expresses the nondeterministic alternatives in the current state q, with input symbol σ and the top stack symbol Z. For any q, $p \in Q$, $\gamma \in \Gamma^*$, and $\mu \in \delta(q, \sigma, Z)$, we can interpret $\mu(p, \gamma)$ as the possibility degree that the GN-FPDA in the current state q and the top stack symbol Z, with input symbol σ, may enter next state p and replace Z with γ by the fuzzy transition μ.

In comparison with Definition 1, the only difference between GN-FPDA and FPDA is their fuzzy transition functions. For any $\sigma \in (\Sigma \cup \{\varepsilon\})$ and $Z \in \Gamma$, the fuzzy transition function in each state q usually has a unique transition labeled by σ and Z in FPDA. That is, nondeterministic choices among transitions with the same input symbol and stack symbol are not allowed in a FPDA, in other words, if $q \overset{\sigma,Z}{\to} \mu_1$ and $q \overset{\sigma,Z}{\to} \mu_2$, then $\mu_1 = \mu_2$. Conversely, there may exist the fuzzy transition function in a state which has more than one transitions involving the same input symbol and stack symbol in a GN-FPDA.

Based on above facts, we shall refer to the FPDA in Definition 1 as general-deterministic fuzzy pushdown automaton (GD-FPDA). Obviously, by identifying each function $\delta : Q\times(\Sigma\cup\varepsilon)\times\Gamma \to \mathcal{F}(Q\times\Gamma^*)$ with a function $\delta' : Q\times(\Sigma\cup\varepsilon)\times\Gamma \to 2^{\mathcal{F}(Q\times\Gamma^*)}$, where δ' is defined as $\delta'(q, \sigma, Z) = \{\delta(q, \sigma, Z)\}$, GD-FPDA can be considered as the special case of GN-FPDA.

Here, the definition of an ID in GN-FPDA is the same as that in GD-FPDA. Intuitively, the GN-FPDA $\mathcal{M} = (Q, \Sigma, \Gamma, \delta, q_0, Z_0, F)$ may switch from an ID to another ID in response to the input string and we thus define a fuzzy relation, denoted by $\Re_{\mathcal{M}}$, as follows.

Next, we show an example for GN-FPDAs.

Example 7. Consider the GN-FPDA $\mathcal{M} = (Q, \Sigma, \Gamma, \delta, q_0, Z_0, F)$, where $Q = \{q_0, q_1, q_2, q_\varepsilon, q_f\}$, $\Sigma = \{0, 1\}$, $\Gamma = \{0, 1, Z_0\}$, and $F = \{\frac{0.6}{q_f}\}$. δ is given below and the transition graph of $\mathcal{M}$ is depicted in Fig. 1.

$$\delta(q_0, 0, Z_0) = \{\frac{0.8}{(q_1, 0Z_0)} + \frac{0.34}{(q_f, 0Z_0)}, \frac{0.8}{(q_2, 0Z_0)} + \frac{0.34}{(q_f, 0Z_0)}\},$$

$$\delta(q_0, 1, Z_0) = \{\frac{0.7}{(q_1, 1Z_0)} + \frac{0.23}{(q_f, 1Z_0)}, \frac{0.7}{(q_2, 1Z_0)} + \frac{0.23}{(q_f, 1Z_0)}\},$$

$$\delta(q_1,0,0) = \{\frac{0.78}{(q_0,\varepsilon)} + \frac{0.45}{(q_\varepsilon,\varepsilon)} + \frac{0.85}{(q_f,\varepsilon)}\},$$

$$\delta(q_1,1,1) = \{\frac{0.75}{(q_0,\varepsilon)} + \frac{0.5}{(q_\varepsilon,\varepsilon)} + \frac{0.58}{(q_f,\varepsilon)}\},$$

$$\delta(q_1,1,0) = \{\frac{0.58}{(q_0,\varepsilon)} + \frac{0.9}{(q_f,\varepsilon)}\}, \delta(q_1,0,1) = \{\frac{0.65}{(q_0,\varepsilon)} + \frac{0.56}{(q_f,\varepsilon)}\},$$

$$\delta(q_2,0,0) = \{\frac{0.78}{(q_0,\varepsilon)} + \frac{0.45}{(q_\varepsilon,\varepsilon)} + \frac{0.85}{(q_f,\varepsilon)}\},$$

$$\delta(q_2,1,1) = \{\frac{0.75}{(q_0,\varepsilon)} + \frac{0.5}{(q_\varepsilon,\varepsilon)} + \frac{0.58}{(q_f,\varepsilon)}\},$$

$$\delta(q_2,1,0) = \{\frac{0.58}{(q_0,\varepsilon)} + \frac{0.9}{(q_f,\varepsilon)}\}, \delta(q_2,0,1) = \{\frac{0.65}{(q_0,\varepsilon)} + \frac{0.56}{(q_f,\varepsilon)}\},$$

$$\delta(q_f,0,Z_0) = \{\frac{0.45}{(q_\varepsilon,\varepsilon)}\}, \delta(q_f,1,Z_0) = \{\frac{0.5}{(q_\varepsilon,\varepsilon)}\}, \delta(q_\varepsilon,\varepsilon,Z_0) = \{\frac{0.6}{(q_\varepsilon,\varepsilon)}\}.$$

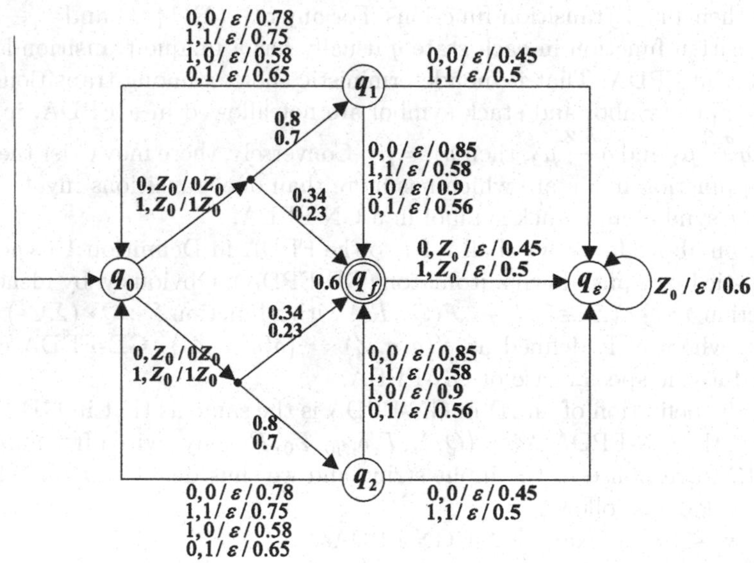

Fig. 1. The transition graph of GN-FPDA $\mathcal{M}$.

Definition 8. *$\Re_{\mathcal{M}}$ is a fuzzy relation on $(Q \times \Sigma^* \times \Gamma^*) \times (Q \times \Sigma^* \times \Gamma^*)$ for any $(p, w, \beta), (q, v, \alpha) \in Q \times \Sigma^* \times \Gamma^*$, that is,*

$$\Re_{\mathcal{M}}((p, w, \beta), (q, v, \alpha)) =$$
$$\begin{cases} \bigvee\{\mu(q, \alpha\backslash tail(\beta)) | \mu \in \delta(p, \varepsilon, head(\beta))\}, & \text{if } v = w, tail(\beta) \leq \alpha, \\ \bigvee\{\mu(q, \alpha\backslash tail(\beta)) | \mu \in \delta(p, head(w), head(\beta))\}, & \text{if } v = tail(w), tail(\beta) \leq \alpha, \\ 0 & \text{otherwise.} \end{cases}$$

Furthermore, $\Re^*_{\mathcal{M}}$ is used to represent the reflexive and transitive closure of $\Re_{\mathcal{M}}$. When no ambiguity occurs, if $\mathcal{M}$ is specific, then we always denote them by $\Re$ and $\Re^*$, respectively.

Definition 9. *Let $\mathcal{M} = (Q, \Sigma, \Gamma, \delta, q_0, Z_0, F)$ be a GN-FPDA.*

(i) The fuzzy language $L_{\aleph}(\mathcal{M}) \in \mathcal{FL}(\Sigma^*)$ accepted by $\mathcal{M}$ by final states is defined for any $\theta \in \Sigma^*$ by

$$L_{\aleph}(\mathcal{M})(\theta) = \bigvee_{q \in Q, \gamma \in \Gamma^*} [\Re^*((q_0, \theta, Z_0), (q, \varepsilon, \gamma)) \wedge F(q)]. \tag{12}$$

(ii) The fuzzy language $N_{\aleph}(\mathcal{M}) \in \mathcal{FL}(\Sigma^*)$ accepted by $\mathcal{M}$ by empty stack is defined for any $\theta \in \Sigma^*$ by

$$N_{\aleph}(\mathcal{M})(\theta) = \bigvee_{q \in Q} [\Re^*((q_0, \theta, Z_0), (q, \varepsilon, \varepsilon))]. \tag{13}$$

As in Theorem 2, it can be seen that the set of fuzzy languages accepted by final states is equivalent to that accepted by empty stack in GD-FPDAs. In the following, we try to extend this equivalence to GN-FPDAs.

Theorem 10. *For any GN-FPDA $\mathcal{M}$, there exists a GN-FPDA $\mathcal{M}'$ such that $N_{\aleph}(\mathcal{M}') = L_{\aleph}(\mathcal{M})$ and vice versa.*

Proof. Firstly, we prove that for any GN-FPDA $\mathcal{M}$, there exists a GN-FPDA $\mathcal{M}'$ such that $N_{\aleph}(\mathcal{M}') = L_{\aleph}(\mathcal{M})$.

Given a GN-FPDA $\mathcal{M} = (Q, \Sigma, \Gamma, \delta, q_0, Z_0, F)$, then we construct a GN-FPDA $\mathcal{M}' = (Q \cup \{q_0', q_\varepsilon\}, \Sigma, \Gamma \cup \{X_0\}, \delta', q_0', X_0, \Phi)$, where for any $\sigma \in \Sigma \cup \{\varepsilon\}, Z \in \Gamma \cup \{X_0\}$,

$$\delta'(q_0', \varepsilon, X_0) = \{1/(q_0, Z_0X_0)\},$$
$$\delta'(q_0', \sigma, Z) = \Phi, \text{ if } \sigma \in \Sigma \text{ or } Z \in \Gamma,$$
$$\delta'(q_\varepsilon, \varepsilon, Z) = \{1/(q_\varepsilon, \varepsilon)\},$$
$$\delta'(q, \varepsilon, Z) = \delta(q, \varepsilon, Z) + \{F(q)/(q_\varepsilon, \varepsilon)\}, \text{ if } q \in Q, Z \in \Gamma,$$
$$\delta'(q, \varepsilon, X_0) = \{F(q)/(q_\varepsilon, \varepsilon)\}, \text{ if } q \in Q,$$
$$\delta'(q, \sigma, Z) = \delta(q, \sigma, Z), \text{ if } q \in Q, \sigma \in \Sigma, Z \in \Gamma,$$
$$\delta'(q, \sigma, X_0) = \Phi, \text{ if } q \in Q, \sigma \in \Sigma.$$

Now, we show that for any $\theta \in \Sigma^*, L_{\aleph}(\mathcal{M})(\theta) \leq N_{\aleph}(\mathcal{M}')(\theta)$. In fact,

$$\begin{aligned}
N_{\aleph}(\mathcal{M}')(\theta) = & \bigvee_{q \in Q \cup \{q_0', q_\varepsilon\}} \Re^{'*}_{\mathcal{M}}((q_0', \theta, X_0), (q, \varepsilon, \varepsilon)) \\
& \geq \Re^{'*}_{\mathcal{M}}((q_0', \theta, X_0), (q_\varepsilon, \varepsilon, \varepsilon)) \\
& \geq \Re^{'}_{\mathcal{M}}((q_0', \theta, X_0), (q_0, \theta, Z_0X_0)) \wedge \Re^{'*}_{\mathcal{M}}((q_0, \theta, Z_0X_0), (q, \varepsilon, \gamma X_0)) \wedge \\
& \quad \Re^{'*}_{\mathcal{M}}((q, \varepsilon, \gamma X_0), (q_\varepsilon, \varepsilon, \varepsilon)).
\end{aligned}$$

Making use of the definition of δ', we obtain

(i) $\Re'_{\mathcal{M}}((q_0', \theta, X_0), (q_0, \theta, Z_0X_0)) = \bigvee\{\mu(q_0, Z_0X_0) | \mu \in \delta'(q_0', \varepsilon, X_0)\} = 1.$
(ii) Let $\gamma = Z_1 \cdots Z_n$ $(n \geq 0)$, then we get

$$\begin{aligned}
& \Re^{'*}_{\mathcal{M}}((q, \varepsilon, \gamma X_0), (q_\varepsilon, \varepsilon, \varepsilon)) \\
& \geq \Re'_{\mathcal{M}}((q, \varepsilon, \gamma X_0), (q_\varepsilon, \varepsilon, Z_2 \cdots Z_n X_0)) \\
& \wedge \Re'_{\mathcal{M}}((q_\varepsilon, \varepsilon, Z_2 \cdots Z_n X_0), (q_\varepsilon, \varepsilon, Z_3 \cdots Z_n X_0)) \wedge \cdots \\
& \wedge \Re'_{\mathcal{M}}((q_\varepsilon, \varepsilon, Z_n X_0), (q_\varepsilon, \varepsilon, X_0)) \wedge \Re'_{\mathcal{M}}((q_\varepsilon, \varepsilon, X_0), (q_\varepsilon, \varepsilon, \varepsilon)) \\
& = F(q) \wedge 1 \wedge \cdots \wedge 1 = F(q).
\end{aligned}$$

(iii) For any $q_i \in Q$, $w_i \in \Sigma^*$, and $\gamma_i \in \Gamma^*$ $(1 \leq i \leq n)$, it follows that

$$\Re_{\mathcal{M}}((q_i, w_i, \gamma_i), (q_{i+1}, w_{i+1}, \gamma_{i+1})) = \Re'_{\mathcal{M}}((q_i, w_i, \gamma_i X_0), (q_{i+1}, w_{i+1}\gamma_{i+1} X_0)).$$

Then, we have

$$\begin{aligned}
& \Re^*_{\mathcal{M}}((q_0, \theta, Z_0), (q, \varepsilon, \gamma)) \\
& = \bigvee [\bigwedge_{i=1}^{n-1} \Re_{\mathcal{M}}((q_i, w_i, \gamma_i), (q_{i+1}, w_{i+1}, \gamma_{i+1}))] \\
& = \bigvee [\bigwedge_{i=1}^{n-1} \Re'_{\mathcal{M}}((q_i, w_i, \gamma_i X_0), (q_{i+1}, w_{i+1}, \gamma_{i+1} X_0))] \\
& \leq \Re^{'*}_{\mathcal{M}}((q_0, \theta, Z_0X_0), (q, \varepsilon, \gamma X_0)),
\end{aligned}$$

where $q_1 = q_0$, $w_1 = \theta$, $\gamma_1 = Z_0$, $q_n = q$, $w_n = \varepsilon$ and $\gamma_n = \gamma$.
From claims (i)–(iii), for any $q \in Q$ and $\gamma \in \Gamma^*$, we have

$$N_{\aleph}(\mathcal{M}')(\theta) \geq \Re^*_{\mathcal{M}}((q_0, \theta, Z_0), (q, \varepsilon, \gamma)) \wedge F(q).$$

Therefore, $L_{\aleph}(\mathcal{M})(\theta) \leq N_{\aleph}(\mathcal{M}')(\theta)$ for any $\theta \in \Sigma^*$.

Similarly, we obtain

$$\begin{aligned}L_{\aleph}(\mathcal{M})(\theta) = &\bigvee_{p\in Q,\gamma\in\Gamma^*}[\Re^*_{\mathcal{M}}((q_0,\theta,Z_0),(p,\varepsilon,\gamma))\wedge F(p)]\\ &\geq \Re^*_{\mathcal{M}}((q_0,\theta,Z_0),(q,\varepsilon,\gamma))\wedge F(q)\\ &= \Re'_{\mathcal{M}}((q_0',\theta,X_0),(q_0,\theta,Z_0X_0))\wedge \Re^*_{\mathcal{M}}((q_0,\theta,Z_0X_0),(q,\varepsilon,\gamma X_0))\wedge F(q)\\ &= \Re'_{\mathcal{M}}((q_0',\theta,X_0),(q_0,\theta,Z_0X_0))\wedge \Re'^*_{\mathcal{M}}((q_0,\theta,Z_0X_0),(q,\varepsilon,\gamma X_0))\wedge F(q)\\ &= \Re'^*_{\mathcal{M}}((q_0',\theta,X_0),(q,\varepsilon,\varepsilon)),\end{aligned}$$

where $q \in Q \cup \{q_0', q_\varepsilon\}$.

So, $L_{\aleph}(\mathcal{M})(\theta) \geq N_{\aleph}(\mathcal{M}')(\theta)$ for any $\theta \in \Sigma^*$. Thus, $L_{\aleph}(\mathcal{M}) = N_{\aleph}(\mathcal{M}')$.

Now, we prove that for any GN-FPDA $\mathcal{M}$, there exists a GN-FPDA $\mathcal{M}'$ such that $L_{\aleph}(\mathcal{M}') = N_{\aleph}(\mathcal{M})$.

Given a GN-FPDA $\mathcal{M} = (Q,\Sigma,\Gamma,\delta,q_0,Z_0,\Phi)$, then we construct a GN-FPDA $\mathcal{M}' = (Q\cup\{q_0',q_f\},\Sigma,\Gamma\cup\{X_0\},\delta',q_0',X_0,\{q_f\})$, where for any $q \in Q\cup\{q_0',q_f\},\sigma\in\Sigma\cup\{\varepsilon\},Z\in\Gamma\cup\{X_0\}$,

$$\begin{aligned}&\delta'(q_0',\varepsilon,X_0) = \{1/(q_0,Z_0X_0)\},\\ &\delta'(q_0',\sigma,Z) = \Phi, \ \text{if}\,\sigma\in\Sigma \ \text{or} \ Z\in\Gamma,\\ &\delta'(q_f,\sigma,Z) = \Phi,\\ &\delta'(q,\sigma,Z) = \delta(q,\sigma,Z), \ \text{if}\,q\in Q, Z\in\Gamma,\\ &\delta'(q,\varepsilon,X_0) = \{1/(q_f,\varepsilon)\}, \ \text{if}\,q\in Q,\\ &\delta'(q,\sigma,X_0) = \Phi, \ \text{if}\,q\in Q,\sigma\in\Sigma.\end{aligned}$$

The proof process is similar to the above proof process and thus it is easy to verify that $L_{\aleph}(\mathcal{M}') = N_{\aleph}(\mathcal{M})$. □

We use $\mathcal{F}_{\aleph}(\Sigma^*)$ to denote the set of all fuzzy languages over Σ accepted by GN-FPDAs.

Theorem 11. $\mathcal{F}_{\mathcal{P}}(\Sigma^*) \subset \mathcal{F}_{\aleph}(\Sigma^*)$.

Proof. Let us review Example 7. Let $f \in \mathcal{FL}(\Sigma^*)$ where $f = L_{\aleph}(\mathcal{M})$. With the help of Theorem 10, we can also take $f = N_{\aleph}(\mathcal{M})$. For $0^n1^n0^n1^n (n \geq 1)$, we compute that $L_{\aleph}(\mathcal{M})(0^n1^n0^n1^n) = 0.58$, namely, $f(0^n1^n0^n1^n) = 0.58$. We assume that f is a fuzzy context-free language, then it satisfies Lemma 5. So, there exists a positive integer N, and for any $\theta \in \Sigma^*$, if $l(\theta) \geq N$, then there exist $u,v,w,x,y \in \Sigma^*$ such that $\theta = uvwxy = 0^N1^N0^N1^N$, $l(vwx) \leq N$, $l(vx) \geq 1$. So, for any nonnegative integer i, $f(uv^iwx^iy) = f(\theta) = 0.58$.

Case 1. If vwx contains either string 0 or string 1, then we can take

(i) $u = \varepsilon; v = 0^h; w = \varepsilon; x = 0^j; y = 1^N0^N1^N$,
(ii) $u = 0^N; v = 1^h; w = \varepsilon; x = 1^j; y = 0^N1^N$,

(iii) $u = 0^N 1^N; v = 0^h; w = \varepsilon; x = 0^j; y = 1^N$,
(iv) $u = 0^N 1^N 0^N; v = 1^h; w = \varepsilon; x = 1^j; y = \varepsilon$,

where $h + j = N$. With respect to (i), if $i = 0$, then $f(uv^0wx^0y) = f(1^N 0^N 1^N)$. For $1^n 0^n 1^n (n \geq 1)$, we compute that $N_{\aleph}(\mathcal{M})(1^n 0^n 1^n) = 0.5$, i.e., $f(1^n 0^n 1^n) = 0.5$.

With respect to (ii), if $i = 0$, then $f(uv^0wx^0y) = f(0^N 0^N 1^N)$. For $0^n 0^n 1^n (n \geq 1)$, we compute that $N_{\aleph}(\mathcal{M})(0^n 0^n 1^n) = 0.5$, i.e., $f(0^n 0^n 1^n) = 0.5$.

With respect to (iii), if $i = 0$, then $f(uv^0wx^0y) = f(0^N 1^N 1^N)$. For $0^n 1^n 1^n (n \geq 1)$, we compute that $N_{\aleph}(\mathcal{M})(0^n 1^n 1^n) = 0.5$, i.e., $f(0^n 1^n 1^n) = 0.5$.

With respect to (iv), if $i = 0$, then $f(uv^0wx^0y) = f(0^N 1^N 0^N)$. For $0^n 1^n 0^n (n \geq 1)$, we compute that $N_{\aleph}(\mathcal{M})(0^n 1^n 0^n) = 0.45$, i.e., $f(0^n 1^n 0^n) = 0.45$.

From the above calculations, we can easily observe that $f(uv^0wx^0y) \neq f(\theta)$.

Case 2. If vwx contains both string 0 and string 1, then we can take

(i) $u = 0^{N-h}; v = 0^h; w = \varepsilon; x = 1^j; y = 1^{N-j} 0^N 1^N$,
(ii) $u = 0^N 1^{N-h}; v = 1^h; w = \varepsilon; x = 0^j; y = 0^{N-j} 1^N$,
(iii) $u = 0^N 1^N 0^{N-h}; v = 0^h; w = \varepsilon; x = 1^j; y = 1^{N-j}$,

where $h + j \leq N$, $h \neq 0$ and $j \neq 0$. By simple calculation, we also have that $f(uv^0wx^0y) \neq f(\theta)$.

Combing Case 1 and Case 2, we conclude that our assumption is invalid, that is, f does not be a fuzzy context-free language. So, the proof is completed. □

Since the concept of FPDAs is coincide with that of GD-FPDAs, an immediate conclusion is presented below.

Corollary 12. $\mathcal{F}_{\mathcal{D}}(\Sigma^*) \subset \mathcal{F}_{\mathcal{P}}(\Sigma^*) \subset \mathcal{F}_{\aleph}(\Sigma^*)$.

4 General-Nondeterministic Fuzzy Context-Free Grammars

Now, we would like to give the definition of general-nondeterministic fuzzy context-free grammars (GN-FCFGs) and study their properties.

Definition 13. *A GN-FCFG $\mathcal{G}$ is a quadruple (V,T,P,S), where all the components are the same as those in Definition 3 excepting the set of productions P defined as follows.*

For any $u \in V$ and $v \in (V \cup T)^*$, P is a finite set of fuzzy productions of the form $u \xrightarrow[\mathcal{G}]{\rho} v$, where $|u| \leq |v|$ and $\rho \in [0,1]$. If $\mathcal{G}$ is specific, then we use $u \xrightarrow{\rho} v$ instead of $u \xrightarrow[\mathcal{G}]{\rho} v$. In comparison with Definition 3, there may exist different possibility degrees of u producing v in P, that is, if $u \xrightarrow{\rho_1} v$ and $u \xrightarrow{\rho_2} v$, then $\rho_1 \neq \rho_2$. So, we use $\bigvee\{\rho | u \xrightarrow{\rho} v\}$ to denote the possibility degree of u producing v.

Here, both $\overset{\rho}{\Rightarrow}$ and $\overset{\rho}{\underset{*}{\Rightarrow}}$ in GN-FCFG are the same as those in FCFG. As usual, by applying a production $u \overset{\rho}{\rightarrow} v$ whose possibility degree is $\bigvee\{\rho|u \overset{\rho}{\rightarrow} v\}$, $\alpha u\beta \overset{\rho}{\Rightarrow} \alpha v\beta$ represents $\alpha u\beta$ directly deriving $\alpha v\beta$ for $\alpha, \beta \in (V \cup T)^*$. What's more, for any $u_i \in (V \cup T)^*$ $(1 \leq i \leq n)$, if $u_1 \overset{\rho_1}{\Rightarrow} u_2 \overset{\rho_2}{\Rightarrow} \cdots \overset{\rho_{n-1}}{\Rightarrow} u_n$, then u_n is said to be derived from u_1, denoted by $u_1 \overset{\rho}{\underset{*}{\Rightarrow}} u_n$, where $\rho = \bigvee\{\rho_1|u_1 \overset{\rho_1}{\rightarrow} u_2\} \wedge \bigvee\{\rho_2|u_2 \overset{\rho_2}{\rightarrow} u_3\} \wedge \cdots \wedge \bigvee\{\rho_{n-1}|u_{n-1} \overset{\rho_{n-1}}{\rightarrow} u_n\}$.

Definition 14. *Let $\mathcal{G} = (V, T, P, S)$ be a GN-FCFG. The fuzzy language $f_{\mathcal{G}}$ generated by $\mathcal{G}$ is a fuzzy subset of T^*, defined as follows:*

$$\begin{aligned} f_{\mathcal{G}}(w) &= \bigvee \bigvee \{\rho|S \overset{\rho}{\underset{*}{\Rightarrow}} w\} \\ &= \bigvee \{\bigvee \{\rho_0|S \overset{\rho_0}{\Rightarrow} w_1\} \wedge \bigvee \{\rho_1|w_1 \overset{\rho_1}{\Rightarrow} w_2\} \wedge \cdots \wedge \bigvee \{\rho_n|w_n \overset{\rho_n}{\Rightarrow} w\}\}, \end{aligned}$$

for any $w \in T^*$.

It should be noted that the fuzzy language generated by a GN-FCFG $\mathcal{G}$ is referred as a general-nondeterministic fuzzy context-free language (GN-FCFL).

Definition 15. *Let $\mathcal{G} = (V, T, P, S)$ be a GN-FCFG. For $A \in V$ and $\alpha \in (V \cup T)^*$, if $A \overset{\rho}{\underset{*}{\Rightarrow}} \alpha$ satisfying $f_{\mathcal{G}}(\alpha) = \bigvee \bigvee \{\rho|A \overset{\rho}{\underset{*}{\Rightarrow}} \alpha\}$, then we say that α is a sentencial form generated by $\mathcal{G}$.*

For the derivation $A \overset{\rho}{\underset{*}{\Rightarrow}} \alpha$, if the leftmost (rightmost) variable of the current sentencial form is replaced in each step of derivation, then we call this derivation the leftmost (rightmost) derivation, denoted by $A \overset{\rho}{\underset{*lm}{\Rightarrow}} \alpha$ $(A \overset{\rho}{\underset{*rm}{\Rightarrow}} \alpha)$. Furthermore, we define the set of fuzzy languages generated by $\mathcal{G}$ with the leftmost (rightmost) derivation as follows:

$$\mathcal{L}(\mathcal{G}_{lm}) = \{\rho/w|w \in T^*, S \overset{\rho}{\underset{*lm}{\Rightarrow}} w\} \text{ satisfying } f_{\mathcal{G}}(w) = \bigvee \bigvee \{\rho|S \overset{\rho}{\underset{*lm}{\Rightarrow}} w\}$$

$$(\mathcal{L}(\mathcal{G}_{rm}) = \{\rho/w|w \in T^*, S \overset{\rho}{\underset{*rm}{\Rightarrow}} w\} \text{ satisfying } f_{\mathcal{G}}(w) = \bigvee \bigvee \{\rho|S \overset{\rho}{\underset{*rm}{\Rightarrow}} w\}).$$

For the convenience of calculation, we also give the next definition.

Definition 16. *Let $\mathcal{G} = (V, T, P, S)$ be a GN-FCFG. The set of fuzzy languages $\mathcal{L}(\mathcal{G})$ generated by $\mathcal{G}$, is as follows:*

$$\mathcal{L}(\mathcal{G}) = \{\rho/w|w \in T^*, S \overset{\rho}{\underset{*}{\Rightarrow}} w\} \text{ satisfying } f_{\mathcal{G}}(w) = \bigvee \bigvee \{\rho|S \overset{\rho}{\underset{*}{\Rightarrow}} w\}. \tag{14}$$

In light of above definitions, we establish the following conclusion which will be used when we prove Theorem 18.

Theorem 17. *Let $\mathcal{G} = (V, T, P, S)$ be a GN-FCFG. Then $\mathcal{L}(\mathcal{G}_{lm}) = \mathcal{L}(\mathcal{G}_{rm}) = \mathcal{L}(\mathcal{G})$.*

Proof. Since the process of proof $\mathcal{L}(\mathcal{G}_{rm}) = \mathcal{L}(\mathcal{G})$ is analogous with that of $\mathcal{L}(\mathcal{G}_{lm}) = \mathcal{L}(\mathcal{G})$, we just proof the latter case. Firstly, we prove that

$$S \overset{\rho}{\underset{*lm}{\Rightarrow}} w \text{ if and only if } S \overset{\rho}{\underset{*}{\Rightarrow}} w, \text{ for any } w \in T^*. \tag{15}$$

Obviously,

$$\text{if } S \overset{\rho}{\underset{*lm}{\Rightarrow}} w, \text{ then } S \overset{\rho}{\underset{*}{\Rightarrow}} w.$$

So, we only need to verify that

$$\text{if } S \overset{\rho}{\underset{n}{\Rightarrow}} w, \text{ then } S \overset{\rho}{\underset{*lm}{\Rightarrow}} w.$$

If $n = 1$, then we are sure that $S \overset{\rho}{\Rightarrow} w$ is the leftmost derivation. Hence, $S \overset{\rho}{\underset{lm}{\Rightarrow}} w$ evidently holds.

If $n \leq k$ $(k > 1)$, then we assume that if $S \overset{\rho}{\underset{n}{\Rightarrow}} w$, then $S \overset{\rho}{\underset{*lm}{\Rightarrow}} w$.

If $n = k+1$, then it suffices to verify that if $S \overset{\rho}{\underset{k+1}{\Rightarrow}} w$, then $S \overset{\rho}{\underset{*lm}{\Rightarrow}} w$. For the derivation $S \overset{\rho}{\underset{k+1}{\Rightarrow}} w$, we suppose that the first step looks like $S \overset{\rho_0}{\Rightarrow} X_1 X_2 \cdots X_m$. Then, we break w into $w = \alpha_1 \alpha_2 \cdots \alpha_m$ such that $X_i \overset{\rho_i}{\underset{n_i}{\Rightarrow}} \alpha_i$ for $n_i \leq k$ $(1 \leq i \leq m)$, where $\rho = \rho_0 \wedge \rho_1 \wedge \cdots \wedge \rho_m$. From the inductive hypothesis, there exist the leftmost derivations $X_i \overset{\rho_i}{\underset{*lm}{\Rightarrow}} \alpha_i$ $(1 \leq i \leq m)$. Then, combining with the first step of $S \overset{\rho}{\underset{k+1}{\Rightarrow}} w$, we obtain the next derivation chain:

$$S \overset{\rho_0}{\Rightarrow} X_1 X_2 \cdots X_m \overset{\rho_1}{\underset{*lm}{\Rightarrow}} \alpha_1 X_2 \cdots X_m \overset{\rho_2}{\underset{*lm}{\Rightarrow}} \cdots \overset{\rho_m}{\underset{*lm}{\Rightarrow}} \alpha_1 \alpha_2 \cdots \alpha_m = w.$$

Thus, $S \overset{\rho}{\underset{*lm}{\Rightarrow}} w$. Therefore, (15) holds.

In fact, to prove $\mathcal{L}(\mathcal{G}_{lm}) = \mathcal{L}(\mathcal{G})$, it is enough to verify that $f_{\mathcal{G}_{lm}} = f_{\mathcal{G}}$. So, utilizing (15), we have

$$f_{\mathcal{G}_{lm}}(w) = \bigvee \bigvee \{\rho | S \overset{\rho}{\underset{*lm}{\Rightarrow}} w\} = \bigvee \bigvee \{\rho | S \overset{\rho}{\underset{*}{\Rightarrow}} w\} = f_{\mathcal{G}}(w),$$

for any $w \in T^*$. Thus, $\mathcal{L}(\mathcal{G}_{lm}) = \mathcal{L}(\mathcal{G})$. □

Now, we show the equivalence between GN-FCFGs and GN-FPDAs. In accordance with Theorem 10, the following proofs only consider GN-FPDAs accepting fuzzy languages by empty stack.

Theorem 18. *For any GN-FCFG $\mathcal{G}$, there exists a GN-FPDA $\mathcal{M}$ such that $N_{\aleph}(\mathcal{M}) = f_{\mathcal{G}}$.*

Proof. Given a GN-FCFG $\mathcal{G} = (V, T, P, S)$, then we construct a GN-FPDA $\mathcal{M} = (\{q\}, T, V \cup T, \delta, q, S, \Phi)$, where

$\delta(q, \varepsilon, A) = \{\rho/(q, \gamma) | A \xrightarrow{\rho} \gamma \in P\}$ for any $A \in V$,

$\delta(q, \sigma, A) = \{\rho/(q, \gamma) | A \xrightarrow{\rho} \sigma\gamma \in P\}$ for any $\sigma \in T, A \in V$.

By means of Theorem 17, it suffices to verify that

$$S \underset{*lm}{\overset{\rho}{\Rightarrow}} \theta\gamma \text{ if and only if } \rho = \Re^*((q_0, \theta, S), (q_0, \varepsilon, \gamma)), \tag{16}$$

where γ is arbitrary.

Firstly, we prove that if $S \underset{i_{lm}}{\overset{\rho}{\Rightarrow}} \theta\gamma$, then $\rho = \Re^i((q_0, \theta, S), (q_0, \varepsilon, \gamma))$.

If $i = 0$, then there must be $\theta = \varepsilon, \gamma = S$. The result evidently holds.

If $i = k$ $(k \geq 1)$, then we assume that if $S \underset{k_{lm}}{\overset{\rho}{\Rightarrow}} \theta\gamma$, then $\rho = \Re^k((q_0, \theta, S), (q_0, \varepsilon, \gamma))$.

If $i = k + 1$, then there must exist intermediate variables $Z, \gamma = \alpha_2\alpha_1$ such that $S \underset{k_{lm}}{\overset{\rho_Z^1}{\Rightarrow}} \theta' Z\alpha_1 \underset{lm}{\overset{\rho_Z^2}{\Rightarrow}} \theta' \sigma\alpha_2\alpha_1$ for $\theta = \sigma_1\sigma_2 \cdots \sigma_n\sigma = \theta' \sigma$ $(\sigma_i, \sigma \in T)$. Then $\rho = \bigvee(\rho_Z^1 \wedge \rho_Z^2)$. For the derivation $S \underset{k_{lm}}{\overset{\rho_Z^1}{\Rightarrow}} \theta' Z\alpha_1$, we have

$$\rho_Z^1 = \Re^k((q, \theta' \sigma, S), (q, \sigma, Z\alpha_1)) = \Re^k((q, \theta', S), (q, \varepsilon, Z\alpha_1)),$$

by using the inductive hypothesis.

Furthermore, we can get $Z \underset{lm}{\overset{\rho_Z^2}{\Rightarrow}} \sigma\alpha_2$ from $\theta' Z\alpha_1 \underset{lm}{\overset{\rho_Z^2}{\Rightarrow}} \theta' \sigma\alpha_2\alpha_1$. According to the definition of δ, we have $\rho_Z^2 = \bigvee\{\mu(q, \alpha_2) | \mu \in \delta(q, \sigma, Z)\}$, that is, $\rho_Z^2 = \Re((q, \sigma, Z), (q, \varepsilon, \alpha_2))$.

In summary, we have

$$\begin{aligned}
&\Re^{k+1}((q, \theta, S), (q, \varepsilon, \gamma)) \\
&= \bigvee[\Re^k((q, \theta' \sigma, S), (q, \sigma, Z\alpha_1)) \wedge \Re((q, \sigma, Z\alpha_1), (q, \varepsilon, \alpha_2\alpha_1))] \\
&= \bigvee[\Re^k((q, \theta', S), (q, \varepsilon, Z\alpha_1)) \wedge \Re((q, \sigma, Z), (q, \varepsilon, \alpha_2))] \\
&= \bigvee[\rho_Z^1 \wedge \rho_Z^2] = \rho.
\end{aligned}$$

Now, we prove that if $\rho = \Re^i((q_0, \theta, S), (q_0, \varepsilon, \gamma))$, then $S \underset{i_{lm}}{\overset{\rho}{\Rightarrow}} \theta\gamma$.

If $i = 0$, then there must be $\theta = \varepsilon, \gamma = S$. Therefore, we have $\rho = \Re^*((q_0, \varepsilon, S), (q_0, \varepsilon, S)) = 1$. Then, it is obvious that $S \underset{*lm}{\overset{1}{\Rightarrow}} S$ holds.

If $i = k$ $(k \geq 1)$, then we assume that if $\rho = \Re^k((q_0, \theta, S), (q_0, \varepsilon, \gamma))$, then $S \underset{k_{lm}}{\overset{\rho}{\Rightarrow}} \theta\gamma$.

If $i = k + 1$, then there exists $\theta = \sigma_1\sigma_2 \cdots \sigma_n\sigma = \theta' \sigma$ $(\sigma_i, \sigma \in T)$ such that

$$\begin{aligned}
\rho &= \Re^{k+1}((q, \theta' \sigma, S), (q, \varepsilon, \gamma)) \\
&= \bigvee[\Re^k((q, \theta' \sigma, S), (q, \sigma, \beta)) \wedge \Re((q, \sigma, \beta), (q, \varepsilon, \gamma))].
\end{aligned}$$

Then, there must exist intermediate variables $Z \in V, \beta = Z\alpha_1$ and $\gamma = \alpha_2\alpha_1$ such that

$$\begin{aligned}\Re((q,\sigma,\beta),(q,\varepsilon,\gamma)) &= \Re((q,\sigma,Z\alpha_1),(q,\varepsilon,\alpha_2\alpha_1))\\ &= \Re((q,\sigma,Z),(q,\varepsilon,\alpha_2)) = \rho_\beta^2.\end{aligned}$$

From the definition of δ, we obtain $\bigvee\{\mu(q,\alpha_2)|\mu \in \delta(q,\sigma,Z)\} = \rho_\beta^2$, that is, $Z \overset{\rho_\beta^2}{\underset{lm}{\Rightarrow}} \sigma\alpha_2$.

Let $\Re^k((q,\theta'\sigma,S),(q,\sigma,\beta)) = \rho_\beta^1$, we can get $\Re^k((q,\theta',S),(q,\varepsilon,\beta)) = \rho_\beta^1$. And then, by using the inductive hypothesis, we have $S \overset{\rho_\beta^1}{\underset{k_{lm}}{\Rightarrow}} \theta'\beta$.

Then, combining $\beta = Z\alpha_1$ and $Z \overset{\rho_\beta^2}{\underset{lm}{\Rightarrow}} \sigma\alpha_2$, we get

$$S \overset{\rho_\beta^1}{\underset{k_{lm}}{\Rightarrow}} \theta'\beta = \theta' Z\alpha_1 \overset{\rho_\beta^2}{\underset{lm}{\Rightarrow}} \theta'\sigma\alpha_2\alpha_1 = \theta\gamma.$$

So, $S \overset{\rho}{\underset{k+1_{lm}}{\Rightarrow}} \theta\gamma$ holds. Therefore, (16) holds. From the generality of γ, we obtain

$$S \overset{\rho}{\underset{*lm}{\Rightarrow}} \theta \text{ if and only if } \rho = \Re^*((q_0,\theta,S),(q_0,\varepsilon,\varepsilon)).$$

Thus, $N_\aleph(\mathcal{M}) = f_\mathcal{G}$. □

Theorem 19. *For any GN-FPDA $\mathcal{M}$, there exists a GN-FCFG $\mathcal{G}$ such that $f_\mathcal{G} = N_\aleph(\mathcal{M})$.*

Proof. Given a GN-FPDA $\mathcal{M} = (Q,\Sigma,\Gamma,\delta,q_0,Z_0,\Phi)$, then we construct GN-FCFG $\mathcal{G} = (V,\Sigma,P,S)$, where

$V = \{S\} \cup \{[q,Z,p]|q,p \in Q, Z \in \Gamma\}$,

$P = \{S \overset{1}{\rightarrow} [q_0,Z_0,q]|q \in Q\} \cup$

$\{[q,Z,q_m] \overset{\rho}{\rightarrow} a[p,Z_1,q_1][q_1,Z_2,q_2]\cdots[q_{m-1},Z_m,q_m]| \bigvee \mu(p,Z_1Z_2\cdots Z_m) = \rho, \mu \in \delta(q,a,Z), a \in \Sigma \cup \{\varepsilon\}, Z, Z_1,\cdots,Z_m \in \Gamma, q,p,q_1,\cdots,q_m \in Q, m \geq 1\} \cup$

$\{[q,Z,p] \overset{\rho}{\rightarrow} a| \bigvee \mu(p,\varepsilon) = \rho, \mu \in \delta(q,a,Z)\}$.

To prove $f_\mathcal{G} = N_\aleph(\mathcal{M})$, it suffices to verify that

$$\rho = \Re^*((q,\theta,Z),(p,\varepsilon,\varepsilon)) \text{ if and only if } [q,Z,p] \overset{\rho}{\underset{*}{\Rightarrow}} \theta, \tag{17}$$

where q and Z are arbitrary.

Firstly, we prove that if $\rho = \Re^i((q,\theta,Z),(p,\varepsilon,\varepsilon))$, then $[q,Z,p] \overset{\rho}{\underset{i}{\Rightarrow}} \theta$.

If $i=1$, then we have that $\rho = \Re((q,\theta,Z),(p,\varepsilon,\varepsilon))$ which indicates that $\theta \in \Sigma \cup \{\varepsilon\}$. So, $\rho = \bigvee\{\mu(p,\varepsilon)|\mu \in \delta(q,\theta,Z)\}$. Then, $[q,Z,p] \overset{\rho}{\Rightarrow} \theta$ holds.

If $i = k$ $(k > 1)$, then we assume that if $\rho = \Re^k((q,\theta,Z),(p,\varepsilon,\varepsilon))$, then $[q,Z,p] \overset{\rho}{\underset{k}{\Rightarrow}} \theta$.

If $i = k+1$, then we let $\theta = a\theta'$ $(a \in \Sigma \cup \{\varepsilon\})$ and $\theta' = a_1 \cdots a_n \in \Sigma^*$ such that $\rho = \bigvee(\rho' \wedge \rho'')$ where

$$\rho' = \Re((q, a\theta', Z), (q_1, \theta', Z_1 Z_2 \cdots Z_n)),$$
$$\rho'' = \Re^k((q_1, \theta', Z_1 Z_2 \cdots Z_n), (p, \varepsilon, \varepsilon)).$$

Then, there must exist states $q_2, \cdots, q_n, q_{n+1} = p$ such that

$$\begin{aligned}
&\Re^{k+1}((q, a\theta', Z), (p, \varepsilon, \varepsilon)) \\
&= \bigvee[\Re((q, a\theta', Z), (q_1, \theta', Z_1 Z_2 \cdots Z_n)) \\
&\wedge \Re^{k_1}((q_1, \theta', Z_1 Z_2 \cdots Z_n), (q_2, a_2 \cdots a_n, Z_2 \cdots Z_n)) \wedge \cdots \\
&\wedge \Re^{k_n}((q_n, a_n, Z_n), (p, \varepsilon, \varepsilon))].
\end{aligned}$$

Thus, we can get

$$\begin{aligned}
\rho' &= \Re((q, a, Z), (q_1, \varepsilon, Z_1 Z_2 \cdots Z_n)), \\
\rho_1 &= \Re^{k_1}((q_1, a_1, Z_1), (q_2, \varepsilon, \varepsilon)), \\
&\cdots, \\
\rho_n &= \Re^{k_n}((q_n, a_n, Z_n), (p, \varepsilon, \varepsilon)),
\end{aligned}$$

and $\rho'' = \rho_1 \wedge \rho_2 \wedge \cdots \wedge \rho_n$. Note that $k_1 + k_2 + \cdots + k_n = k$. So, by the inductive hypothesis, it follows that

$$[q_1, Z_1, q_2] \overset{\rho_1}{\underset{*}{\Rightarrow}} a_1,$$
$$[q_2, Z_2, q_3] \overset{\rho_2}{\underset{*}{\Rightarrow}} a_2,$$
$$\cdots,$$
$$[q_n, Z_n, p] \overset{\rho_n}{\underset{*}{\Rightarrow}} a_n.$$

Furthermore, since $\rho' = \Re((q, a, Z), (q_1, \varepsilon, Z_1 Z_2 \cdots Z_n))$, we obtain

$$\rho' = \bigvee\{\mu(q_1, Z_1 Z_2 \cdots Z_n) | \mu \in \delta(q, a, Z)\}.$$

Then, according to the definition of $\mathcal{G}$, we have

$$[q, Z, p] \overset{\rho'}{\rightarrow} a[q_1, Z_1, q_2][q_2, Z_2, q_3] \cdots [q_n, Z_n, p].$$

In summary, we get

$$\begin{aligned}
&\overset{\rho'}{\Rightarrow} a[q_1, Z_1, q_2][q_2, Z_2, q_3] \cdots [q_n, Z_n, p] \\
&\overset{\rho_1}{\underset{*}{\Rightarrow}} aa_1[q_2, Z_2, q_3] \cdots [q_n, Z_n, p] \\
&\Rightarrow \cdots \\
&\overset{\rho_n}{\underset{*}{\Rightarrow}} aa_1 a_2 \cdots a_n = \theta,
\end{aligned}$$

and $\rho' \wedge \rho'' = \rho' \wedge \rho_1 \wedge \rho_2 \wedge \cdots \wedge \rho_n$.

Now, we prove that if $[q, Z, p] \overset{\rho}{\underset{i}{\Rightarrow}} \theta$, then $\rho = \Re^i((q, \theta, Z), (p, \varepsilon, \varepsilon))$. The proof process is analogous with the above proof process, and thus we omit it here.

Therefore, (17) holds. From the generality of q, Z, we let $q = q_0, Z = S$ and obtain

$$\rho = \Re^*((q_0, \theta, S), (p, \varepsilon, \varepsilon)) \text{ if and only if } [q_0, S, p] \overset{\rho}{\underset{*}{\Rightarrow}} \theta.$$

Thus, $f_{\mathcal{G}} = N_{\aleph}(\mathcal{M})$. □

4.1 Closure Properties of General-Nondeterministic Fuzzy Context-Free Languages

We are now in a position to consider the closure properties of some operations on the set of GN-FCFLs. To this end, we need to draw the following conclusion.

Theorem 20. *Let T be a finite set of terminals. Then (i) $\emptyset$; (ii) $\{1/\varepsilon\}$; (iii) $\forall \sigma \in T, a \in [0, 1], \{a/\sigma\}$ are all GN-FCFLs.*

Proof. For (i), let $\mathcal{G}_1 = (\{S, A\}, \{\sigma\}, \{S \overset{0.8}{\rightarrow} \sigma A\}, S)$. Clearly, $\mathcal{L}(\mathcal{G}_1) = \emptyset$.

For (ii), let $\mathcal{G}_2 = (\{S, A\}, \{\sigma\}, \{S \overset{1}{\rightarrow} \varepsilon\}, S)$. Clearly, $\mathcal{L}(\mathcal{G}_2) = \{1/\varepsilon\}$.

For (iii), let $\mathcal{G}_3 = (\{S\}, \{\sigma\}, \{S \overset{a}{\rightarrow} \sigma\}, S)$. Clearly, $\mathcal{L}(\mathcal{G}_3) = \{a/\sigma\}$. □

Theorem 21. *The set of GN-FCFLs is closed under union.*

Proof. Let f_1 and f_2 be GN-FCFLs. Then there exist GN-FCFG $\mathcal{G}_1 = (V_1, T_1, P_1, S_1)$ and GN-FCFG $\mathcal{G}_2 = (V_2, T_2, P_2, S_2)$ where $V_1 \cap V_2 = \emptyset$, such that $f_1 = f_{\mathcal{G}_1}, f_2 = f_{\mathcal{G}_2}$ respectively. We construct GN-FCFG $\mathcal{G} = (V_1 \cup V_2 \cup \{S\}, T_1 \cup T_2, P, S)$, where S $\notin V_1 \cup V_2$ is an new start symbol and $P = P_1 \cup P_2 \cup \{S \overset{1}{\rightarrow} S_1, S \overset{1}{\rightarrow} S_2\}$.

We note $\mathcal{L}_1 = \{f_1(w)/w | w \in T_1^*, S_1 \overset{f_1(w)}{\underset{*}{\Rightarrow}} w\}$ and $\mathcal{L}_2 = \{f_2(w)/w | w \in T_2^*, S_2 \overset{f_2(w)}{\underset{*}{\Rightarrow}} w\}$, respectively. If any $\rho/w \in \mathcal{L}_1 \cup \mathcal{L}_2$ where $f_1(w)/w \in \mathcal{L}_1, f_2(w)/w \in \mathcal{L}_2$ and $\rho = f_1(w) \vee f_2(w)$, then we have $S_1 \overset{f_1(w)}{\underset{\mathcal{G}_1}{\rightarrow}} w$ or $S_2 \overset{f_2(w)}{\underset{\mathcal{G}_2}{\rightarrow}} w$. We define the set of fuzzy languages generated by $\mathcal{G}$ as $\mathcal{L} = \{f(w)/w | w \in (T_1 \cup T_2)^*, S \overset{f(w)}{\underset{*}{\Rightarrow}} w\}$ satisfying $f(w) = f_1(w) \vee f_2(w)$. According to the set of productions P, we obtain $S \overset{1}{\underset{\mathcal{G}}{\rightarrow}} S_1 \overset{f_1(w)}{\underset{\mathcal{G}}{\rightarrow}} w$ or $S \overset{1}{\underset{\mathcal{G}}{\rightarrow}} S_2 \overset{f_2(w)}{\underset{\mathcal{G}}{\rightarrow}} w$. Then, we get $S \overset{\rho}{\underset{\mathcal{G}}{\rightarrow}} w$ satisfying

$$\rho = (1 \wedge f_1(w)) \vee (1 \wedge f_2(w)) = f_1(w) \vee f_2(w).$$

Thus, $\rho/w \in \mathcal{L}$, i.e., $\mathcal{L}_1 \cup \mathcal{L}_2 \subseteq \mathcal{L}$.

Inversely, if $\rho/w \in \mathcal{L}$, then $S \overset{\rho}{\underset{\mathcal{G}}{\rightarrow}} w$. From the set of productions P, we can see that $S \overset{1}{\underset{\mathcal{G}}{\rightarrow}} S_1 \overset{f_1(w)}{\underset{\mathcal{G}}{\rightarrow}} w$ or $S \overset{1}{\underset{\mathcal{G}}{\rightarrow}} S_2 \overset{f_2(w)}{\underset{\mathcal{G}}{\rightarrow}} w$. If $S \overset{1}{\underset{\mathcal{G}}{\rightarrow}} S_1 \overset{f_1(w)}{\underset{\mathcal{G}}{\rightarrow}} w$ is reasonable, then we have that only variables of $\mathcal{G}_1$ may appear on the derivation chain $S \underset{\mathcal{G}}{\overset{1}{\to}} S_1 \underset{\mathcal{G}}{\overset{f_1(w)}{\to}} w$. However, it is P_1 that only contains variables of $\mathcal{G}_1$. So, only productions of P_1 are applied to the derivation $S_1 \underset{\mathcal{G}}{\overset{f_1(w)}{\to}} w$. Therefore, we have $S_1 \underset{\mathcal{G}_1}{\overset{f_1(w)}{\to}} w$, i.e., $f_1(w)/w \in \mathcal{L}_1$. Similarly, it is easy to verify $f_2(w)/w \in \mathcal{L}_2$. Then $\rho = f_1(w) \vee f_2(w)$.

Hence, $\rho/w \in \mathcal{L}_1 \cup \mathcal{L}_2$, i.e., $\mathcal{L} \subseteq \mathcal{L}_1 \cup \mathcal{L}_2$.

Thus, $f_1 \cup f_2$ is a GN-FCFL. □

Theorem 22. *The set of GN-FCFLs is closed under concatenation.*

Proof. Let f_1 and f_2 be GN-FCFLs. Then there exist GN-FCFG $\mathcal{G}_1 = (V_1, T_1, P_1, S_1)$ and GN-FCFG $\mathcal{G}_2 = (V_2, T_2, P_2, S_2)$ where $V_1 \cap V_2 = \emptyset$, such that $f_1 = f_{\mathcal{G}_1}, f_2 = f_{\mathcal{G}_2}$ respectively.

From (i) of Theorem 20, if either f_1 or f_2 is empty, then it is obvious that $f_1 f_2$ is a GN-FCFL. So, we consider the case that both f_1 and f_2 are nonempty. We construct GN-FCFG $\mathcal{G} = (V_1 \cup V_2 \cup \{S\}, T_1 \cup T_2, P, S)$, where S $\notin V_1 \cup V_2$ is an new start symbol and $P = P_1 \cup P_2 \cup \{S \overset{1}{\to} S_1 S_2\}$.

Then, we note $\mathcal{L}_1 = \{f_1(w)/w | w \in T_1^*, S_1 \underset{*}{\overset{f_1(w)}{\Rightarrow}} w\}$ and $\mathcal{L}_2 = \{f_2(\psi)/\psi | \psi \in T_2^*, S_2 \underset{*}{\overset{f_2(\psi)}{\Rightarrow}} \psi\}$, respectively. If any $\rho/w\psi \in \mathcal{L}_1\mathcal{L}_2$ where $f_1(w)/w \in \mathcal{L}_1, f_2(\psi)/\psi \in \mathcal{L}_2$ and $\rho = f_1(w) \wedge f_2(\psi)$, then we have $S_1 \underset{\mathcal{G}_1}{\overset{f_1(w)}{\to}} w$ and $S_2 \underset{\mathcal{G}_2}{\overset{f_2(\psi)}{\to}} \psi$. Taking advantage of the set of productions P, we get $S \underset{\mathcal{G}}{\overset{1}{\to}} S_1 S_2 \underset{\mathcal{G}_1}{\overset{f_1(w)}{\to}} w S_2 \underset{\mathcal{G}_2}{\overset{f_2(\psi)}{\to}} w\psi$. We define the set of fuzzy languages generated by $\mathcal{G}$ as $\mathcal{L} = \{f(w\psi)/w\psi | w\psi \in (T_1^* T_2^*), S \underset{*}{\overset{f(w\psi)}{\Rightarrow}} w\psi\}$. From the set of productions P, we know that $P_1, P_2 \subseteq P$. So, there exists

$$S \underset{\mathcal{G}}{\overset{1}{\to}} S_1 S_2 \underset{\mathcal{G}}{\overset{f_1(w)}{\to}} w S_2 \underset{\mathcal{G}}{\overset{f_2(\psi)}{\to}} w\psi,$$

satisfying

$$\rho = 1 \wedge f_1(w) \wedge f_2(\psi) = f_1(w) \wedge f_2(\psi).$$

Therefore, $\rho/w\psi \in \mathcal{L}$, i.e., $\mathcal{L}_1\mathcal{L}_2 \subseteq \mathcal{L}$.

Inversely, if $\forall \vartheta/\theta \in \mathcal{L}$, then $S \underset{\mathcal{G}}{\overset{\vartheta}{\to}} \theta$. In fact, each derivation of $\mathcal{G}$ must take the form $S \underset{\mathcal{G}}{\overset{\rho}{\to}} w\psi$ where $\rho = f_1'(w) \wedge f_2'(\psi)$, $f_1'(w)/w \in \mathcal{L}_1$ and $f_2'(\psi)/\psi \in \mathcal{L}_2$. From the set of productions P, we have $S \underset{\mathcal{G}}{\overset{1}{\to}} S_1 S_2 \underset{\mathcal{G}}{\overset{f_1'(w)}{\to}} w S_2 \underset{\mathcal{G}}{\overset{f_2'(\psi)}{\to}} w\psi$. For the derivation $S_1 S_2 \underset{\mathcal{G}}{\overset{f_1'(w)}{\to}} w S_2$ in the above derivation chain, only productions of P_1 are applied to the process of replacing S_1 by w. Thus, we have $S_1 S_2 \underset{\mathcal{G}_1}{\overset{f_1'(w)}{\to}} w S_2$, namely, $f_1'(w)/w \in \mathcal{L}_1$. Similarly, it is easy to verify that $f_2'(\psi)/\psi \in \mathcal{L}_2$. Then, we get $\rho = 1 \wedge f_1'(w) \wedge f_2'(\psi) = f_1'(w) \wedge f_2'(\psi)$.

So, for $\forall \vartheta/\theta \in \mathcal{L}$, there must exist $f_1(w)/w \in \mathcal{L}_1$ and $f_2(\psi)/\psi \in \mathcal{L}_2$ satisfying $\theta = w\psi$, $\vartheta = f_1(w) \wedge f_2(\psi)$, respectively. Therefore, $\vartheta/\theta \in \mathcal{L}_1\mathcal{L}_2$, i.e., $\mathcal{L} \subseteq \mathcal{L}_1\mathcal{L}_2$.

Thus, $f_1 f_2$ is a GN-FCFL. □

Theorem 23. *The set of GN-FCFLs is closed under Kleene closure.*

Proof. Let f_1 be a GN-FCFL. There exists a GN-FCFG $\mathcal{G}_1 = (V_1, T_1, P_1, S_1)$ such that $f_1 = f_{\mathcal{G}_1}$. From (ii) of Theorem 20, if f_1 is empty, then it is obvious that f_1^* is a GN-FCFL. So, we consider the case that f_1 is nonempty. We construct GN-FCFG $\mathcal{G} = (V_1 \cup \{S\}, T_1, P, S)$ where S $\notin V_1$ is an new start symbol and $P = P_1 \cup \{S \xrightarrow{1} S_1 S,\ S \xrightarrow{1} \varepsilon\}$.

We note $\mathcal{L}_1 = \{f_1(w_i)/w_i | w_i \in T_1^*, S_1 \overset{f_1(w_i)}{\underset{*}{\Rightarrow}} w_i\}$ $(1 \leq i \leq n)$. For any $\rho/w \in \mathcal{L}_1^*$, we break w into $w = w_1 w_2 \cdots w_n$ such that $\rho_i/w_i \in \mathcal{L}_1$ $(1 \leq i \leq n)$ and $\rho = \bigwedge_{i=1}^{n} \rho_i$. Then, it follows that $S_1 \underset{\mathcal{G}_1}{\overset{\rho_i}{\rightarrow}} w_i\,(1 \leq i \leq n)$. We define the set of fuzzy languages generated by $\mathcal{G}$ as $\mathcal{L} = \{f(w)/w | w \in T_1^*, S \overset{f(w)}{\underset{*}{\Rightarrow}} w\}$ satisfying $f(w) = \bigwedge_{i=1}^{n} f_1(w_i)$. By using the set of productions P, we have the next derivation chain:

$$S \underset{\mathcal{G}}{\overset{1}{\rightarrow}} S_1 S \underset{\mathcal{G}}{\overset{\rho_1}{\rightarrow}} w_1 S \underset{\mathcal{G}}{\overset{1}{\rightarrow}} w_1 S_1 S \underset{\mathcal{G}}{\overset{\rho_2}{\rightarrow}} \cdots \underset{\mathcal{G}}{\overset{\rho_n}{\rightarrow}} w_1 w_2 \cdots w_n S \underset{\mathcal{G}}{\overset{1}{\rightarrow}} w_1 w_2 \cdots w_n \varepsilon = w,$$

satisfying $\rho = 1 \wedge \rho_1 \wedge 1 \wedge \rho_2 \wedge \cdots \wedge \rho_n \wedge 1$. Therefore, $\rho/w \in \mathcal{L}$, i.e., $\mathcal{L}_1^* \subseteq \mathcal{L}$.

Inversely, we prove that if $\rho/w \in \mathcal{L}$, then $\rho/w \in \mathcal{L}_1^*$. The proof process is analogous with that of Theorem 22 and then we omit it here.

Thus, f_1^* is a GN-FCFL. □

Theorem 24. *If f_1 is a GN-FCFL and f_2 is a fuzzy regular language, then $f_1 \cap f_2$ is a GN-FCFL.*

Proof. In [32,33], it is shown that a fuzzy language $L_C(\mathcal{M})$ accepted by a deterministic fuzzy automaton $\mathcal{M}$ is a fuzzy regular language, defined for any $\theta \in \Sigma^*$ by $L_C(\mathcal{M})(\theta) = F(\delta^*(q_0, \theta))$. Let f_1 be a GN-FCFL and f_2 be a fuzzy regular language. Then, there exist a GN-FPDA $\mathcal{M}_1 = (Q_1, \Sigma, \Gamma, \delta_1, q_{01}, Z_0, F_1)$ and a deterministic fuzzy automaton $\mathcal{M}_2 = (Q_2, \Sigma, \delta_2, q_{02}, F_2)$ such that $f_1 = L_\aleph(\mathcal{M}_1), f_2 = L_C(\mathcal{M}_2)$, respectively.

Now, we construct a GN-FPDA $\mathcal{M} = (Q_1 \times Q_2, \Sigma, \Gamma, \delta, [q_{01}, q_{02}], Z_0, F_1 \times F_2)$, where for any $([q,p], \sigma, z) \in (Q_1 \times Q_2) \times (\Sigma \cup \{\varepsilon\}) \times \Gamma$,

$$\bigvee\{\mu([q', p'], \gamma) | \mu \in \delta([q,p], \sigma, Z)\} = \bigvee\{\mu(q', \gamma) | \mu \in \delta_1(q, \sigma, Z)\},$$
$$p' = \delta_2(p, \sigma) \quad \text{and} \quad (F_1 \times F_2(q,p)) = F_1(q) \wedge F_2(p).$$

Since there may be ε-moves made by $\mathcal{M}_1$ but there must not be ε-moves made by $\mathcal{M}_2$ in the processing of an input string, we define $\delta_2(p,\varepsilon)=p$ for any $p \in Q_2$. So, when $\sigma=\varepsilon$, we define

$$\bigvee\{\mu([q',p],\gamma)|\mu \in \delta([q,p],\varepsilon,Z)\} = \bigvee\{\mu(q',\gamma)|\mu \in \delta_1(q,\varepsilon,Z)\}.$$

For any $\theta \in \Sigma^*$, it is easy to verify that

$$\bigvee\{\mu([q,p],\gamma)|\mu \in \delta([q_{01},q_{02}],\theta,Z)\} = \rho \in (0,1] \text{ if and only if}$$
$$\bigvee\{\mu(q,\gamma)|\mu \in \delta_1(q_{01},\theta,Z)\} = \rho \text{ and } \delta_2(q_{02},\theta)=p.$$

Furthermore, we note that the set of final states in $\mathcal{M}$ is the Cartesian product of the set of final states in $\mathcal{M}_1$ and the set of final states in $\mathcal{M}_2$. So, we have that $(q,p) \in (F_1 \times F_2)$ if and only if $q \in F_1$ and $p \in F_2$, namely, $(F_1 \times F_2(q,p)) = F_1(q) \wedge F_2(p)$.

Therefore, for any $\theta \in \Sigma^*$, we obtain

$$L_{\aleph}(\mathcal{M})(\theta) = \bigvee_{(q,p)\in Q_1\times Q_2,\gamma\in\Gamma^*} [\Re^*(([q_{01},q_{02}],\theta,Z_0),([q,p],\varepsilon,\gamma))] \wedge (F_1 \times F_2(q,p))$$

if and only if

$$L_{\aleph}(\mathcal{M}_1)(\theta) = \bigvee_{q\in Q_1,\gamma\in\Gamma^*} [\Re^*((q_{01},\theta,Z_0),(q,\varepsilon,\gamma))] \wedge F_1(q), \text{ and } L_C(\mathcal{M}_2) = F_2(p).$$

Thus, $L_{\aleph}(\mathcal{M}) = L_{\aleph}(\mathcal{M}_1) \cap L_C(\mathcal{M}_2)$. □

5 Conclusions

This paper introduces a new kind of fuzzy pushdown automata called general-nondeterministic fuzzy pushdown automata as shown in Definition 6. Compared with previous models, developed by Su in [22], Xing et al. in [25] and Han in [26], our new model always has nondeterministic feature. It is verified that GN-FPDAs are more powerful than FPDAs in recognition ability. Interestingly, an hierarchy of the sets of fuzzy languages accepted by several kinds of fuzzy pushdown automata is presented. Moreover, the study of GN-FCFGs motivates us to consider the closure properties of the set of GN-FCFLs under some operations.

Acknowledgements. This paper was supported by the Research Project of the Fundamental Science (Natural Science) for Higher School in Jiangsu under Grant 21KJD520001.

References

1. Cao, Y., Ezawa, Y.: Nondeterministic fuzzy automata. Inf. Sci. **191**, 86–97 (2012)
2. Crisan, S., Tebrean, B.: Low cost, high quality vein pattern recognition device with liveness Detection. Workflow and implementations. Measurement **108**, 207–216 (2017)
3. Li, Y., Droste, M., Lei, L.: Model checking of linear-time properties in multi-valued systems. Inf. Sci. **377**, 51–74 (2017)
4. Yang, C., Li, Y.: ϵ-bisimulation relations for fuzzy automata. IEEE Trans. Fuzzy Syst. **26**(4), 2017–2029 (2018)
5. Yang, C., Li, Y.: Approximate bisimulations and state reduction of fuzzy automata under fuzzy similarity measures. Fuzzy Sets Syst. **391**(15), 72–95 (2020)
6. Ying, M.: A formal model of computing with words. IEEE Trans. Fuzzy Syst. **10**(5), 640–652 (2002)
7. Nguyen, P.H.D., Tran, D.Q., Lines, B.C.: Empirical inference system for highway project delivery selection using fuzzy pattern recognition. J. Constr. Eng. Manag. **146**, 04020141 (2020)
8. Wee, W.G.: On Generalizations of Adaptive Algorithm and Application of the Fuzzy Sets Concept to Pattern Classification. Purdue University, West Lafayette (1967). https://dl.acm.org/doi/book/10.5555/905166
9. Cao, Y., Chen, G., Kerre, E.: Bisimulations for fuzzy-transition systems. IEEE Trans. Fuzzy Syst. **19**(3), 540–552 (2015)
10. Li, Y.: Finite automata theory with membership values in lattices. Inf. Sci. **181**(5), 1003–1017 (2011)
11. Li, Y., Shao, X., Tong, S.: Adaptive fuzzy prescribed performance control of non-triangular structure nonlinear systems. IEEE Trans. Fuzzy Syst. **28**(10), 2416–2426 (2019)
12. Lee, E.T., Zadeh, L.A.: Note on fuzzy languages. Inf. Sci. **1**, 421–434 (1969)
13. Malik, D.S., Mordeson, J.N.: On fuzzy regular languages. Inf. Sci. **88**(1–4), 263–273 (1994)
14. Mordeson, J.N., Malik, D.S.: Fuzzy Automata and Languages: Theory and Applications. Chapman & Hall/CRC, Boca Raton (2002). https://www.abe.pl/pl/book/9781584882251/fuzzy-automata-languages-theory-applications
15. Bucurescu, I., Pascu, A.: Fuzzy pushdown automata. Int. J. Comput. Math. **10**(2), 109–119 (1981)
16. Clemente, L., Lasota, S.: Reachability relations of timed pushdown automata. J. Comput. Syst. Sci. **117**, 202–241 (2021)
17. Ghorani, M.: On characterization of fuzzy tree pushdown automata. Soft. Comput. **23**, 1123–1131 (2019). https://doi.org/10.1007/s00500-017-2829-7
18. Ghorani, M., Garhwal, S., Moghari, S.: Lattice-valued tree pushdown automata: pumping lemma and closure properties. Int. J. Approximate Reasoning **142**, 301–323 (2022)
19. Guillon, B., Pighizzini, G., Prigioniero, L.: Non-self-embedding grammars, constant-height pushdown automata, and limited automata. Int. J. Found. Comput. Sci. **31**, 1133–1157 (2020)
20. Jancar, P.: Equivalence of pushdown automata via first-order grammars. J. Comput. Syst. Sci. **115**, 86–112 (2021)
21. Kalra, N., Kumar, A.: Fuzzy state grammar and fuzzy deep pushdown automaton. J. Intell. Fuzzy Syst. **31**(1), 249–258 (2016)

22. Su, L.: Pushdown automata accepted fuzzy context free language. J. UEST China **21**, 187–190 (1992)
23. Wu, Q., Wang, X., Wang, Y.: Application of fuzzy pushdown automaton on prediction of quality control for spinning yarn. Inf. Technol. Control **50**(1), 76–88 (2021)
24. Xing, H.: Fuzzy pushdown automata. Fuzzy Sets Syst. **158**(13), 1437–1449 (2007)
25. Xing, H., Qiu, D., Liu, F.: Automata theory based on complete residuated lattice-valued logic: pushdown automata. Fuzzy Sets Syst. **160**(8), 1125–1140 (2009)
26. Han, Z., Li, Y.: Pushdown automata and context-free grammars based on quantum logic. J. Softw. **21**(9), 2107–2117 (2010)
27. Cao, Y., Ezawa, Y., Sun, S., Wang, H., Chen, G.: A behavioral distance for fuzzy-transition systems. IEEE Trans. Fuzzy Syst. **21**(4), 735–747 (2013)
28. Nithya, V., Senthilkumar, S.: Detection and avoidance of input validation attacks in web application using deterministic push down automata. J. Autom. Inf. Sci. **51**(9), 32–51 (2019)
29. Esparza, J., Kucera, A., Mayr, R.: Model checking probabilistic pushdown automata. Log. Methods Comput. Sci. **2**(1–2), 1–31 (2006)
30. Droste, M., Kuich, W., Vogler, H.: Handbook of Weighted Automata. Springer, Berlin (2009). https://doi.org/10.1007/978-3-642-01492-5
31. Li, T., Li, P.: Fuzzy Computing Theory. Academic Press, Beijing (2016)
32. Bělohávek, R.: Determinism and fuzzy automata. Inf. Sci. **143**(1–4), 205–209 (2002)
33. Li, Y., Wang, Q.: The universal fuzzy automaton. Fuzzy Sets Syst. **249**, 27–48 (2014)

Joint Degree Distribution of Growing Multiplex Network Model with Nonlinear Preferential Attachment Rule

Youjun Lu[1(✉)], Yongqiu Guan[1], Jiaying Wei[1], Yanjun Liang[1], Li Fu[2], Feiyu Zuo[1], and Yunfeng Deng[1]

[1] College of Data Science and Information Engineering, Guizhou Minzu University, Guiyang, China
yjlu111@126.com

[2] Department of Information Engineering, Guiyang Institute of Information Science and Technology, Guiyang, China

Abstract. Many complex systems in real life are made up of several subsystems that evolve through time. Multiplex growth network models, in which edges reflect different types between the same vertex set, can be used to represent such systems. Here we put forward a new multiplex growth network model based on nonlinear preferential attachment rule. Firstly, we derive the general joint degree distribution expression of the model via the rate equation approach at the steady-state. Secondly, by using the Z-transform theory, we obtain the joint degree distribution of the model corresponding to the weight function $f(k) = k$ and $f(k) = c > 0$. Finally, we apply Monte Carlo simulation to check the correctness of the theoretical analysis, the research shows that the theoretical results are corroborated with Monte Carlo simulations.

Keywords: Multiplex network model · Nonlinear preferential attachment rule · Joint degree distribution

1 Introduction

The network framework is widely utilized for studying various complex systems and their properties, by means of mapping primary elements onto vertices and interactions onto edges, such as the World Wide Web [1], the Internet [2], protein networks [3], social networks [4], scientific collaboration networks [5] and others. Many scholars have worked over the last few decades to develop a collection of models that characterize the crucial properties of these real-world complex systems [6–11]. Although many real-world complex systems involve different types of edges between vertices, the standard model assumes that the interaction between vertices is equivalent. As a result, common assumptions could omit crucial details regarding the structure and function of the original complex system. In reality,

Supported by organization x.

Z. Cai et al. (Eds.): NCTCS 2022, CCIS 1693, pp. 26–42, 2022.
https://doi.org/10.1007/978-981-19-8152-4_2

these systems can be easily described by multiplex network, the vertices in the network are components of distinct network layers, and each layer corresponding to a certain kind of edge. Especially, multiplex structures can be found in a variety of places, such as social networks, transportation and communication systems [12–15] and so on. The edge connections with multiple relationships between the same vertex pairs are a common feature of these systems.

Various multiplex network models have been presented for describing and simulating the structure and behavior of these systems in recent years. For example, Kim et al. proposed a modeling framework based on network layer coevolution, in which the chance that an existing vertex will gain an edge from the new addition is a function of the degree of other vertices at all layers in [16]. In [17,18], Nicosia et al. proposed a broad multiplex network model based on nonlinear preferential attachment rule, which was inspired by the classical model [7]. Both uniform and preferential growth were considered by Fotouhi and Momeni [19,20], who presented a new multiplex network growth model with any number of layers. A variety of measuring methods have been established to characterize the structure and features of multiplex networks, including degree centrality and node ranking [22–25], clustering coefficient [26], degree correlation [27], and community structure [28–31]. Furthermore, some academics are interested in investigating dynamic process on a variety of multiplex topologies, such as diffusion process [32–35], propagation [36,37], cooperation [38–40], synchronization [41,42] and random walks [43] and others. In multilayer networks, different connection pattern is represented by different layers usually. In the standard multilayer network evolution model, only potential connections between new vertices and existing vertices in each layer are taken into account at any one time, whereas potential connections between existing vertices in each layer are ignored. In [21], Lu et al. proposed a two-layer network growth model with nonlinear preferential attachment rules to describe this phenomenon. However, there are not only one or two connection patterns in complex systems in real life, but more than two connection patterns. Therefore, we extend the two-layer network growth model with nonlinear preferential attachment rules in [21] to the multiplex growth network model with any number of layers, which is related to probability p, the number of network edges m_l added to each layer at each time, and the weight function f. The general joint degree distribution of multiplex growth network model is studied. The joint degree distribution of two weight functions $f(k) = k$ and $f(k) = c > 0$ corresponding to multiplex growth network model is analyzed respectively. It is found that the joint degree distribution is related to probability p and the number of network edges m_l added to each layer at each time.

The paper is organized as follows. In Sect. 2, there are some definitions and notations are given, according to the nonlinear preferential attachment rule, we propose a new multiplex growth network model with arbitrary number of layers. In Sect. 3, the general joint degree distribution of a multiplex growth network model in steady state is derived using the rate equation approach. Moreover, we analyze the joint degree distribution of the multiplex growth network model corresponding to the weight function $f(k) = k$ and $f(k) = c > 0$ via Z-transform theory, separately. In Sect. 4, we apply Monte Carlo simulation to ensure that the theoretical result are true. Finally, the conclusions are given in Sect. 5.

2 Definitions and Model

2.1 Definitions and Notations

A multilayer network [27] that comprising L layers can be completely described by $\mathcal{M} = (\mathcal{G}, \mathcal{C})$, where we denote by $\mathcal{G} = \{G_l : l \in \{1, 2, \cdots, L\}\}$ a family of graphs $G_l = (X_l, E_l)$, and by $\mathcal{C} = \{E_{lr} \subseteq X_l \times X_r : l \neq r \in \{1, 2, \cdots, L\}\}$ the set of interconnections between vertices in layers l and r. The elements of $\mathcal{C}$ are called inter-layer connections, and the elements of each E_l are called intra-layer connections of $\mathcal{M}$. The set of vertices of each layer G_l is given by $X_l = \{x_1^l, x_2^l \cdots, x_{N_l}^l\}$, where N_l is the number of vertices in layer l. The adjacency matrix of each layer G_l is denoted by $A^{[l]} = (a_{ij}^l) \in R^{N_l \times N_l}$, where $a_{ij}^l = 1$ if $(x_i^l, x_j^l) \in E_l$, otherwise $a_{ij}^l = 0$, for $1 \leq i, j \leq N_l$ and $1 \leq l \leq L$. The inter-layer adjacency matrix corresponding to E_{lr} is the matrix $A^{[l,r]} = (a_{ij}^{lr}) \in R^{N_l \times N_r}$, where $a_{ij}^{lr} = 1$ if $(x_i^l, x_j^r) \in E_{lr}$, otherwise $a_{ij}^{lr} = 0$.

A multiplex network [22] can be thought of as a multi-layer network by taking $X_1 = X_2 = \cdots = X_L = X$ and the only possible type of inter-layer connections are $E_{lr} = \{(x, x) : x \in X\}$ for every $l \neq r \in \{1, 2, \cdots, L\}$. In other words, multiplex networks consist of a fixed set of vertices connected by different types of edges. In the multiplex network $\mathcal{M} = (\mathcal{G}, \mathcal{C})$, the degree of a vertex $i \in X$ is characterized by vector $\mathrm{K} = (k_i^{[1]}, k_i^{[2]}, \cdots, k_i^{[L]})$, where $k_i^{[l]}$ is the degree of vertex i in layer l, i.e. $k_i^{[l]} = \sum_j a_{ij}^{[l]}$. Let N be the total number of vertices of the networks, and $N(\mathrm{K})$ be the number of vertices whose degree vector is K. We denote by $P(\mathrm{K})$ the fraction of vertices whose degree vector is K. Hence, the joint degree distribution of the multiplex network is given by $P(\mathrm{K}) = N(\mathrm{K})/N$.

2.2 Multiplex Growth Network Model

The nonlinear preferential attachment rule means that the probability $\Pi_{i \to j}^{[l]}$ of a newborn vertex i connecting an existing vertex j in layer l is proportional to a non-negative function f, respectively, i.e.,

$$\Pi_{i \to j}^{[l]} = \frac{f(k_j^{[l]})}{\Sigma_v f(k_v^{[l]})}, \quad l = 1, 2, \cdots, L. \tag{1}$$

where $k_j^{[l]}$ is the degree of vertex j in layer l, f is called the weight function, which is defined as if $1 \leq m \leq k \leq M \leq \infty$, then $f(k) > 0$, otherwise $f(k) = 0$, where m is the minimum degree and M is the maximum degree [10].

In the following, we generalize two layer growth network model with nonlinear preferential attachment rule in [21] to $L > 2$ layers, and record it as a multiplex growth network model $\mathcal{M}_L = (\mathcal{G}_L, \mathcal{C})$, where $\mathcal{G}_L = \{G_l(p, m_l, f)[t] :$

$l \in \{1, 2, \cdots, L\}; 0 \leq t \leq T\}$ and $\mathcal{C} = \{E_{lr} \subseteq X_l \times X_r : l \neq r \in \{1, 2, \cdots, L\}\}$. The network layer $G_l(p, m_l, f)[t]$ at time t is related to the probability p, the number of edges m_l added the network layer l and the weight function f, T is the evolution time of the multiplex growth network model $\mathcal{M}_L = (\mathcal{G}_L, \mathcal{C})$.

The construction algorithm of the multiplex growth network model $\mathcal{M}_L = (\mathcal{G}_L, \mathcal{C})$ with $\mathcal{G}_L = \{G_l(p, m_l, f)[t] : l \in \{1, 2, \cdots, L\}; 0 \leq t \leq T\}$ is as follows.

Algorithm 1: $\mathcal{M}_L$ Construction Algorithm

```
Input: p, m_l, f, T;
Output: M_L = (G_L, C);
Start from initial network G_l(p, m_l, f)[0] in each layer l;
while t ≤ T do
    Generate a random number r ∈ (0, 1);
    if r < p then
        Add a new vertex and L − 1 replica vertices;
        Each newly added vertex has m_l new edges that with probability
        Π^[l]_{i→j} are attached to existing vertices of the same layer.
    else
        Add m_l new edges to each layer, respectively;
        Each new edge that with probability Π^[l]_{i→j} are connected to vertex
        of the corresponding layer.
    end
end
```

In the multiplex growth network model $\mathcal{M}_L = (\mathcal{G}_L, \mathcal{C})$, each layer is formed of an undirected and unweighted network model and all layers have the same vertices. In this case, the vertex degree distribution in each layer is provided by the vertex degree distribution of the single layer growth network model proposed by [44]. Figure 1 shows the evolution process of the multiplex growth network model $\mathcal{M}_L = (\mathcal{G}_L, \mathcal{C})$ with $L = 3, m_1 = 1, m_2 = 2$ and $m_3 = 3$ at time $t = 0, 1, 2$.

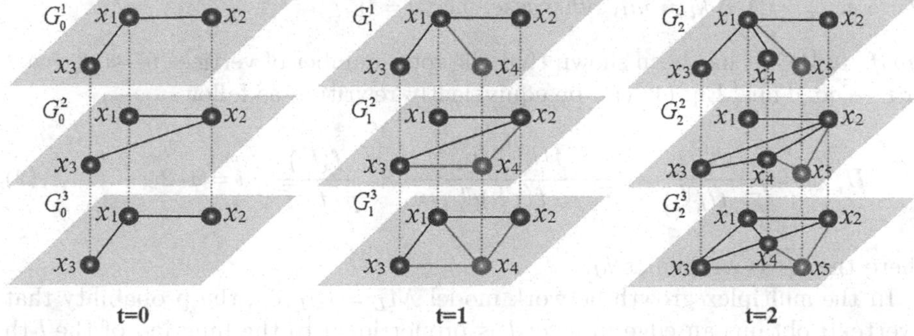

Fig. 1. The evolution process of the multiplex growth network model $\mathcal{M}_L = (\mathcal{G}_L, \mathcal{C})$.

3 Joint Degree Distribution in Multiplex Network Model

In this section, we are interested in the general joint degree distribution of the multiplex growth network model $\mathcal{M}_L = (\mathcal{G}_L, \mathcal{C})$ with $\mathcal{G}_L = \{G_l(p, m_l, f)[t] : l \in \{1, 2, \cdots, L\}; 0 \leq t \leq T\}$. In the following, the steady-state joint degree distribution expression of the weight function f corresponding to the multiplex growth network model $\mathcal{M}_L = (\mathcal{G}_L, \mathcal{C})$ is proved via the rate equation approach [19], which is widely used for studying the evolution of degrees of individual vertices. Taking into account the general characteristics of the weight function f, we also study the joint degree distribution of the weight function $f(k) = k$ and $f(k) = c > 0$ corresponding to the multiplex growth network model $\mathcal{M}_L = (\mathcal{G}_L, \mathcal{C})$ using z-transform theory.

3.1 General Weight Function *f*

We denote by $\overline{f}_l = \sum_{r \geq m} f(r^{[l]}) Q_r$ the average weight of graph vertices in the layer l, and we denote the number of vertices having the connectivity degree r at time t in layer l by $d^l_{r,t}$, Q_r is the probability that a randomly selected vertex has degree r. Here, We demonstrate that the general joint degree distribution expression for the multiplex growth network model $\mathcal{M}_L = (\mathcal{G}_L, \mathcal{C})$ with $\mathcal{G}_L = \{G_l(p, m_l, f)[t] : l \in \{1, 2, \cdots, L\}; 0 \leq t \leq T\}$ via the rate equation approach.

Theorem 1. *In the multiplex growth network model $\mathcal{M}_L = (\mathcal{G}_L, \mathcal{C})$ with $\mathcal{G}_L = \{G_l(p, m_l, f)[t] : l \in \{1, 2, \cdots, L\}; 0 \leq t \leq T\}$. Suppose the average weight of graph vertices is $\overline{f}_l \neq 0$ in layer l, then the general joint degree distribution expression $P(\mathrm{K})$ is given by*

$$P(\mathrm{K}) = \frac{\sum\limits_{l=1}^{L} \prod\limits_{i=1, i \neq l}^{L} \overline{f}_i m_l f(k_l - 1) \cdot P(\mathrm{K} - \mathrm{e}_l)}{\frac{p}{2-p} \prod\limits_{l=1}^{L} \overline{f}_l + \sum\limits_{l=1}^{L} \prod\limits_{i=1, i \neq l}^{L} \overline{f}_i m_l f(k_l)} + \frac{\frac{p}{2-p} \prod\limits_{l=1}^{L} \overline{f}_l \prod\limits_{l=1}^{L} \delta_{k_l, m_l}}{\frac{p}{2-p} \prod\limits_{l=1}^{L} \overline{f}_l + \sum\limits_{l=1}^{L} \prod\limits_{i=1, i \neq l}^{L} \overline{f}_i m_l f(k_l)}.$$

where $\delta_{k_l, m_l} = 1$ if $k_l = m_l$, otherwise, $\delta_{k_l, m_l} = 0$.

Proof. In [44], it has been shown that the total number of vertices $n_t \approx n_0 + p \cdot t$ for $t \to \infty$. Thus, Eq. (1) can be equivalently rewritten as follows:

$$\Pi^{[l]}_{i \to j} = \frac{f(k^{[l]}_j)}{\Sigma_v f(k^{[l]}_v)} = \frac{f(k^{[l]}_j)/n_t}{\Sigma_{r \geq m} f(r^{[l]}) d^l_{r,t}/n_t} = \frac{f(k_l)}{p \cdot t \cdot \overline{f}_l}, \quad l = 1, 2, \cdots, L. \tag{2}$$

where the $k^{[l]}_j$ is written as k_l.

In the multiplex growth network model $\mathcal{M}_L = (\mathcal{G}_L, \mathcal{C})$, the probability that a vertex i obtains an edge in layer l is proportional to the function of the l-th component k_l of degree vector K. If vertex x with degree k receives an edge in layer l, then its degree will change to $\mathrm{K} + \mathrm{e}_l$, where e_l is the unit vector in l-th dimension, that is to say, it is a vector whose elements are all zero except its l-th element, which is unity. We denote by $N_t(\mathrm{K})$ the number of vertices that have degree vector K at arbitrary time t, and the rate equation for $N_t(\mathrm{K})$ is given by

$$\begin{aligned} N_{t+1}(\mathrm{K}) &= 2(1-p)\sum_{l=1}^{L} m_l \frac{f(k_l-1)\cdot N_t(\mathrm{K}-\mathrm{e}_l) - f(k_l)\cdot N_t(\mathrm{K})}{p\cdot t\cdot \overline{f_l}} + p\prod_{l=1}^{L}\delta_{k_l,m_l} \\ &\quad + p\sum_{l=1}^{L} m_l \frac{f(k_l-1)\cdot N_t(\mathrm{K}-\mathrm{e}_l) - f(k_l)\cdot N_t(\mathrm{K})}{p\cdot t\cdot \overline{f_l}} + N_t(\mathrm{K}) \\ &= (2-p)\sum_{l=1}^{L} m_l \frac{f(k_l-1)\cdot N_t(\mathrm{K}-\mathrm{e}_l) - f(k_l)\cdot N_t(\mathrm{K})}{p\cdot t\cdot \overline{f_l}} \\ &\quad + N_t(\mathrm{K}) + p\prod_{l=1}^{L}\delta_{k_l,m_l}. \end{aligned} \tag{3}$$

Assuming that $N_t(\mathrm{K}) \to n_t \cdot P(\mathrm{K}) \approx p\cdot t\cdot P(\mathrm{K})$ is valid for $t\to\infty$, and combing this with Eq. (3), we can obtain the following expression for $P(\mathrm{K})$,

$$P(\mathrm{K}) = \frac{2-p}{p}\left(\sum_{l=1}^{L} m_l \frac{f(k_l-1)\cdot P(\mathrm{K}-\mathrm{e}_l) - f(k_l)\cdot P(\mathrm{K})}{\overline{f_l}}\right) + \prod_{l=1}^{L}\delta_{k_l,m_l}. \tag{4}$$

Solving Eq. (4), we can obtain the following general joint degree distribution expression $P(\mathrm{K})$. Namely,

$$P(\mathrm{K}) = \frac{\sum\limits_{l=1}^{L}\prod\limits_{i=1,i\neq l}^{L}\overline{f_i} m_l f(k_l-1)\cdot P(\mathrm{K}-\mathrm{e}_l)}{\frac{p}{2-p}\prod\limits_{l=1}^{L}\overline{f_l} + \sum\limits_{l=1}^{L}\prod\limits_{i=1,i\neq l}^{L}\overline{f_i} m_l f(k_l)} + \frac{\frac{p}{2-p}\prod\limits_{l=1}^{L}\overline{f_l}\prod\limits_{l=1}^{L}\delta_{k_l,m_l}}{\frac{p}{2-p}\prod\limits_{l=1}^{L}\overline{f_l} + \sum\limits_{l=1}^{L}\prod\limits_{i=1,i\neq l}^{L}\overline{f_i} m_l f(k_l)} \tag{5}$$

3.2 The Weight Function $f(k) = k$

Here, we use Z-transform and inverse Z-transform to investigate the joint degree distribution $P(\mathrm{K})$ of the multiplex growth network model $\mathcal{M}_L = (\mathcal{G}_L, \mathcal{C})$ with $\mathcal{G}_L = \{G_l(p, m_l, f)[t] : l \in \{1, 2, \cdots, L\}; 0 \le t \le T\}$ corresponding to the weight function $f(k) = k$. If the weight function $f(k) = k$, then the nonlinear preferential attachment probability reduces to the linear preferential attachment probability was given in [7].

Theorem 2. *In the multiplex growth network model* $\mathcal{M}_L = (\mathcal{G}_L, \mathcal{C})$ *with* $\mathcal{G}_L = \{G_l(p, m_l, f)[t] : l \in \{1, 2, \cdots, L\}; 0 \le t \le T\}$*, if the weight function* $f(k) = k$*, then the joint degree distribution* $P(\mathrm{K})$ *is given by*

$$P(\mathrm{K}) = \frac{2\Gamma\left(\sum\limits_{l=1}^{L} m_l + \frac{2}{2-p}\right)}{(2-p)\prod\limits_{l=1}^{L}\Gamma(m_l)} \frac{\Gamma\left(\sum\limits_{l=1}^{L}(k_l - m_l) + 1\right)\prod\limits_{l=1}^{L}\Gamma(k_l)}{\prod\limits_{l=1}^{L}\Gamma(k_l - m_l + 1)\Gamma\left(\sum\limits_{l=1}^{L} k_l + \frac{2}{2-p} + 1\right)}.$$

where $\Gamma(x) = \int_0^{+\infty} t^{x-1}e^{-t}dt$ *is Gamma function for* $x > 0$.

Proof. In the multiplex growth network model $\mathcal{M}_L = (\mathcal{G}_L, \mathcal{C})$, if the weight function $f(k) = k$, then by Theorem 1, we have

$$P(\mathrm{K}) = \sum_{l=1}^{L} \frac{(k_l - 1) \cdot P(\mathrm{K} - \mathrm{e}_l)}{\sum_{l=1}^{L} k_l + \frac{2}{2-p}} + \frac{2}{(2-p)\sum_{l=1}^{L} k_l + 2} \prod_{l=1}^{L} \delta_{k_l, m_l}. \tag{6}$$

In order to solve Eq. (6), we define the following new sequence

$$m(\mathrm{K}) = \frac{\Gamma\left(\sum_{l=1}^{L} k_l + \frac{2}{2-p} + 1\right)}{\prod_{l=1}^{L} \Gamma(k_l)} P(\mathrm{K}). \tag{7}$$

By Eq. (7), we observe that the following holds for $l = 1, 2, \cdots, L$.

$$\frac{k_l - 1}{\sum_{l=1}^{L} k_l + \frac{2}{2-p}} P(\mathrm{K} - \mathrm{e}_l) = \frac{\prod_{l=1}^{L} \Gamma(k_l)}{\Gamma\left(\sum_{l=1}^{L} k_l + \frac{2}{2-p} + 1\right)} m(\mathrm{K} - \mathrm{e}_l). \tag{8}$$

Combing Eqs. (6) and Eq. (8), we can obtain

$$m(\mathrm{K}) = \sum_{l=1}^{L} m(\mathrm{K} - \mathrm{e}_l) + \frac{2\Gamma\left(\sum_{l=1}^{L} k_l + \frac{2}{2-p}\right)}{(2-p)\prod_{l=1}^{L} \Gamma(k_l)} \prod_{l=1}^{L} \delta_{k_l, m_l}. \tag{9}$$

Now, we define the Z-transform of sequence $m(\mathrm{K})$ as follows:

$$\varphi(Z) = \sum_{k_1=m_1}^{\infty} \sum_{k_2=m_2}^{\infty} \cdots \sum_{k_L=m_L}^{\infty} m(\mathrm{K}) \prod_{l=1}^{L} {z_l}^{-k_l}. \tag{10}$$

where $Z = (z_1, z_2, \cdots, z_L)$. Then the inverse Z transform is given by

$$m(\mathrm{K}) = \frac{1}{(2\pi i)^L} \oint \cdots \oint \varphi(Z) \prod_{l=1}^{L} {z_l}^{k_l - 1} dz_1 \cdots dz_L. \tag{11}$$

Taking the Z-transform of every term in Eq. (9), we have

$$\varphi(Z) = \varphi(Z) \sum_{l=1}^{L} {z_l}^{-1} + \frac{2\Gamma\left(\sum_{l=1}^{L} m_l + \frac{2}{2-p}\right)}{(2-p)\prod_{l=1}^{L} \Gamma(m_l)} \prod_{l=1}^{L} {z_l}^{-m_l}. \tag{12}$$

Solving Eq. (12), we can obtain

$$\varphi(Z) = \frac{2\Gamma\left(\sum\limits_{l=1}^{L} m_l + \frac{2}{2-p}\right)}{(2-p)\prod\limits_{l=1}^{L}\Gamma(m_l)} \frac{\prod\limits_{l=1}^{L} z_l^{-m_l}}{1-\sum\limits_{l=1}^{L} z_l^{-1}}. \tag{13}$$

Combing Eq. (11) with Eq. (13), we can obtain the following expression for $m(\mathrm{K})$,

$$\begin{aligned}
m(\mathrm{K}) &= \frac{1}{(2\pi i)^L}\oint\cdots\oint \frac{2\Gamma\left(\sum\limits_{l=1}^{L} m_l+\frac{2}{2-p}\right)}{(2-p)\prod\limits_{l=1}^{L}\Gamma(m_l)} \frac{\prod\limits_{l=1}^{L} z_l^{k_l-m_l-1}}{1-\sum\limits_{l=1}^{L} z_l^{-1}} dz_1\cdots dz_L \\
&= \frac{\Delta}{(2\pi i)^L}\oint\cdots\oint \prod_{l=1}^{L} z_l^{k_l-m_l-1}\sum_{n=0}^{\infty}\left(\sum_{l=1}^{L} z_l^{-1}\right)^n dz_1\cdots dz_L \\
&= \frac{\Delta}{(2\pi i)^L}\oint\cdots\oint \sum_{n=0}^{\infty}\sum_{\sum_{l=1}^{L} r_l=n}\binom{n}{r_1, r_2, \cdots, r_L}\prod_{l=1}^{L} z_l^{k_l-m_l-r_l-1} dz_1\cdots dz_L \\
&= \frac{2\Gamma\left(\sum\limits_{l=1}^{L} m_l+\frac{2}{2-p}\right)}{(2-p)\prod\limits_{l=1}^{L}\Gamma(m_l)}\binom{n}{k_1-m_1, k_2-m_2, \cdots, k_L-m_L} \\
&= \frac{2\Gamma\left(\sum\limits_{l=1}^{L} m_l+\frac{2}{2-p}\right)}{(2-p)\prod\limits_{l=1}^{L}\Gamma(m_l)} \frac{\Gamma\left(\sum_{l=1}^{L}(k_l-m_l)+1\right)}{\prod\limits_{l=1}^{L}\Gamma(k_l-m_l+1)}.
\end{aligned} \tag{14}$$

where

$$\Delta = \frac{2\Gamma\left(\sum\limits_{l=1}^{L} m_l+\frac{2}{2-p}\right)}{(2-p)\prod\limits_{l=1}^{L}\Gamma(m_l)}.$$

Inserting Eq. (14) into Eq. (7), then we can obtain that the joint degree distribution $P(\mathrm{K})$ for the model corresponding to the weight function $f(k) = k$. The solutions is

$$P(\mathrm{K}) = \frac{2\Gamma\left(\sum\limits_{l=1}^{L} m_l+\frac{2}{2-p}\right)}{(2-p)\prod\limits_{l=1}^{L}\Gamma(m_l)} \frac{\Gamma\left(\sum\limits_{l=1}^{L}(k_l-m_l)+1\right)\prod\limits_{l=1}^{L}\Gamma(k_l)}{\prod\limits_{l=1}^{L}\Gamma(k_l-m_l+1)\Gamma\left(\sum\limits_{l=1}^{L} k_l+\frac{2}{2-p}+1\right)}. \tag{15}$$

In particular, when $p = 1$, Theorem 2 is consistent with the results in [20]. Now let us consider some special cases in order to gain insight into the pattern. For $L = 1$, we have

$$P(k) = \frac{2}{2-p} \frac{\Gamma(k)\Gamma\left(m + \frac{2}{2-p}\right)}{\Gamma(m)\Gamma\left(k + \frac{2}{2-p} + 1\right)}, k \geq m. \tag{16}$$

This result agrees with single layer growth network model's degree distribution, obtained for instance in [44]. For $L = 2$ and $k = k_1 \geq m_1$, $l = k_2 \geq m_2$, we noticed that this result accords with the joint degree distribution of the two layer growth network model in [21]. Namely,

$$P(k,l) = \frac{2\Gamma\left(m_1 + m_2 + \frac{2}{2-p}\right)\Gamma(k)\Gamma(l)}{(2-p)\Gamma(m_1)\Gamma(m_2)\Gamma\left(k + l + \frac{2}{2-p} + 1\right)} \times \frac{\Gamma(k + l - m_1 - m_2 + 1)}{\Gamma(k - m_1 + 1)\Gamma(l - m_2 + 1)} \tag{17}$$

3.3 The Weight Function $f(k) = c > 0$

In the following, we study the joint degree distribution $P(\mathrm{K})$ of the multiplex growth network model $\mathcal{M}_L = (\mathcal{G}_L, \mathcal{C})$ with $\mathcal{G}_L = \{G_l(p, m_l, f)[t] : l \in \{1, 2, \cdots, L\}; 0 \leq t \leq T\}$, corresponding to the weight function $f(k) = c > 0$ via Z-transform and inverse Z-transform theory. If the weight function $f(k) = c > 0$, then the nonlinear preferential attachment probability reduces to the uniform random attachment probability.

Theorem 3. *In the multiplex growth network model $\mathcal{M}_L = (\mathcal{G}_L, \mathcal{C})$ with $\mathcal{G}_L = \{G_l(p, m_l, f)[t] : l \in \{1, 2, \cdots, L\}; 0 \leq t \leq T\}$, if the weight function $f(k) = c > 0$, then the joint degree distribution $P(\mathrm{K})$ is given by*

$$P(\mathrm{K}) = \frac{p \prod_{l=1}^{L} m_l^{k_l - m_l} \Gamma\left(\sum_{l=1}^{L}(k_l - m_l) + 1\right)}{(2-p)\left(\sum_{l=1}^{L} m_l + \frac{p}{2-p}\right)^{1 + \sum_{l=1}^{L}(k_l - m_l)} \prod_{l=1}^{L} \Gamma(k_l - m_l + 1)}.$$

where $\Gamma(x) = \int_0^{+\infty} t^{x-1} e^{-t} dt$ is Gamma function for $x > 0$.

Proof. In the multiplex growth network model $\mathcal{M}_L = (\mathcal{G}_L, \mathcal{C})$, if the weight function $f(k) = c > 0$, then by Theorem 1, we can get

$$\begin{aligned} P(\mathrm{K}) &= \frac{\sum_{l=1}^{L} m_l P(\mathrm{K} - \mathrm{e}_l)}{\sum_{l=1}^{L} m_l + \frac{p}{2-p}} + \frac{\frac{p}{2-p} \prod_{l=1}^{L} \delta_{k_l, m_l}}{\sum_{l=1}^{L} m_l + \frac{p}{2-p}} \\ &= \sum_{l=1}^{L} q_l \cdot P(\mathrm{K} - \mathrm{e}_l) + B \prod_{l=1}^{L} \delta_{k_l, m_l}. \end{aligned} \tag{18}$$

where

$$q_l = \frac{m_l}{A}, B = \frac{p}{(2-p)A}, A = \sum_{l=1}^{L} m_l + \frac{p}{2-p}. \tag{19}$$

Here, in order to solve Eq. (18), we also define the Z-transform of sequence $P(\mathrm{K})$ as follows:

$$\Phi(Z) = \sum_{k_1=m_1}^{\infty} \sum_{k_2=m_2}^{\infty} \cdots \sum_{k_L=m_L}^{\infty} P(\mathrm{K}) \prod_{l=1}^{L} {z_l}^{-k_l}. \tag{20}$$

where $Z = (z_1, z_2, \cdots, z_L)$, then the inverse transform is given by

$$P(\mathrm{K}) = \frac{1}{(2\pi i)^L} \oint \oint \ldots \oint \Phi(Z) \prod_{l=1}^{L} {z_l}^{k_l - 1} dz_1 dz_2 \cdots dz_L. \tag{21}$$

Taking the Z-transform of every term in Eq. (18), we have

$$\Phi(Z) = \Phi(Z) \sum_{l=1}^{L} q_l {z_l}^{-1} + B \prod_{l=1}^{L} z_l^{-m_l}. \tag{22}$$

Solving Eq. (22), we obtain

$$\Phi(Z) = \frac{B \prod\limits_{l=1}^{L} z_l^{-m_l}}{1 - \sum\limits_{l=1}^{L} q_l z_l^{-1}}. \tag{23}$$

Plugging Eq. (23) into Eq. (21), we can get

$$\begin{aligned}
P(\mathrm{K}) &= \frac{1}{(2\pi i)^L} \oint \cdots \oint \frac{B \prod\limits_{l=1}^{L} z_l^{k_l - m_l - 1}}{1 - \sum\limits_{l=1}^{L} q_l z_l^{-1}} dz_1 \cdots dz_L \\
&= \frac{B}{(2\pi i)^L} \oint \cdots \oint \prod_{l=1}^{L} z_l^{k_l - m_l - 1} \sum_{n=0}^{\infty} \left(\sum_{l=1}^{L} q_l z_l^{-1} \right)^n dz_1 \cdots dz_L \\
&= \frac{B}{(2\pi i)^L} \oint \cdots \oint \sum_{n=0}^{\infty} \sum_{\sum_{l=1}^{L} r_l = n} \binom{n}{r_1, r_2, \cdots, r_L} \prod_{l=1}^{L} q_l^{r_l} z_l^{k_l - m_l - r_l - 1} dz_1 \cdots dz_L \\
&= B \binom{n}{k_1 - m_1, k_2 - m_2, \cdots, k_L - m_L} \prod_{l=1}^{L} q_l^{k_l - m_l} \\
&= \frac{B \cdot \Gamma\left(\sum_{l=1}^{L} (k_l - m_l) + 1\right) \prod\limits_{l=1}^{L} q_l^{k_l - m_l}}{\prod\limits_{l=1}^{L} \Gamma(k_l - m_l + 1)}.
\end{aligned} \tag{24}$$

Combing Eq. (19) and Eq. (24), the joint degree distribution for the weight function $f(k) = c > 0$ is given by

$$P(\mathrm{K}) = \frac{p \prod_{l=1}^{L} m_l^{k_l - m_l} \Gamma\left(\sum_{l=1}^{L}(k_l - m_l) + 1\right)}{(2-p)\left(\sum_{l=1}^{L} m_l + \frac{p}{2-p}\right)^{1+\sum_{l=1}^{L}(k_l - m_l)} \prod_{l=1}^{L} \Gamma(k_l - m_l + 1)}. \quad (25)$$

In particular, Theorem 2 is consistent with the results in [20] when $p = 1$. We now think of the particular cases $L = 1, 2$ and make this expression easier to obtain more insight into the pattern for general L. For $L = 1$ and $k = k_1 \geq m$, we have

$$P(k) = \frac{p}{(2-p)\cdot m + p}\left(\frac{(2-p)\cdot m}{(2-p)\cdot m + p}\right)^{k-m}. \quad (26)$$

This result agrees with the degree distribution of the preferential attachment model for a single layer, obtained in [44]. For $L = 2$ and $k = k_1 \geq m_1$, $l = k_2 \geq m_2$, this result agrees with the $P(k, l)$ in [21].

$$P(k,l) = \frac{p m_1^{k-m_1} m_2^{l-m_2}}{(2-p)\left(m_1 + m_2 + \frac{p}{2-p}\right)^{k-m_1+l-m_2+1}} \times \frac{\Gamma(k + l - m_1 - m_2 + 1)}{\Gamma(k - m_1 + 1)\Gamma(l - m_2 + 1)}. \quad (27)$$

4 Simulation Results

We apply Monte Carlo simulations in this part to check the accuracy of the prior theoretical analysis. We consider in the following simulations the initial seed networks are start graphs with $n_0 = 10$ vertices in all layers, and $t = 4000$. The results are averaged over 100 Monte Carlo simulations. For the sake of clarity and without loss of generality, we here focus on the multiplex growth network model $\mathcal{M}_2 = (\mathcal{G}_2, \mathcal{C})$ and $\mathcal{M}_3 = (\mathcal{G}_3, \mathcal{C})$.

Figure 2 and 3 demonstrates the logarithm of the inverse of the joint degree distribution for the weight function $f(k) = k$, respectively. Thanks to the joint degree distribution decay fast in k and l in Eq. (17), the logarithm of this function's inverse has been depicted for a smoother output and better visibility. Suppose $p = 0.4, m_1 = 3, m_2 = 3$ and $m_1 = 10, m_2 = 3$ in Fig. 2 and $p = 0.8, m_1 = 3, m_2 = 3$ and $m_1 = 3, m_2 = 10$ in Fig. 3. It is easy to see from Fig. 2(a) and Fig. 3(a) that the joint degree distribution obtains its maximum at $k = m_1$ and $l = m_2$, and the contours are symmetric with respect to the bisector because m_1 and m_2 are equal. We also observed that the contours are skewed towards the k axis because $m_1 > m_2$ in Fig. 2(b), and the contours are skewed towards the l axis because $m_1 < m_2$ in Fig. 3(b).

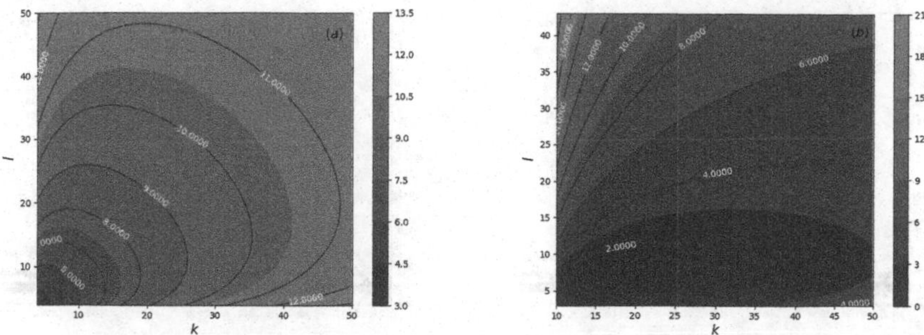

Fig. 2. The logarithm of the inverse of the $P(k,l)$ for the weight function $f(k) = k$ with parameters $p = 0.4$ in Eq. (17). (a) $m_1 = 3$ and $m_2 = 3$, (b) $m_1 = 10$ and $m_2 = 3$.

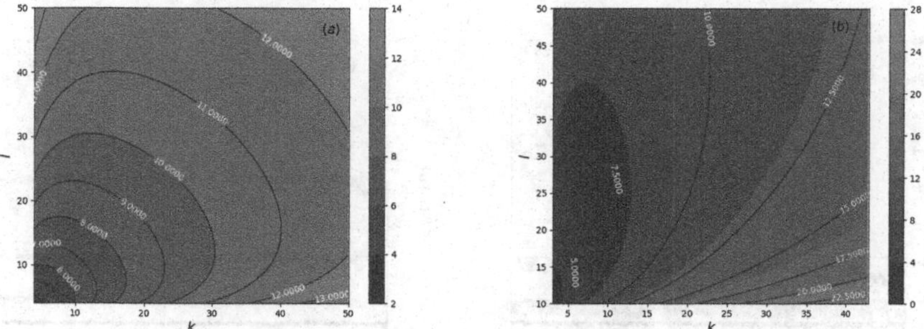

Fig. 3. The logarithm of the inverse of the $P(k,l)$ for the weight function $f(k) = k$ with parameters $p = 0.8$ in Eq. (17). (a) $m_1 = 3$ and $m_2 = 3$, (b) $m_1 = 3$ and $m_2 = 10$.

Figure 4 and 5 illustrates the variations trends of the simulation joint degree distribution and the theoretical joint degree distribution over time t for the multiplex growth network model $\mathcal{M}_2 = (\mathcal{G}_2, \mathcal{C})$ and $\mathcal{M}_3 = (\mathcal{G}_3, \mathcal{C})$ corresponding to the weight function $f(k) = k$, respectively. In Fig. 4 and Fig. 5, the horizontal solid line stands for the theoretical joint degree distribution which accords with the multiplex growth network model $\mathcal{M}_2 = (\mathcal{G}_2, \mathcal{C})$ and $\mathcal{M}_3 = (\mathcal{G}_3, \mathcal{C})$, and the circle solid line, square solid line, thin diamond line, star solid line represents the simulation results, respectively. We observe from Fig. 4 and Fig. 5 that the Monte Carlo simulation results visibly converge to theoretical results with the increasing of time t.

Figure 6 and 7 displays the logarithm of the inverse of the joint degree distribution for the weight function $f(k) = 10$, respectively. In Fig. 6, we let $p = 0.4, m_1 = 3, m_2 = 3$ and $m_1 = 3, m_2 = 6$. In Fig. 7, we let $p = 0.8, m_1 = 3, m_2 = 3$ and $m_1 = 6, m_2 = 3$. In Fig. 6(a) and Fig. 7(a), we see that the joint degree distribution attains its maximum at $k = m_1$ and $l = m_2$, and the contours are symmetric with respect to the bisector because m_1 and

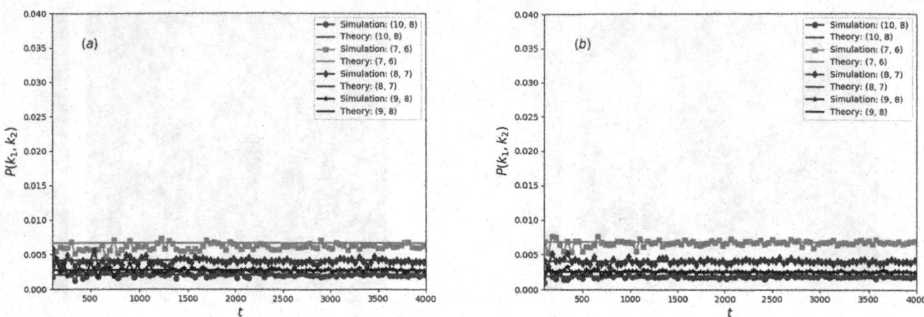

Fig. 4. Comparison between the theoretical joint degree distribution and the steady state joint degree distribution for the weight function $f(k) = k$ with parameters $m_1 = 3$, $m_2 = 4$. (a) $p = 0.4$, (b) $p = 0.8$.

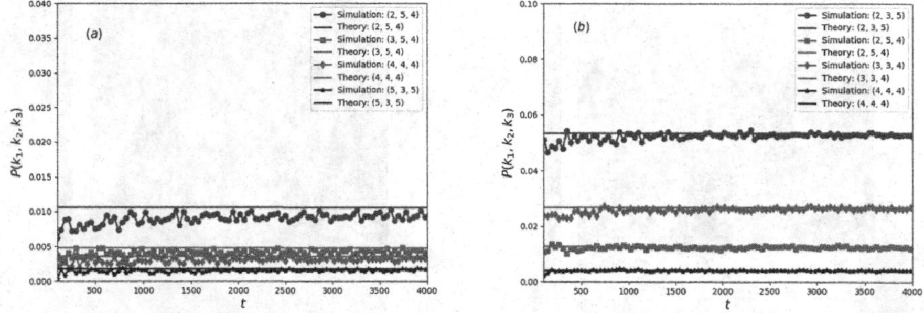

Fig. 5. Comparison between the theoretical joint degree distribution and the steady state joint degree distribution for the weight function $f(k) = k$ with parameters $m_1 = 2$, $m_2 = 3$ and $m_3 = 4$. (a) $p = 0.4$, (b) $p = 0.8$.

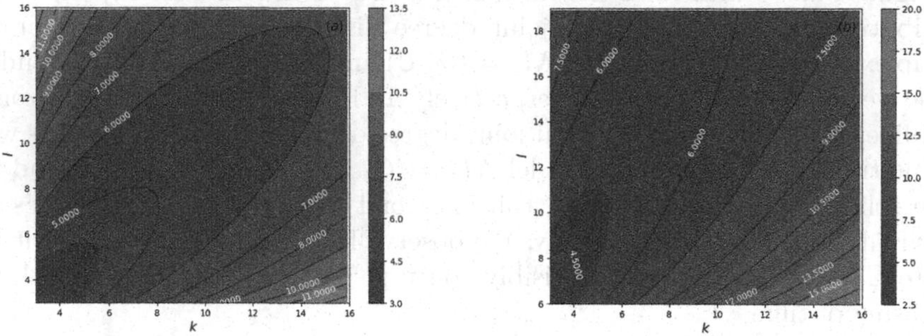

Fig. 6. The logarithm of the inverse of the $P(k, l)$ for the weight function $f(k) = 10$ with parameters $p = 0.4$ in Eq. (27). (a) $m_1 = 3$ and $m_2 = 3$, (b) $m_1 = 3$ and $m_2 = 6$.

m_2 are equal. In Fig. 6(b), the contours are skewed towards the l axis because $m_1 < m_2$ and the contours are skewed towards the k axis because $m_1 > m_2$ in Fig. 7(b).

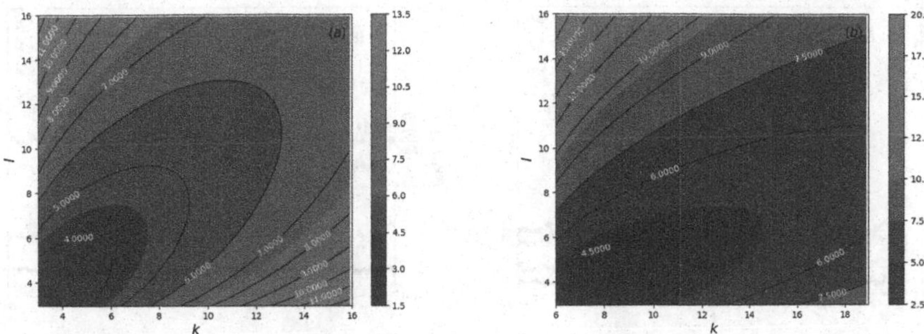

Fig. 7. The logarithm of the inverse of the $P(k, l)$ for the weight function $f(k) = 10$ with parameters $p = 0.8$ in Eq. (27). (a) $m_1 = 3$ and $m_2 = 3$, (b) $m_1 = 6$ and $m_2 = 3$.

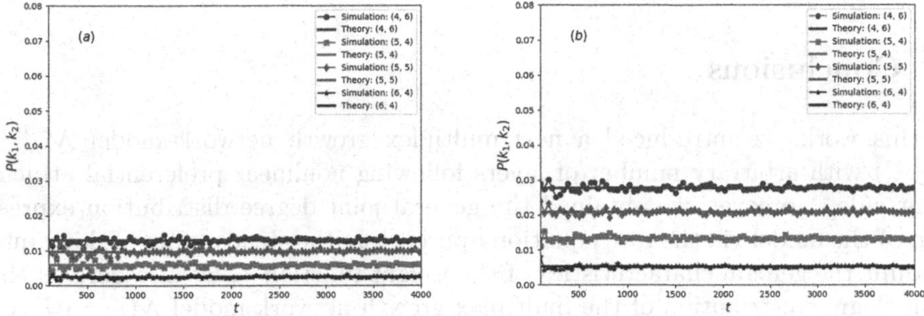

Fig. 8. Comparison between the theoretical joint degree distribution and the steady state joint degree distribution for the weight function $f(k) = 10$ with parameters $m_1 = 3$, $m_2 = 4$. (a) $p = 0.4$, (b) $p = 0.8$.

We also perform Monte Carlo simulations for the model of the weight function $f(k) = 10$. Figure 8 and 9 shows the variations trends of the simulation joint degree distribution and the theoretical joint degree distribution over time t for the multiplex growth network model $\mathcal{M}_2 = (\mathcal{G}_2, \mathcal{C})$ and $\mathcal{M}_3 = (\mathcal{G}_3, \mathcal{C})$ corresponding to the weight function $f(k) = 10$, respectively. In Fig. 8 and Fig. 9, the horizontal solid stands for the theoretical joint degree distribution which accord with the Eq. (25) for $L = 2, 3$, and the circle solid line, square solid line, thin diamond line, star solid line denotes the simulation results, respectively. We observe from Fig. 8 and 9 that the Monte Carlo simulation results visibly converge to theoretical results given by Eq. (25) for $L = 2, 3$ with the increasing of time t.

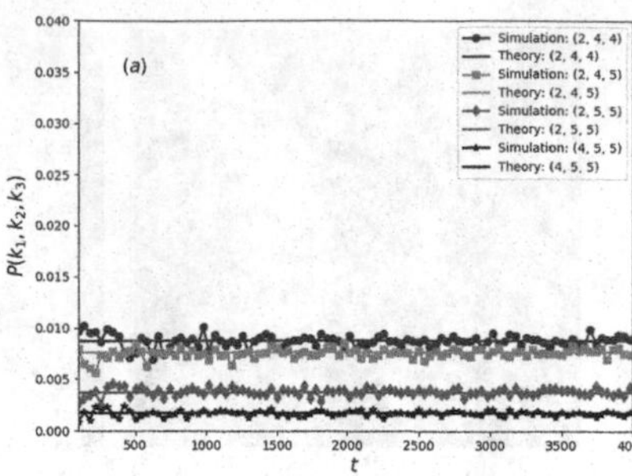

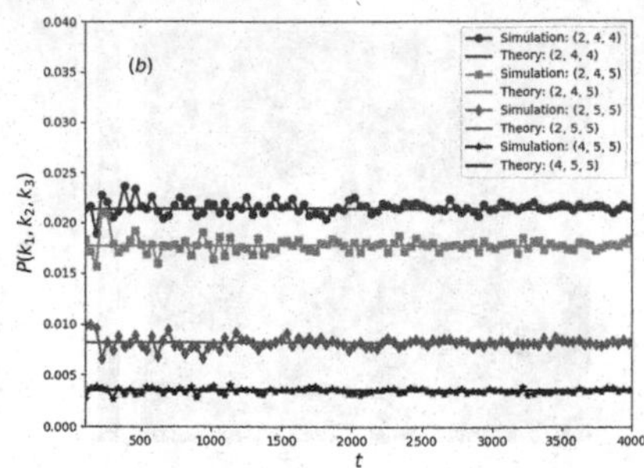

Fig. 9. Comparison between the steady state joint degree distribution and the theoretical joint degree distribution for the weight function $f(k) = 10$ with parameters $m_1 = 2$, $m_2 = 3$ and $m_3 = 4$. (a) $p = 0.4$, (b) $p = 0.8$.

5 Conclusions

In this work, we introduced a new multiplex growth network model $\mathcal{M}_L = (\mathcal{G}_L, \mathcal{C})$ with arbitrary number of layers following nonlinear preferential attachment rule. Moreover, we obtained the general joint degree distribution expression of the model via the rate equation approach in the steady state. Taking into account the general characteristics of the weight function f, we also derived the joint degree distribution of the multiplex growth network model $\mathcal{M}_L = (\mathcal{G}_L, \mathcal{C})$ corresponding to the weight function $f(k) = k$ and $f(k) = c > 0$, respectively. The probability p and the number of edges m_l added to the network layer at each time t are discovered to be linked to the joint degree distribution $P(k, l)$. In particular, the nonlinear preferential attachment probability reduces to the linear preferential attachment probability and uniform random attachment probability if the weight function $f(k) = k$ and $f(k) = c > 0$, separately. To verify our theoretical results, we perform Monte Carlo simulations for the multiplex growth network model $\mathcal{M}_L = (\mathcal{G}_L, \mathcal{C})$ ctions. Experiments indicate that our theoretical findings are coincide with Monte Carlo simulations well.

Acknowledgements. This work was supported by the National Natural Science Foundation of China (Grant No. 62162012), the National Science and Technology Project of Guizhou Province (Grant Nos. [2019]1159, [2020]1Y277, [2021]016, [2020]1Y263), the Natural Science Research Project of the Guizhou Provincial Department of Education(Grant No. QJHKY[2018]087, QJJ[2022]015), and the Guizhou Minzu University Fund Project (Grant Nos. [2019]YB01, [2019]YB02, [2019]YB03).

References

1. Murphy, J.: Artificial intelligence, rationality, and the world wide web. IEEE Intell. Syst. **33**(1), 98–103 (2018)
2. Pastor-Satorras, R., Vázquez, A., Vespignani, A.: Dynamical and correlation properties of the internet. Phys. Rev. Lett. **87**(25), 258701 (2001)

3. Boltz, T.A., Devkota, P., Wuchty, S.: Collective influencers in protein interaction networks. Sci. Rep. **9**, 3948 (2019)
4. Tabassum, S., Pereira, F.S.F., Fernandes, S., et al.: Social network analysis: an overview. WIREs Data Min. Knowl. Discov. **8**, e1256 (2018)
5. Lu, C., Zhang, Y., Ahn, Y.Y., Ding, Y., et al.: Co-contributorship network and division of labor in individual scientific collaborations. J. Assoc. Inf. Sci. Technol. **71**(10), 1–17 (2020)
6. Watts, D.J., Strogatz, S.H.: Collective dynamics of small world networks. Nature **393**(6684), 440–442 (1998)
7. Barabasi, A.L., Albert, R.: Emergence of scaling in random networks. Science **286**(5439), 509–512 (1999)
8. Bianconi, G., Barabasi, A.L.: Bose-Einstein condensation in complex networks. Phys. Rev. Lett. **86**(24), 5632–5635 (2001)
9. Li, X., Chen, G.R.: A local-world evolving network model. Phys. A **328**(1–2), 274–286 (2003)
10. Zadorozhnyi, V.N., Yudin, E.B.: Growing network: models following nonlinear preferential attachment rule. Phys. A **428**, 111–132 (2015)
11. Xiong, K., Zeng, C., Liu, Z.: Effect of degree correlation on the thermal transport in complex networks. Nonlinear Dyn. **94**, 3067–3075 (2018). https://doi.org/10.1007/s11071-018-4545-y
12. Lewis, K., Kaufman, J., Gonzalez, M., et al.: Tastes, ties, and time: a new social network dataset using Facebook.com. Soc. Netw. **30**(4), 330–342 (2008)
13. Szell, M., Lambiotte, R., Thurner, R.: Multirelational organization of large-scale social networks in an online world. PNAS **107**(31), 13636–13641 (2010)
14. Barigozzi, M., Fagiolo, G., Garlaschelli, D.: Multinetwork of international trade: a commodity-specific analysis. Phys. Rev. E **81**(1), 046104 (2010)
15. Halu, A., Mukherjee, S., Bianconi, G.: Emergence of overlap in ensembles of spatial multiplexes and statistical mechanics of spatial interacting network ensembles. Phys. Rev. E **89**(1), 012806 (2014)
16. Kim, J.Y., Goh, K.I.: Coevolution and correlated multiplexity in multiplex networks. Phys. Rev. Lett. **111**(5), 058702 (2013)
17. Nicosia, V., Bianconi, G., Latora, V., et al.: Growing multiplex networks. Phys. Rev. Lett. **111**(5), 058701 (2013)
18. Nicosia, V., Bianconi, G., Latora, V., et al.: Nonlinear growth and condensation in multiplex networks. Phys. Rev. E Stat. Nonlinear Soft Matter Phys. **90**(4), 042807 (2013)
19. Fotouhi, B., Momeni, N.: Inter-layer degree correlations in heterogeneously growing multiplex networks. In: Mangioni, G., Simini, F., Uzzo, S.M., Wang, D. (eds.) Complex Networks VI. SCI, vol. 597, pp. 159–170. Springer, Cham (2015). https://doi.org/10.1007/978-3-319-16112-9_16
20. Momeni, N., Fotouhi, B.: Growing multiplex networks with arbitrary number of layers. Phys. Rev. E Stat. Nonlinear Soft Matter Phys. **92**(6), 062812 (2015)
21. Lu, Y., Xu, D., Zhou, J.: Degree correlations in two layer growth model with nonlinear preferential attachment rule. In: Du, D., Li, L., Zhu, E., He, K. (eds.) NCTCS 2017. CCIS, vol. 768, pp. 167–181. Springer, Singapore (2017). https://doi.org/10.1007/978-981-10-6893-5_13
22. Solá, L., Romance, M., Criado, R., et al.: Eigenvector centrality of nodes in multiplex networks. Chaos **23**, 033131 (2013)
23. Tudisco, F., Arrigo, F., Gautier, A.: Node and layer eigenvector centralities for multiplex networks. SIAM J. Appl. Math. **78**(2), 853–876 (2018)

24. Cangfeng, D., Kan, L.: Centrality ranking in multiplex networks using topologically biased random walks. Neurocomputing **312**, 263–275 (2018)
25. Tortosa, L., Vicent, J.F., Yeghikyan, G.: An algorithm for ranking the nodes of multiplex networks with data based on the PageRank concept. Appl. Math. Comput. **392**, 125676 (2021)
26. Baxter, G.J., Cellai, D., Dorogovtsev, S.N., et al.: Cycles and clustering in multiplex networks. Phys. Rev. E **94**(6), 062308 (2016)
27. Boccaletti, S., Bianconi, G., Criado, R., et al.: The structure and dynamics of multilayer networks. Phys. Rep. **544**(1), 1–122 (2014)
28. Mucha, P.J., Richardson, T., Macon, K., et al.: Community structure in time-dependent, multiscale, and multiplex networks. Science **32**(5980), 876–878 (2010)
29. Newman, M.J., Girvan, M.: Finding and evaluating community structure in networks. Phys. Rev. E **69**(2), 026113 (2004)
30. Didier, G., Brun, C., Baudot, A.: Identifying communities from multiplex biological networks. PeerJ **3**, e1525 (2015)
31. Ma, X., Dong, D., Wang, Q.: Community detection in multi-layer networks using joint nonnegative matrix factorization. IEEE Trans. Knowl. Data Eng. **31**(2), 273–286 (2018)
32. Gomez, S., Diaz-Guilera, A., Gomez-Gardenes, J., et al.: Diffusion dynamics on multiplex networks. Phys. Rev. Lett. **110**(2), 028701 (2013)
33. Guo, Q., Lei, Y., Jiang, X., et al.: Epidemic spreading with activity-driven awareness diffusion on multiplex network. Chaos **26**(4), 043110 (2016)
34. Tejedor, A., Longjas, A., Foufoula-Georgiou, E., et al.: Diffusion dynamics and optimal coupling in multiplex networks with directed layers. Phys. Rev. X **8**, 031071 (2018)
35. Gao, S., Chang, L., Wang, X., et al.: Cross-diffusion on multiplex networks. New J. Phys. **22**, 053047 (2020)
36. Jaquez, R.B., Ramos, L.A.A., Schaum, A.: Spreading control in two-layer multiplex networks. Entropy **22**(10), 1157 (2020)
37. Yu, X., Yang, Q., Ai, K., et al.: Information spreading on two-layered multiplex networks with limited contact. IEEE Access **8**, 104316–104325 (2020)
38. Gómez-Gardenes, J., Reiñares, I., Arenas, A., et al.: Evolution of cooperation in multiplex networks. Sci. Rep. **2**, 620 (2012)
39. Pereda, M.: Evolution of cooperation under social pressure in multiplex networks. Phys. Rev. E **94**(3), 032314 (2016)
40. Yu, J., Liu, Z., Han, X.: Cooperation evolution in multiplex networks with the heterogeneous diffusion model. IEEE Access **9**, 86074–86082 (2021)
41. Leyva, I., Sendiña-Nadal, I., Sevilla-Escoboza, R., Vera-Avila, V.P., et al.: Relay synchronization in multiplex networks. Sci. Rep. **8**, 8629 (2017)
42. Jalan, S., Rathore, V., Kachhvah, A.D., et al.: Inhibition-induced explosive synchronization in multiplex networks. Phys. Rev. E **99**(6), 062305 (2019)
43. Guo, Q., Cozzo, E., Zheng, Z., et al.: Levy random walks on multiplex networks. Sci. Rep. **6**, 37641 (2016)
44. Lu, Y.J., Xu, D.Y., Zhou, J.C.: Vertex degree distribution in growth models with nonlinear preferential attachment rule. J. Beijing Univ. Posts Telecommun. **39**(5), 116–123 (2016)

Coherence of Quantum States Based on Mutually Unbiased Bases in $\mathbb{C}^4$

Xudong Ma[1] and Yongming Li[1,2(✉)]

[1] School of Computer Science, Shaanxi Normal University, Xi'an 710119, Shaanxi, China
liyongm@snnu.edu.cn

[2] School of Mathematics and Statistics, Shaanxi Normal University, Xi'an 710119, Shaanxi, China

Abstract. Recently, many measures have been put forward to quantify the coherence of quantum states relative to a given basis. We extend the relationship between mutually unbiased basis (MUBs) and quantum coherence to a higher dimension. Results include arbitrary complete sets of MUBs from $\mathbb{C}^2$ to $\mathbb{C}^4$, and the form of arbitrary 2×2 Unitary matrix and any density matrix of qubit states in respect of complete sets of MUBs. We construct a set of three MUBs by tensor product and further think of complete sets of five MUBs in $\mathbb{C}^4$. Taking the Bell diagonal state as an example, we analyze the coherence of quantum states under MUBs and calculate the corresponding upper and lower bounds. The results show that in addition to selecting the unbiased basis which is often used, we can consider more sets of MUBs, which may be helpful to the analysis of quantum states.

Keywords: Coherence · Mutually unbiased bases · Coherence measure

1 Introduction

In order to determine an unknown quantum state completely, we must rely on quantum measurement. It is necessary to make a large number of copies and multiple different basis measurements to reconstruct the unknown quantum state. It has been shown that Mutual Unbiased Basis (MUBs) plays a special role in determining the state of a finite-dimensional quantum system [1].

Mutual unbiased bases (MUBs) are quite symmetric orthogonal bases in complex Hilbert spaces. They form a set of minimum measurement bases and provide the best way to determine quantum states [1–3]. MUBs are applied in detection of quantum entanglement [4], quantum state tomography (QST) [5] and quantum error correction (QEC) [6], etc. Many features of MUBs are reviewed in reference [7]. When d is a prime power, the size of maximal MUBs sets is $d+1$. Constructing a set of at least four mutually unbiased bases in dimension six or proving that there are no seven MUBs in 6-dimensional complex Hilbert space [8], it is an open question until now.

Z. Cai et al. (Eds.): NCTCS 2022, CCIS 1693, pp. 43–60, 2022.
https://doi.org/10.1007/978-981-19-8152-4_3

Quantum coherence plays an important role in the theory of quantum mechanics. In quantum information theory, quantum coherence is a necessary condition for the existence of quantum entanglement and non-entanglement quantum correlation (such as quantum discord, quantum defect, etc.) [14].

Recently, Baumgratz et al. proposed a rigorous mathematical framework for quantifying quantum coherence from the point of view of quantum resource theory, and obtained two well-defined measures of quantum coherence (relative entropy coherence and l_1 norm coherence) [10]. With the development of quantum coherence theory, the basic properties of different coherence measures have been well studied such as robustness of coherence [11], modified trace distance of coherence [12], skew information-based coherence [9], geometric coherence [13] and the extension of various quantum coherence measures studies [14–19]. The theory of quantum coherence has been well developed not only in physical theory, but also in many research fields such as quantum thermodynamics [20,21], quantum biology [22–24] and quantum medicine [25,26], etc.

In this paper, we extend the relationship between mutually unbiased basis (MUBs) and quantum coherence to a higher dimension. In Sect. 2, we provide some concepts that will be used in this article. In Sect. 3, we study the form of arbitrary complete sets of MUBs in $\mathbb{C}^2$. We prove the form of arbitrary 2×2 unitary matrix and analyze the forms of any qubit states with respect to these complete sets of MUBs. In Sect. 4, we construct a set of three MUBs by tensor product in $\mathbb{C}^4$. Taking the Bell diagonal state as an example, we analyze the its coherence of MUBs and calculate the corresponding upper and lower bounds. In Sect. 5, we further consider a complete set of five MUBs in $\mathbb{C}^4$ and the form of any unitary matrix which can be used to construct arbitrary MUBs. We make a summary in Sect. 6.

2 Preliminaries

In this section, we provide some concepts that will be used in this article.

Two orthonormal bases $\mathcal{A} = \{|a_i\rangle\}_{i=1}^{d}$ and $\mathcal{B} = \{|b_j\rangle\}_{j=1}^{d}$ of the d-dimensional Hilbert space $\mathbb{C}^d$ are said to be mutually unbiased if for every pair of basis vectors $|a_i\rangle \in \mathcal{A}$ and $|b_j\rangle \in \mathcal{B}$, it holds that

$$|\langle a_i|b_j\rangle| = \frac{1}{\sqrt{d}}, \forall i, j = 1, ..., d. \tag{1}$$

Fix an orthonormal basis $\{|i\rangle\}_{i=1}^{d}$ of $\mathbb{C}^d$, the set of all incoherent states is denoted by $\mathcal{I}$ [10], i.e.,

$$\mathcal{I} = \left\{ \delta \in \mathbb{C}^d \mid \delta = \sum_i p_i |i\rangle\langle i|, \ p_i \geq 0, \ \sum_i p_i = 1 \right\}.$$

Let Λ be a completely positive trace preserving (CPTP) map

$$\Lambda(\rho) = \sum_n K_n \rho K_n^{\dagger},$$

where K_n are Kraus operators satisfying $\sum_n K_n^\dagger K_n = I_d$ with the identity operator I_d. In [10], the authors proposed the conditions that a well-defined coherence measure C should satisfy:
(C_1) (Faithfulness) $C(\rho) \geq 0$ and $C(\rho) = 0$ iff ρ is incoherent;
(C_2) (Monotonicity) $C(\Lambda(\rho)) \leq C(\rho)$ for any incoherent operation Λ;
(C_3) (Convexity) $C(\cdot)$ is a convex function of ρ; i.e.,

$$\sum_n p_n C(\rho_n) \geq C\left(\sum_n p_n \rho_n\right),$$

where $\rho = \sum_n p_n \rho_n$ with $p_n \geq 0$ and $\sum_n p_n = 1$;
(C_4) (Strong monotonicity) $C(\cdot)$ does not increase on average under selective incoherent operations, i.e.,

$$C(\rho) \geq \sum_n p_n C(\varrho_n),$$

where $p_n = Tr\left(K_n \rho K_n^\dagger\right)$ forms a probability distribution, $\varrho_n = \frac{K_n \rho K_n^\dagger}{p_n}$ are the postmeasurement states.

It is obvious that in such a framework the definition of coherence strongly depends on the fixed basis. This can be easily understood because the bases could not be arbitrarily changed in the practical scenario. Under fixed reference basis, the l_1 norm of coherence of state ρ is defined by [10]

$$C_{l_1}(\rho) = \min_{\delta \in \mathcal{I}} |\rho - \delta|_{l_1} = \sum_{i \neq j} |\langle i|\rho|j\rangle|, \tag{2}$$

the geometric measure of coherence C_g is defined by [27]

$$C_g(\rho) = 1 - \max_{\delta \in \mathcal{I}} F(\rho, \delta), \tag{3}$$

where the maximum is taken over all incoherent states $\delta \in \mathcal{I}$. $F(\rho, \delta)$ is the fidelity of two density operators ρ and δ. Next we focus on the relative entropy of coherence. The relative entropy of coherence is defined as [10]

$$C_r(\rho) = \min_{\delta \in \mathcal{I}} S(\rho||\delta) = S(\rho_{diag}) - S(\rho), \tag{4}$$

where ρ_{diag} comes from ρ by vanishing off-diagonal elements, $S(\rho) = -Tr(\rho log_2 \rho)$ is the von Neumann entropy [28].

3 The Geometric Measure of Coherence of Quantum States Under Complete MUBs in $\mathbb{C}^2$

In $\mathbb{C}^2$, a set of three complete MUBs is readily obtained from the eigenvectors of the three Pauli matrices σ_z, σ_x and σ_y:

$$\begin{cases} A_1 = \{\alpha_{11}, \alpha_{12}\} = \{|0\rangle, |1\rangle\}; \\ A_2 = \{\alpha_{21}, \alpha_{22}\} = \left\{\frac{1}{\sqrt{2}}(|0\rangle + |1\rangle), \frac{1}{\sqrt{2}}(|0\rangle - |1\rangle)\right\}; \\ A_3 = \{\alpha_{31}, \alpha_{32}\} = \left\{\frac{1}{\sqrt{2}}(|0\rangle + i|1\rangle), \frac{1}{\sqrt{2}}(|0\rangle - i|1\rangle)\right\}. \end{cases} \tag{5}$$

If this set of bases is applied to any 2×2 unitary matrix, can it still meet the requirements of unbiased bases? The answer is that the partial unitary matrix are satisfied.

Let $U = \begin{pmatrix} u_{11} & u_{12} \\ u_{21} & u_{22} \end{pmatrix}$ be a unitary matrix, $U^{-1} = U^{\dagger}$, we have $\frac{1}{|U|}\begin{pmatrix} u_{22} & -u_{12} \\ -u_{21} & u_{11} \end{pmatrix} = \begin{pmatrix} \bar{u_{11}} & \bar{u_{21}} \\ \bar{u_{12}} & \bar{u_{22}} \end{pmatrix}$. Thus, $u_{22} = |\, U \,|\bar{u_{11}}$, $u_{12} = -|\, U \,|\bar{u_{21}}$. Since the column vector group of U is a standard orthogonal basis of $\mathbb{C}^2$, we have $|\, u_{11} \,|^2 + |\, u_{21} \,|^2 = 1$. $(|\, u_{11} \,|, |\, u_{21} \,|)$ is a point on the unit circle, which is in the first quadrant or on the positive axis of the x-axis and y-axis. It exists $\theta (0 \leq \theta \leq \frac{\pi}{2})$, such that $|\, u_{11} \,| = r\cos\theta$, $|\, u_{21} \,| = r\sin\theta$. Therefore, $u_{11} = \cos\theta e^{i\theta_1}$, $u_{21} = \sin\theta e^{i\theta_2}$, where $0 \leq \theta_j \leq 2\pi, j = 1, 2$. Considering that the determinant module of the unitary matrix is 1, so $|\, U \,| = e^{i\theta_3}$, where $0 \leq \theta j \leq 2\pi$. Thus, $u_{12} = -\sin\theta e^{i(\theta_3 - \theta_2)}$, $u_{22} = \cos\theta e^{i(\theta_3 - \theta_1)}$. Therefore, the unitary matrix

$$U = \begin{pmatrix} \cos\theta e^{i\theta_1} & -\sin\theta e^{i(\theta_3-\theta_2)} \\ \sin\theta e^{i\theta_2} & \cos\theta e^{i(\theta_3-\theta_1)} \end{pmatrix} \tag{6}$$

is obtained, where $0 \leq \theta \leq \frac{\pi}{2}, 0 \leq \theta_j \leq 2\pi, j = 1, 2, 3$.

Under the unitary transformations of

$$\begin{cases} A_1 U = (a_1, a_2) = \begin{pmatrix} \cos\theta e^{i\theta_1} & -\sin\theta e^{i(\theta_3-\theta_2)} \\ \sin\theta e^{i\theta_2} & \cos\theta e^{i(\theta_3-\theta_1)} \end{pmatrix}, \\ A_2 U = (b_1, b_2) = \frac{1}{\sqrt{2}} \begin{pmatrix} \cos\theta e^{i\theta_1} + \sin\theta e^{i\theta_2} & -\sin\theta e^{i(\theta_3-\theta_2)} + \cos\theta e^{i(\theta_3-\theta_1)} \\ \cos\theta e^{i\theta_1} - \sin\theta e^{i\theta_2} & -\sin\theta e^{i(\theta_3-\theta_2)} - \cos\theta e^{i(\theta_3-\theta_1)} \end{pmatrix}, \\ A_3 U = (c_1, c_3) = \frac{1}{\sqrt{2}} \begin{pmatrix} \cos\theta e^{i\theta_1} + \sin\theta e^{i\theta_2} & -\sin\theta e^{i(\theta_3-\theta_2)} + \cos\theta e^{i(\theta_3-\theta_1)} \\ i\cos\theta e^{i\theta_1} - i\sin\theta e^{i\theta_2} & -i\sin\theta e^{i(\theta_3-\theta_2)} - i\cos\theta e^{i(\theta_3-\theta_1)} \end{pmatrix}. \end{cases} \tag{7}$$

According to the unbiased requirement, vectors $|a_1\rangle$, $|b_1\rangle$ and $|c_1\rangle$ should satisfy the following relations,

$$\begin{aligned} |\langle a_1|b_1\rangle| &= \left| \frac{1}{\sqrt{2}} \left[\cos^2\theta - \sin^2\theta + \sin\theta\cos\theta e^{i(\theta_2-\theta_1)} + \sin\theta\cos\theta e^{i(\theta_1-\theta_2)}\right] \right| \\ &= \left| \frac{1}{\sqrt{2}} [\cos 2\theta + \sin 2\theta \cos(\theta_1 - \theta_2)] \right|. \end{aligned} \tag{8}$$

By further solving the above formula, we can get

$$\begin{aligned} \cos 2\theta + \sin 2\theta \cos(\theta_1 - \theta_2) &= 1, \\ 2\sin\theta\cos\theta\cos(\theta_1 - \theta_2) &= 1 - \cos 2\theta, \\ \cos\theta\cos(\theta_1 - \theta_2) &= \sin\theta. \end{aligned}$$

Similarly,

$$|\langle b_1|c_1\rangle| = \left| \frac{1}{2} [1 + \sin 2\theta \cos(\theta_1 - \theta_2) + i(1 - \sin 2\theta \cos(\theta_1 - \theta_2)] \right|. \tag{9}$$

If $\alpha = \sin\theta\cos\theta\cos(\theta_1 - \theta_2)$, we have

$$\sqrt{(\frac{1+2\alpha}{2})^2 + (\frac{1-2\alpha}{2})^2} = \frac{1}{\sqrt{2}},$$
$$\sqrt{\frac{1}{2} + 2\alpha^2} = \frac{1}{\sqrt{2}},$$
$$\sin\theta\cos\theta\cos(\theta_1 - \theta_2) = 0.$$

Obviously, the above equations both satisfy (1) when $\theta = 0$ and $\theta = \frac{\Pi}{2}$. Matrix U have the following two forms,

$$U_1 = \begin{pmatrix} e^{i\delta_1} & 0 \\ 0 & e^{i\delta_2} \end{pmatrix}, U_2 = \begin{pmatrix} 0 & e^{i\nu_1} \\ e^{i\nu_2} & 0 \end{pmatrix} \tag{10}$$

.

Considering the following relationships
$|U| = 1 \Leftrightarrow \cos^2\theta e^{i\theta_3} + \sin^2\theta e^{i\theta_3} = 1 \Leftrightarrow e^{i\theta_3} = 1$,
We can further obtain any element

$$\mathcal{U} = \begin{pmatrix} \cos\theta e^{i\theta_1} & -\sin\theta e^{-i\theta_2} \\ \sin\theta e^{i\theta_2} & \cos\theta e^{-i\theta_1} \end{pmatrix} \tag{11}$$

of a two-dimensional special unitary group from arbitrary 2×2 Unitary matrix and any density matrix in Eq. (6), where $0 \le \theta \le \frac{\pi}{2}, 0 \le \theta_j \le 2\pi, j = 1, 2$. If $\alpha = 2\theta, \phi = \theta_1 - \theta_2 + \frac{\pi}{2}, \psi = \theta_1 + \theta_2 - \frac{\pi}{2}$, then

$$\mathcal{U} = \begin{pmatrix} \cos\frac{\alpha}{2} e^{i(\frac{\phi+\psi}{2})} & -\sin\frac{\alpha}{2} e^{-i(\frac{\phi-\psi}{2})} \\ \sin\frac{\alpha}{2} e^{-i(\frac{\phi-\psi}{2})} & \cos\frac{\alpha}{2} e^{i(\frac{\phi+\psi}{2})} \end{pmatrix}, \tag{12}$$

where $0 \le \alpha \le \pi, 0 \le \phi \le 2\pi, 0 \le \psi \le 2\pi$.

$\mathcal{U}_1 = \begin{pmatrix} e^{i\frac{\phi}{2}} & 0 \\ 0 & e^{-i\frac{\psi}{2}} \end{pmatrix}$ when $\theta = 0$ and $\psi = 0$,

$\mathcal{U}_2 = \begin{pmatrix} \cos\frac{\alpha}{2} & -\sin\frac{\alpha}{2} \\ \sin\frac{\alpha}{2} & \cos\frac{\alpha}{2} \end{pmatrix}$ when $\phi = 0$ and $\psi = 0$,

$\mathcal{U}_3 = \begin{pmatrix} e^{i\frac{\psi}{2}} & 0 \\ 0 & e^{-i\frac{\psi}{2}} \end{pmatrix}$ when $\theta = 0$ and $\phi = 0$.

Therefore, any 2×2 unitary matrix can be decomposed into

$$\mathcal{U} = e^{i\varphi}\mathcal{U}_1\mathcal{U}_2\mathcal{U}_3 = e^{i\varphi} \begin{pmatrix} e^{i\frac{\phi}{2}} & 0 \\ 0 & e^{-i\frac{\phi}{2}} \end{pmatrix} \begin{pmatrix} \cos\frac{\alpha}{2} & -\sin\frac{\alpha}{2} \\ \sin\frac{\alpha}{2} & \cos\frac{\alpha}{2} \end{pmatrix} \begin{pmatrix} e^{i\frac{\psi}{2}} & 0 \\ 0 & e^{-i\frac{\psi}{2}} \end{pmatrix}, \tag{13}$$

where φ, ϕ, θ and ψ are arbitrary real numbers. To sum up, we can get the same result that Nielsen introduced in the book [29]. Based on the above inference, we can further consider three kinds of useful rotation operators

$$\mathcal{R}_x(\theta) = \begin{pmatrix} \cos\frac{\theta}{2} & -i\sin\frac{\theta}{2} \\ -i\sin\frac{\theta}{2} & \cos\frac{\theta}{2} \end{pmatrix} \mathcal{R}_y(\theta) = \begin{pmatrix} \cos\frac{\theta}{2} & -\sin\frac{\theta}{2} \\ \sin\frac{\theta}{2} & \cos\frac{\theta}{2} \end{pmatrix} \mathcal{R}_z(\theta) = \begin{pmatrix} e^{-i\frac{\theta}{2}} & 0 \\ 0 & e^{i\frac{\theta}{2}} \end{pmatrix}, \tag{14}$$

which will give physical practical significance to our results.

By unitary transformation we can get

$$\begin{cases} A_1U_1 = \begin{pmatrix} e^{i\delta_1} & 0 \\ 0 & e^{i\delta_2} \end{pmatrix} \\ A_2U_1 = \frac{1}{\sqrt{2}}\begin{pmatrix} e^{i\delta_1} & e^{i\delta_2} \\ e^{i\delta_1} & -e^{i\delta_2} \end{pmatrix} \\ A_3U_1 = \frac{1}{\sqrt{2}}\begin{pmatrix} e^{i\delta_1} & e^{i\delta_2} \\ ie^{i\delta_1} & -ie^{i\delta_2} \end{pmatrix} \end{cases} \quad \begin{cases} A_1U_2 = \begin{pmatrix} 0 & e^{i\nu_1} \\ e^{i\nu_2} & 0 \end{pmatrix} \\ A_2U_2 = \frac{1}{\sqrt{2}}\begin{pmatrix} e^{i\nu_2} & e^{i\nu_1} \\ -e^{i\nu_2} & e^{i\nu_1} \end{pmatrix} \\ A_3U_2 = \frac{1}{\sqrt{2}}\begin{pmatrix} e^{i\nu_2} & e^{i\nu_1} \\ -ie^{i\nu_2} & ie^{i\nu_1} \end{pmatrix} \end{cases}. \tag{15}$$

Through the calculation, we can find out $\{A_1U_1, A_2U_1, A_3U_1\}$ and $\{A_1U_2, A_2U_2, A_3U_2\}$ still constitute complete sets of MUBs in $\mathbb{C}^2$.

We now present the density matrix expression of mixed qubit states with respect to the MUBs $\{A_1, A_2, A_3\}$. For single-qubit state $\rho = \frac{1}{2}(\boldsymbol{I} + \boldsymbol{r}\cdot\boldsymbol{\sigma})$, where $\boldsymbol{r} = (r_1, r_2, r_3)$ is a real three-dimensional vector such that $|\boldsymbol{r}|^2 = r_1^2 + r_2^2 + r_3^2 \le 1$ and $\boldsymbol{\sigma} = (\sigma_x, \sigma_y, \sigma_z)$, where σ_i $(i = 1, 2, 3)$ are Pauli matrices.

Obviously, under the basis $A = \{|0\rangle, |1\rangle\}$, ρ has the expression

$$\rho_{A_1} = A_1^\dagger \rho A_1 = \frac{1}{2}\begin{pmatrix} 1+z & x-iy \\ x+iy & 1-z \end{pmatrix} \tag{16}$$

By immediately computing, we get the density matrix expressions ρ_{A_2} and ρ_{A_3} of ρ with respect to the basis A_2 and A_3,

$$\rho_{A_2} = A_2^\dagger \rho A_2 = \frac{1}{2}\begin{pmatrix} 1+x & z+iy \\ z-iy & 1-x \end{pmatrix}, \rho_{A_3} = A_3^\dagger \rho A_3 = \frac{1}{2}\begin{pmatrix} 1+y & z-ix \\ z+ix & 1-y \end{pmatrix}. \tag{17}$$

Likewise, we can get the expressions $\rho_{A_1U_1}$, $\rho_{A_2U_1}$, $\rho_{A_3U_1}$ and $\rho_{A_1U_2}$, $\rho_{A_2U_2}$, $\rho_{A_3U_2}$ of ρ with respect to the MUBs $\{A_1U_1, A_1U_2, A_1U_3\}$ and $\{A_2U_1, A_2U_2, A_2U_3\}$, severally,

$$\begin{cases} \rho_{A_1U_1} = U_1^\dagger \rho_{A_1} U_1 = \frac{1}{2}\begin{pmatrix} 1+z & e^{i(\delta_2-\delta_1)}(x-iy) \\ e^{i(\delta_2-\delta_1)}(x+iy) & 1-z \end{pmatrix}, \\ \rho_{A_2U_1} = U_1^\dagger \rho_{A_2} U_1 = \frac{1}{2}\begin{pmatrix} 1+x & e^{i(\delta_2-\delta_1)}(z+iy) \\ e^{i(\delta_2-\delta_1)}(z-iy) & 1-x \end{pmatrix}, \\ \rho_{A_3U_1} = U_1^\dagger \rho_{A_2} U_1 = \frac{1}{2}\begin{pmatrix} 1+y & e^{i(\delta_2-\delta_1)}(z-ix) \\ e^{i(\delta_2-\delta_1)}(z+ix) & 1-y \end{pmatrix}. \end{cases} \tag{18}$$

and

$$\begin{cases} \rho_{A_1U_2} = U_2^\dagger \rho_{A_1} U_2 = \frac{1}{2}\begin{pmatrix} 1+z & e^{i(\nu_2-\nu_1)}(x-iy) \\ e^{i(\nu_2-\nu_1)}(x+iy) & 1-z \end{pmatrix}, \\ \rho_{A_2U_2} = U_2^\dagger \rho_{A_2} U_2 = \frac{1}{2}\begin{pmatrix} 1+x & e^{i(\nu_2-\nu_1)}(z+iy) \\ e^{i(\nu_2-\nu_1)}(z-iy) & 1-x \end{pmatrix}, \\ \rho_{A_3U_2} = U_2^\dagger \rho_{A_3} U_2 = \frac{1}{2}\begin{pmatrix} 1+y & e^{i(\nu_2-\nu_1)}(z-ix) \\ e^{i(\nu_2-\nu_1)}(z+ix) & 1-y \end{pmatrix}. \end{cases} \tag{19}$$

In [13], the authors introduced the geometric measure of coherence defined by $C_g(\rho) = 1 - max_{\sigma \in I} F(\rho, \sigma)$, where $F(\rho, \sigma) = (Tr\sqrt{\sqrt{\sigma}\rho\sqrt{\sigma}})^2$ is the fidelity of two density operators ρ and σ. For qubit states, $C_g(\rho) = \frac{1-\sqrt{1-4|\rho_{12}|^2}}{2}$ [13]. For single-qubit state, $x^2 + y^2 + z^2 = 2tr\rho^2 - 1$. Then we have

$$\begin{aligned}
C_g(sum) &= C_g(\rho_{A_1U_1}) + C_g(\rho_{A_2U_1}) + C_g(\rho_{A_3U_1}) \\
&= \frac{1}{2}[1 - \sqrt{1-(x^2+y^2)} + 1 - \sqrt{1-(y^2+z^2)}1 - \sqrt{1-(x^2+z^2)}] \\
&\leq \frac{3}{2}[1 - \sqrt{1-(x^2+y^2+z^3)}] \\
&= \frac{3}{2}[1 - \sqrt{2-2tr\rho^2}].
\end{aligned} \tag{20}$$

Applying the ordinary Lagrange multiplier method yields by constraint $x^2 + y^2 + z^2 \leq 1$,

$$C_g(sum) \geq \frac{3}{2} - \frac{\sqrt{3}}{2}\sqrt{3 - 2(x^2+y^2+z^2)}. \tag{21}$$

The equality holds if and only if $|x| = |y| = |z| = \frac{\sqrt{3}}{3}$.
Considering $tr\rho^2 = 1$ when ρ is a pure state, we have

$$\frac{3}{2} - \frac{\sqrt{3}}{2} \leq C_g(\rho_{A_1U_1}) + C_g(\rho_{A_2U_1}) + C_g(\rho_{A_3U_1}) \leq \frac{3}{2} \tag{22}$$

and

$$\frac{3}{2} - \frac{\sqrt{3}}{2} \leq C_g(\rho_{A_1U_2}) + C_g(\rho_{A_2U_2}) + C_g(\rho_{A_3U_2}) \leq \frac{3}{2}. \tag{23}$$

4 The l_1 Norm of Coherence of Bell-Diagonal States Under Self-tensor MUBs in $\mathbb{C}^4$

In this section we consider extending $\mathbb{C}^2$ to $\mathbb{C}^4$ in the form of self-tensors. Based on the idea of the Sect. 3, we have

$$\begin{cases}
C_1 = A_1 \otimes A_1 = \begin{pmatrix} 1&0&0&0 \\ 0&1&0&0 \\ 0&0&1&0 \\ 0&0&0&1 \end{pmatrix}, \\
C_2 = A_2 \otimes A_2 = \frac{1}{2}\begin{pmatrix} 1&1&1&1 \\ 1&-1&1&-1 \\ 1&1&-1&-1 \\ 1&-1&-1&1 \end{pmatrix}, \\
C_3 = A_3 \otimes A_3 = \frac{1}{2}\begin{pmatrix} 1&1&1&1 \\ i&-i&i&-i \\ i&i&-i&-i \\ -1&1&1&-1 \end{pmatrix},
\end{cases} \tag{24}$$

and unitary matrix

$$\begin{cases} W_1 = U_1 \otimes U_1 = \begin{pmatrix} e^{i(\delta_1+\delta_1)} & 0 & 0 & 0 \\ 0 & e^{i(\delta_1+\delta_2)} & 0 & 0 \\ 0 & 0 & e^{i(\delta_1+\delta_2)} & 0 \\ 0 & 0 & 0 & e^{i(\delta_2+\delta_2)} \end{pmatrix}, \\ W_2 = U_2 \otimes U_2 = \begin{pmatrix} 0 & 0 & 0 & e^{i(\nu_1+\nu_1)} \\ 0 & 0 & e^{i(\nu_1+\nu_2)} & 0 \\ 0 & e^{i(\nu_1+\nu_2)} & 0 & 0 \\ e^{i(\nu_2+\nu_2)} & 0 & 0 & 0 \end{pmatrix}. \end{cases} \tag{25}$$

Under the unitary transformations of

$$\begin{cases} C_1W_1 = \begin{pmatrix} e^{i(\delta_1+\delta_1)} & 0 & 0 & 0 \\ 0 & e^{i(\delta_1+\delta_2)} & 0 & 0 \\ 0 & 0 & e^{i(\delta_1+\delta_2)} & 0 \\ 0 & 0 & 0 & e^{i(\delta_2+\delta_2)} \end{pmatrix}, \\ C_2W_1 = \frac{1}{2} \begin{pmatrix} e^{i(\delta_1+\delta_1)} & e^{i(\delta_1+\delta_2)} & e^{i(\delta_1+\delta_2)} & e^{i(\delta_2+\delta_2)} \\ e^{i(\delta_1+\delta_1)} & -e^{i(\delta_1+\delta_2)} & e^{i(\delta_1+\delta_2)} & -e^{i(\delta_2+\delta_2)} \\ e^{i(\delta_1+\delta_1)} & e^{i(\delta_1+\delta_2)} & -e^{i(\delta_1+\delta_2)} & -e^{i(\delta_2+\delta_2)} \\ e^{i(\delta_1+\delta_1)} & -e^{i(\delta_1+\delta_2)} & -e^{i(\delta_1+\delta_2)} & -e^{i(\delta_2+\delta_2)} \end{pmatrix}, \\ C_3W_1 = \frac{1}{2} \begin{pmatrix} e^{i(\delta_1+\delta_1)} & e^{i(\delta_1+\delta_2)} & e^{i(\delta_1+\delta_2)} & e^{i(\delta_2+\delta_2)} \\ ie^{i(\delta_1+\delta_1)} & -ie^{i(\delta_1+\delta_2)} & ie^{i(\delta_1+\delta_2)} & -ie^{i(\delta_2+\delta_2)} \\ ie^{i(\delta_1+\delta_1)} & ie^{i(\delta_1+\delta_2)} & -ie^{i(\delta_1+\delta_2)} & -ie^{i(\delta_2+\delta_2)} \\ -e^{i(\delta_1+\delta_1)} & -e^{i(\delta_1+\delta_2)} & -e^{i(\delta_1+\delta_2)} & -e^{i(\delta_2+\delta_2)} \end{pmatrix}. \end{cases} \tag{26}$$

$$\begin{cases} C_1W_2 = \begin{pmatrix} 0 & 0 & 0 & e^{i(\nu_1+\nu_1)} \\ 0 & 0 & e^{i(\nu_1+\nu_2)} & 0 \\ 0 & e^{i(\nu_1+\nu_2)} & 0 & 0 \\ e^{i(\nu_2+\nu_2)} & 0 & 0 & 0 \end{pmatrix}, \\ C_2W_2 = \frac{1}{2} \begin{pmatrix} e^{i(\nu_2+\nu_2)} & e^{i(\nu_1+\nu_2)} & e^{i(\nu_1+\nu_2)} & e^{i(\nu_1+\nu_1)} \\ -e^{i(\nu_2+\nu_2)} & e^{i(\nu_1+\nu_2)} & -e^{i(\nu_1+\nu_2)} & e^{i(\nu_1+\nu_1)} \\ -e^{i(\nu_2+\nu_2)} & -e^{i(\nu_1+\nu_2)} & e^{i(\nu_1+\nu_2)} & e^{i(\nu_1+\nu_1)} \\ -e^{i(\nu_2+\nu_2)} & -e^{i(\nu_1+\nu_2)} & -e^{i(\nu_1+\nu_2)} & e^{i(\nu_1+\nu_1)} \end{pmatrix}, \\ C_3W_2 = \frac{1}{2} \begin{pmatrix} e^{i(\nu_2+\nu_2)} & e^{i(\nu_1+\nu_2)} & e^{i(\nu_1+\nu_2)} & e^{i(\nu_1+\nu_1)} \\ -ie^{i(\nu_2+\nu_2)} & ie^{i(\nu_1+\nu_2)} & -ie^{i(\nu_1+\nu_2)} & ie^{i(\nu_1+\nu_1)} \\ -ie^{i(\nu_2+\nu_2)} & -ie^{i(\nu_1+\nu_2)} & ie^{i(\nu_1+\nu_2)} & ie^{i(\nu_1+\nu_1)} \\ -e^{i(\nu_2+\nu_2)} & e^{i(\nu_1+\nu_2)} & -e^{i(\nu_1+\nu_2)} & -e^{i(\nu_1+\nu_1)} \end{pmatrix}. \end{cases} \tag{27}$$

It is easy to verify that $\{C_1W_1, C_2W_1, C_3U_1\}$ and $\{C_1W_2, C_2W_2, C_3W_2\}$ still constitute sets of MUBs. Next, we will consider the relation of the coherence of quantum states in above MUBs. We chose Bell-diagonal state, a representative two-qubit states which has a simple structure and is a good example of understanding more complex structure. For any two-qubit states under the basis $C = \{|00\rangle, |01\rangle, |10\rangle, |11\rangle\}$, which Hilbert space is $\mathbb{C}^2 \otimes \mathbb{C}^2$, X state can be written as

$$\rho = \frac{1}{4}(\boldsymbol{I} \otimes \boldsymbol{I} + \sum_{i=1}^{3} c_i \sigma_i \otimes \sigma_i + \boldsymbol{r} \cdot \boldsymbol{\sigma} \otimes \boldsymbol{I} + \boldsymbol{I} \otimes \boldsymbol{s} \cdot \boldsymbol{\sigma}), \tag{28}$$

where $\boldsymbol{I}$ is $2 \otimes 2$ unit operator, σ_i (i = 1, 2, 3) are the Pauli matrices, $\boldsymbol{r}$ $\boldsymbol{s}$ are the three-dimensional Bloch vectors associated with subsystems A, B and c_i denote the elements in the correlation matrix that represents the interaction of particles. When Bloch vectors $\boldsymbol{r}$, $\boldsymbol{s} = 0$, state ρ is Bell-diagonal states.

$$\rho_{Bell} = \frac{1}{4}(I \otimes I + \sum_{i=1}^{3} c_i \sigma_i \otimes \sigma_i) = \frac{1}{4}\begin{pmatrix} 1+c_3 & 0 & 0 & c_1-c_2 \\ 0 & 1-c_3 & c_1+c_2 & 0 \\ 0 & c_1+c_2 & 1-c_3 & 0 \\ c_1-c_2 & 0 & 0 & 1+c_3 \end{pmatrix}, \tag{29}$$

where σ_i $(i = 1, 2, 3)$ are Pauli matrices, and $c_1, c_2, c_3 \in [-1, 1]$. The density matrix of ρ_{Bell} in base C_1 is

$$\rho_{C_1} = C_1^{\dagger} \rho_{Bell} C_1 = \frac{1}{4}\begin{pmatrix} 1+c_3 & 0 & 0 & c_1-c_2 \\ 0 & 1-c_3 & c_1+c_2 & 0 \\ 0 & c_1+c_2 & 1-c_3 & 0 \\ c_1-c_2 & 0 & 0 & 1+c_3 \end{pmatrix}, \tag{30}$$

The density matrix of ρ_{Bell} in base C_2 is

$$\rho_{C_2} = C_2^{\dagger} \rho_{Bell} C_2 = \frac{1}{4}\begin{pmatrix} 1+c_1 & 0 & 0 & c_3-c_2 \\ 0 & 1-c_1 & c_3+c_2 & 0 \\ 0 & c_3+c_2 & 1-c_1 & 0 \\ c_3-c_2 & 0 & 0 & 1+c_1 \end{pmatrix}, \tag{31}$$

The density matrix of ρ_{Bell} in base C_3 is

$$\rho_{C_3} = C_3^{\dagger} \rho_{Bell} C_3 = \frac{1}{4}\begin{pmatrix} 1+c_2 & 0 & 0 & c_3-c_1 \\ 0 & 1-c_2 & c_3+c_1 & 0 \\ 0 & c_3+c_1 & 1-c_2 & 0 \\ c_3-c_1 & 0 & 0 & 1+c_2 \end{pmatrix}. \tag{32}$$

Similarly, we can obtain the expressions $\rho_{C_1W_1}$, $\rho_{C_2W_1}$, $\rho_{C_3W_1}$ and $\rho_{C_1W_2}$, $\rho_{C_2W_2}$, $\rho_{C_3W_2}$ of ρ with respect to the MUBs $\{C_1W_1, C_2W_1, C_3W_1\}$ and $\{C_1W_2, C_2W_2, C_3W_2\}$, severally,

$$\begin{aligned} \rho_{C_1W_1} &= W_1^{\dagger} \rho_{C_1} W_1 \\ &= \frac{1}{4}\begin{pmatrix} 1+c_3 & 0 & 0 & (c_1-c_2)e^{2i(\delta_2-\delta_1)} \\ 0 & 1-c_3 & c_1+c_2 & 0 \\ 0 & c_1+c_2 & 1-c_3 & 0 \\ (c_1-c_2)e^{2i(\delta_1-\delta_2)} & 0 & 0 & 1+c_3 \end{pmatrix}, \end{aligned} \tag{33}$$

$$\rho_{C_2W_1} = W_1^\dagger \rho_{C_2} W_1 = \frac{1}{4}\begin{pmatrix} 1+c_1 & 0 & 0 & (c_3-c_2)e^{2i(\delta_2-\delta_1)} \\ 0 & 1-c_1 & c_3+c_2 & 0 \\ 0 & c_3+c_2 & 1-c_1 & 0 \\ (c_3-c_2)e^{2i(\delta_1-\delta_2)} & 0 & 0 & 1+c_1 \end{pmatrix}, \tag{34}$$

$$\rho_{C_3W_1} = W_1^\dagger \rho_{C_3} W_1 = \frac{1}{4}\begin{pmatrix} 1+c_2 & 0 & 0 & (c_3-c_1)e^{2i(\delta_2-\delta_1)} \\ 0 & 1-c_2 & c_3+c_1 & 0 \\ 0 & c_3+c_1 & 1-c_2 & 0 \\ (c_3-c_1)e^{2i(\delta_1-\delta_2)} & 0 & 0 & 1+c_2 \end{pmatrix}, \tag{35}$$

$$\rho_{C_1W_2} = W_2^\dagger \rho_{C_1} W_2 = \frac{1}{4}\begin{pmatrix} 1+c_3 & 0 & 0 & (c_1-c_2)e^{2i(\nu_1-\nu_2)} \\ 0 & 1-c_3 & c_1+c_2 & 0 \\ 0 & c_1+c_2 & 1-c_3 & 0 \\ (c_1-c_2)e^{2i(\nu_2-\nu_1)} & 0 & 0 & 1+c_3 \end{pmatrix}, \tag{36}$$

$$\rho_{C_2W_2} = W_2^\dagger \rho_{C_2} W_2 = \frac{1}{4}\begin{pmatrix} 1+c_1 & 0 & 0 & (c_3-c_2)e^{2i(\nu_1-\nu_2)} \\ 0 & 1-c_1 & c_3+c_2 & 0 \\ 0 & c_3+c_2 & 1-c_1 & 0 \\ (c_3-c_2)e^{2i(\nu_2-\nu_1)} & 0 & 0 & 1+c_1 \end{pmatrix}, \tag{37}$$

$$\rho_{C_3W_2} = W_2^\dagger \rho_{C_3} W_2 = \frac{1}{4}\begin{pmatrix} 1+c_2 & 0 & 0 & (c_3-c_1)e^{2i(\nu_1-\nu_2)} \\ 0 & 1-c_2 & c_3+c_1 & 0 \\ 0 & c_3+c_1 & 1-c_2 & 0 \\ (c_3-c_1)e^{2i(\nu_2-\nu_1)} & 0 & 0 & 1+c_2 \end{pmatrix}. \tag{38}$$

According to the definition of l_1 norm of coherence, we have

$$\begin{aligned} C_{l_1(\rho_{(C_1W_1)})} &= \frac{1}{2}(|c_1+c_2|+|c_1-c_2|) = \max\{|c_1|,|c_2|\}, \\ C_{l_1(\rho_{(C_2W_1)})} &= \frac{1}{2}(|c_3+c_2|+|c_3-c_2|) = \max\{|c_2|,|c_3|\}, \\ C_{l_1(\rho_{(C_3W_1)})} &= \frac{1}{2}(|c_3+c_1|+|c_3-c_1|) = \max\{|c_3|,|c_1|\}. \end{aligned} \tag{39}$$

$$\begin{aligned} C_{l_1(\rho_{(C_1W_2)})} &= \frac{1}{2}(|c_1+c_2|+|c_1-c_2|) = \max\{|c_1|,|c_2|\}, \\ C_{l_1(\rho_{(C_2W_2)})} &= \frac{1}{2}(|c_3+c_2|+|c_3-c_2|) = \max\{|c_2|,|c_3|\}, \\ C_{l_1(\rho_{(C_3W_2)})} &= \frac{1}{2}(|c_3+c_1|+|c_3-c_1|) = \max\{|c_3|,|c_1|\}. \end{aligned} \tag{40}$$

From Eq. (33) to Eq. (38), let $c_1 = c_2 = c_3 = \frac{4p}{3} - 1$, where $0 \le p \le 1$, then Bell-diagonal states ρ_B change to the following Werner state

$$\rho_{WerW_1} = \rho_{WerW_2} = \begin{pmatrix} \frac{p}{3} & 0 & 0 & 0 \\ 0 & -\frac{p}{3}+\frac{1}{2} & \frac{2p}{3}-\frac{1}{2} & 0 \\ 0 & \frac{2p}{3}-\frac{1}{2} & -\frac{p}{3}+\frac{1}{2} & 0 \\ 0 & 0 & 0 & \frac{p}{3} \end{pmatrix}. \quad (41)$$

Obviously, the l_1 norms of coherence of Werner states ρ_W remains the same in bases C_1, C_2, C_3 by $C_{l_1(\rho_{(C_1W_1)})}$, $C_{l_1(\rho_{(C_2W_1)})}$, $C_{l_1(\rho_{(C_3W_1)})}$ or $C_{l_1(\rho_{(C_1W_2)})}$, $C_{l_1(\rho_{(C_2W_2)})}$, $C_{l_1(\rho_{(C_3W_2)})}$, that is,
$C_{l_1(\rho_{(C_1W_1)})} = C_{l_1(\rho_{(C_2W_1)})} = C_{l_1(\rho_{(C_3W_1)})} = C_{l_1(\rho_{(C_1W_2)})} = C_{l_1(\rho_{(C_2W_2)})} = C_{l_1(\rho_{(C_3W_2)})} = \left|\frac{4p}{3} - 1\right|$.

Similarly, let $c_1 = \frac{4F-1}{3}, c_2 = -\frac{4F-1}{3}, c_3 = \frac{4F-1}{3}$, where $0 \le F \le 1$, then Bell-diagonal states ρ_B turn into the following isotropic state

$$\rho_{IsoW_1} = \begin{pmatrix} \frac{F}{3}+\frac{1}{6} & 0 & 0 & (\frac{2F}{3}-\frac{1}{6})e^{2i(\delta_2-\delta_1)} \\ 0 & \frac{1}{3}-\frac{F}{3} & 0 & 0 \\ 0 & 0 & \frac{1}{3}-\frac{F}{3} & 0 \\ (\frac{2F}{3}-\frac{1}{6})e^{2i(\delta_1-\delta_2)} & 0 & 0 & \frac{F}{3}+\frac{1}{6} \end{pmatrix} \quad (42)$$

and

$$\rho_{IsoW_2} = \begin{pmatrix} \frac{F}{3}+\frac{1}{6} & 0 & 0 & (\frac{2F}{3}-\frac{1}{6})e^{2i(\nu_1-\nu_2)} \\ 0 & \frac{1}{3}-\frac{F}{3} & 0 & 0 \\ 0 & 0 & \frac{1}{3}-\frac{F}{3} & 0 \\ (\frac{2F}{3}-\frac{1}{6})e^{2i(\nu_2-\nu_1)} & 0 & 0 & \frac{F}{3}+\frac{1}{6} \end{pmatrix}. \quad (43)$$

The l_1 norms of coherence of isotropic states ρ_{Iso} remains the same in bases C_1, C_2, C_3 by $C_{l_1(\rho_{(C_1W_1)})}$, $C_{l_1(\rho_{(C_2W_1)})}$, $C_{l_1(\rho_{(C_3W_1)})}$ or $C_{l_1(\rho_{(C_1W_2)})}$, $C_{l_1(\rho_{(C_2W_2)})}$, $C_{l_1(\rho_{(C_3W_2)})}$, that is, $C_{l_1(\rho_{(C_1W_1)})} = C_{l_1(\rho_{(C_2W_1)})} = C_{l_1(\rho_{(C_3W_1)})} = C_{l_1(\rho_{(C_1W_2)})} = C_{l_1(\rho_{(C_2W_2)})} = C_{l_1(\rho_{(C_3W_2)})} = \left|\frac{4F-1}{3}\right|$.

5 The l_1 Norm of Coherence and the Relative Entropy of Coherence Under Complete MUBs in $\mathbb{C}^4$

In this section, we consider a more complex situation. We choose five complete MUBs in $\mathbb{C}^4$,

$$D_1 = \begin{pmatrix} 1&0&0&0 \\ 0&1&0&0 \\ 0&0&1&0 \\ 0&0&0&1 \end{pmatrix}, D_2 = \frac{1}{2}\begin{pmatrix} 1&1&1&1 \\ 1&1&-1&-1 \\ 1&-1&-1&1 \\ 1&-1&1&-1 \end{pmatrix},$$

$$D_3 = \frac{1}{2}\begin{pmatrix} 1&1&1&1 \\ -1&-1&1&1 \\ -i&i&i&-i \\ -i&i&-i&i \end{pmatrix}, D_4 = \frac{1}{2}\begin{pmatrix} 1&1&1&1 \\ -i&-i&i&i \\ -i&i&i&-i \\ -1&1&-1&1 \end{pmatrix}, D_5 = \frac{1}{2}\begin{pmatrix} 1&1&1&1 \\ -i&-i&i&i \\ -1&1&-1&1 \\ -i&i&i&-i \end{pmatrix}. \quad (44)$$

We find matrix U have the following eight forms based on the idea of constructing matrix U in Sect. 3, all of which can satisfy the definition of unbiased basis construction.

$$\left\{\begin{array}{l} W_a = \begin{pmatrix} e^{i\delta_1} & 0 & 0 & 0 \\ 0 & e^{i\delta_2} & 0 & 0 \\ 0 & 0 & e^{i\delta_3} & 0 \\ 0 & 0 & 0 & e^{i\delta_4} \end{pmatrix}, \\ W_b = \begin{pmatrix} 0 & 0 & e^{i\delta_1} & 0 \\ 0 & 0 & 0 & e^{i\delta_2} \\ e^{i\delta_3} & 0 & 0 & 0 \\ 0 & e^{i\delta_4} & 0 & 0 \end{pmatrix}, \\ W_c = \begin{pmatrix} 0 & e^{i\delta_1} & 0 & 0 \\ 0 & 0 & e^{i\delta_2} & 0 \\ 0 & 0 & 0 & e^{i\delta_3} \\ e^{i\delta_4} & 0 & 0 & 0 \end{pmatrix}, \\ W_d = \begin{pmatrix} 0 & 0 & 0 & e^{i\delta_1} \\ e^{i\delta_2} & 0 & 0 & 0 \\ 0 & e^{i\delta_3} & 0 & 0 \\ 0 & 0 & e^{i\delta_4} & 0 \end{pmatrix}. \end{array}\right. \left\{\begin{array}{l} W_e = \begin{pmatrix} 0 & 0 & 0 & e^{i\nu_1} \\ 0 & 0 & e^{i\nu_2} & 0 \\ 0 & e^{i\nu_3} & 0 & 0 \\ e^{i\nu_4} & 0 & 0 & 0 \end{pmatrix}, \\ W_f = \begin{pmatrix} 0 & e^{i\nu_1} & 0 & 0 \\ e^{i\nu_2} & 0 & 0 & 0 \\ 0 & 0 & 0 & e^{i\nu_3} \\ 0 & 0 & e^{i\nu_4} & 0 \end{pmatrix}, \\ W_g = \begin{pmatrix} 0 & 0 & e^{i\nu_1} & 0 \\ 0 & e^{i\nu_2} & 0 & 0 \\ e^{i\nu_3} & 0 & 0 & 0 \\ 0 & 0 & 0 & e^{i\nu_4} \end{pmatrix}, \\ W_h = \begin{pmatrix} e^{i\nu_1} & 0 & 0 & 0 \\ 0 & 0 & 0 & e^{i\nu_2} \\ 0 & 0 & e^{i\nu_3} & 0 \\ 0 & e^{i\nu_4} & 0 & 0 \end{pmatrix}. \end{array}\right. \tag{45}$$

For convenience, let's take W_a and W_e as an example. Under the unitary transformations of

$$\left\{\begin{array}{l} D_1 W_a = \begin{pmatrix} e^{i\delta_1} & 0 & 0 & 0 \\ 0 & e^{i\delta_2} & 0 & 0 \\ 0 & 0 & e^{i\delta_3} & 0 \\ 0 & 0 & 0 & e^{i\delta_4} \end{pmatrix}, \\ D_2 W_a = \frac{1}{2} \begin{pmatrix} e^{i\delta_1} & e^{i\delta_2} & e^{i\delta_3} & e^{i\delta_4} \\ e^{i\delta_1} & e^{i\delta_2} & -e^{i\delta_3} & -e^{i\delta_4} \\ e^{i\delta_1} & -e^{i\delta_2} & -e^{i\delta_3} & e^{i\delta_4} \\ e^{i\delta_1} & -e^{i\delta_2} & e^{i\delta_3} & -e^{i\delta_4} \end{pmatrix}, \\ D_3 W_a = \frac{1}{2} \begin{pmatrix} e^{i\delta_1} & e^{i\delta_2} & e^{i\delta_3} & e^{i\delta_4} \\ -e^{i\delta_1} & -e^{i\delta_2} & e^{\delta_3} & e^{i\delta_4} \\ -ie^{i\delta_1} & ie^{\delta_2} & ie^{i\delta_3} & -ie^{i\delta_4} \\ -ie^{i\delta_1} & ie^{i\delta_2} & -ie^{i\delta_3} & ie^{i\delta_4} \end{pmatrix}, \\ D_4 W_a = \frac{1}{2} \begin{pmatrix} e^{i\delta_1} & e^{i\delta_2} & e^{i\delta_3} & e^{i\delta_4} \\ -ie^{i\delta_1} & -ie^{i\delta_2} & ie^{i\delta_3} & ie^{i\delta_4} \\ -ie^{i\delta_1} & ie^{i\delta_2} & ie^{i\delta_3} & -ie^{i\delta_4} \\ -e^{i\delta_1} & e^{i\delta_2} & -e^{i\delta_3} & e^{i\delta_4} \end{pmatrix}, \\ D_5 W_a = \frac{1}{2} \begin{pmatrix} e^{i\delta_1} & e^{i\delta_2} & e^{i\delta_3} & e^{i\delta_4} \\ -ie^{i\delta_1} & -ie^{i\delta_2} & ie^{i\delta_3} & ie^{i\delta_4} \\ -ie^{i\delta_1} & ie^{i\delta_2} & ie^{i\delta_3} & -ie^{i\delta_4} \\ -e^{i\delta_1} & e^{i\delta_2} & -e^{i\delta_3} & e^{i\delta_4} \end{pmatrix}. \end{array}\right. \left\{\begin{array}{l} D_1 W_e = \begin{pmatrix} 0 & 0 & 0 & e^{i\nu_1} \\ 0 & 0 & e^{i\nu_2} & 0 \\ 0 & e^{i\nu_3} & 0 & 0 \\ e^{i\nu_4} & 0 & 0 & 0 \end{pmatrix}, \\ D_2 W_e = \frac{1}{2} \begin{pmatrix} e^{i\nu_4} & e^{i\nu_3} & e^{i\nu_2} & e^{i\nu_1} \\ -e^{i\nu_4} & -e^{i\nu_3} & e^{i\nu_2} & e^{i\nu_1} \\ e^{i\nu_4} & -e^{i\nu_3} & -e^{i\nu_2} & e^{i\nu_1} \\ -e^{i\nu_4} & e^{i\nu_3} & -e^{i\nu_2} & e^{i\nu_1} \end{pmatrix}, \\ D_3 W_e = \frac{1}{2} \begin{pmatrix} e^{i\nu_4} & e^{i\nu_3} & e^{i\nu_2} & e^{i\nu_1} \\ e^{i\nu_4} & e^{i\nu_3} & -e^{i\nu_2} & -e^{i\nu_1} \\ -ie^{i\nu_4} & ie^{i\nu_3} & ie^{i\nu_2} & -ie^{i\nu_1} \\ ie^{i\nu_4} & -ie^{i\nu_3} & ie^{i\nu_2} & -ie^{i\nu_1} \end{pmatrix}, \\ D_4 W_e = \frac{1}{2} \begin{pmatrix} e^{i\nu_4} & e^{i\nu_3} & e^{i\nu_2} & e^{i\nu_1} \\ ie^{i\nu_4} & ie^{i\nu_3} & -ie^{i\nu_2} & -ie^{i\nu_1} \\ -ie^{i\nu_4} & ie^{i\nu_3} & ie^{i\nu_2} & -ie^{i\nu_1} \\ e^{i\nu_4} & -e^{i\nu_3} & e^{i\nu_2} & -e^{i\nu_1} \end{pmatrix}, \\ D_5 W_e = \frac{1}{2} \begin{pmatrix} e^{i\nu_4} & e^{i\nu_3} & e^{i\nu_2} & e^{i\nu_1} \\ ie^{i\nu_4} & ie^{i\nu_3} & -ie^{i\nu_2} & -ie^{i\nu_1} \\ e^{i\nu_4} & -e^{i\nu_3} & e^{i\nu_2} & -e^{i\nu_1} \\ -ie^{i\nu_4} & ie^{i\nu_3} & ie^{i\nu_2} & -ie^{i\nu_1} \end{pmatrix}. \end{array}\right. \tag{46}$$

It is easy to verify that $\{D_1W_a, D_2W_a, D_3W_a, D_4W_a, D_5W_a\}$, $\{D_1W_b, D_2W_b, D_3W_b, D_4W_b, D_5W_b\}$, $\{D_1W_c, D_2W_c, D_3W_c, D_4W_c, D_5W_c\}$, $\{D_1W_d, D_2W_d, D_3W_d, D_4W_d, D_5W_d\}$, $\{D_1W_e, D_2W_e, D_3W_e, D_4W_e, D_5W_e\}$, $\{D_1W_f, D_2W_f, D_3W_f, D_4W_f, D_5W_f\}$, $\{D_1W_g, D_2W_g, D_3W_g, D_4W_g, D_5W_g\}$, $\{D_1W_h, D_2W_h, D_3W_h, D_4W_h, D_5W_h\}$ still constitute complete sets of MUBs.

The density matrix of ρ_{Bell} in base D_1 is

$$\rho_{D_1} = D_1^\dagger \rho_{Bell} D_1 = \frac{1}{4}\begin{pmatrix} 1+c_3 & 0 & 0 & c_1-c_2 \\ 0 & 1-c_3 & c_1+c_2 & 0 \\ 0 & c_1+c_2 & 1-c_3 & 0 \\ c_1-c_2 & 0 & 0 & 1+c_3 \end{pmatrix}, \tag{47}$$

The density matrix of ρ_{Bell} in base D_2 is

$$\rho_{D_2} = D_2^\dagger \rho_{Bell} D_2 = \frac{1}{4}\begin{pmatrix} 1+c_1 & 0 & c_3-c_2 & 0 \\ 0 & 1-c_1 & 0 & c_3+c_2 \\ c_3-c_2 & 0 & 1+c_1 & 0 \\ 0 & c_3+c_2 & 0 & 1-c_1 \end{pmatrix}, \tag{48}$$

The density matrix of ρ_{Bell} in base D_3 is

$$\rho_{D_3} = D_3^\dagger \rho_{Bell} D_3 = \frac{1}{4}\begin{pmatrix} 1 & -ic_2 & c_3 & ic_1 \\ ic_2 & 1 & -ic_1 & c_3 \\ c_3 & ic_1 & 1 & -ic_2 \\ -ic_1 & c_3 & ic_2 & 1 \end{pmatrix}, \tag{49}$$

The density matrix of ρ_{Bell} in base D_4 is

$$\rho_{D_4} = D_4^\dagger \rho_{Bell} D_4 = \frac{1}{4}\begin{pmatrix} 1+c_2 & 0 & c_3-c_1 & 0 \\ 0 & 1-c_2 & 0 & c_3+c_1 \\ c_3-c_1 & 0 & 1+c_2 & 0 \\ 0 & c_3+c_1 & 0 & 1-c_2 \end{pmatrix}, \tag{50}$$

The density matrix of ρ_{Bell} in base D_5 is

$$\rho_{D_5} = D_5^\dagger \rho_{Bell} D_5 = \frac{1}{4}\begin{pmatrix} 1 & ic_1 & -ic_2 & c_3 \\ -ic_1 & 1 & c_3 & ic_2 \\ ic_2 & c_3 & 1 & -ic_1 \\ c_3 & -ic_2 & ic_1 & 1 \end{pmatrix}. \tag{51}$$

Similarly, we can obtain the expressions $\rho_{D_1W_a}, \rho_{D_2W_a}, \rho_{D_3W_a}, \rho_{D_4W_a}, \rho_{D_5W_a}$

$$\begin{aligned}\rho_{D_1W_a} &= W_a^\dagger \rho_{D_1} W_a \\ &= \frac{1}{4}\begin{pmatrix} 1+c_3 & 0 & 0 & (c_1-c_2)e^{i(\delta_4-\delta_1)} \\ 0 & 1-c_3 & (c_1+c_2)e^{i(\delta_3-\delta_2)} & 0 \\ 0 & (c_1+c_2)e^{i(\delta_2-\delta_3)} & 1-c_3 & 0 \\ (c_1-c_2)e^{i(\delta_1-\delta_4)} & 0 & 0 & 1+c_3 \end{pmatrix},\end{aligned} \tag{52}$$

$$\rho_{D_2W_a} = W_a^\dagger \rho_{D_2} W_a = \frac{1}{4}\begin{pmatrix} 1+c_1 & 0 & (c_3-c_2)e^{i(\delta_3-\delta_1)} & 0 \\ 0 & 1-c_1 & 0 & (c_3+c_2)e^{i(\delta_4-\delta_2)} \\ (c_3-c_2)e^{i(\delta_1-\delta_3)} & 0 & 1+c_1 & 0 \\ 0 & (c_3+c_2)e^{i(\delta_2-\delta_4)} & 0 & 1-c_1 \end{pmatrix}, \tag{53}$$

$$\rho_{D_3W_a} = W_a^\dagger \rho_{D_3} W_a = \frac{1}{4}\begin{pmatrix} 1 & -ic_2e^{i(\delta_2-\delta_1)} & c_3e^{i(\delta_3-\delta_1)} & ic_1e^{i(\delta_4-\delta_1)} \\ ic_2e^{i(\delta_1-\delta_2)} & 1 & -ic_1e^{i(\delta_3-\delta_2)} & c_3e^{i(\delta_4-\delta_2)} \\ c_3e^{i(\delta_1-\delta_3)} & ic_1e^{i(\delta_2-\delta_3)} & 1 & -ic_2e^{i(\delta_4-\delta_3)} \\ -ic_1e^{i(\delta_1-\delta_4)} & c_3e^{i(\delta_2-\delta_4)} & ic_2e^{i(\delta_3-\delta_4)} & 1 \end{pmatrix}, \tag{54}$$

$$\rho_{D_4W_a} = W_a^\dagger \rho_{D_4} W_a = \frac{1}{4}\begin{pmatrix} 1+c_2 & 0 & (c_3-c_1)e^{i(\delta_3-\delta_1)} & 0 \\ 0 & 1-c_2 & 0 & (c_3+c_1)e^{i(\delta_4-\delta_2)} \\ (c_3-c_1)e^{i(\delta_1-\delta_3)} & 0 & 1+c_2 & 0 \\ 0 & (c_3+c_1)e^{i(\delta_2-\delta_4)} & 0 & 1-c_2 \end{pmatrix}, \tag{55}$$

$$\rho_{D_5W_a} = W_a^\dagger \rho_{D_5} W_a = \frac{1}{4}\begin{pmatrix} 1 & ic_1e^{i(\delta_2-\delta_1)} & -ic_2e^{i(\delta_3-\delta_1)} & c_3e^{i(\delta_4-\delta_1)} \\ -ic_1e^{i(\delta_1-\delta_2)} & 1 & c_3e^{i(\delta_3-\delta_2)} & ic_2e^{i(\delta_4-\delta_2)} \\ ic_2e^{i(\delta_1-\delta_3)} & c_3e^{i(\delta_2-\delta_3)} & 1 & -ic_1e^{i(\delta_4-\delta_3)} \\ c_3e^{i(\delta_1-\delta_4)} & -ic_2e^{i(\delta_2-\delta_4)} & ic_1e^{i(\delta_3-\delta_4)} & 1 \end{pmatrix}, \tag{56}$$

and the expressions $\rho_{D_1W_e}$, $\rho_{D_2W_e}$, $\rho_{D_3W_e}$, $\rho_{D_4W_e}$, $\rho_{D_5W_e}$

$$\rho_{D_1W_e} = W_e^\dagger \rho_{D_1} W_e = \frac{1}{4}\begin{pmatrix} 1+c_3 & 0 & 0 & (c_1-c_2)e^{i(\nu_1-\nu_4)} \\ 0 & 1-c_3 & (c_1+c_2)e^{i(\nu_2-\nu_3)} & 0 \\ 0 & (c_1+c_2)e^{i(\nu_3-\nu_2)} & 1-c_3 & 0 \\ (c_1-c_2)e^{i(\nu_4-\nu_1)} & 0 & 0 & 1+c_3 \end{pmatrix}, \tag{57}$$

$$\rho_{D_2W_e} = W_e^\dagger \rho_{D_2} W_e = \frac{1}{4}\begin{pmatrix} 1-c_1 & 0 & (c_3+c_2)e^{i(\nu_2-\nu_4)} & 0 \\ 0 & 1+c_1 & 0 & (c_3-c_2)e^{i(\nu_1-\nu_3)} \\ (c_3+c_2)e^{i(\nu_4-\nu_2)} & 0 & 1-c_1 & 0 \\ 0 & (c_3-c_2)e^{i(\nu_3-\nu_1)} & 0 & 1+c_1 \end{pmatrix}, \tag{58}$$

$$\rho_{D_3W_e} = W_e^\dagger \rho_{D_3} W_e = \frac{1}{4}\begin{pmatrix} 1 & -ic_2e^{i(\nu_3-\nu_4)} & c_3e^{i(\nu_2-\nu_4)} & ic_1e^{i(\nu_1-\nu_4)} \\ ic_2e^{i((\nu_4-\nu_3))} & 1 & -ic_1e^{i(\nu_2-\nu_3)} & c_3e^{i(\nu_1-\nu_3)} \\ c_3e^{i(\nu_4-\nu_2)} & ic_1e^{i(\nu_3-\nu_2)} & 1 & -ic_2e^{i(\nu_1-\nu_2)} \\ -ic_1e^{i(\nu_4-\nu_1)} & c_3e^{i(\nu_3-\nu_1)} & ic_2e^{i(\nu_2-\nu_1)} & 1 \end{pmatrix}, \tag{59}$$

$$\rho_{D_4W_e} = W_e^\dagger \rho_{D_4} W_e = \frac{1}{4}\begin{pmatrix} 1-c_2 & 0 & (c_3-c_1)e^{i(\nu_2-\nu_4)} & 0 \\ 0 & 1+c_2 & 0 & (c_3+c_1)e^{i(\nu_1-\nu_3)} \\ (c_3-c_1)e^{i(\nu_4-\nu_2)} & 0 & 1-c_2 & 0 \\ 0 & (c_3+c_1)e^{i(\nu_3-\nu_1)} & 0 & 1+c_2 \end{pmatrix}, \tag{60}$$

$$\rho_{D_5W_e} = W_e^\dagger \rho_{D_5} W_e = \frac{1}{4}\begin{pmatrix} 1 & ic_1e^{i(\nu_3-\nu_4)} & -ic_2e^{i(\nu_2-\nu_4)} & c_3e^{i(\nu_1-\nu_4)} \\ -ic_1e^{i(\nu_4-\nu_3)} & 1 & c_3e^{i(\nu_2-\nu_3)} & ic_2e^{i(\nu_1-\nu_3)} \\ ic_2e^{i(\nu_4-\nu_2)} & c_3e^{i(\nu_3-\nu_2)} & 1 & -ic_1e^{i(\nu_1-\nu_2)} \\ c_3e^{i(\nu_4-\nu_1)} & -ic_2e^{i(\nu_3-\nu_1)} & ic_1e^{i(\nu_2-\nu_1)} & 1 \end{pmatrix}. \tag{61}$$

According to the definition of Eq. (2), we have

$$\begin{aligned} C_{l_1(\rho_{(D_1W_a)})} =& \frac{1}{4}\Big(\left|e^{i(\delta_4-\delta_1)}(c_1-c_2)\right| + \left|e^{i(\delta_1-\delta_4)}(c_1-c_2)\right| \\ &+ \left|e^{i(\delta_2-\delta_3)}(c_1+c_2)\right| + \left|e^{i(\delta_3-\delta_2)}(c_1+c_2)\right|\Big) \\ =& \frac{1}{2}(|c_1-c_2|+|c_1+c_2|) \\ =& \max\{|c_1|,|c_2|\}, \end{aligned} \tag{62}$$

$$\begin{aligned} C_{l_1(\rho_{(D_2W_a)})} =& \frac{1}{4}\Big(\left|e^{i(\delta_3-\delta_1)}(c_3-c_2)\right| + \left|e^{i(\delta_1-\delta_3)}(c_3-c_2)\right| \\ &+ \left|e^{i(\delta_4-\delta_2)}(c_3+c_2)\right| + \left|e^{i(\delta_2-\delta_4)}(c_3+c_2)\right|\Big) \\ =& \frac{1}{2}(|c_3-c_2|+|c_3+c_2|) \\ =& \max\{|c_3|,|c_2|\}, \end{aligned} \tag{63}$$

$$\begin{aligned} C_{l_1(\rho_{(D_4W_a)})} =& \frac{1}{4}\Big(\left|e^{i(\delta_3-\delta_1)}(c_3-c_1)\right| + \left|e^{i(\delta_1-\delta_3)}(c_3-c_1)\right| \\ &+ \left|e^{i(\delta_4-\delta_2)}(c_3+c_1)\right| + \left|e^{i(\delta_2-\delta_4)}(c_3+c_1)\right|\Big) \\ =& \frac{1}{2}(|c_3-c_1|+|c_3+c_1|) \\ =& \max\{|c_3|,|c_1|\}, \end{aligned} \tag{64}$$

$$C_{l_1(\rho_{(D_3W_e)})} = C_{l_1(\rho_{(D_5W_e)})} = |c_1|+|c_2|+|c_3|. \tag{65}$$

We can obtain the following l_1 norm of coherence measures bounds

$$\begin{aligned} &0 \le \frac{1}{2}(|c_1|+|c_2|) \le C_{l_1(\rho_{(D_1W_a)})} \le |c_1|+|c_2| \le 2, \\ &0 \le \frac{1}{2}(|c_3|+|c_2|) \le C_{l_1(\rho_{(D_2W_a)})} \le |c_3|+|c_2| \le 2, \\ &0 \le \frac{1}{2}(|c_3|+|c_1|) \le C_{l_1(\rho_{(D_4W_a)})} \le |c_3|+|c_1| \le 2, \\ &0 \le C_{l_1(\rho_{(D_3W_a)})} \le 3, \\ &0 \le C_{l_1(\rho_{(D_5W_a)})} \le 3. \end{aligned} \tag{66}$$

Let $C_{l_1(\rho_{(D_{sum}W_a)})} = C_{l_1(\rho_{(D_1W_a)})} + C_{l_1(\rho_{(D_2W_a)})} + C_{l_1(\rho_{(D_3W_a)})} + C_{l_1(\rho_{(D_4W_a)})} + C_{l_1(\rho_{(D_5W_a)})}$, we have

$$0 \le 2(|c_1|+|c_2|+|c_3|) \le C_{l_1(\rho_{(D_{sum}W_a)})} \le 4(|c_1|+|c_2|+|c_3|) \le 12. \tag{67}$$

Moreover, since $C_{l_1}(\rho_{D_1W_a}) = C_{l_1}(\rho_{D_1W_e})$, $C_{l_1}(\rho_{D_2W_a}) = C_{l_1}(\rho_{D_2W_e})$, $C_{l_1}(\rho_{D_3W_a}) = C_{l_1}(\rho_{D_3W_e})$, $C_{l_1}(\rho_{D_4W_a}) = C_{l_1}(\rho_{D_4W_e})$ and $C_{l_1}(\rho_{D_5W_a}) = C_{l_1}(\rho_{D_5W_e})$, we can get the same boundary

$$\begin{aligned}
&0 \le \frac{1}{2}(|c_1| + |c_2|) \le C_{l_1(\rho_{(D_1 W_e)})} \le |c_1| + |c_2| \le 2,\\
&0 \le \frac{1}{2}(|c_3| + |c_2|) \le C_{l_1(\rho_{(D_2 W_e)})} \le |c_3| + |c_2| \le 2,\\
&0 \le \frac{1}{2}(|c_3| + |c_1|) \le C_{l_1(\rho_{(D_4 W_e)})} \le |c_3| + |c_1| \le 2,\\
&0 \le C_{l_1(\rho_{(D_3 W_e)})} \le 3,\\
&0 \le C_{l_1(\rho_{(D_5 W_e)})} \le 3.
\end{aligned} \tag{68}$$

Therefore, $C_{l_1(\rho_{(D_{sum} W_e)})} = C_{l_1(\rho_{(D_1 W_e)})} + C_{l_1(\rho_{(D_2 W_e)})} + C_{l_1(\rho_{(D_3 W_e)})} + C_{l_1(\rho_{(D_4 W_e)})} + C_{l_1(\rho_{(D_5 W_e)})}$,

$$0 \le 2(|c_1| + |c_2| + |c_3|) \le C_{l_1(\rho_{(D_{sum} W_e)})} \le 4(|c_1| + |c_2| + |c_3|) \le 12. \tag{69}$$

Next, we consider the relative entropy coherence. Through the calculation, we find that the eigenvalues of $\rho_{(C_1 W_a)}$, $\rho_{(C_2 W_a)}$, $\rho_{(C_3 W_a)}$, $\rho_{(C_4 W_a)}$, $\rho_{(C_5 W_a)}$ and $\rho_{(C_1 W_e)}$, $\rho_{(C_2 W_e)}$, $\rho_{(C_3 W_e)}$, $\rho_{(C_4 W_e)}$, $\rho_{(C_5 W_e)}$ are the same.

$$\begin{aligned}
S(\rho) =& -\sum_i \lambda_i log_2 \lambda_i\\
=& 2 - \frac{1}{4}[(1 - c_1 - c_2 - c_3) log_2 (1 - c_1 - c_2 - c_3)\\
&+ (1 - c_1 + c_2 + c_3) log_2 (1 - c_1 + c_2 + c_3)\\
&+ (1 + c_1 - c_2 + c_3) log_2 (1 + c_1 - c_2 + c_3)\\
&+ (1 + c_1 + c_2 - c_3) log_2 (1 + c_1 + c_2 - c_3)].
\end{aligned} \tag{70}$$

$$\begin{aligned}
&Cr(\rho_{(D_1 W_a)}) = 2 - S(\rho) - \frac{1}{2}[(1 + c_3) log_2 (1 + c_3) + (1 - c_3) log_2 (1 - c_3)],\\
&Cr(\rho_{(D_2 W_a)}) = 2 - S(\rho) - \frac{1}{2}[(1 + c_1) log_2 (1 + c_1) + (1 - c_1) log_2 (1 - c_1)],\\
&Cr(\rho_{(D_3 W_a)}) = 2 - S(\rho),\\
&Cr(\rho_{(D_4 W_a)}) = 2 - S(\rho) - \frac{1}{2}[(1 + c_2) log_2 (1 + c_2) + (1 - c_2) log_2 (1 - c_2)],\\
&Cr(\rho_{(D_5 W_a)}) = 2 - S(\rho).
\end{aligned} \tag{71}$$

$$\begin{aligned}
&Cr(\rho_{(D_1 W_e)}) = 2 - S(\rho) - \frac{1}{2}[(1 + c_3) log_2 (1 + c_3) + (1 - c_3) log_2 (1 - c_3)],\\
&Cr(\rho_{(D_2 W_e)}) = 2 - S(\rho) - \frac{1}{2}[(1 + c_1) log_2 (1 + c_1) + (1 - c_1) log_2 (1 - c_1)],\\
&Cr(\rho_{(D_3 W_e)}) = 2 - S(\rho),\\
&Cr(\rho_{(D_4 W_e)}) = 2 - S(\rho) - \frac{1}{2}[(1 + c_2) log_2 (1 + c_2) + (1 - c_2) log_2 (1 - c_2)],\\
&Cr(\rho_{(D_5 W_e)}) = 2 - S(\rho).
\end{aligned} \tag{72}$$

This is an entropic measure of coherence which has a clear physical interpretation, as $C_r(\rho)$ equals the optimal rate of the distilled maximally coherent states by IO in the asymptotic limit of many copies of ρ [30].

6 Summary

In this work, we extend the relationship between mutually unbiased basis(MUBs) and quantum coherence to a higher dimension. Results include arbitrary complete sets of MUBs form $\mathbb{C}^2$ to $\mathbb{C}^4$, and the form of arbitrary 2×2 unitary matrix and any density matrix of qubit states with respect to these complete sets of MUBs. We construct a set of three MUBs by tensor product in $\mathbb{C}^4$ and further think of complete sets of five MUBs in $\mathbb{C}^4$. Taking the Bell diagonal state as an example, we analyze the quantum state coherence of MUBs and calculate the corresponding upper and lower bounds. The results show that in addition to selecting the unbiased basis which is often used, we can consider more sets of complete MUBs, which may be helpful to the analysis of quantum states. This construction method will have better results for other coherent measures which is valuable in the practical sense of physics.

Acknowledgements. This paper was supported by National Science Foundation of China (Grant Nos: 12071271, 11671244, 62001274), the Higher School Doctoral Subject Foundation of Ministry of Education of China (Grant No: 20130202110001) and the Research Funds for the Central Universities (GK202003070). Special thanks to Professor Yuanhong Tao for her enlightening academic report. Useful suggestions given by Dr. Ruonan Ren, Dr. Ping Li, Dr. Mingfei Ye and Yongxu Liu are also acknowledged.

References

1. Bandyopadhyay, S.: A new proof for the existence of mutually unbiased bases. Algorithmica **34**(4), 512–528 (2002). https://doi.org/10.1007/s00453-002-0980-7
2. Ivonovic, I.D.: Geometrical description of quantal state determination. J. Phys. A: Gen. Phys. **14**(12), 3241–3245 (1981)
3. Wootters, W.K.: Optimal state-determination by mutually unbiased measurements. Ann. Phys. **191**(2), 363–381 (1989)
4. Spengler, C.: Entanglement detection via mutually unbiased bases. Phys. Rev. A **86**(2), 022311 (2012)
5. Melko, R.G.: Restricted Boltzmann machines in quantum physics. Nat. Phys. **15**(9), 887–892 (2019)
6. Ryan-Anderson, C.: Realization of real-time fault-tolerant quantum error correction. Phys. Rev. X **11**(4), 041058 (2021)
7. Durt, T.: On mutually unbiased bases. Int. J. Quantum. Inform. **8**(4), 535–640 (2010)
8. Horodecki, P.: Five open problems in quantum information theory. PRX Quantum **3**(1), 010101 (2022)
9. Luo, S.: Partial coherence with application to the monotonicity problem of coherence involving skew information. Phys. Rev. A **96**(2), 022136 (2017)
10. Baumgratz, T.: Quantifying coherence. Phys. Rev. Lett. **113**(14), 140401 (2014)
11. Napoli, C.: Robustness of coherence: an operational and observable measure of quantum coherence. Phys. Rev. Lett. **116**(15), 150502 (2016)
12. Chen, B.: Notes on modified trace distance measure of coherence. Quantum Inf. Process. **17**(5), 1–9 (2018). https://doi.org/10.1007/s11128-018-1879-9

13. Pires, D.: Geometric lower bound for a quantum coherence measure. Phys. Rev. A **91**(4), 042330 (2015)
14. Hu, M.-L.: Quantum coherence and geometric quantum discord. Phys. Rep. **762**, 1–100 (2018)
15. Mu, H.: Quantum uncertainty relations of two quantum relative entropies of coherence. Phys. Rev. A **102**(2), 022217 (2020)
16. Luo, Y.: Inequivalent multipartite coherence classes and two operational coherence monotones. Phys. Rev. A **99**(4), 042306 (2019)
17. Lian, Y.: Protocol of deterministic coherence distillation and dilution of pure states. Laser Phys. Lett. **17**(8), 085201 (2020)
18. Ren, R.: Tighter sum uncertainty relations based on metric-adjusted skew information. Phys. Rev. A **104**(5), 052414 (2021)
19. Ye, M.: Operational characterization of weight-based resource quantifiers via exclusion tasks in general probabilistic theories. Quantum Inf. Process. **20**(9), 1–28 (2021). https://doi.org/10.1007/s11128-021-03251-5
20. Vinjanampathy, S.: Quantum thermodynamics. Contemp. Phys. **57**(4), 545–579 (2016)
21. Kosloff, R.: Quantum thermodynamics: a dynamical viewpoint. Entropy **15**(6), 2100–2128 (2013)
22. Lambert, N.: Quantum biology. Nat. Phys. **9**(1), 10–18 (2013)
23. Cao, J.: Quantum biology revisited. Sci. Adv. **6**(14), eaaz4888 (2020)
24. McFadden, J.: The origins of quantum biology. Proc. R. Soc. Lond. Ser. A **474**(2220), 20180674 (2018)
25. Solenov, D.: The potential of quantum computing and machine learning to advance clinical research and change the practice of medicine. Mo. Med. **115**(5), 463–467 (2018)
26. Hassanzadeh, P.: Towards the quantum-enabled technologies for development of drugs or delivery systems. J. Controlled Release **324**, 260–279 (2020)
27. Streltsov, A.: Measuring quantum coherence with entanglement. Phys. Rev. Lett. **115**(2), 020403 (2015)
28. Bengtsson, I., Życzkowski, K.: Geometry of Quantum States: An Introduction to Quantum Entanglement, 2nd edn. Cambridge University Press, Cambridge (2017)
29. Nielsen, M.A., Chuang, I.L.: Quantum Computation and Quantum Information: 10th Anniversary Edition, 10th edn. Cambridge University Press, New York (2011)
30. Winter, A.: Operational resource theory of coherence. Phys. Rev. Lett. **116**(12), 120404 (2016)

Determining the Sampling Size with Maintaining the Probability Distribution

Jiaoyun Yang[1,2], Zhenyu Ren[1,2(✉)], Junda Wang[3], and Lian Li[1,2]

[1] School of Computer Science and Information Engineering, Hefei University of Technology, Hefei 230601, China
{jiaoyun,llian}@hfut.edu.cn, silvery@xy.hfut.edu.cn

[2] National Smart Eldercare International Science and Technology Cooperation Base, Hefei University of Technology, Hefei 230601, China

[3] Department of Computer Science, University of Rochester, Rochester 14627, USA
jwang212@ur.rochester.edu

Abstract. Sampling is a fundamental method in data science, which can reduce the dataset size and decrease the computational complexity. A basic sampling requirement is identically distributed sampling, which requires maintaining the probability distribution. Numerous sampling methods are proposed. However, how to estimate the sampling boundary under the constraint of the probability distribution is still unclear. In this paper, we formulate a Probably Approximate Correct (PAC) problem for sampling, which limits the distribution difference in the given error boundary with the given confidence level. We further apply Hoeffding's inequality to estimate the sampling size by decomposing the joint probability distribution into conditional distributions based on Bayesian networks. In the experiments, we simulate 5 Bayesian datasets with size 1, 000, 000 and give out the sampling size with different error boundaries and confidence levels. When the error boundary is 0.05, and the confidence level is 0.99, at least 80% samples could be excluded according to the estimated sampling size.

Keywords: Sampling size · Probably approximate correct · Probability distribution · Bayesian network

1 Introduction

Data volume has grown at an exponential rate with the rapid development of the Internet over the past dozens of years. According to statistics, Google needs to process hundreds of petabytes of data daily, Facebook generates 10 petabytes of log data every month, Baidu needs to process nearly 100 petabytes of data every day, and Taobao generates tens of terabytes of online transaction data every day [3]. Massive data resource brings many challenges to data analysis and data mining. One of these challenges is that data analysis and data mining based

Z. Cai et al. (Eds.): NCTCS 2022, CCIS 1693, pp. 61–74, 2022.
https://doi.org/10.1007/978-981-19-8152-4_4

on the entire dataset is time-consuming. Currently, there are two strategies to solve this problem: sampling and distributed system [14]. Even if we have enough computer resources, the cost is still expensive sometimes and we still hope to use sampling techniques to cut costs and accelerate data analysis.

Sampling aims to select a portion of samples as a subset to represent the whole dataset. It reduces the dataset size, thereby reducing the computational complexity. As only a small part of samples are chosen, some information may be ignored. Therefore, identically distributed sampling is usually required to guarantee data analysis performance. The assumption behind this is that if the distribution of the sampled subset is identical to that of the original dataset, the statistics information will be identical, and the sampled subset could be regarded as the representation of the original dataset. Many sampling methods have been designed according to this requirement, including purposive sampling, random sampling, stratified sampling, cluster sampling, systematic sampling, multistage sampling, and quota sampling [17].

Although these sampling methods have been widely used, the sampling size is still unclear for most applications. A common sense is the more the better. However, a larger sampling size indicates a higher computational complexity. Researchers have started to explore the sampling size with different utility constraints. Glenn estimated the sampling size according to the size in similar studies and presented two tables with varying combinations of precision, confidence level and variability for checking the sampling size [10, 17]. Cochran developed an equation to get the sampling size by combining the precision level and the estimated dichotomous proportion based on the abscissa of the normal curve that cuts off an area α at the tails [5]. Yamane provided a simplified formula to calculate the sampling size of the finite population when the estimated dichotomous proportion is 0.5 [18]. Jones et al. estimated the sampling size under statistical power constraints [11]. Kock et al. estimated the minimal sampling size required for the partial least squares structural equation model [12]. Alwosheel et al. used the MCMC method to estimate the sampling size required for the neural network model [1]. Yan et al. developed a dynamic programming algorithm based on Hoeffding's inequality to solve the minimal sampling size under a given error boundary [19]. Silva et al. designed a heuristic search strategy based on the performance of machine learning methods to find the minimal sampling size [16].

Most of these current methods focus on low-dimensional data or specific applications. When handling high-dimensional datasets, there are two challenges. One is that the distribution of the original dataset is hard to obtain. The simple idea is to treat each variable independently, however, this simplifies the distribution and the correlations between variables are ignored, which will introduce high bias. A widely used strategy to overcome the curse of dimensionality is to decompose the high-dimensional distribution into low-dimensional conditional distributions. For example, Zhang et al. in Google implemented a low-dimensional edge distribution based on Bayesian networks to approximate the original high-dimensional distribution [22]. Chen et al. decomposed the high-dimensional distribution into a low-dimensional conditional distribution based on a probability map model [4]. The other challenge is how to evaluate the distribution difference to guide the sampling. Recently, Yang et al. proposed using the chi-square test to conduct the distribution test and utilized this test to design a heuristic sampling method to obtain the required subset, while the sampling boundary for general sampling methods is still unclear [20,21].

This paper aims to determine the sampling boundary with the probability distribution constraint. We first formulate a Probably Approximate Correct (PAC) problem for sampling, which requires limiting the distribution difference within the given error boundary at the given confidence level. Then, we decompose the joint distribution into conditional distributions based on the Bayesian network to handle the high-dimensional challenge and apply Hoeffding's inequality to establish the sampling boundary under the random sampling assumption. Finally, we conducted experimental studies on 5 Bayesian datasets with size $1,000,000$. The experimental results show that when using random sampling, at least 80% samples could be excluded when the error boundary is 0.05 and the confidence level is 0.99 for these datasets. Meanwhile, we also validate the closeness of our established sampling boundary to the real one.

The remaining of this paper is organized as follows. In Sect. 2, we introduce the distribution decomposition formula and Hoeffding's inequality. In Sect. 3, we formulate the problem and present the process of determining the sampling size. In Sect. 4, we report the experimental results. In Sect. 5, we conclude this paper.

2 Related Works

2.1 Distribution Decomposition

Let D be a dataset, and $X = (x_1, x_2, \ldots, x_n)$ be a sample in D. x_i represents the i-th variable of D. The Bayesian network $\mathcal{N}$ on the variable set $\{x_1, x_2, \ldots, x_n\}$ is a probabilistic graphical model. It is a directed acyclic graph (DAG) in which each node represents a variable and each directed edge represents a direct dependence between the two variables connected by this directed edge. For convenience, we still use x_i as the notion of the node in the Bayesian network if it represents the variable x_i. For any two nodes x_i and x_j, if there exists a directed edge from x_j to x_i, then we call x_j a parent of x_i and correspondingly call x_i a child of x_j. We refer to the set of all parents of x_i as its parent set $\pi(x_i)$. We define $\theta_{ijk} = P(x_i = k \mid \pi(x_i) = j)$. It represents the probability when the variable x_i takes the k-th value and the parent set $\pi(x_i)$ takes the j-th combination.

Figure 1 illustrates a simple example of a Bayesian network. It has four nodes: x_1, x_2, x_3 and x_4. Every node has two values and they both are encoded by 1 and 2, respectively. There is a conditional probability table that contains θ_{ijk} for each node. The conditional probability table of node x_i represents the conditional distribution $P(x_i|\pi(x_i))$. These four tables can describe the full distribution of this Bayesian network.

The Bayesian network $\mathcal{N}$ has n conditional distributions $P(x_1|\pi(x_1))$, ..., $P(x_n|\pi(x_n))$. Let $\theta_{ijk} = P(x_i = k|\pi(x_i) = j)$ denote the probability that x_i takes the k-th value with the condition that $\pi(x_i)$ takes the j-th combination.

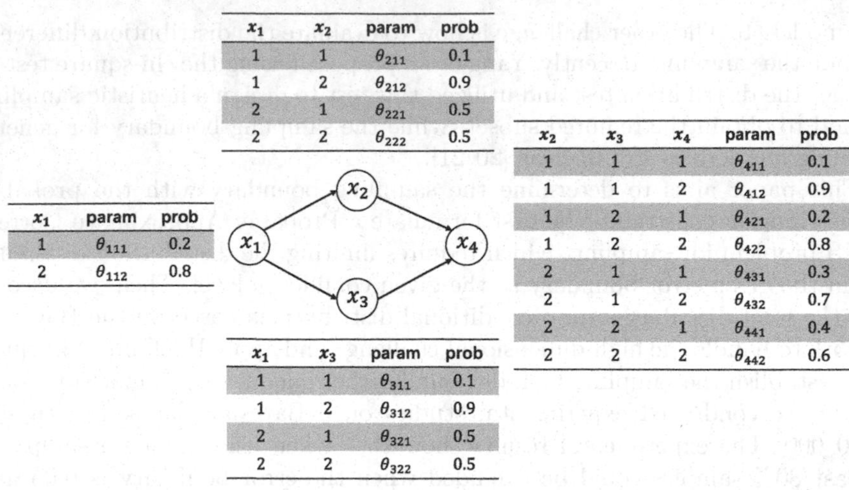

Fig. 1. An example of the Bayesian network with four conditional probability tables.

Then $\Theta = \{\theta_{ijk} | 1 \leq i \leq n, 1 \leq j \leq r_i, 1 \leq k \leq p_i\}$ denotes all of these conditional distributions, where n, r_i, and p_i denote the number of variables, the number of values x_i could get, and the combination number of the values of x_i's parents, respectively. According to the related reference [7], the Bayesian network's full distribution can be factorized as the product of all conditional distributions. This fact can be summarized as the following equation

$$P(X) = P(x_1, x_2, \ldots, x_n) = \prod_{i=1}^{n} P(x_i | \pi(x_i)) \tag{1}$$

We call Eq. (1) the Bayesian network's distribution decomposition formula. Hence, the set Θ can represent the Bayesian network's full distribution.

2.2 Hoeffding's Inequality

Let $X_1, X_2, \ldots, X_n$ be n mutually independent random variables and $X_i \in [a_i, b_i], i = 1, 2, 3, \ldots, n$. These random variables' mean is represented by

$$\overline{X} = \frac{X_1 + X_2 + \cdots + X_n}{n}$$

Hoeffding's inequality [9] is

$$\forall t > 0, P(|\overline{X} - E\overline{X}| \geq t) \leq exp\left\{-\frac{2n^2t^2}{\sum_{i=1}^{n}(b_i - a_i)^2}\right\} \tag{2}$$

It is worth noting that Hoeffding's inequality (2) still holds when the random variable series $X_1, X_2, \ldots, X_n$ from a population of size n drawn without replacement.

For convenience, we summarize the notations used in this paper in Table 1.

Table 1. Table of notations.

Notation	Description
$\mathcal{N}$	A Bayesian network
D	A dataset with size N
D'	A subset with size N' drawn without replacement from the dataset D
$X = (x_1, x_2, \ldots, x_n)$	A sample from the dataset D. It has n variables
$\pi(x_i)$	The parent set of the node x_i in $\mathcal{N}$
p_i	The number of unique values of x_i
r_i	The number of all combinations of $\pi(x_i)$
$M_{ijk} = count\{x_i = k, \pi(x_i) = j, X \in D\}$	The number of samples that x_i takes the k-th value and $\pi(x_i)$ takes the j-th combination in D
$m_{ijk} = count\{x_i = k, \pi(x_i) = j, X \in D'\}$	The number of samples that x_i takes the k-th value and $\pi(x_i)$ takes the j-th combination in D'
$M_{ij+} = count\{\pi(x_i) = j, X \in D\}$	The number of samples that $\pi(x_i)$ takes the j-th combination in D
$m_{ij+} = count\{\pi(x_i) = j, X \in D'\}$	The number of samples that $\pi(x_i)$ takes the j-th combination in D'
$\theta_{ijk} = P(x_i = k \mid \pi(x_i) = j, X \in D)$	The probability that x_i takes the k-th value with the condition that $\pi(x_i)$ takes the j-th combination in D
$\gamma_{ij} = P(\pi(x_i) = j, X \in D)$	The probability that $\pi(x_i)$ takes the j-th combination in D

3 Method

3.1 Problem Formulation

Most sampling methods are probabilistic sampling, which means each sample has some chance of being chosen or not. This means the sampling results would vary for different sampling executions. The apparent problem is that there is a probability for the satisfiability of the constraint that the distribution difference is within the given error boundary. Therefore, we adopt the idea of Probably Approximate Correct (PAC) learning to formulate the sampling problem.

Let's first introduce the definition of the PAC algorithm, and then we will formulate the sampling size determination problem.

Definition 1. An algorithm A is called a PAC algorithm for a problem T, if for all $0 < \epsilon, \lambda < 1$, we have

$$P(E(A(u), F(u)) < \epsilon) > \lambda$$

Here, u denotes an element or a dataset. $A(u)$ and $F(u)$ are the approximate result of algorithm A and the real result of problem T, respectively. E is the error definition. ϵ and λ denote the error boundary and the confidence level, respectively. This equation means that for the constraint the error between the approximate result $A(u)$ and the real result $F(u)$ is less than ϵ, and the probability of the satisfiability of this constraint is greater than λ.

For our problem, we want to know how many samples we need to draw from the original dataset so that the distribution difference between the sampled subset and the original dataset satisfies the given error boundary. For simplification, we assume the samples are chosen randomly, i.e., A denotes the random sampling algorithm. $A(u)$ represents the distribution of the sampled subset. $F(u)$ represents the distribution of the original dataset.

According to Eq. (1), the distribution of a dataset could be factorized into the product of several conditional distributions, denoted as $\Theta = \{\theta_{ijk}\}$. Therefore, we use $\Theta' = \{\theta'_{ijk}\}$ and $\Theta = \{\theta_{ijk}\}$ to represent the distribution of the sampled subset D' and the original dataset D, respectively. The distribution difference could be defined as the absolute error, i.e. $|\theta'_{ijk} - \theta_{ijk}|$. We need each conditional distribution to satisfy the error boundary, therefore, the problem is to estimate the minimum sampling size K_t that if the sampling size N' is no less than K_t, the distribution difference satisfies the following equation:

$$P\left(\bigwedge_{ijk}\left(\left|\theta'_{ijk} - \theta_{ijk}\right| < \epsilon_t\right) \middle| N' \geq K_t\right) > \lambda_t \tag{3}$$

where $0 < \epsilon_t < 1$ and $0 < \lambda_t < 1$. This equation means if we draw at least K_t samples from D, we could guarantee all the conditional distribution difference is less than ϵ_t with the confidence level λ_t.

3.2 Sampling Size Estimation

According to problem formulation (3), we aim to solve a lower boundary estimation about the sampling size N'. For simplicity, we first only consider one conditional distribution and simplify the probability inequality (3) as below:

$$P\left(\left|\theta'_{ijk} - \theta_{ijk}\right| < \epsilon_t\right) \tag{4}$$

We hope to get a lower boundary of the formula (4). So we apply Hoeffding's inequality (2) to this problem. The result is shown in Lemma 1.

Lemma 1.

$$P\left(\left|\theta'_{ijk} - \theta_{ijk}\right| < \epsilon_t\right) \geq 1 - 2exp\{-2m_{ij+}\epsilon_t^2\}$$

Proof. As we only guarantee one conditional distribution θ_{ijk}, we could just consider the subset $D_{ij+} = \{X | X = (x_1, x_2, \ldots, x_n) \in D, \pi(x_i) = j\}$. The size of D_{ij+} is M_{ij+}, i.e., the number of samples that $\pi(x_i)$ takes the j-th combination in D. Assume that we uniformly draw m_{ij+} samples without replacement from D_{ij+}. Define m_{ij+} random variables as

$$Y_{ijk}^{(l)} = \begin{cases} 0, x_i^{(l)} = k \\ 1, x_i^{(l)} \neq k \end{cases}$$

where $l = 1, 2, \ldots, m_{ij+}$. The expectation and variance of $Y_{ijk}^{(l)}$ respectively are

$$EY_{ijk}^{(l)} = \theta_{ijk}$$
$$DY_{ijk}^{(l)} = \theta_{ijk}(1 - \theta_{ijk})$$

We know $\theta'_{ijk} = \frac{m_{ijk}}{m_{ij+}} = \frac{1}{m_{ij+}} \sum_{l=1}^{m_{ij+}} Y_{ijk}^{(l)}$ and $E\theta'_{ijk} = \theta_{ijk}$, where m_{ijk} denotes the number of samples that x_i takes the k-th value and $\pi(x_i)$ takes the j-th combination in D', and m_{ij+} denotes the number of samples that $\pi(x_i)$ takes the j-th combination in D'. Hence, we can use Hoeffding's inequality (2) to get a lower boundary about the probability inequality (4).

$$P\left(\left|\theta'_{ijk} - \theta_{ijk}\right| < \epsilon_t\right) = 1 - P\left(\left|\theta'_{ijk} - \theta_{ijk}\right| \geq \epsilon_t\right) \geq 1 - 2exp\{-2m_{ij+}\epsilon_t^2\}$$

□

In Lemma 1, the right hand of the probability inequality only contains m_{ij+}. However, we want a lower boundary about the sampling size N'. Inspired by $M_{ij+} = N\gamma_{ij}$, where $\gamma_{ij} = P(\pi(x_i) = j, X \in D)$, we think m_{ij+} is near $N'\gamma_{ij}$.

The mathematical expression is

$$lb < m_{ij+} - N'\gamma_{ij} < ub$$

Let $-lb = ub = N'\epsilon_g$. Then, the above inequality is transformed into

$$\left|\gamma'_{ij} - \gamma_{ij}\right| < \epsilon_g$$

where $\gamma'_{ij} = \frac{m_{ij+}}{N'}$ and $0 < \epsilon_g < 1$.

Lemma 2. *When* $\left|\gamma'_{ij} - \gamma_{ij}\right| < \epsilon_g$ *and* $\gamma_{ij} > \epsilon_g$,

$$P\left(\left|\theta'_{ijk} - \theta_{ijk}\right| < \epsilon_t\right) > 1 - 2exp\{-2\,N'(\gamma_{ij} - \epsilon_g)\epsilon_t^2\}$$

where $\gamma'_{ij} = \frac{m_{ij+}}{N'}$ *and* $0 < \epsilon_g < 1$

Proof. The two conditions, $\left|\gamma'_{ij} - \gamma_{ij}\right| < \epsilon_g$ and $\gamma_{ij} > \epsilon_g$, imply that

$$0 < N'(\gamma_{ij} - \epsilon_g) < m_{ij+} < N'(\gamma_{ij} + \epsilon_g)$$

Then we have

$$2exp\{-2m_{ij+}\epsilon_t^2\} < 2exp\{-2\,N'(\gamma_{ij} - \epsilon_g)\epsilon_t^2\}$$

We introduce the above inequality into Lemma 1 and get a new probability inequality with the right side containing N' rather than m_{ij+}.

$$\begin{aligned} &P\left(\left|\theta'_{ijk} - \theta_{ijk}\right| < \epsilon_t\right) \\ &\geq 1 - 2exp\{-2m_{ij+}\epsilon_t^2\} \\ &> 1 - 2exp\{-2\,N'(\gamma_{ij} - \epsilon_g)\epsilon_t^2\} \end{aligned}$$

□

In Lemma 2, let $1 - 2exp\{-2\,N'(\gamma_{ij} - \epsilon_g)\epsilon_t^2\} > \lambda_t$. Then we get

$$N' > -\frac{log\frac{1-\lambda_t}{2}}{2(\gamma_{ij} - \epsilon_g)\epsilon_t^2}$$

The log represents the natural logarithm. Let $K_t = \left\lceil -(log\frac{1-\lambda_t}{2})/(2(\gamma_{ij} - \epsilon_g)\epsilon_t^2) \right\rceil$. When the sampling size $N' \geq K_t$ we can ensure that the absolute error between θ'_{ijk} and θ_{ijk} is less than ϵ_t with the confidence level λ_t. Hence, we get a sampling size K_t for a single θ_{ijk}. Next, we need to generalize this result to the sampling size for all θ_{ijk} in Θ.

Theorem 1 calculates the sampling size for Θ through the function $f_t(N')$. The minimal positive integer that satisfies $f_t(N') < 0$ is denoted by K_t. We take the minimal one between K_t and N as the sampling size because K_t may be greater than the dataset's size N.

Theorem 1. *When $\left|\gamma'_{ij} - \gamma_{ij}\right| < \epsilon_g$ and $\gamma_{ij} > \epsilon_g$ hold simultaneously for all i and j, there exists a positive integer K_t such that*

$$P\left(\bigwedge_{ijk}\left(\left|\theta'_{ijk} - \theta_{ijk}\right| < \epsilon_t\right)\middle| N' \geq K_t\right) > \lambda_t$$

where K_t is the minimal integer that satisfies the following inequality (The function $f_t(N')$ is monotone decreasing).

$$f_t(N') = \sum_{ij} p_i exp\{-2N'(\gamma_{ij} - \epsilon_g)\epsilon_t^2\} - \frac{1-\lambda_t}{2} < 0$$

Proof. In the below process, the first inequality scaling uses the probability inequality $P(\bigwedge_{i=1}^n A_i) \geq \sum_{i=1}^n P(A_i) - (n-1)$ and the second inequality scaling uses Lemma 2.

$$
\begin{aligned}
&P\left(\bigwedge_{ijk}\left(\left|\theta'_{ijk}-\theta_{ijk}\right|<\epsilon_t\right)\right)\\
&\geq \sum_{ijk} P\left(\left|\theta'_{ijk}-\theta_{ijk}\right|<\epsilon_t\right)-\left(\sum_{ijk}1-1\right)\\
&> \sum_{ijk}\left(1-2exp\{-2N'(\gamma_{ij}-\epsilon_g)\epsilon_t^2\}\right)-\left(\sum_{ijk}1-1\right)\\
&= 1-2\sum_{ijk} exp\{-2N'(\gamma_{ij}-\epsilon_g)\epsilon_t^2\}\\
&= 1-2\sum_{ij} p_i exp\{-2N'(\gamma_{ij}-\epsilon_g)\epsilon_t^2\}
\end{aligned}
$$

Let $1-2\sum_{ij} p_i exp\{-2N'(\gamma_{ij}-\epsilon_g)\epsilon_t^2\} > \lambda_t$. After transforming we get

$$\sum_{ij} p_i exp\{-2N'(\gamma_{ij}-\epsilon_g)\epsilon_t^2\} - \frac{1-\lambda_t}{2} < 0$$

Let $f_t(N') = \sum_{ij} p_i exp\{-2N'(\gamma_{ij}-\epsilon_g)\epsilon_t^2\} - \frac{1-\lambda_t}{2}$. Next, we only need to prove that there exists K_t such that $f_t(K_t) < 0$. We know three corollaries as follows:

(1) When $N' = 0$, $f_t(0) = \sum_{ij} p_i - \frac{1-\lambda_t}{2} > 0$;
(2) When $N' \to +\infty$, $f_t(N') \to -\frac{1-\lambda_t}{2} < 0$;
(3) $f_t(N')$ is strictly monotone decreasing about the independent variable N'.

Hence, there is a positive integer $K_t > 0$ such that $f_t(N') < 0$ □

4 Experiment

In this section, we show the experiments about sampling size estimation with satisfying the distribution constraint. As we decompose the joint distribution into conditional distributions based on the Bayesian network, we simulated 5 datasets with size 1,000,000 according to 5 Bayesian networks, including ASIA, SACHS, ALARM, WIN95PTS, and ANDES.

1. **ASIA:** The ASIA [13] is a small Bayesian network used for diagnosing chest diseases, including tuberculosis, lung cancer, and bronchitis. It has 8 nodes and 8 edges and all nodes have two kinds of values.
2. **SACHS:** The SACHS [15] is a small Bayesian network used to understand native-state tissue signaling biology, complex drug actions and dysfunctional signaling in diseased cells. It consists of 11 nodes and 17 edges. All nodes have three kinds of values.

3. **ALARM:** The ALARM [2] is a medium Bayesian network used for disease diagnosis. It consists of 37 nodes and 46 edges. Each node has two, three, or four kinds of unique values.
4. **WIN95PTS:** The WIN95PTS [8] is a large Bayesian network developed by Microsoft and edited for style by Norsys Software Corp. It consists of 76 nodes and 112 edges. All nodes have two kinds of values.
5. **ANDES:** The ANDES [6] is a very large Bayesian network, an Intelligent Tutoring System that teaches Newtonian physics via coached problem solving. It consists of 223 nodes and 338 edges. And all nodes have two kinds of values.

Based on these 5 Bayesian networks' parameters, we use the Gibbs sampler to generate these 5 Bayesian datasets.

To our best knowledge, there are few works on estimating the sampling size for high-dimensional datasets with maintaining the probability distribution. Hence, we only compare the estimated sampling size calculated by Theorem 1 against the real one estimated by the simulation experiment. Our theory has two critical parameters: the error boundary ϵ_t and the confidence level λ_t. We estimate the real sampling size by fixing the error boundary ϵ_t and observing the real success rate. We randomly take the specified number of samples from the original dataset 3000 times. The number ranges from 0 to the size of each dataset. Then we count how many times the sampled results satisfy the error boundary ϵ_t and calculate the real success rate. Finally, we find the smallest number that the real success rate is equal to or greater than λ_t, and we apply this number as the real sampling size that satisfies the error boundary ϵ_t and the confidence level λ_t.

The estimated and real sampling sizes are shown in Table 2. We set the error boundary ϵ_t as 0.05 and check the results for different confidence levels on five datasets. The theoretical sampling sizes of these five Bayesian datasets are all greater than the real ones, which means our theory can ensure the distribution difference is less than ϵ_t with the confidence level λ_t. When the Bayesian network becomes more complex, the theoretical sampling size does not always become larger. This is because the sampling size calculated by Theorem 1 is related to the size of the set Θ rather than the number of nodes and edges of the Bayesian network. This means the theoretical sampling size is related to the complexity of the distribution, and if there are more conditional distributions to maintain, the sampling size will become larger. Compared with the size of the original dataset, i.e., $1,000,000$, we can find that the theoretically estimated sampling size is less than 20% of the total dataset size. It means original datasets have a large proportion of redundant samples from the perspective of distribution maintenance.

Note that, in Theorem 1, the estimated sampling size is related to $\gamma_{ij} - \epsilon_g$, where γ_{ij} denotes the probability that $\pi(x_i)$ takes the j-th combination in D. In our experiments, ϵ_g is set as 0.01. We also eliminate the γ_{ij} that satisfies $\gamma_{ij} \leq 2\epsilon_g$. This is because if a probability is too small, we must obtain a large number of samples to satisfy this probability. The total number of γ_{ij} and the number of eliminated γ_{ij} for five Bayesian networks is shown in Table 3. These

Table 2. The sampling size on 5 Bayesian datasets of size 10,000,000 with the error boundary $\epsilon_t = 0.05$ and the confidence level $\lambda_t = 0.95$ or 0.99.

Dataset	$\lambda_t = 0.95$		$\lambda_t = 0.99$	
	Estimated	Real	Estimated	Real
ASIA	47181	11000	63028	20000
SACHS	81676	26000	102731	37000
ALARM	121697	26000	148937	40000
WIN95PTS	61352	17000	80642	27000
ANDES	139228	20000	168872	27000

small probabilities could also be ignored for some statistical analysis. At the same time, we also validate whether the condition $\left|\gamma'_{ij} - \gamma_{ij}\right| < \epsilon_g$ is satisfied. We find that this condition always holds for all confidence levels.

The error boundary ϵ_t and the confidence level λ_t are two critical parameters in our theory. Their values greatly influence the final result, especially the parameter ϵ_t. The confidence level is usually set as 0.95 or 0.99 in mathematical statistics. So the parameter λ_t in this paper is also set as 0.95 or 0.99. The parameter ϵ_t will vary with the requirement of the distribution difference. ϵ_t is smaller, the theoretically estimated sampling size is larger. To quantify the impact of ϵ_t on the sampling size, we set ϵ_t as 0.1, 0.08, 0.06, 0.04, 0.02 and 0.01, respectively. Then we calculate the theoretical sampling size and estimate the real one with $\lambda_t = 0.95$ or 0.99.

Table 3. The total number of γ_{ij} and the number of eliminated γ_{ij} for five Bayesian datasets. C_g is the former and D_g is the latter.

	ASIA	SACHS	ALARM	WIN95PTS	ANDES
C_g	18	89	243	532	1157
D_g	3	34	131	383	321

Figure 2 illustrates how the error boundary ϵ_t influences the sampling size. When ϵ_t is greater than 0.04, the theoretical sampling size is close to the real one. But the theoretical sampling size greatly exceeds the real one when ϵ_t is less than 0.02. In particular, when $\epsilon_t = 0.01$, the theoretical sampling size equals the size of the dataset.

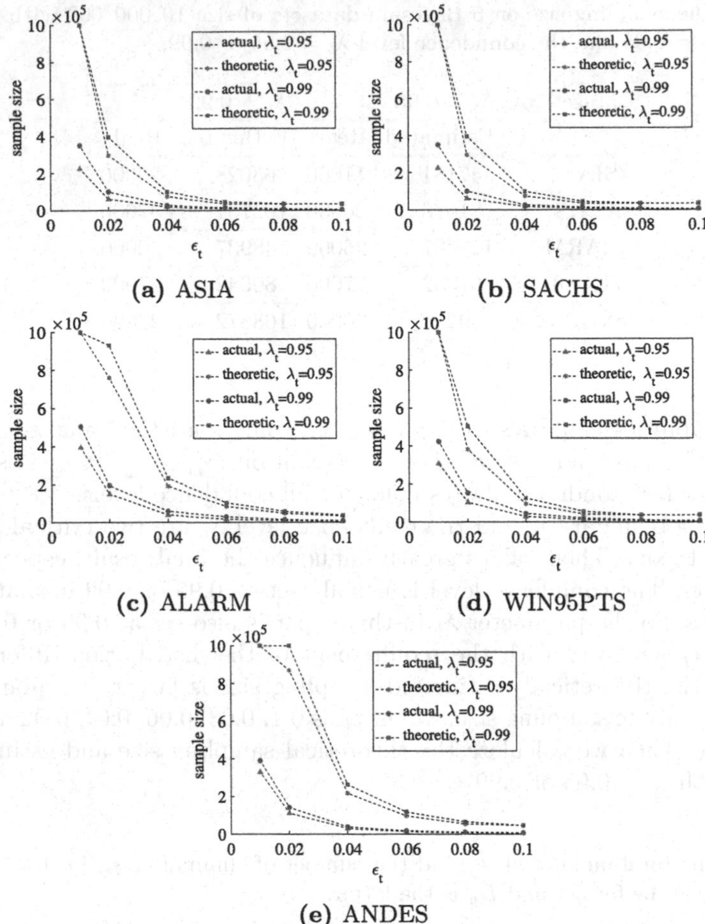

Fig. 2. The impact of the error boundary ϵ_t on the theoretical and real sampling size for different datasets with the confidence level $\lambda_t = 0.95$ and 0.99.

5 Conclusion

The distribution of a dataset is important. Many statistical properties rely on the distribution. In this paper, we theoretically estimate the sampling size of the high-dimensional dataset while maintaining the distribution using the random sampling technique. Specifically, we apply the PAC framework to formulate this sampling estimation problem. As the joint distribution is hard to obtain, we decompose the joint distribution into conditional distributions based on Bayesian networks. Then, we use Hoeffding's inequality to estimate the sampling size for conditional distributions instead of the full distribution. The experimental study on five Bayesian datasets shows the effectiveness of our theory.

Acknowledgements. This work was partially supported by the National Natural Science Foundation of China (No. 62072153), the Anhui Provincial Key Technologies R&D Program (2022h11020015), the International Science and technology cooperation project of the Shenzhen Science and Technology Commission (GJHZ20200731095804014), the Program of Introducing Talents of Discipline to Universities (111 Program) (B14025).

References

1. Alwosheel, A., van Cranenburgh, S., Chorus, C.G.: Is your dataset big enough? sample size requirements when using artificial neural networks for discrete choice analysis. J. Choice Model. **28**, 167–182 (2018)
2. Beinlich, I.A., Suermondt, H.J., Chavez, R.M., Cooper, G.F.: The alarm monitoring system: a case study with two probabilistic inference techniques for belief networks. In: Hunter, J., Cookson, J., Wyatt, J. (eds.) AIME 89, vol. 38, pp. 247–256. Springer, Cham (1989). https://doi.org/10.1007/978-3-642-93437-7_28
3. Chen, M., Mao, S., Liu, Y.: Big data: a survey. Mobile Netw. Appl. **19**(2), 171–209 (2014). https://doi.org/10.1007/s11036-013-0489-0
4. Chen, R., Xiao, Q., Zhang, Y., Xu, J.: Differentially private high-dimensional data publication via sampling-based inference. In: Proceedings of the 21th ACM SIGKDD International Conference on Knowledge Discovery and Data Mining, pp. 129–138 (2015)
5. Cochran, W.G.: Sampling Techniques. John Wiley, Hoboken (1977)
6. Conati, C., Gertner, A.S., VanLehn, K., Druzdzel, M.J.: On-line student modeling for coached problem solving using Bayesian networks. In: Jameson, A., Paris, C., Tasso, C. (eds.) User Modeling. ICMS, vol. 383, pp. 231–242. Springer, Vienna (1997). https://doi.org/10.1007/978-3-7091-2670-7_24
7. Friedman, N., Geiger, D., Goldszmidt, M.: Bayesian network classifiers. Mach. Learn. **29**(2), 131–163 (1997). https://doi.org/10.1023/A:1007465528199
8. Heckerman, D., Breese, J.: Decision-theoretic troubleshooting: a framework for repair and experiment. In: Proceedings of the Twelfth Conference on Uncertainty in Artificial Intelligence, pp. 124–132 (1996)
9. Hoeffding, W.: Probability inequalities for sums of bounded random variables. In: Fisher, N.I., Sen, P.K. (eds.) The collected works of Wassily Hoeffding, pp. 409–426. Springer, New York (1994). https://doi.org/10.1007/978-1-4612-0865-5_26
10. Israel, G.D.: Sampling the evidence of extension program impact. Citeseer (1992)
11. Jones, S., Carley, S., Harrison, M.: An introduction to power and sample size estimation. Emerg. Med. J.: EMJ **20**(5), 453 (2003)
12. Kock, N., Hadaya, P.: Minimum sample size estimation in PLS-SEM: the inverse square root and gamma-exponential methods. Information Syst. J. **28**(1), 227–261 (2018)
13. Lauritzen, S.L., Spiegelhalter, D.J.: Local computations with probabilities on graphical structures and their application to expert systems. J. Roy. Stat. Soc.: Ser. B (Methodol.) **50**(2), 157–194 (1988)
14. Liu, Z., Zhang, A.: A survey on sampling and profiling over big data (technical report). arXiv preprint arXiv:2005.05079 (2020)
15. Sachs, K., Perez, O., Pe'er, D., Lauffenburger, D.A., Nolan, G.P.: Causal protein-signaling networks derived from multiparameter single-cell data. Science **308**(5721), 523–529 (2005)

16. Silva, J., Ribeiro, B., Sung, A.H.: Finding the critical sampling of big datasets. In: Proceedings of the Computing Frontiers Conference, pp. 355–360 (2017)
17. Singh, A.S., Masuku, M.B.: Sampling techniques & determination of sample size in applied statistics research: an overview. Int. J. Econ. Commer. Manage. **2**(11), 1–22 (2014)
18. Yamane, T.: Statistics: An introductory analysis. Technical report (1967)
19. Yan, Y., Chen, L.J., Zhang, Z.: Error-bounded sampling for analytics on big sparse data. Proc. VLDB Endowment **7**(13), 1508–1519 (2014)
20. Yang, J.Y., Wang, J.D., Zhang, Y.F., Cheng, W.J., Li, L.: A heuristic sampling method for maintaining the probability distribution. J. Comput. Sci. Technol. **36**(4), 896–909 (2021)
21. Yang, J., Wang, J., Cheng, W., Li, L.: Sampling to maintain approximate probability distribution under chi-square test. In: Sun, X., He, K., Chen, X. (eds.) NCTCS 2019. CCIS, vol. 1069, pp. 29–45. Springer, Singapore (2019). https://doi.org/10.1007/978-981-15-0105-0_3
22. Zhang, J., Cormode, G., Procopiuc, C.M., Srivastava, D., Xiao, X.: Privbayes: private data release via Bayesian networks. ACM Trans. Database Syst. (TODS) **42**(4), 1–41 (2017)

Approximation Algorithms

The Polynomial Randomized Algorithm to Compute Bounded Degree Graph for TSP Based on Frequency Quadrilaterals

Yong Wang[1,2](✉)

[1] North China Electric Power University, Beijing 102206, China
yongwang@ncepu.edu.cn
[2] Tarim University, Alar 843300, Xinjiang, China

Abstract. It is the first time that bounded degree graph is proven to be computed for a big class of TSP in polynomial time based on frequency quadrilaterals. As TSP conforms to the properties of frequency quadrilaterals, a polynomial algorithm is given to reduce complete graph of TSP to bounded degree graph in which the optimal Hamiltonian cycle is preserved with a probability above 0.5. For TSP on such bounded degree graphs, there are more competitive exact and approximation algorithms.

Keywords: Traveling salesman problem · Frequency quadrilateral · Bounded degree graph · Randomized algorithm

1 Introduction

Traveling Salesman Problem (TSP) is extensively studied in computer science and operations research for searching the optimal Hamiltonian cycle (OHC) [1] in short time. Given complete graph K_n on n vertices $V = \{1, 2, \cdots, n\}$, a distance function $d(u, v) > 0$ is given for any pair of vertices $u, v \in V$. $d(u, v) = d(v, u)$ is considered for the symmetric TSP. The objective of TSP is to find the Hamiltonian cycle (HC) with the minimum distance, i.e. OHC, in K_n. In the following, we assume the distance between any two vertices is bounded as the computation time according to n is regarded here. In addition, we assume the distances of edges satisfy the triangle inequality since every edge in one cycle can be replaced by the shortest path with the same endpoints.

As a hard problem in combinatorial optimization, many exact and approximation algorithms have been designed for TSP over last sixty years [2]. However, the computation time of the exact algorithms for TSP on complete graph is hard to reduce to be below $O(2^n)$ [3]. The approximation ratio of approximation algorithms is also difficult to decrease, even for metric TSP [4]. On the other hand,

Supported by State Key Lab of Alternate Electrical Power System with Renewable Energy Sources, China.

Z. Cai et al. (Eds.): NCTCS 2022, CCIS 1693, pp. 77–95, 2022.
https://doi.org/10.1007/978-981-19-8152-4_5

there are better exact algorithms for TSP on sparse graphs [5]. Moreover, we have further better exact and approximation algorithms for TSP on bounded degree and genus graphs, see the literatures in the next section. These outcomes motivate researchers to try to convert TSP on complete graph into those on sparse graphs so that the current promising algorithms can be applied.

In previous papers [6,7], the scholars found many ordinary edges excluding from OHC. As these edges are eliminated, sparse graph is obtained. However, these algorithms cannot guarantee to generate one bounded degree or genus graph. It is the first time that bounded degree graph is figured out from complete graph for TSP in polynomial time and OHC is preserved with a probability above $\frac{1}{2}$. This result is derived based on the properties of frequency quadrilaterals [8] not only for metric TSP. Thus, bounded degree graph can be computed for a big class of TSP having such frequency quadrilaterals.

Except the literature review in Sect. 2 and a brief introduction of frequency property for the OHC edges in Sect. 3, the main contributions of this paper are included in Sects. 4 and 5.

In Sect. 4, we first prove that the probability $p_{3,5}(e)$ defined in Sect. 3 is bigger than $\frac{2}{3}$ for the OHC edges according to the frequency quadrilaterals in K_n. Secondly, we show that $p_{3,5}(e)$ of every OHC edge does not decrease with respect to the preserved frequency quadrilaterals after many ordinary edges are eliminated according to their $p_{3,5}(e)$ or frequency. Thus, it is safe to eliminate the edges with small $p_{3,5}(e)$ or frequency from K_n and dense graphs whereas the OHC edges are intact. These discoveries are the base for computing sparse bounded degree graph.

In Sect. 5, the iterative algorithm is provided to convert complete graph into sparse bounded degree graph for TSP. At each iteration, $\frac{1}{3}$ of the edges having the smallest $p_{3,5}(e)$ are cut until the residual graph contains a small number of quadrilaterals. We show that the maximum probability that the OHC edge having the smallest $p_{3,5}(e)$ is cut is smaller than $\frac{1}{3}$ at each iteration. After a finite cycles of edges elimination, the cumulative probability that this OHC edge is preserved is bigger than $\frac{1}{2}$ as it is contained in one or two quadrilaterals.

As each OHC edge is contained in one or two quadrilaterals, many ordinary edges are eliminated and bounded degree graph is generated. This bears out the randomized algorithm which reduces K_n to bounded degree graph where OHC is preserved with a probability above $\frac{1}{2}$. Based on bounded degree graph, TSP can be resolved in less than $O(2^n)$ time, see the proof in paper [5]. Moreover, there are more competitive approximation algorithms.

2 Literature Review

Fifty years ago, Karp [9] showed that TSP is NP-complete. It says there are no exact polynomial algorithms for TSP unless $P = NP$. The exact algorithms usually consume $O(\lambda^n)$ time where $\lambda > 1$. Held and Karp [10], and independently Bellman [11] presented the dynamic programming approach running time $O(n^2 2^n)$. Björklund [12] gave the exact algorithm consuming $O^*(1.657^n)$ time based on Monte Carlo method while it stands with an exponentially small probability of error. Most of the applied exact algorithms are designed based on branch and bound [13] and cutting plane [14,15] which generally run long time for TSP instances of big size. The approximation algorithms are also studied by researchers. The running time of the approximation algorithms has close relationship with the approximation ratio. For example for Euclidean TSP, the nearer the approximation to the optimal solution is, the longer the computation time will be [16].

Recently, the improved exact and approximation algorithms are studied for TSP on bounded degree and genus graphs. Björklund, Husfeldt, Kaski and Koivisto [5] augured that OHC in bounded degree graph can be found in $O(\xi_{\Delta}^n)$ time, where $\xi_{\Delta} = (2^{\Delta+1} - 2\Delta - 2)^{1/(\Delta+1)}$ is up to the maximum vertex degree Δ. They presented the computation time of exact algorithm for TSP on graphs of the maximum degree 3–8. For TSP on cubic graph, Eppstein [17] first gave the exact algorithm with running time $O(1.260^n)$. Later, Liśkiewicz and Schuster [18] improved the computation time to $O(1.2553^n)$. The current best time is $O(1.2312^n)$ owing to Xiao and Nagamochi [19]. In above papers, they also presented the time of algorithms to resolve TSP on 4-regular graph. It mentions that the sub-exponential algorithm for TSP on planar graph is provided by Dorn, Penninkx, Bodlaender, and Fomin [20].

Besides the improved exact algorithms, there are competitive approximation algorithms for TSP on bounded degree and genus graphs. Given TSP on cubic and subcubic graphs, the $\frac{4}{3}$-approximation algorithm is designed owing to Boyd, Sitters, van der Ster and Stougie [21]. Moreover, Correa and Larré [22] stated that the approximation ratio is strictly below $\frac{4}{3}$ for TSP on cubic graph. For metric TSP on planar graph, Klein [23] presented the linear approximation scheme which searches the $(1+\epsilon)$-optimal tour within $O(c^{1/\epsilon^2}n)$ time. Given TSP on bounded-genus graph, the polynomial-time approximation scheme is proposed by Borradaile, Demaine and Tazari [24]. For the asymmetric TSP on sparse graph, the results are also interesting. Svensson, Tarnawski and Végh [25] designed the 506-approximation algorithm for the triangle asymmetric TSP based on local connectivity. Soon, the approximation ratio is improved to $22+\epsilon$ for $\epsilon > 0$ owing to Traub and Vygen [26]. As the asymmetric TSP is on genus-g graph, Erickson and Sidiropoulos [27] have designed the $O\left(\frac{\log(g)}{\log\log(g)}\right)$–approximation algorithm. Kawarabayashi and Sidiropoulos [28] have approximated the Euler genus of bounded degree graph. Thus, the algorithm for TSP on bounded genus graph can be applied to TSP on bounded degree graph having limited genus.

These results demonstrate that it is essential to convert complete graph into sparse graph for reducing the computing time of algorithms for TSP. The experiments also illustrated that the computation time for resolving TSP instances on sparse graphs is much reduced. For example, Jonker and Volgenant [6] found many ordinary edges not in OHC based on 2-*opt* move. After these ordinary edges are trimmed, the computation time of the exact algorithm is reduced to half. In similarity, Hougardy and Schroeder [7] presented the combinatorial algorithm based on 3-*opt* move which eliminated more ordinary edges for the TSP

instances. They assigned big weights to these eliminated edges and submitted them to Concorde Package (exact algorithm). The Concorde was accelerated more than 11 times for resolving several big size of TSP instances on the changed graphs. To enhance the search engine, Taillard and Helsgaun [29] found a set of candidate edges. The experiments illustrated that the small number of candidate edges are useful for search package to find the solutions of high quality quickly. Turkensteen, Ghosh, Goldengorin and Sierksma [30] depended on the tolerances of edges rather than edges' weights for neglecting the ordinary edges. The branch and bound algorithm becomes quite efficient under the guidance of the preserved edges and the computation time is greatly decreased.

Different from the previous methods for computing sparse graphs for TSP, Wang and Remmel [8] eliminated the ordinary edges with respect to the frequency of edges computed with the frequency quadrilaterals. The frequency quadrilaterals have good properties to be used for distinguishing the OHC edges from most of the other edges. As the frequency of each edge is computed with the frequency quadrilaterals, the frequency of an OHC edge is generally much bigger than that of an ordinary edge. As the minimum frequency of the OHC edges is taken as threshold to cut edges having the smaller frequency, a big percentage of ordinary edges are eliminated [8] and the sparse graphs are obtained.

Given a quadrilateral on four vertices, six frequency quadrilaterals are derived [8] according to the distances of edges. They assumed the six frequency quadrilaterals are uniformly distributed in K_n. Based upon all the frequency quadrilaterals, they derived the probability $p_{3,5}(e) > \frac{2}{3}$ for the OHC edges and $p_{3,5}(e)$ notes the probability that edge e has the frequency 3 and 5 in a frequency quadrilateral containing e. In the next, Wang and Remmel [31,32] gave two iterative algorithms for computing sparse graph for TSP. According to the frequency of edges computed with frequency quadrilaterals, many ordinary edges are eliminated whereas the OHC edges are still preserved.

Although the algorithms work well to compute the sparse bounded degree graphs for the real-world TSP instances, the frequency change for the OHC edges is not known in the iterations. One will ask why the OHC edges can keep the big frequency according to the preserved graphs as that computed with respect to K_n? In addition, the lower bound of $p_{3,5}(e)$ is not proven for the OHC edges. As we choose N frequency quadrilaterals containing an edge to compute its frequency, it is not clear whether the frequency of the OHC edges is much bigger than that of most ordinary edges. To answer these questions, this paper is written and the contents in the following sections will convince us sparse bounded degree graph can be computed for a big class of TSP based on frequency quadrilaterals.

3 The Probability of Frequency for Edges in OHC

In this section, the probability that an edge has frequency 3, 5 is computed for the OHC edges based on frequency quadrilaterals [8].

Here quadrilateral means K_4 on four vertices A, B, C and D in K_n. We assume the order of the four vertices is $A < B < C < D$ which is induced by the natural ordering on $\{1, 2, \cdots, n\}$. Quadrilateral $ABCD$ contains six edges (A, B), (B, C), (C, D), (A, D), (A, C) and (B, D). The distances of the six edges are noted as $d(A, B)$, $d(B, C)$, $d(C, D)$, $d(A, D)$, $d(A, C)$ and $d(B, D)$, respectively. The corresponding frequency quadrilateral $ABCD$ is computed with the six optimal four-vertex paths with appointed endpoints. The computations of the optimal four-vertex paths and frequency quadrilateral are given as follows.

For example, given two endpoints A and B in $ABCD$, there are two paths visiting the four vertices. We assume they have different distances. The shorter path is considered as the optimal four-vertex path for A and B. There are six pairwise vertices $\{A, B\}$, $\{B, C\}$, $\{C, D\}$, $\{D, A\}$, $\{A, C\}$ and $\{B, D\}$. We naturally compute six optimal four-vertex paths according to the distances of edges. For an edge e in $ABCD$, the frequency $f(e)$ is the number of the optimal four-vertex paths containing e. As e is noted with vertices A and B, i.e., $e = (A, B)$, $f(e)$ is also represented as $f(A, B)$.

The frequency of edges is up to the three sum distances $d(A, B) + d(C, D)$, $d(A, C) + d(B, D)$ and $d(A, D) + d(B, C)$. Since the distances of edges are bounded, they can be compared. In the same manner, we assume they are unequal. For example, if $d(A, B) + d(C, D) < d(A, C) + d(B, D) < d(A, D) + d(B, C)$, the six optimal four-vertex paths are computed as (C, A, B, D), (A, C, D, B), (B, A, C, D), (A, B, D, C), (A, B, C, D) and (B, A, D, C). Thus, one can compute the frequency quadrilateral $ABCD$ illustrated in Fig. 1(a). As the three sum distances are arranged differently, another frequency quadrilateral can be computed. Since the three sum distances have six permutations, there are totally six frequency quadrilaterals $ABCD$. The other five frequency quadrilaterals $ABCD$ are shown in Fig. 1(b)–(f). Under each frequency quadrilateral, the distance inequality array is given according to the distances of edges in $ABCD$.

In every frequency quadrilateral, the frequency of edges is 1, 3 or 5. Moreover, the two opposite edges have the same frequency and the adjacent edges containing one vertex have different frequencies. For edge e in $ABCD$, let $p_1(e)$, $p_3(e)$ and $p_5(e)$ be the probability that it is assigned by the frequency 1, 3 and 5, respectively. Based on the six frequency quadrilaterals $ABCD$, each frequency 1, 3 and 5 of e occurs twice. Thus, $p_1(e) = p_3(e) = p_5(e) = \frac{1}{3}$ is computed and the expected frequency is 3.

Given a quadrilateral $ABCD$, if the three sum distances are unequal, the corresponding frequency quadrilateral may be one of the six frequency quadrilaterals. There are $\binom{n}{4}$ quadrilaterals in K_n. Every quadrilateral is a $ABCD$. Based on the six frequency quadrilaterals (a)–(f) for $ABCD$, let the six frequency quadrilaterals be uniformly distributed in K_n.

An edge e is contained in $\binom{n-2}{2}$ quadrilaterals in K_n. If there are no restrictions, every corresponding frequency quadrilateral is selected from the $\binom{n}{4}$ frequency quadrilaterals. On average, the probability $p_1(e) = p_3(e) = p_5(e) = \frac{1}{3}$ holds. It is the average probability for all edges.

For an OHC edge, Wang and Remmel [8] found $n-3$ frequency quadrilaterals where the frequency is 5 and 3. In the rest frequency quadrilaterals, the average probability $p_1(e) = p_3(e) = p_5(e) = \frac{1}{3}$ is considered. In this case, the probability

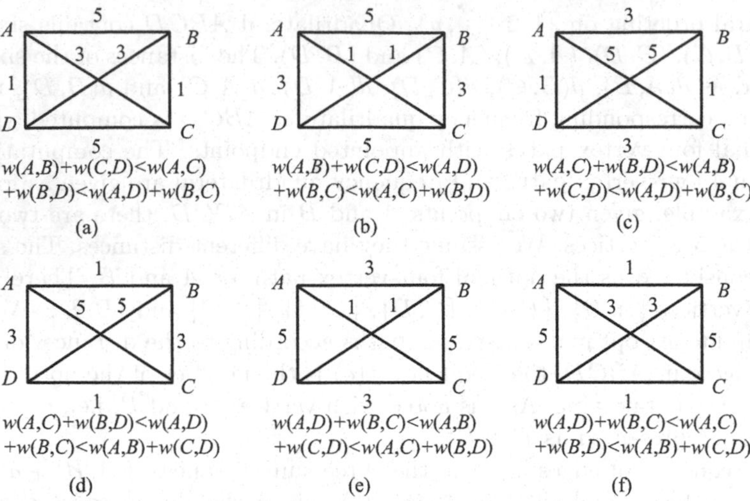

Fig. 1. The six frequency quadrilaterals for a quadrilateral $ABCD$.

that an OHC edge has the frequency 1, 3 and 5 is derived as Formulae (1) where $p_{3,5}(e) = p_3(e) + p_5(e)$.

$$p_{3,5}(e) = \frac{2}{3} + \frac{2}{3(n-2)},$$
$$p_1(e) = \frac{1}{3} - \frac{2}{3(n-2)} \tag{1}$$

As N frequency quadrilaterals containing e are chosen to compute the total frequency $F(e)$ or $F(A,B)$, it is equal to $\sum_{i=1}^{N} f_i(e)$ where $f_i(e)$ is the frequency of e in the ith frequency quadrilateral. The average frequency is $\bar{f}(e) = \frac{1}{N}\sum_{i=1}^{N} f_i(e)$. The OHC edges will have the frequency $F(e) > 3N$ or $\bar{f}(e) > 3$ according to the probability (1). Thus, the edges meeting the condition of $F(e) < 3N$ or $\bar{f}(e) < 3$ can be neglected for reducing the number of the concerned edges as one searches OHC.

4 Proof of the Probability for Edges in *OHC*

Based on the probability (1), the authors proved that the probability $p_5(e)$, $p_3(e)$ and $p_1(e)$ keeps constant for the OHC edges as n is big enough [33]. It means $p_5(e)$, $p_3(e)$ and $p_1(e)$ for the OHC edges computed according to some subgraphs in K_n is nearly equal to that computed according to K_n. They also showed that the OHC edges have frequency 5 and 3 in most of the frequency quadrilaterals containing them. However, the probability (1) is not proven in previous papers. In the following, we will prove the probability for the OHC edges. The frequency consistency is stated first for the proof. The frequency consistency was introduced in one recent paper [34] but the proof method is not constructive. Here the construction method is adopted to complete the proof.

Lemma 1. *Given a frequency quadrilateral $ABCD$ in K_n on vertex set V, if $f(A,B) > f(A,C)$ (or $f(A,B) < f(A,C)$) exists, $f(A,B) > f(A,C)$ (or $f(A,B) < f(A,C)$) holds with a probability above $\frac{2}{3}$ in another frequency quadrilateral $ABCE$, where $E \in V \backslash \{A,B,C,D\}$.*

The frequency consistency states an edge (A,B) has a big probability to maintain the same frequency in two frequency quadrilaterals containing A, B and another vertex C. The probability of frequency consistency is noted as δ and $\frac{2}{3} \leq \delta \leq 1$. We take $f(A,B) > f(A,C)$ as an example to prove the probability. The case of $f(A,B) < f(A,C)$ can be proven in the same manner.

Proof. As $f(A,B) > f(A,C)$ in the frequency quadrilateral $ABCD$, the distance inequality $d(A,B) + d(C,D) < d(A,C) + d(B,D)$ must hold in $ABCD$ (see Fig. 1). There are three cases (a), (b) and (e) in Fig. 1 according to $d(A,B) + d(C,D) < d(A,C) + d(B,D)$. Moreover, $d(A,D) + d(B,C) < d(A,C) + d(B,D)$ occurs twice among the three cases. As every type of frequency quadrilateral $ABCD$ has the equal probability, $d(A,D) + d(B,C) < d(A,C) + d(B,D)$ occurs with the probability $\frac{2}{3}$ and $d(A,B) + d(C,D) < d(A,D) + d(B,C)$ does as well.

When vertex D is replaced by another vertex $E \neq A,B,C,D$, a second quadrilateral $ABCE$ is generated. $ABCD$ and $ABCE$ are contained in $K_5 = ABCDE$. The optimal tour in $ABCDE$ will be constructed for proving the probability $\geq \frac{2}{3}$ of $f(A,B) > f(A,C)$ occurring in frequency quadrilateral $ABCE$. We first demonstrate that the optimal tour of $ABCDE$ rarely contains both (A,C) and (B,D).

If the optimal tour in $ABCDE$ contains both (A,C) and (B,D), there are four feasible tours (a_1) (A,B,D,E,C,A), (a_2) (A,C,D,B,E,A), (a_3) (A,C,E,B,D,A) and (a_4) (A,C,B,D,E,A). According to the distance inequality arrays in Fig. 1(a), (b) and (e), the four cycles will become shorter with some probability. For the tours (a_1) and (a_2), the shorter tour will be generated after (A,C) and (B,D) are substituted with (A,D) and (B,C) with the probability $\frac{2}{3}$. For each case of (a_3) and (a_4), the shorter tour is generated after (A,C) and (B,D) are replaced by (A,B) and (C,D) with the probability 1. Thus, tours (a_3) and (a_4) are never optimal. Plus the other eight tours, there are ten tours in $ABCDE$. If every tour has the equal probability to be optimal, the optimal tour containing both (A,C) and (B,D) occurs with a probability at most $\frac{1}{5}$. Since this probability is small, both (A,C) and (B,D) are rarely contained in the optimal tour of $ABCDE$. In the following, we first consider the optimal tours not including both (A,C) and (B,D).

Either (A,C) or (B,D) is deleted from $ABCDE$, one corresponding residual graph is obtained. The six tours in each of the residual graphs are found and the twelve tours (a)–(l) are shown in Fig. 2. Each tour is pictured as one pentagon. The layout of the five vertices A,B,C,D,E on the K_5 is the same as that of tour (a). Three frame edges of $ABCE$ are outlined along each tour and one frame edge is inside the tour. The edges (A,B) or (A,C) is noted with thin lines if they are not contained in the four frame edges. In the two groups of cycles (a)–(f) and (g)–(l), four of them are identical. The eight cycles contain neither (A, C) nor (B, D) and they are collected in the rounded rectangle in Fig. 2. In each group of (a)–(f) and (g)–(l), (A, B) is contained in four of them whereas (A, C) or (B, D) is only contained in two of them. If each cycle has the equal probability to be optimal, (A, B) has the big probability $\frac{2}{3}$ contained in the optimal tour whereas (A, C) or (B, D) has the small probability $\frac{1}{6}$. In the next, we demonstrate that $f(A, B) > f(A, C)$ occurs with a probability above $\frac{2}{3}$ in frequency $ABCE$ under the help of the possible optimal tours in Fig. 2.

Given a cycle in Fig. 2 is optimal, we build quadrilateral $ABCE$ along the tour, for example the case (a) in Fig. 2. Using two vertex-disjoint optimal tour edges in $ABCD$, the distance inequality related to two pairs of vertex-disjoint edges in $ABCE$ can be derived, i.e., $d(A, E) + d(B, C) < d(A, C) + d(B, E)$. Thus, one can derive three frequency quadrilaterals $ABCE$ conforming to this inequality. Meanwhile, three frequency pairs $(f(A, B), f(A, C))$ are obtained according to the three frequency quadrilaterals $ABCE$. The three frequency pairs are (5, 1), (3, 1) and (1, 3). Since each frequency quadrilateral $ABCE$ occurs with the equal probability, $f(A, B) > f(A, C)$ occurs with the probability $\frac{2}{3}$. On average, $f(A, B) > f(A, C)$ holds in frequency quadrilateral $ABCE$.

In the same manner, the distance inequality related to $ABCE$ is built with respect to each of the other possible optimal tours in Fig. 2. The three frequency quadrilaterals $ABCE$ are derived and the frequency pairs $(f(A, B), f(A, C))$ as well according to corresponding distance inequality. These results are given under the tours (a)–(l) in Fig. 2. In total, there are eight cases (a), (b), (c), (g), (h), (i), (k) and (l) where $f(A, B) > f(A, C)$ occurs with the probability above $\frac{2}{3}$. It says $f(A, B) > f(A, C)$ in these frequency quadrilaterals $ABCE$. In the other $ABCE$s built according to the rest four cycles (d), (j), (e) and (f), $f(A, B) < f(A, C)$ is considered. In total, $f(A, B) > f(A, C)$ occurs with the probability $\frac{2}{3}$ in frequency quadrilateral $ABCE$.

In the above analysis, we assume every tour in $ABCDE$ occurs with the equal probability. In fact, the cycles in $ABCDE$ occur with different probabilities due to the distance inequality related to $ABCD$ derived according to each possible optimal tour. Based on the precondition $d(A, B) + d(C, D) < d(A, C) + d(B, D)$, there are three frequency quadrilaterals $ABCD$ in Fig. 1 and the corresponding distance inequality arrays. However, the distance inequality related to $ABCD$ derived according to the optimal tour of $ABCDE$ may comply with 1, 2 or 3 of the distance inequality arrays. Thus, the occurring probabilities of these cycles will be different.

Given a possible optimal tour, we fist build $ABCD$ along the tour and then derive the distance inequality related to $ABCD$ under the constraints of the optimal tour. The distance inequality is compared with the three distance inequality arrays including $d(A, B) + d(C, D) < d(A, C) + d(B, D)$. If the distance inequality conforms to k $(k \leq 3)$ of the three distance inequality arrays, the occurring probability of this tour is computed as $\frac{k}{3}$.

For example (a) and (b) in Fig. 2, $d(A,B)+d(C,D)<d(A,C)+d(B,D)$ and $d(A,D)+d(B,C)<d(A,C)+d(B,D)$ are derived with respect to the two possible optimal tours, respectively. For cycle (a) in Fig. 2, the inequality $d(A,B)+d(C,D)<d(A,C)+d(B,D)$ conforms to the three distance inequality arrays. For the inequality $d(A,D)+d(B,C)<d(A,C)+d(B,D)$ derived according to tour (b), it only conforms to two of the three distance inequality arrays. Thus, the occurring probability of tour (a) is $\frac{3}{2}$ times of that of tour (b).

In this way, one can derive the relationships between the occurring probabilities for the cycles in $ABCDE$. Note the occurring probability p_{oc} of cycle (a) as p_0. The occurring probability of the other cycles is computed and illustrated in Table 1. It is clearly that the tours containing (A,B) and (C,D) have the bigger occurring probability than those containing (A,C) and (B,D) do.

Come back to the four cycles (a_1), (a_2), (a_3) and (a_4) containing both (A,C) and (B,D). Under the constraint of the distance inequalities, each cycle of (a_1) and (a_2) occurs with the probability $\frac{p_0}{3}$ whereas the cycles (a_3), (a_4) occur with the probability zero so they are never optimal.

Based on the precondition $d(A,B)+d(C,D)<d(A,C)+d(B,D)$, ten tours may be optimal in $ABCDE$. Moreover, every tour occurs with its own probability p_{oc} shown in Table 1. The total occurring probability of the ten possible optimal tours is 1 so we obtain $p_0=\frac{1}{6}$.

In the end, we compute the probability of $f(A,B)>f(A,C)$ in frequency quadrilateral $ABCE$. Based on the distance inequality related to $ABCE$ built according to each possible optimal tour, one can derive the probability $q_>$ of $f(A,B)>f(A,C)$ in frequency quadrilateral $ABCE$. The value of $q_>$ for each case is given in Table 1. As $f(A,B)>f(A,C)$ occurs with a probability above $\frac{2}{3}$, $f(A,B)>f(A,C)$ holds in frequency quadrilateral $ABCE$. In view of the six cases where $q_>\geq\frac{2}{3}$ in Table 1, the total probability of $f(A,B)>f(A,C)$ is computed as $\delta=p_0+\frac{2p_0}{3}+p_0+\frac{2p_0}{3}+\frac{p_0}{3}+\frac{p_0}{3}=4p_0=\frac{2}{3}$.

Since both (A,C) and (B,D) are seldom contained in the optimal tour of $ABCDE$ (the probability is $\frac{1}{9}$), the twelve cycles in Fig. 2 can be taken as the possible optimal tours. If only the twelve cycles in Fig. 2 are considered, $p_0=\frac{3}{26}$ is derived and the total probability of $f(A,B)>f(A,C)$ occurs with a probability $\delta=\frac{19}{26}>\frac{2}{3}$ in frequency quadrilateral $ABCE$. □

We have done experiments to testify the probability of frequency consistency. As $ABCE$ is built from $ABCD$, $d(C,E)$ and $d(B,E)$ pick values from the same interval at random while $d(A,B)$ and $d(A,C)$ keep unchanged. The experimental result has a good fit. Since we assume the distances of edges are bounded in K_n, all edges are assigned the distances in one interval. The frequency consistency will work well for such TSP which contains a big class of TSP.

Based on the frequency consistency, Theorem 1 is given as follows.

Theorem 1. *If there is only one OHC in K_n, the probability that an OHC edge e has the frequency 3, 5 in a random frequency quadrilateral containing e is above $\frac{2}{3}$.*

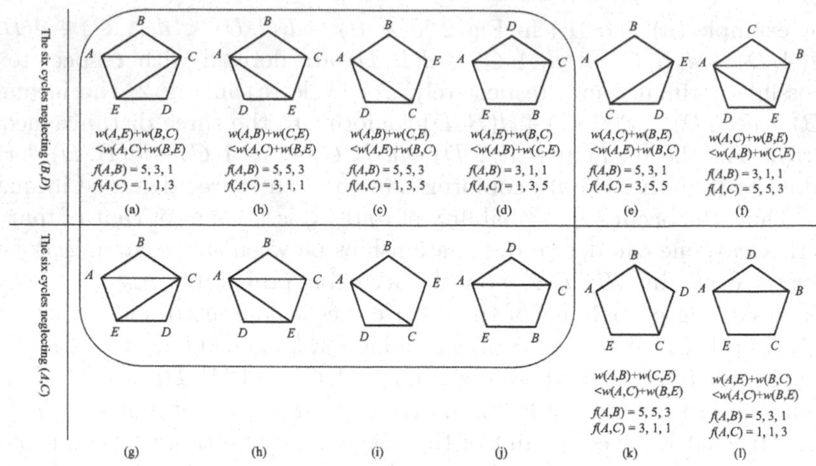

Fig. 2. Twelve tours in $ABCDE$ after (A, C) or (B, D) is cut.

Table 1. Occurring probability of each tour in $ABCDE$.

Cycle	(a)/(g)	(b)/(h)	(c)/(i)	(d)/(j)	(e)	(f)	(k)	(l)	(a_1)	(a_2)	(a_3)	(a_4)
p_{oc}	p_0	$\frac{2p_0}{3}$	p_0	$\frac{2p_0}{3}$	$\frac{2p_0}{3}$	$\frac{p_0}{3}$	$\frac{2p_0}{3}$	$\frac{p_0}{3}$	$\frac{p_0}{3}$	$\frac{p_0}{3}$	0	0
$q_>$	$\frac{2}{3}$	1	$\frac{2}{3}$	$\frac{1}{3}$	$\frac{1}{3}$	0	1	$\frac{2}{3}$	$\frac{2}{3}$	0	$\frac{1}{3}$	$\frac{1}{3}$

Proof. The OHC of K_n is illustrated in Fig. 3. (A, B) and (C, D) are two vertex-disjoint OHC edges. (A, B) has $n - 3$ such vertex-disjoint edges (C, D) along OHC. In each of these quadrilaterals $ABCD$, $d(A, B) + d(C, D) < d(A, C) + d(B, D)$ holds since $(A, B), (C, D) \in OHC$. Based on the three frequency quadrilaterals (a), (b) and (e) conforming to the distance inequality in Fig. 1, the three frequency pairs (5, 3), (5, 1) and (3, 1) are obtained for $(f(A, B), f(A, C))$. Since each of the frequency pairs (5, 3), (5, 1) and (3, 1) occurs with the equal probability, $f(A, B) > f(A, C)$ holds in frequency quadrilateral $ABCD$. As vertex D is replaced by a different vertex E, another quadrilateral $ABCE$ is generated in Fig. 3. In frequency quadrilateral $ABCE$, $f(A, B) > f(A, C)$ occurs with a probability above $\frac{2}{3}$ according to Lemma 1.

Except the four vertices A, B, C and D, there are other $n-4$ vertices $E \in V$. Thus, there are $n-4$ frequency quadrilaterals $ABCE$ in which $f(A, B) > f(A, C)$ holds with a probability above $\frac{2}{3}$. Moreover, considering the $n-3$ vertex-disjoint edges (C, D) on OHC, there will be $(n-3)(n-4)$ such frequency quadrilaterals $ABCE$. Because each $ABCE$ appears twice as (C, D) moves along OHC, the number of the quadrilaterals $ABCE$ becomes $\binom{n-3}{2}$. As $f(A, B) > f(A, C)$ exists, $f(A, B)$ is equal to 3 or 5 in each of the frequency quadrilaterals $ABCE$. This case occurs with the probability above $\frac{2}{3}$. Thus, there are at least $\frac{2\binom{n-3}{2}}{3} + n - 3$ frequency quadrilaterals in which (A, B) has the frequency 5 or 3.

(A, B) is contained in $\binom{n-2}{2}$ quadrilaterals in K_n. Therefore, the probability that (A, B) has the frequency 3 and 5 is bigger than $\frac{2}{3} + \frac{2}{3(n-2)} > \frac{2}{3}$. The probability model (1) is proven for the OHC edges. □

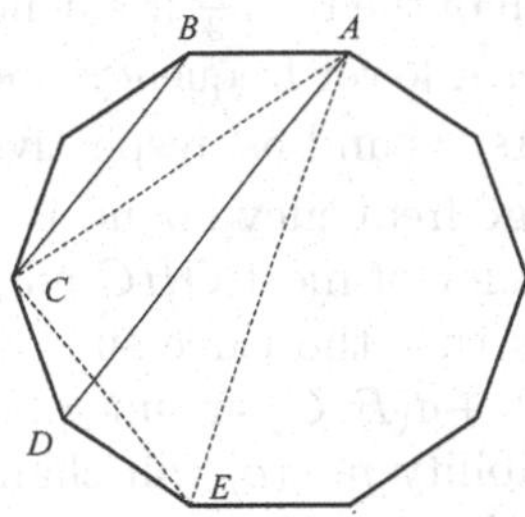

Fig. 3. *ABCD* and *ABCE* along *OHC*.

We assume K_{n+1} stems from K_n by adding one vertex. Given OHCs in K_n and K_{n+1} include an identical edge e, let's see what happens to the probability of frequency consistency δ if the probability $p_{3,5}(e)$ approaches $\frac{2}{3}$ according to K_n. Note $p^n_{3,5}(e)$ and $p^{n+1}_{3,5}(e)$ as the probability $p_{3,5}(e)$ of e according to K_n and K_{n+1}, respectively, and $p^n_{3,5}(e)$ is close to $\frac{2}{3}$. According to K_n, the number of frequency quadrilaterals where $f(e) = 3, 5$ is computed as $p^n_{3,5}(e)\binom{n-2}{2}$. As another vertex is added to K_n, $n - 2$ more quadrilaterals containing e is generated. Among the $n - 2$ frequency quadrilaterals, $p^n_{3,5}(e)(n - 2)$ of them stem from the frequency quadrilaterals in K_n where $f(e) = 3, 5$. Using the probability of frequency consistency $\delta \leq 1$, the number of frequency quadrilaterals where $f(e) = 3, 5$ in K_{n+1} is computed as $p^n_{3,5}(e)\binom{n-2}{2} + \delta p^n_{3,5}(e)(n - 2)$. Thus, $p^{n+1}_{3,5}(e) = \frac{p^n_{3,5}(e)\binom{n-2}{2}+\delta p^n_{3,5}(e)(n-2)}{\binom{n-1}{2}}$ is derived.

Because $p^{n+1}_{3,5}(e) \geq \frac{2}{3}$, $\delta \geq 1$ is derived as $p^n_{3,5}(e) = \frac{2}{3}$. Since $\delta \leq 1$, $p^n_{3,5}(e)$ must be bigger than $\frac{2}{3}$. When $p^n_{3,5}(e)$ is small, δ is much bigger than $\frac{2}{3}$ for producing more 3s and 5s in the generated frequency quadrilaterals for guaranteeing $p^{n+1}_{3,5}(e) > \frac{2}{3}$. Thus, $p^n_{3,5}(e)$ will increase according to n until it is much greater than $\frac{2}{3}$. On the other hand, if $p^n_{3,5}(e)$ is much bigger than $\frac{2}{3}$, the generated frequency quadrilaterals where e has 3, 5 will occupy a big percentage owing to the probability of frequency consistency ($\delta \geq \frac{2}{3}$). In this case, $p^{n+1}_{3,5}(e) \approx p^n_{3,5}(e)$ exists. That's why $p_{3,5}(e)$ of most of the OHC edges is much bigger than $\frac{2}{3}$. Many experiments [8,33] illustrated that only a few $p_{3,5}(e)$s of the OHC edges are close to but bigger than $\frac{2}{3}$. For all of the other OHC edges, $p_{3,5}(e)$ is much bigger than $\frac{2}{3}$. For an ordinary edge, $p_{3,5}(e)$ does not have these properties. This result implies us to find the OHC edges according to $p_{3,5}(e)$ with respect to some subgraphs of K_n.

Since only $n - 3$ quadrilaterals $ABCD$ are considered to derive $p_{3,5}(e)$, the probability (1) is conservative. Here, we use it to compute one lower frequency bound and one lower average frequency bound for the OHC edges. As we choose N frequency quadrilaterals containing an OHC edge (A, B), there will be at least $\frac{2N}{3}$ frequency quadrilaterals where the frequency of (A, B) is either 5 or 3. Among the $\frac{2N}{3}$ frequency quadrilaterals, the number of 5s will be $\frac{2}{3} \times \frac{2N}{3}$ due to the inequality $d(A, B) + d(C, D) < d(A, C) + d(B, D)$. In this case, the number of 3s is $\frac{1}{3} \times \frac{2N}{3}$. In each of the rest $\frac{N}{3}$ frequency quadrilaterals, we assume (A, B) has 1 in the worst case. A lower frequency bound is computed as $\frac{29N}{9}$. On average, (A, B) will have $\frac{N}{9}$ 1s, 3s and 5s, respectively, among the $\frac{N}{3}$ frequency quadrilaterals. A lower average frequency bound is computed as $\frac{35N}{9}$.

For big graphs, the frequency of most OHC edges will approach $5N$ as n is big enough [33]. It reminders that the three sum distances $d(A, B) + d(C, D)$, $d(A, C) + d(B, D)$ and $d(A, D) + d(B, C)$ are unequal in $ABCD$. As two or three of them are equal, the probability $p_{3,5}(e)$ will change [35]. If a graph contains many equal-weight edges, it is hard to choose the right optimal four-vertex paths with respect to OHC. In this case, the numerical results will deviate from theory due to the usage of many inappropriate optimal four-vertex paths which do not contain the OHC edges.

Moreover, if the frequency of (A, B) is known in frequency quadrilateral $ABCD$, it will keep the same frequency in another frequency quadrilateral $ABCE$ with a probability above $\frac{2}{3}$. Theorem 2 is given as below.

Theorem 2. *If $f(A, B) = 5$ exists in a frequency quadrilateral $ABCD$, (A, B) has the frequency 5 in another frequency quadrilateral $ABCE$ with a probability above $\frac{2}{3}$ where $E \in V \backslash \{A, B, C, D\}$.*

Proof. Since $f(A, B) = 5$ exists in frequency quadrilateral $ABCD$, the frequency inequality $f(A, B) > f(A, C)$ and $f(A, B) > f(B, C)$ hold. Based on the property of frequency consistency, $f(A, B) > f(A, C)$ and $f(A, B) > f(B, C)$ occur with a probability above $\frac{2}{3}$ in frequency quadrilateral $ABCE$. Thus, $f(A, B) = 5$ occurs with a probability greater than $\frac{2}{3}$ in frequency quadrilateral $ABCE$. □

Theorem 2 also holds for (A, B) maintaining 1 or 3 from $ABCD$ to $ABCE$. As $f(A, B) = 3$ appears in frequency quadrilateral $ABCD$, it will have 3 or 5 in frequency quadrilateral $ABCE$ with probability above $\frac{2}{3}$ for $d(A, B) + d(C, D) < d(A, C) + d(B, D)$ or $d(A, B) + d(C, D) < d(A, D) + d(B, C)$.

We assume a dense or big graph containing many edges or vertices stems from certain sparse or small graph containing a small number of edges or vertices. In addition, all these graphs are Hamiltonian. Given such a sparse or small graph, it contains a small number of quadrilaterals. Every quadrilateral corresponds to one of the frequency quadrilaterals in Fig. 1. Thus, each edge in the sparse or small graph has the fixed $p_1(e)$, $p_3(e)$ and $p_5(e)$. As more edges or vertices are added to the sparse or small graph, the edges in the original graph will be included in more and more generated quadrilaterals. We assume the generated quadrilaterals also have the frequency quadrilaterals in Fig. 1. The frequency of e in the original frequency quadrilaterals will be transferred to most of the generated frequency quadrilaterals. Based on the frequency consistency, one can estimate $p_1(e)$, $p_3(e)$ and $p_5(e)$ for e in the expanded dense or big graph, such as K_n, based on those computed according to sparse or small graph.

In reverse, $p_1(e)$, $p_3(e)$ and $p_5(e)$ of e computed according to K_n can be estimated by a small number of frequency quadrilaterals with high accuracy according to certain sparse or small subgraphs in K_n. We call the subgraph containing the minimum number of quadrilaterals as the *kernel graph* of e with respect to the fixed $p_1(e), p_3(e)$ and $p_5(e)$ computed according to K_n. The set of quadrilaterals in the kernel graph are taken as the *kernel quadrilaterals* for e. The kernel graph may not be unique for an edge and the numbers of kernel quadrilaterals for two edges may also be different. One can search a limited number of quadrilaterals to construct one kernel graph for e with respect to $p_1(e)$, $p_3(e)$ and $p_5(e)$. The union of the kernel graphs for a set of concerned edges, such as the OHC edges, will form certain sparse graph. In the next section, an algorithm is given to convert K_n of TSP to such sparse graph for OHC. As K_n is changed into sparse graph, $p_1(e)$, $p_3(e)$ and $p_5(e)$ of $e \in OHC$ is nearly unchanged if the quadrilaterals (and edges) generated according to the kernel quadrilaterals are eliminated.

5 An Iterative Algorithm

We first argue that K_n of TSP can be reduced to bounded degree graph according to the probability $p_1(e)$, $p_3(e)$ and $p_5(e)$ of edges. Then, we provide the polynomial randomized algorithm to compute the bounded degree graph.

Proposition 1. *Based on the frequency quadrilaterals, K_n of TSP can be reduced to bounded degree graph in which an OHC edge is contained in at most c quadrilaterals where c is some constant.*

Proof. Given K_n of TSP, $p_1(e)$, $p_3(e)$ and $p_5(e)$ of edges $e \in OHC$ is computed and $p_{3,5}(e) > \frac{2}{3}$ holds. For each of the OHC edges, there is one kernel graph contains a finite number of kernel quadrilaterals. Among the numbers of the kernel quadrilaterals, the maximum value is c. According to the c kernel quadrilaterals, $p_1(e)$, $p_3(e)$ and $p_5(e)$ of e is the same as or nearly equal to that computed with all frequency quadrilaterals containing e in K_n.

There must be one vertex $v \in e$ and it is also contained in the c quadrilaterals. Since v is contained in the maximum number of quadrilaterals, it has the maximum degree noted as Δ. The relationship between Δ and c is $c = \binom{\Delta-1}{2}$. The maximum vertex degree is computed as $\Delta = \lceil \sqrt{2c} + 1.5 \rceil$. Thus, a bounded degree graph is computed based on frequency quadrilaterals. □

Since $p_{3,5}(e)$ or $\bar{f}(e) = p_1(e) + 3p_3(e) + 5p_5(e)$ plays an important role to cultivate the OHC edges in either subgraphs or K_n, it is used to reduce K_n to sparse graphs [31,32]. In the next, the iterative algorithm is revised for computing bounded degree graph for TSP. Moreover, we demonstrate that $p_{3,5}(e)$ of the OHC edges does not decrease according to the preserved quadrilaterals after many edges with the smallest $p_{3,5}(e)$ or $\bar{f}(e)$ are cut.

The algorithm of edges elimination has been introduced in papers [31, 32]. Here the fundamental of the algorithm is further analyzed. As we choose N frequency quadrilaterals for an edge, an OHC edge has more than $\frac{2N}{3}$ 3s and 5s in these frequency quadrilaterals. Meanwhile, the number of 1s will be smaller than $\frac{N}{3}$. For an ordinary edge, $p_1(e) \geq \frac{1}{3}$ exists in most cases. Thus, there will be above $\frac{N}{3}$ 1s in N frequency quadrilaterals. As an edge is trimmed according to the frequency threshold 3 with respect to the N frequency quadrilaterals, an OHC edge will be cut smaller than $\frac{N}{3}$ times whereas an ordinary edge will be cut at least $\frac{N}{3}$ times. According to the frequency threshold 3, the probability that an OHC edge is eliminated is smaller than $\frac{1}{3}$. On the other hand, the probability that an ordinary edge is trimmed is bigger than $\frac{1}{3}$.

One binomial distribution is built to illustrate whether $e \in OHC$ is cut according to the probability threshold $p_{3,5}(e) = \frac{2}{3}$. Let X be the random variable representing the number of frequency quadrilaterals where e has the frequency 1 among N random frequency quadrilaterals. As $X = k (1 \leq k \leq N)$, the binomial distribution is given as $P(X = k) = \binom{N}{k}(1 - p_{3,5}(e))^k (p_{3,5}(e))^{N-k}$. For an ordinary edge, $p_{3,5}(e) \leq \frac{2}{3}$ is considered and the binomial distribution function reaches the maximum value at $k \geq \lceil \frac{N}{3} \rceil$ or $\lceil \frac{N}{3} \rceil + 1$. As $k > \frac{N}{3}$ appears for an edge, it will be trimmed according to $p_{3,5}(e) = \frac{2}{3}$.

Since $p_{3,5}(e) \geq \frac{2}{3}$ for $e \in OHC$, it will be preserved according to the probability threshold $\frac{2}{3}$. In one trial of edges elimination, the probability that e is trimmed is smaller than $\frac{1}{3}$. If a OHC edges are trimmed by accident, the probability of such event will be smaller than $\left(\frac{1}{3}\right)^a$. One sees OHC will be preserved with a big probability. Starting from K_n, we first eliminate $\frac{1}{3}$ of the edges with the smallest $p_{3,5}(e) < \frac{2}{3}$. As the preserved graph contains many quadrilaterals, the edges elimination can be repeated until terminal conditions are met.

Based on above analysis, the iterative algorithm [31, 32] is designed to eliminate ordinary edges from K_n for computing sparse graphs. At each iteration, the frequency of each edge is computed with N frequency quadrilaterals, and then $\frac{1}{3}$ of the edges with the smallest frequency are cut. The experiments illustrated that bounded degree graphs are computed [32]. We changed the algorithm [32] in which the edges are eliminated according to $p_{3,5}(e)$ rather than $\bar{f}(e)$ of edges. In addition, the terminal condition is also given for preserving OHC to bounded degree graph. The Algorithm 1 is shown as below.

At each iteration, $\frac{1}{3}$ of the edges with the smallest $p_{3,5}(e)$ are trimmed for each vertex. The maximum vertex degree decreases exponentially in proportion to $\frac{2}{3}$. The algorithm will run $\left\lceil \log_{1.5} \frac{n-1}{\sqrt{2c}+1.5} \right\rceil$ iterations for computing one graph with the maximum vertex degree $\lceil \sqrt{2c} + 1.5 \rceil$. The time complexity of the algorithm is $O(Nn^2)$. As the value of c is set too small, a big percentage of the preserved edges may not be contained in any quadrilaterals at the end of the algorithm although they have several adjacent edges. In the experiments [31, 32], the frequency quadrilaterals containing smaller than six edges are deduced and used to compute $\bar{f}(e)$ of edges. The results illustrated that the algorithm can be executed one or two more cycles. The sparser graphs are computed and OHC is still preserved for most TSP instances. Even though according to the frequency quadrilaterals containing less than six edges, the OHC edges still have the bigger $p_{3,5}(e)$ or $\bar{f}(e)$ than most of the ordinary edges.

Algorithm 1: The algorithm for computing bounded degree graph.

Input: $K_n = (V, E)$, the distance matrix and constant c
Output: One residual graph of bounded degree
$k := 0$, $d_{max} := n - 1$;
while $d_{max} > \lceil \sqrt{2c} + 1.5 \rceil$ **do**
  Compute $p_{3,5}(e)$ of each edge with N frequency quadrilaterals;
  Order the edges containing an vertex according to $p_{3,5}(e)$;
  Eliminate $\frac{1}{3}$ of the edges with the smallest $p_{3,5}(e) < \frac{2}{3}$;
  $k := k + 1$ and d_{max} is updated;
end

In the following, we will prove that $p_{3,5}(e)$ of the OHC edges does not decrease with respect to the preserved graphs even though most of the ordinary edges are trimmed according to $p_{3,5}(e)$.

Theorem 3. *As a portion of edges with the smallest probability $p_{3,5}(e)$ are cut from K_n (or preserved dense graph), $p_{3,5}(e)$ of $e \in OHC$ does not become smaller with respect to the following preserved graphs if it is contained in c quadrilaterals where c is some constant.*

Proof. $p_{3,5}(e) > \frac{2}{3}$ holds for $e \in OHC$ according to the frequency quadrilaterals in K_n. Given $e \in OHC$, we construct the quadrilaterals for e with its two adjacent edges containing one vertex v. At first, there are $M \leq n - 1$ edges containing v in the original graph. Thus, there are $\binom{M-1}{2}$ quadrilaterals containing e. $p_{3,5}(e)$ notes the probability that e has frequency 3 and 5 based on the $\binom{M-1}{2}$ frequency quadrilaterals.

According to $p_{3,5}(g)$ of all edges g containing v, K of the M edges having the lowest $p_{3,5}(e) < \frac{2}{3}$ are eliminated. The number of the preserved quadrilaterals containing e becomes $\binom{M-K-1}{2}$ and the number of the destructed quadrilaterals containing e is $\binom{K}{2} + (M - K - 1)K$. According to the frequency quadrilaterals in the preserved graph, the probability that e has 3 and 5 is noted as $q_{3,5}(e)$. It mentions that the destructed frequency quadrilaterals stem from the $\binom{M-K-1}{2}$ preserved quadrilaterals by adding the eliminated K edges.

Based on Lemma 1, the frequency 1, 3, and 5 of e in the preserved frequency quadrilaterals will be transferred to the destructed frequency quadrilaterals with a probability above $\frac{2}{3}$. $p_{3,5}(e)$ is computed as formula (2) based on the $\binom{M-K-1}{2}$ preserved quadrilaterals and frequency consistency. In formula (2), η is the probability that frequency 1 changes to 3 or 5 for e from a frequency quadrilateral to another generated frequency quadrilateral. $\eta < \frac{1}{3}$ holds based on Theorem 2. Since $p_{3,5}(e) > \frac{2}{3}$ according to K_n, $q_{3,5}(e) > \frac{2}{3}$ is derived as e is contained in a few quadrilaterals for $\frac{\binom{M-K-1}{2}}{\binom{M-1}{2}} < 1$. One sees $p_{3,5}(e)$ does not decrease after edges elimination once $K \geq 1$ and $M - K \geq 3$.

In Algorithm 1, the edges with the smallest $p_{3,5}(e) < \frac{2}{3}$ are trimmed step by step. Since the OHC edges maintain the high $p_{3,5}(e) > \frac{2}{3}$, they are preserved in the edges elimination process. As $K = 1$, $M = 4$ is derived. In this case, $p_{3,5}(e) > \frac{2}{3}$ still holds with respect to the three quadrilaterals ($c = 3$) containing e in the preserved graph. Algorithm 1 can be executed once even though four edges containing v are left. After the edge with the smallest $p_{3,5}(e)$ is cut, only one quadrilateral containing e and v is remained and the degree of v is 3. In this case, the bounded degree graph is computed by Algorithm 1. □

$$p_{3,5}(e) = \frac{q_{3,5}(e)\binom{M-K-1}{2} + \left[\frac{2}{3}q_{3,5}(e) + \eta(1-q_{3,5}(e))\right]\left[\binom{M-1}{2} - \binom{M-K-1}{2}\right]}{\binom{M-1}{2}},$$

$$\Rightarrow q_{3,5}(e) > 1 - \frac{\left[(\frac{1}{3}+\eta)q_{3,5}(e) - \eta\right]\binom{M-K-1}{2}}{(\frac{2}{3}-\eta)\binom{M-1}{2}}$$

$$\Rightarrow q_{3,5}(e) > \frac{2}{3} \text{ as } \frac{\binom{M-K-1}{2}}{\binom{M-1}{2}} \leq 1. \quad (2)$$

Theorem 4. *Based on the frequency quadrilaterals, there is a polynomial algorithm reducing K_n to bounded degree graph for TSP and OHC is preserved with a probability above $\frac{1}{2}$.*

Proof. Theorem 3 guarantees the polynomial Algorithm 1 to compute bounded degree graph. In the next, we prove the probability that OHC is preserved to the bounded degree graph.

In the extreme case, $e \in OHC$ has the probability $p_1(e) = \frac{1}{3} - \frac{2}{3(n-2)}$. A binomial distribution is built to estimate the cumulative probability that it is preserved after a number of cycles of edges elimination as Algorithm 1 is executed. As N frequency quadrilaterals containing e are chosen, the probability that there are $X = k (0 \leq k \leq N)$ 5s and 3s conforms to the binomial distribution $X \sim \mathcal{B}(N, p_{3,5}(e))$, i.e., $P(X = k) = \binom{N}{k}(p_{3,5}(e))^k(1-p_{3,5}(e))^{N-k}$. As we know, the number k is smaller than $\frac{2N}{3}$ for the trimmed edges at each iteration.

Since the trials of edges elimination are independent to each other in the iteration, the cumulative probability that $e \in OHC$ is trimmed is computed as $Pr(X < \frac{2N}{3}) = \sum_{k=1}^{\frac{2N}{3}-1} P(X = k)$. Because $p_{3,5}(e) > \frac{2}{3}$ for $e \in OHC$, $Pr(X < \frac{2N}{3}) < \frac{1}{2}$ holds. The cumulative probability that e is preserved is bigger than $\frac{1}{2}$ after edges elimination.

As this OHC edge is not trimmed, the other OHC edges will be preserved since they have the bigger $p_{3,5}(e)$. Thus, OHC is preserved to bounded degree graph with a probability above $\frac{1}{2}$. According to the bounded degree graph, TSP can be resolved in less than $O(2^n)$ time, see [5]. □

As $p_1(e) \ll \frac{1}{3}$ or the number of quadrilaterals containing e is big enough, $p_{3,5}(e)$ will be bigger than $\frac{2}{3}$. In this case, the probability that $e \in OHC$ is preserved is 1. If $p_1(e)$ is bigger than but close to $\frac{1}{3}$, the probability that this e is eliminated is smaller than $\frac{1}{2}$. As a OHC edges are eliminated, the probability of such event will be smaller than $\left(\frac{1}{2}\right)^a$.

Until now, bounded degree graph is computed for TSP. In paper [32], it shows the eliminated edges are either edges owing big distances or edges having big sum distances with the non-adjacent edges in most quadrilaterals. That's to say, the ordinary edges with large distances will be trimmed without doubts. Besides the OHC edges, the bounded degree graph contain the relatively short ordinary edges and it is locally connected. One can find OHC or good approximations in such a graph.

6 Conclusion

A polynomial randomized algorithm is designed to reduce K_n to bounded degree graph for TSP based on frequency quadrilaterals. According to TSP on bounded degree graph, the computation time of algorithms for TSP will be reduced. In the future, the properties of the bounded degree graphs, such as connectivity and genus, will be further studied. If some bounded degree graph loses a few OHC edges, we will study the approximations it includes.

References

1. Cook, W.J.: In Pursuit of the Traveling Salesman: Mathematics at the Limits of Computation. Princeton University Press, Princeton (2011)
2. Gutin, G., Punnen, A.-P.: The Traveling Salesman Problem and Its Variations. Combinatorial Optimization, Springer, London (2007)
3. de Berg, M., Bodlaender, H.-L., Kisfaludi-Bak, S., Kolay, S.: An ETH-tight exact algorithm for Euclidean TSP. In: The 59th Symposium on Foundations of Computer Science, FOCS 2018, pp. 450–461. IEEE, New York (2018)
4. Karlin, A.-R., Klein, N., Gharan, S.-O.: A (slightly) improved approximation algorithm for metric TSP. In: The 53rd Symposium on Theory of Computing, STOC 2021, pp. 32–45. ACM, New York (2021)
5. Björklund, A., Husfeldt, T., Kaski, P., Koivisto, M.: The traveling salesman problem in bounded degree graphs. ACM Trans. Algorithms **8**(2), 1–18 (2012)
6. Jonker, R., Volgenant, T.: Nonoptimal edges for the symmetric traveling salesman problem. Oper. Res. **32**(4), 837–846 (1984)
7. Hougardy, S., Schroeder, R.T.: Edge elimination in TSP instances. In: Kratsch, D., Todinca, I. (eds.) WG 2014. LNCS, vol. 8747, pp. 275–286. Springer, Cham (2014). https://doi.org/10.1007/978-3-319-12340-0_23
8. Wang, Y., Remmel, J.-B.: A binomial distribution model for travelling salesman problem based on frequency quadrilaterals. J. Graph Algorithms Appl. **20**(2), 411–434 (2016)
9. Karp, R.: On the computational complexity of combinatorial problems. Networks (USA) **5**(1), 45–68 (1975)
10. Held, M., Karp, R.: A dynamic programming approach to sequencing problems. J. Sco. Ind. Appl. Math. **10**(1), 196–210 (1962)

11. Bellman, R.: Dynamic programming treatment of the travelling salesman problem. J. ACM **9**(1), 61–63 (1962)
12. Björklund, A.: Determinant sums for undirected Hamiltonicity. In: The 51st Symposium on Foundations of Computer Science, FOCS 2010, pp. 173–182. IEEE, New York (2010)
13. Yuan, Y., Cattaruzza, D., Ogier, M., Semet, F.: A branch-and-cut algorithm for the generalized traveling salesman problem with time windows. Eur. J. Oper. Res. **286**(3), 849–866 (2020)
14. Applegate, D.-L., et al.: Certification of an optimal TSP tour through 85900 cities. Oper. Res. Lett. **37**(1), 11–15 (2009)
15. Cook, W.: The traveling salesman problem: postcards from the edge of impossibility (Plenary talk). In: The 30th European Conference on Operational Research, Dublin, Ireland (2019)
16. Kisfaludi-Bak, S., Nederlof, J., Wegrzycki, K.: A gap-ETH-tight approximation scheme for Euclidean TSP arXiv:2011.03778v2 (2021)
17. Eppstein, D.: The traveling salesman problem for cubic graphs. J. Graph Algorithms Appl. **11**(1), 61–81 (2007)
18. Liśkiewicz, M., Schuster, M.R.: A new upper bound for the traveling salesman problem in cubic graphs. J. Discret. Algorithms **27**, 1–20 (2014)
19. Xiao, M.-Y., Nagamochi, H.: An exact algorithm for TSP in degree-3 graphs via circuit procedure and amortization on connectivity structure. Algorithmica **74**(2), 713–741 (2016). https://doi.org/10.1007/s00453-015-9970-4
20. Dorn, F., Penninkx, E., Bodlaender, H.-L., Fomin, F.-V.: Efficient exact algorithms on planar graphs: exploiting sphere cut decompositions. Algorithmica **58**(3), 790–810 (2010). https://doi.org/10.1007/s00453-009-9296-1
21. Boyd, S., Sitters, R., van der Ster, S., Stougie, L.: The traveling salesman problem on cubic and subcubic graphs. Math. Program. **144**(1–2), 227–245 (2014). https://doi.org/10.1007/s10107-012-0620-1
22. Correa, J.-R., Larré, O., Soto, J.-A.: TSP tours in cubic graphs: beyond 4/3. SIAM J. Discret. Math. **29**(2), 915–939 (2015)
23. Klein, P.: A linear-time approximation scheme for TSP in undirected planar graphs with edge-weights. SIAM J. Comput. **37**(6), 1926–1952 (2008)
24. Borradaile, G., Demaine, E.-D., Tazari, S.: Polynomial-time approximation schemes for subset-connectivity problems in bounded-genus graphs. Algorithmica **68**(2), 287–311 (2014). https://doi.org/10.1007/s00453-012-9662-2
25. Svensson, O., Tarnawski, J., Végh, L.-A.: A constant-factor approximation algorithm for the asymmetric traveling salesman problem arXiv:1708.04215pdf (2019)
26. Traub, V., Vygen, J.: An improved approximation algorithm for ATSP. In: The 52nd Symposium on Theory of Computing, STOC 2020, pp. 1–13. ACM, New York (2020)
27. Erickson, J., Sidiropoulos, A.: A near-optimal approximation algorithm for asymmetric TSP on embedded graphs arXiv:1304.1810v2 (2013)
28. Kawarabayashi, K., Sidiropoulos, A.: Polylogarithmic approximation for Euler genus on bounded degree graphs. In: The 51st Symposium on the Theory of Computing, STOC 2019, pp. 164–175. ACM, New York (2019)
29. Taillard, E.-D., Helsgaun, K.: POPMUSIC for the traveling salesman problem. Eur. J. Oper. Res. **272**(2), 420–429 (2019)
30. Turkensteen, M., Ghosh, D., Goldengorin, B., Sierksma, G.: Tolerance-based branch and bound algorithms for the ATSP. Eur. J. Oper. Res. **189**(3), 775–788 (2008)

31. Wang, Y., Remmel, J.: A method to compute the sparse graphs for traveling salesman problem based on frequency quadrilaterals. In: Chen, J., Lu, P. (eds.) FAW 2018. LNCS, vol. 10823, pp. 286–299. Springer, Cham (2018). https://doi.org/10.1007/978-3-319-78455-7_22
32. Wang, Y.: Bounded degree graphs computed for traveling salesman problem based on frequency quadrilaterals. In: Li, Y., Cardei, M., Huang, Y. (eds.) COCOA 2019. LNCS, vol. 11949, pp. 529–540. Springer, Cham (2019). https://doi.org/10.1007/978-3-030-36412-0_43
33. Wang, Y.: Sufficient and necessary conditions for an edge in the optimal Hamiltonian cycle based on frequency qudrilaterals. J. Optim. Theory Appl. **181**(2), 671–683 (2019). https://doi.org/10.1007/s10957-018-01465-9
34. Wang, Y., Han, Z.: The frequency of the optimal Hamiltonian cycle computed with frequency quadrilaterals for traveling salesman problem. In: Zhang, Z., Li, W., Du, D.-Z. (eds.) AAIM 2020. LNCS, vol. 12290, pp. 513–524. Springer, Cham (2020). https://doi.org/10.1007/978-3-030-57602-8_46
35. Wang, Y.: Special frequency quadrilaterals and an application. In: Sun, X., He, K., Chen, X. (eds.) NCTCS 2019. CCIS, vol. 1069, pp. 16–26. Springer, Singapore (2019). https://doi.org/10.1007/978-981-15-0105-0_2

An Approximation Algorithm for the Minimum Soft Capacitated Disk Multi-coverage Problem

Han Dai(✉)

School of Mathematics and Statistics, Yunnan University, Kunming 650504, China
18283649705@163.com

Abstract. Given a set U of n users and a set S of m sensors on the plane, each sensor s has the same integer capacity C, and each user u has an integer demand d_u. Each sensor s regulates its power p_s to form a circular coverage area $disk(s, r_s)$ (i.e. a disk with s as the center and r_s as the radius), the relationship between the power p_s and its coverage radius r_s is: $p_s = c \cdot r_s^{\alpha}$, where $c > 0$, $\alpha \geq 1$ are constants. The minimum soft capacitated disk multi-coverage problem is to find a set of disks supported by the power $\{p_s\}_{s \in S}$ such that the number of users assigned to one copy of each disk $disk(s, r_s)$ is at most C, each user u is allocated at least d_u times, and minimize the number of selected disks. We obtain a 4-approximation of this problem based on an LP rounding algorithm.

Keywords: Soft capacity · Multi-coverage · LP rounding · Approximation algorithm

1 Introdunction

Capacity coverage problem has been studied by a large number of scholars, and the set cover problem with capacity is a very classic capacity coverage problem. The set cover problem is that, given a set of elements E and a set of sets $\mathcal{S}$ defined on the elements, it is to find a subset $\mathcal{S}' \subseteq \mathcal{S}$ such that each element $e \in E$ is covered by a set $S \in \mathcal{S}'$ contain it and minimize the number of the sets of selected subsets $\mathcal{S}'$. The set cover problem with capacity is a generalization of the set cover problem. Each set S both has an integer capacity C_S, and each set S covers elements that do not exceed its capacity.

Capacity constraints are further divided into hard capacity constraints and soft capacity constraints. The set cover problem with hard capacity constraints is that each set $S \in \mathcal{S}$ is selected at most $m(S)$ times, and allocate at most $C_S m(S)$ elements of each set S. Wolsey [10] uses a greedy algorithm to obtain an $O(logn)$-approximation for this problem and this approximation is currently the best approximation for this problem. The set cover problem of the soft capacity constraint is that each set $S \in \mathcal{S}$ can be allowed to open an infinite number of copies.

Z. Cai et al. (Eds.): NCTCS 2022, CCIS 1693, pp. 96–104, 2022.
https://doi.org/10.1007/978-981-19-8152-4_6

The coverage problem in geometric space is rarely studied. Bandyapadhyay et al. [1] first studied this problem, and designed an LP rounding algorithm for the metric set cover problem with hard capacity constraints and obtained a two-standard approximation of $(21, 9)$ to this problem, which allows each selected ball to be expanded by a factor of 9. And the special case of the same capacity can get a two-standard approximation of $(21, 6.47)$, which each ball only needs to be expanded by a factor of 6.47. For the Euclidean capacity coverage problem in R^d space, Bandyapadhyay et al. [1] devised a plane subdivision technique and propose to an $O(\epsilon^{-4d}log(\frac{1}{\epsilon}), 1+\epsilon)$-approximation, which allows the ball to be expanded by an arbitrarily small constant. Later, Bandyapadhyay [2] improved the results on the metric capacity coverage problem, obtaining an $O(1)$-approximation and only needing to expand by a factor of 5 each ball, and for the special case of the same capacity, each ball only needs to expand 4.24 times.

The power cover problem is a variant of the set cover problem. Given a set U of n users and a set S of m sensors on the plane, adjusting the power of each sensor $s \in S$ generates a sensing radius r_s and the relationship between the two is: $p_s = c \cdot r_s^\alpha$, where $c > 0$ and $\alpha \geq 0$ are constants. The minimum power cover problem is to find a power assignment such that all users $u \in U$ are covered and minimize the total power of the sensor $s \in S$. Li et al. [4] studied the minimum power partial cover problem, requiring at least k users to be covered and designed a primal dual algorithm to obtain a 3^α-approximation. Recently, Dai et al. [3] improved this algorithm and obtained an $O(\alpha)$-approximation on the plane.

The minimum power partial cover problem with penalty is a generalization of the minimum power partial cover problem, which requires that uncovered points will be given a penalty. Liu et al. [7] obtained a 3^α-approximation based on the primal dual algorithm. And for the minimum power cover problem with submodular penalty, Liu et al. [6] proposed a $(3^\alpha + 1)$-approximation. A polynomial time approximation scheme (PTAS) is proposed for the case when the penalty is linear. Later, Liu et al. [8] devised a primal-dual algorithm to obtain a $(5 \cdot 2^\alpha + 1)$- approximation for the minimum power partial coverage problem with submodular penalty on a plane. If each point v has a cover requirement, the minimum power multiple coverage problem is posed, which requires finding a power assignment such that each point v is at least covered by its coverage requirement. When all points and sensors are on a line, Liang et al. [5] proposed an optimal algorithm based on dynamic programming when the maximum covering requirement of points is upper bounded by a constant. Ran et al. [9] designed a PTAS for the minimum power partial multiple coverage problem.

The minimum power coverage problem with capacity constraints is a difficult problem to solve. In this paper, we study the minimum soft capacitated disk multi-coverage problem, where the disk is generated by power of the sensor. The main structure of this paper is as follows, the second part introduces the basic knowledge related to the minimum soft capacitated disk multi-coverage problem; the third part introduces the linear programming of this problem; the fourth part introduces an LP rounding algorithm and related theoretical proofs for this problem. Finally, the fifth part summarizes the problem.

2 Preliminary

On the plane, given a set of n users U, a set of m sensors S, each sensor s has the same integer capacity of C and each user u has an integer requirement of d_u. Each sensor s can adjust its power p_s, the coverage of any sensor s with power p_s is a circular area with radius r_s and the relationship between p_s and r_s is :

$$p_s = c \cdot r_s^{\alpha} \text{ where } c > 0, \alpha \geq 1 \text{ are constants.} \tag{1}$$

we use the disk $disk(s, r_s)$ to represent the circular coverage area with center s and radius r_s, any user $u \in disk(s, r_s)$ indicates that user u can be covered by sensor s.

In this paper, we consider the minimum soft capacitated disk multi-coverage (MSCDM) problem. The minimum soft capacitated disk multi-coverage problem is to find a set of disks supported by the power $\{p_s\}_{s \in S}$ such that the number of users assigned to one copy of each disk $disk(s, r_s)$ is at most C, each user u is assigned at least d_u times and minimizing the number of selected disks.

In the optimal solution of the MSCDM problem, for each disk in the optimal solution, there will be at least one point on its boundary, otherwise the radius of the disk can be reduced to cover the same point. Therefore, each sensor has at most n disks of different radius, and all sensors have at most mn disks to be considered. Next, we use D to denote such a disk and $\mathcal{D}$ to denote the set of all disks. For any $D \in \mathcal{D}$, we use $U(D)$ to represent the set of users covered by the disk D. For any $\mathcal{D}' \subseteq \mathcal{D}$, we use $U(\mathcal{D}')$ to represent the user set covered by the union of all disks in $\mathcal{D}'$, p_D represents the power of the disk D, r_D represents the radius of the disk D and c_D represents the center of the disk D. In addition, since each sensor s has the same integer capacity C, all the disks D of different radius produced by each sensor s have the capacity C. Here, we assume that the power of all sensors is unlimited.

So we can also define the MSCDM problem as follows, given a set of users U and a set of disks $\mathcal{D}$ on the plane, each disk D has a power p_D and an identical integer capacity C, each user u has an integer demand d_u. The MSCDM problem is to find an allocation scheme such that the number of points where each disk D is selected once allocated does not exceed its capacity C, each point $u \in U$ is allocated at least d_u times, and the total number of selected disks is minimized.

3 Linear Programming for the MSCDM Problem

We define that for any user $u \in U$ and $D \in \mathcal{D}$, if the user $u \in U(D)$ is assigned to the disk D, $x_{uD} = 1$; if the disk $D \in \mathcal{D}$ is selected, $y_D = 1$. The integer linear programming of the MSCDM is given as follows:

$$\begin{aligned}
&\min \sum_{D:D\in\mathcal{D}} y_D \\
s.t.\ \ & x_{uD} \le y_D,\ \forall u \in V(D),\ \forall D \in \mathcal{D}, \\
& \sum_{u:u\in D} x_{uD} \le y_D \cdot C,\ \forall D \in \mathcal{D}, \\
& \sum_{D:D\in\mathcal{D}} x_{uD} \ge d_u,\ \forall u \in U(D), \\
& x_{uD} \in N_0,\ \forall u \in U,\ \forall D \in \mathcal{D}, \\
& y_D \in N_0,\ \forall D \in \mathcal{D},
\end{aligned} \tag{2}$$

where the first constraint indicates that the user $u \in U(D)$ is assigned to the disk $D \in \mathcal{D}$ and the disk D must be selected; the second constraint indicates that the number of users allocated to the disk D does not exceed its capacity; the third constraint indicates that the user $u \in U(D)$ is assigned at least d_u times. Relax constraints $x_{uD} \in N_0$, $y_D \in N_0$ to $x_{uD} \ge 0$ and $y_D \ge 0$, the corresponding relaxed linear programming is as follows:

$$\begin{aligned}
&\min \sum_{D:D\in\mathcal{D}} y_D \\
s.t.\ \ & x_{uD} \le y_D,\ \forall u \in U(D),\ \forall D \in \mathcal{D}, \\
& \sum_{u:u\in D} x_{uD} \le y_D \cdot C,\ \forall D \in \mathcal{D}, \\
& \sum_{D:D\in\mathcal{D}} x_{uD} \ge d_u,\ \forall u \in U(D), \\
& x_{uD} \ge 0,\ \forall u \in U,\ \forall D \in \mathcal{D}, \\
& y_D \ge 0,\ \forall D \in \mathcal{D},
\end{aligned} \tag{3}$$

4 An LP Rounding Algorithm

In this section, we solve linear programming (3) and obtain its optimal solution (x^*, y^*). Next we use an LP rounding algorithm to get a feasible solution $(\bar{x}, \bar{y})$, where $\bar{y}$ is an integer and $\bar{x}$ may be a fraction. Define two basic concepts, let the heavy disk set be

$$\mathcal{D}_H = \{D \in \mathcal{D} | y_D > \frac{1}{2}\},$$

and the light disk set be

$$\mathcal{D}_L = \{D \in \mathcal{D} | 0 < y_D \le \frac{1}{2}\}.$$

The detailed steps of our algorithm are as follows. First, we initialize $(\bar{x}, \bar{y})$ to (x^*, y^*), for each user $u \in U$, while $\sum_{D\in\mathcal{D}_L, \bar{x}_{uD}>0} \bar{y}_D > \frac{1}{2}d_u$, find a subset of light disks $\mathcal{D}_{L_u} \subseteq \mathcal{D}_L$ that covers the user u currently satisfying

$$\sum_{D\in\mathcal{D}_{L_u}, \bar{x}_{uD}>0} \bar{y}_D > \frac{1}{2}d_u.$$

We select a disk with the largest radius D_{max} in $\mathcal{D}_{L_u}$ (if there is more than one disk with the largest radius, choose one of them), set $\bar{y}_{D_{max}} := \sum_{D \in \mathcal{D}_{L_u}} \bar{y}_D$. Let $\mathcal{D}_{LH}$ be the set of disks that become heavier, add D_{max} to the set of disks $\mathcal{D}_{LH}$, and set $\bar{y}_{D_{max}} := \lceil \bar{y}_{D_{max}} \rceil$ (disk D_{max} becomes a heavy disk).

Then, expand the radius of each disk $D \in \mathcal{D}_{LH}$ by three times, let $\mathcal{D}^3_{LH}$ represent such a set of disks. For any user $u \in U(\mathcal{D}_{L_u})$, let D^3_{max} be the disk with the radius of D_{max} expanded by three times, and set $\bar{x}_{uD^3_{max}} := \bar{x}_{uD_{max}} + \sum_{D \in \mathcal{D}_{L_u} \setminus \{D_{max}\}} \bar{x}_{uD}$. For each disk $D \in \mathcal{D}_{L_u} \setminus \{D_{max}\}$, set $\bar{x}_{uD} := 0$ and $\bar{y}_D := 0$.

Finally, we get a variable-heavy disk set $\mathcal{D}^3_{LH}$ covering user u and an initial heavy disk set $\mathcal{D}_{IH_u}$ covering user u. Let the set of all heavy disks covering user u after the LP rounding be $\bar{\mathcal{D}}_{H_u}$. Obviously there is,

$$\bar{\mathcal{D}}_{H_u} = \mathcal{D}^3_{LH} \cup \mathcal{D}_{IH_u}.$$

for any user $u \in U$, Select $2\lceil \bar{y}_D \rceil$ copies of each disk $D \in \bar{\mathcal{D}}_{H_u}$.

That is, according to the LP rounding algorithm we find a feasible solution $(\bar{x}, \bar{y})$, where $\bar{y}$ is integral. Our algorithm pseudocode is shown in Algorithm 1.

Lemma 1. *The Algorithm 1 computes a feasible solution $(\bar{x}, \bar{y})$ to the program (2), where $\bar{y}$ is integral.*

Proof. For any user $u \in U(D)$, let $\mathcal{D}_u$ denote all disks covering user u. According to Algorithm 1, we consider each disk in $\mathcal{D}_{L_u} \subseteq \mathcal{D}_u$, the disk D_{max} with the largest radius in $\mathcal{D}_{L_u}$ becomes heavier. For the disk D^3_{max} we have

$$\begin{aligned} \bar{x}_{uD^3_{max}} &= x^*_{uD_{max}} + \sum_{D: D \in \mathcal{D}_{L_u} \setminus \{D_{max}\}} x^*_{vD} \\ &\le y^*_{D_{max}} + \sum_{D: D \in \mathcal{D}_{L_u} \setminus \{D_{max}\}} y^*_D \\ &= \bar{y}_{D_{max}} = \bar{y}_{D^3_{max}} \end{aligned}$$

For any user $u \in U(D)$ and the disk $D \in \mathcal{D}_{L_u} \setminus \{D_{max}\}$, we have $\bar{x}_{uD} = \bar{y}_D = 0$. And for the disk $D \in \mathcal{D}_u \setminus \mathcal{D}_{L_u}$, we have $\bar{x}_{uD} = x^*_{uD} \le y^*_D = \bar{y}_D$, the first constraint of (2) is satisfied.

By the Algorithm 1, D^3_{max} can cover all users in $\mathcal{D}_{L_u}$. Since through the triangle inequality, for any disk $D' \in \mathcal{D}_{L_u}$ we have

$$\begin{aligned} d(u, c(D_{max})) &\le d(u, c(D')) + d(c(D'), c(D_{max})) \\ &\le r(D') + 2r(D_{max}) \\ &\le 3r(D_{max}) = r(D^3_{max}) \end{aligned}$$

and D^3_{max} has enough capacity to satisfy all users in $\mathcal{D}_{L_u}$ because

$$\begin{aligned} \sum_{u \in U(\mathcal{D}_{L_u})} \bar{x}_{uD^3_{max}} &= \sum_{D \in \mathcal{D}_{L_u}} \sum_{u \in D} \bar{x}_{uD} = \sum_{D \in \mathcal{D}_{L_u}} \sum_{u \in D} x^*_{uD} \\ &\le \sum_{D \in \mathcal{D}_{L_u}} y^*_D C = \bar{y}_{D_{max}} C = \bar{y}_{D^3_{max}} C. \end{aligned}$$

the second constraint of (2) is satisfied.

Algorithm 1: ROUNDING

Input: A user set U; a disk set $\mathcal{D}$; an integer capacity C; a demand function $d : U \rightarrow N_0$;
Output: A feasible multiple cover $\mathcal{F}$.

Initial, set $(\bar{x}, \bar{y}) := (x^*, y^*)$, $\mathcal{D}_{LH} := \phi$, $\mathcal{D}^3_{LH} := \phi$, $\bar{\mathcal{D}}_{H_u} := \phi$.
for $u \in U$ **do**
  while $\sum_{D \in \mathcal{D}_L, \bar{x}_{uD}>0} \bar{y}_D > \frac{1}{2} d_u$ **do**
    Find a subset $\mathcal{D}_{L_u} \subseteq \mathcal{D}_L$ of light disks covering user u such that $\sum_{D \in \mathcal{D}_{L_u}, \bar{x}_{uD}>0} \bar{y}_D > \frac{1}{2} d_u$.
    for $D \in \mathcal{D}_{L_u}$ **do**
      $D_{max} := \arg\max_{D \in \mathcal{D}_{L_u}} r_D$ and set $\bar{y}_{D_{max}} := \sum_{D: D \in \mathcal{D}_{L_u}} \bar{y}_D$.
      $\mathcal{D}_{LH} := \mathcal{D}_{LH} \cup \{D_{max}\}$, $\bar{y}_{D_{max}} := \lceil \bar{y}_{D_{max}} \rceil$.
    Increase the disk D_{max} radius by 3 times, let D^3_{max} denote such a disk.
    $\mathcal{D}^3_{LH} := \mathcal{D}^3_{LH} \cup \{D^3_{max}\}$
    for $u \in U(\mathcal{D}_{L_u})$ **do**
      Set $\bar{x}_{uD^3_{max}} := \bar{x}_{uD_{max}} + \sum_{D \in \mathcal{D}_{L_u} \setminus \{D_{max}\}} \bar{x}_{uD}$.
      for $D \in \mathcal{D}_{L_u} \setminus \{D_{max}\}$ **do**
        for $u \in U(D)$ **do**
          Set $\bar{x}_{uD} := 0$ and $\bar{y}_D := 0$.
  Set $\bar{\mathcal{D}}_{H_u} = \mathcal{D}^3_{LH} \cup \mathcal{D}_{H_u}$.
  for $D \in \bar{\mathcal{D}}_{H_u}$ **do**
    Select $2\lceil \bar{y}_D \rceil$ copies of each disk.
Output $\mathcal{F}$ which is a feasible multiple cover.

Then, for any user $u \in U(D)$, it is obvious that

$$\sum_{D \in \mathcal{D}_{L_u}} \bar{x}_{uD} = \sum_{D \in \mathcal{D}_{L_u}, \bar{x}_{uD}>0} \bar{x}_{uD} \leq \sum_{D \in \mathcal{D}_{L_u}, \bar{x}_{uD}>0} \bar{y}_D \leq \frac{1}{2} d_u,$$

where $\mathcal{D}_{L_u}$ is the set of all light disks covering the user u after the LP rounding. In order to ensure that each user u is assigned at least d_v times, so each user u is assigned to the disk $D \in \bar{\mathcal{D}}_{H_u}$ at least $\frac{1}{2} d_u$ times, where $\bar{\mathcal{D}}_{H_u}$ is all the heavy disks covering user u after the LP rounding, i.e., for any user $u \in U(D)$ satisfy

$$\sum_{D: D \in \bar{\mathcal{D}}_{H_u}} \bar{x}_{uD} \geq \frac{1}{2} d_u.$$

that is, to satisfy

$$d_u \leq 2 \sum_{D: D \in \bar{\mathcal{D}}_{H_u}} \bar{x}_{uD} \leq 2 \sum_{D: D \in \bar{\mathcal{D}}_{H_u}} \bar{y}_D \leq 2 \sum_{D: D \in \bar{\mathcal{D}}_{H_u}} \lceil \bar{y}_D \rceil$$

So for any user $u \in U$, $2\lceil \bar{y}_D \rceil$ copies of each disk $D \in \bar{\mathcal{D}}_{H_u}$ need to be selected, the third constraint of (2) is satisfied.

Lemma 2. *We can find a feasible solution* $(\bar{z}, \bar{y})$ *with the same feasible multi-coverage in polynomial time, where* $\bar{z}, \bar{y}$ *are both integers.*

Proof. Let $\mathcal{F}$ be a feasible multi-coverage for the program (2) and $f(\mathcal{F})$ be the maximum value of the number of users covered by $\mathcal{F}$. For each disk $D \in \mathcal{F}$, let $m(D)$ be the number of copies of disk D that appear in $\mathcal{F}$. We build a directed associative graph $G = (V, U, E)$, in which a copy of each disk in $\mathcal{F}$ is used as a vertex of the vertex set V of the graph G, that is,

$$V = \{v_i(D) | D \in \mathcal{F}, 1 \leq i \leq m(D)\},$$

For each vertex $v_i(D) \in V, 1 \leq i \leq m(D)$, $u \in U(D)$, there is an edge $(v_i(D), u) \in E$ with a capacity of 1. Add a source point s and for each vertex $v_i(D) \in V$, $1 \leq i \leq m(D)$, add an edge $(s, v_i(D)) \in E$ with an integer capacity of C. Add another sink point t and for each user $u \in U$, add an edge $(u, t) \in E$ of an integer capacity d_u.

Consider the maximum flow of this network, since the maximum flow of this network is an integer, we can get another solution that contains the same disk. For the MSCDM problem, $\mathcal{F}$ is a feasible solution iff

$$f(\mathcal{F}) = \sum_{u \in U} d_u,$$

Since all capacities are integers, integer feasible solutions $(\bar{z}, \bar{y})$ can be found, that is, a feasible capacity assignment scheme can be obtained.

According to the Algorithm 1, we can find that the cost of disk $D \in \mathcal{D}^3_{LH}$ is expanded by a constant factor. We can derive the following Lemma 3 and Theorem 1.

Lemma 3. *For any user* $u \in U$, $\sum_{D \in \mathcal{D}^3_{LH}} \bar{y}_D \leq 2 \sum_{D: D \in \mathcal{D}_u \setminus \mathcal{D}_{L_u} \cup \mathcal{D}_{IH_u}} y^*_D$, *Where* $\mathcal{D}_{IH_u}$ *is the initial heavy disk covering user* u.

Proof. Let $(\hat{x}, \hat{y})$ be a feasible solution of (2), since for each user $u \in U$ and each disk $D \in \mathcal{D}^3_{LH}$, $\hat{y}_D > \frac{1}{2} d_u$, $\bar{y}_D := \lceil \hat{y}_D \rceil$. If $d_u = 1$, there is $\bar{y}_D := 1$, then

$$\sum_{D: D \in \mathcal{D}^3_{LH}} \bar{y}_D = \sum_{D \in \mathcal{D}^3_{LH}} 1 \leq \sum_{D \in \mathcal{D}^3_{LH}} 2\hat{y}_D = \sum_{D \in \mathcal{D}_{LH}} 2\hat{y}_D = 2 \sum_{D: D \in \mathcal{D}_u \setminus \mathcal{D}_{L_u} \cup \mathcal{D}_{IH_u}} y^*_D$$

Otherwise, we have

$$\begin{aligned}
\sum_{D: D \in \mathcal{D}^3_{LH}} \bar{y}_D &= \sum_{D \in \mathcal{D}^3_{LH}} \lceil \hat{y}_D \rceil \leq \sum_{D \in \mathcal{D}^3_{LH}} (\hat{y}_D + 1) \\
&= \sum_{D \in \mathcal{D}^3_{LH}} \hat{y}_D + \sum_{D \in \mathcal{D}^3_{LH}} 1 \leq (1 + \frac{2}{d_u}) \sum_{D: D \in \mathcal{D}^3_{LH}} \hat{y}_D \\
&\leq (1 + \frac{2}{d_{u_{min}}}) \sum_{D: D \in \mathcal{D}^3_{LH}} \hat{y}_D = (1 + \frac{2}{d_{u_{min}}}) \sum_{D: D \in \mathcal{D}_{LH}} \hat{y}_D \\
&\leq 2 \sum_{D: D \in \mathcal{D}_u \setminus \mathcal{D}_{L_u} \cup \mathcal{D}_{IH_u}} y^*_D
\end{aligned}$$

where the second inequality is based on $1 < \frac{2\hat{y}_D}{d_u}$; the last inequality is based on $d_{u_{min}} \geq 2$ and $d_{u_{min}}$ is the minimum coverage requirement for user $u \in U$. □

Theorem 1. *Algorithm 1 can obtain a 4-approximation for the MSCDM problem.*

Proof. For any user $u \in U$, we select $2\lceil \bar{y}_D \rceil$ copies of each disk in $\bar{\mathcal{D}}_{H_u}$. Let $(\hat{x}, \hat{y})$ be a feasible solution of (2), since for each disk $D \in \mathcal{D}^3_{LH}$, $\bar{y}_D := \lceil \hat{y}_D \rceil$, for each disk $D \in \mathcal{D}_{IH_u}$, $\bar{y}_D := y^*_D$ and have

$$\bar{\mathcal{D}}_{H_u} = \mathcal{D}^3_{LH} \cup \mathcal{D}_{IH_u},$$

then for any user $u \in U$, we have

$$\begin{aligned}
\sum_{D:D\in\bar{\mathcal{D}}_{H_u}} 2\lceil \bar{y}_D \rceil &= \sum_{D:D\in\mathcal{D}^3_{LH}} 2\lceil \bar{y}_D \rceil + \sum_{D:D\in\mathcal{D}_{IH_u}} 2\lceil \bar{y}_D \rceil \\
&= \sum_{D:D\in\mathcal{D}^3_{LH}} 2\bar{y}_D + \sum_{D:D\in\mathcal{D}_{IH_u}} 2\lceil y^*_D \rceil \\
&\leq 4 \sum_{D:D\in\mathcal{D}_u\setminus\mathcal{D}_{L_u}\cup\mathcal{D}_{IH_u}} y^*_D + 4 \sum_{D:D\in\mathcal{D}_{IH_u}} y^*_D \\
&\leq 4 \sum_{D\in\mathcal{D}_u} y^*_D \leq 4 \sum_{D\in\mathcal{D}} y^*_D \leq 4OPT
\end{aligned}$$

where the first inequality is based on the lemma 3; the second inequality is based on $\sum_{D:D\in\mathcal{D}_{L_u}\cup\mathcal{D}_{IH_u}\cup\mathcal{D}_{LH}} y^*_D \leq \sum_{D:D\in\mathcal{D}_u} y^*_D$; the last inequality is based on $\sum_{D:D\in\mathcal{D}} y^*_D \leq OPT$, where OPT is the optimal value of integer programming (1).

5 Conclusion

In this paper, we study the minimum soft capacitated disk multi-coverage problem, where the disk is generated by power, and a 4-approximation algorithm is designed by using an LP rounding algorithm and the geometric properties of the disk set.

The minimum soft capacitated power cover problem requires us to take power as a cost and be able to combine the geometric properties of the disk. the minimum soft capacitated power multi-coverage problem is a generalization of the minimum soft capacitated power cover problem, this problem has not been studied yet. It is a challenge to obtain a constant approximation like the MSCDM problem.

References

1. Bandyapadhyay, S.; Bhowmick, S., Inamdar, T., Varadarajan.: Capacitated covering problems in geometric spaces. Discrete Comput. Geom. **63**(4), 768–798(2020)
2. Bandyapadhyay, S.: Improved bounds for metric capacitated covering problems. arXiv preprint arXiv:2006.12454(2020)
3. Dai, H., Deng, B., Li, W., Liu, X.: A note on the minimum power partial cover problem on the plane. J. Comb. Optim. **44**(2), 970–978 (2022)
4. Li, M., Ran, Y., Zhang, Z.: A primal-dual algorithm for the minimum power partial cover problem. J. Comb. Optim. **39**, 725–746 (2020). https://doi.org/10.1007/s10878-020-00567-3
5. Liang, W., Li, M., Zhang, Z., Huang, X.: Minimum power partial multi-cover on a line. Theor. Comput. Sci. **864**, 118–128 (2021)
6. Liu, X., Li, W., Dai, H.: Approximation algorithms for the minimum power cover problem with submodular/linear penalties. Theor. Comput. Sci. **923**, 256–270 (2022)
7. Liu, X., Li, W., Xie, R.: A primal-dual approximation algorithm for the k-prize-collecting minimum power cover problem. Optim. Lett. 1–13 (2021). https://doi.org/10.1007/s11590-021-01831-z
8. Liu, X., Dai, H., Li, S., Li, W.: k-prize-collecting minimum power cover problem with submodular penalties on a plane. Chin. Sci.: Inf. Sci. **52**(6), 947–959 (2022)
9. Ran, Y., Huang, X., Zhang, Z., Du, D.: Approximation algorithm for minimum power partial multi-coverage in wireless sensor networks. J. Glob. Optim. **80**, 661–677 (2021). https://doi.org/10.1007/s10898-021-01033-y
10. Wolsey, L.A.: An analysis of the greedy algorithm for the submodular set covering problem. Combinatorica **2**, 385–393 (1982)

A 1/2 Approximation Algorithm for Energy-Constrained Geometric Coverage Problem

Huan Lan(✉)

School of Mathematics and Statistics, Yunnan University,
Kunming 650504, People's Republic of China
lanhuan0714@163.com

Abstract. This paper studies the energy-constrained geometric coverage problem, which is to find an energy allocation that maximizes sensor coverage benefits while satisfying budget constraints. In this paper, we give a *Greedy+* algorithm with 1/2-approximation. The time complexity is $O(m^2n^2)$. This algorithm is an improvement of the greedy algorithm. In each iteration of the greedy algorithm, the single element with the largest revenue that satisfy budget constraints is added. The solution with the largest revenue as the output of the algorithm. We show that the approximation ratio of the algorithm is tight.

Keywords: *Greedy+* algorithm · Geometric coverage problems · Energy-constrained

1 Introduction

With the development of wireless communication technology, wireless sensor networks are used more and more frequently in commercial or industrial monitoring and tracking tasks such as signal coverage. [1] The problem of minimum energy coverage is one of the hotspots in wireless sensor network research. It assumes that all sensors and users are on the plane. The sensor s can form a variable radius disk $D(s, r(s))$ by adjusting the energy. The radius $r(s)$ of the disk $D(s, r(s))$ and energy is related as follows: $p(s) = r(s)^\alpha$ where the attenuation factor $\alpha \geq 1$. A user is covered by sensor s if it is within the service disk $D(s, r(s))$ of sensor s. The minimum energy coverage problem is that sensor covers all users and the goal is to use the least amount of energy. The problem is NP-hard when $\alpha > 1$ [2,3].

With the study of the energy coverage problem, some coverage requirements and constraints are considered. Li et al. [4] and Dai et al. [5] consider the minimum energy partial coverage problem, which finds a minimum energy allocation scheme such that at least k users are covered. Abu-Affash et al. [6] study the minimum-energy multi-coverage problem, which finds a minimum-energy allocation scheme such that each user satisfies the multi-coverage requirement.

Z. Cai et al. (Eds.): NCTCS 2022, CCIS 1693, pp. 105–114, 2022.
https://doi.org/10.1007/978-981-19-8152-4_7

Ran et al. [7] study the minimum-energy partial multi-coverage problem, which finds a minimum-energy allocation scheme such that at least k users satisfy the multi-coverage requirement. Liu et al. [8–10] consider covering the reward and punishment problem. They study the minimum energy partial coverage problem with submodular penalty cost and the minimum energy coverage problem of k reward collection. Li et al. study the trade-offs between energy and performance of sensor [11]. Lan et al. [12] study the energy-constrained geometric coverage problem, which is to maximize the coverage gain for the sensor under energy constraints.

This paper studies the energy-constrained geometric coverage problem. The problem is given an user set U, a sensor set S, energy budget P and user coverage benefit $w_u, u \in U$. The goal is to find an energy allocation that maximizes coverage gains while satisfying the energy constraints.

1.1 Related Work

The minimum energy coverage problem is to find the minimum energy distribution scheme so that all the user is covered. When $\alpha > 1$, Alt et al. [3] and Biló et al. [2] proved that the problem is NP-hard. When the sensor and the user are on the same line, the problem is in P [2]. When the sensor and the user are on the same line and $\alpha = 1$, Lev-Tov et al. [13] designed a polynomial time approximation scheme (PTAS) and Rezende et al. [14] designed the first fully polynomial time approximation scheme (FPTAS). When the sensor and user are in the plane and $\alpha > 1$, Biló et al. [2] give a polynomial-time approximation scheme (PTAS). When all sensor centers are on a straight line, Pedersen et al. [15] give an exact algorithm for the norm of L_1, L_∞.

For the energy-constrained maximum coverage problem, Lan et al. [12] give a greedy algorithm with $1-1/\sqrt{e}$-approximation. The algorithm selects the disk with the largest unit return in each iteration. After the iteration is over, the obtained solution is compared with the maximum profit disk. The algorithm selects the solution with greater profit as the output.

The knapsack constrained submodular function maximization problem is to find a subset that satisfies the knapsack constraint and maximizes the submodular function. When the cost is a modular function, Wolsey et al. [16] give an improved greedy algorithm with $(1 - 1/e^\beta)$-approximation where β is the root of $e^x = 2 - x$. Khuller et al. [17] give an improved Wolsey's algorithm for the maximum coverage problem under budget constraints with $1/2(1 - 1/e)$-approximate. Subsequently, Tang et al. [18] improved the approximate ratio lower bound $(1 - 1/\sqrt{e})$ of the algorithm through further analysis. In addition, Khuller et al. [17] give an algorithm that combines three elements of enumeration and a greedy algorithm with $(1 - 1/e)$-approximation, but requires $O(n^5)$ times of function computation. This result was subsequently improved by Ariel et al. [19] and Feldman et al. [20]. The same approximate ratio can be obtained in the case of enumerating two elements, and the number of function calculations is reduced to $O(n^4)$ times. Dmitrii et al. [21] give an *Greed*$^+$ algorithm with 1/2-approximation which add a single element to each iteration of the greedy algorithm. Feldman et al. [20] give an algorithm with 0.6174-approximation which enumerating an element and combining *Greed*$^+$ and requiring $O(n^3)$ times of function calculations.

When the cost function is a submodular function, Zhang et al. [22] generalized the greedy algorithm to submodular costs, they obtained a generalized greedy algorithm approximated by $1/2(1-1/e)$, but with a reduced budget.

The energy-constrained geometric coverage problem is also a special case of the maximum coverage problem with grouped budgets. The problem is to find a subset in each group that satisfies the constraint, the sum of their costs does not exceed the constraint, and the goal is to maximize the benefit of the subset. Chekuri et al. [23] give the greedy algorithm for all constraint are cardinality constraints and the group budget constraint with $1/(1+\alpha)$-approximation and $1/[6(1+\alpha)]$-approximation, respectively, where α is the approximate ratio of the sub-algorithm. Farbstein et al. [24] give an algorithm with $\alpha/(3+2\alpha)$-approximation in the group budget constraint problem. Recently, Guo et al. [25] used linear programming and rounding techniques to give a pseudo-polynomial time algorithm with $(1-1/e)$-approximation. They extend the algorithm to the maximum coverage problem under the constraints of cardinality grouping budget and total cost.

1.2 Our Work

This paper studies the energy-constrained geometric coverage problem, which is to find an energy allocation that maximizes sensor coverage benefits while satisfying budget constraints. In this paper, we give a *Greedy+* algorithm with 1/2-approximation. This algorithm is an improvement of the greedy algorithm [12]. The *Greedy+* algorithm is to add a disk that satisfies the constraints with the largest profit in each iteration of the greedy algorithm. until all disks have been considered.

The first Section will introduce the source of the problem and related work; the second Section mainly describes the energy-constrained geometric coverage problem; the third Section will introduce *Greedy+* algorithm and the corresponding approximation proof; the fourth Section is the summary of the problem.

2 Preliminaries

This section presents a detailed description of the energy-constrained geometric coverage problem and related knowledge.

Given a set U and a set function $f: 2^U \to \mathbb{R}$. f is monotonic if and only if $\forall X \subseteq Y$, $f(X) \leq f(Y)$. f is submodular if and only if $\forall X \subseteq Y \subseteq U$, $u \notin Y$,

$$f(X \cup \{u\}) - f(X) \geq f(Y \cup \{u\}) - f(Y). \tag{1}$$

We use $f(u \mid X) = f(X \cup \{u\}) - f(X)$ to represent the increment brought by adding u.

Definition 1. (Energy-constrained geometric coverage problem). *There are n users on the plane to form a ground set $U = \{u_1, u_2, \ldots, u_n\}$ and each point has a corresponding weight $w : U \to \mathbb{R}^+$. There are m sensors to form a set $S = \{s_1, s_2, \ldots, s_m\}$ and each sensor $s \in S$ can form a circular coverage area $D(s, r(s))$ by adjusting the energy $p(s)$. The relationship between energy and radius is $p(s) = r(s)^\alpha$, $\alpha \geq 1$. Given $P \in \mathbb{R}^+$, the energy-constrained geometric coverage problem is to give an energy distribution $p : S \to \mathbb{R}_{\geq 0}$ such that the sensor energy satisfy the constraints of $\sum_{s\in S} p(s) \leq P$ and the sum of the weights of the covered points is the largest.*

For any instance of an energy-constrained geometric coverage problem, a sensor has at most n optional disks. (Because we assume that there is at least one user on the boundary of each disk. If there are no users on the boundary, the energy distribution of the sensor can be reduced to achieve the same coverage effect. Then there is an optimal solution with users on the boundary.) Let the radius of the optional disk of s_i are $r_{i1} \leq r_{i2} \leq \cdots \leq r_{in}$. Let D_{ij} denote $D(s_i, r_{ij})$ and $U(D_{ij})$ is the set of users covered by the disk D_{ij}. The optional disk set of s_i is $\mathcal{D}_i = \{D_{i0}, D_{i1}, \ldots, D_{in}\}$, where D_{i0} indicates that the sensor does not distribute energy and no users are covered. $\mathcal{D} = \mathcal{D}_1 \cup \cdots \cup \mathcal{D}_m$. The energy-constrained geometric coverage problem can be viewed as each sensor selects a disk from the set of candidate disks to maximize the coverage benefits under energy constraints. So the energy-constrained geometric coverage problem is a special case of the maximum coverage problem under group budgets where only one element can be selected per group.

3 *Greedy+* Algorithm

This chapter will introduce the *Greedy+* algorithm for energy-constrained geometric coverage problems. The algorithm is to add the single element with the largest gain increment in each iteration of the greedy algorithm. The solution with the largest revenue as the output of the algorithm.

In the energy-constrained geometric coverage problem, the disks of the same sensor have an inclusion relationship ($D_{i1} \subseteq D_{i2} \subseteq \cdots \subseteq D_{in}$). We define

$$c(D^*) = \sum_{i=1}^{m} \max_{D_{ij} \in D^* \cap \mathcal{D}_i} \{r_{ij}^\alpha\}, \quad f(D^*) = \sum_{u \in \cup_{D \in D^*} U(D)} w(u). \tag{2}$$

Before proving the approximation ratio of the *Greedy+* algorithm, Some definitions are as follows. For any instance I, let OPT be the optimal solution of the instance. There is only one disk per sensor in OPT. D_g^i is the solution after adding i disk to the greedy algorithm. d_g^i is the $i-th$ disk add to D_g. o_1 is the most expensive disk in OPT. In order to facilitate the subsequent approximate ratio proof, let $f(OPT) = 1$ and $P = 1$. We define c^* so that $1 - c(o_1) - c^*$ is the cost of the greedy solution that the largest index solution cost is less than $1 - c(o_1)$.

Algorithm 1: *Greedy+* algorithm

Input: Objective function $f(\cdot)$, cost function $c(\cdot)$, budget P
Output: D^*

Initially, let $D_g = \emptyset$, $S = \emptyset$ and $D' = \mathcal{D}$.
while $D' \neq \emptyset$ **do**
  $s = \arg\max_{d \in D', c(D_g \cup d) \leq P}[f(D_g \cup d) - f(D_g)]$
  if $f(S) < f(D_g \cup s)$ **then**
    $S = D_g \cup s$
  for $i = 1, 2, \ldots, m$ **do**
    $d_i \in \arg\max_{d \in Disk_i} \frac{f(D_g \cup d) - f(D_g)}{c(D_g \cup d) - c(D_g)}$
  $d' \in \arg\max\limits_{i} \frac{f(D_g \cup d_i) - f(D_g)}{c(D_g \cup d_i) - c(D_g)}$
  if $c(D_g \cup d') \leq P$ **then**
    $D_g := D_g \cup d'$
  Remove all elements $d \in D'$ with $f(d \cup D_g) - f(D_g) = 0$ or $c(d \cup D_g) > P$
$D^* := \{ \arg\max\limits_{d \in S \cap Disk_i} c(d) \mid i = 1, 2, \ldots, m\}$

Definition 2. *Any* $x \in [0, 1]$, *i is the smallest index such that* $c(D_g^i) > x$, *defines:*

$$g(x) = f(D_g^{i-1}) + [x - c(D_g^{i-1})]\frac{f(d_g^i \mid D_g^{i-1})}{c(d_g^i \mid D_g^{i-1})}. \tag{3}$$

$g'(x)$ is the right derivative of g.

Definition 3. *Any* $x \in [0, 1]$, *i is the smallest index such that* $c(D_g^i) > x$, *defines:*

$$g_+(x) = g(x) + f(v \mid D_g^{i-1}) \tag{4}$$

$$v = \arg\max_{d \in \mathcal{D} \setminus D_g^{i-1}, c(d \cup D_g^{i-1}) \leq 1} f(d \mid D_g^{i-1}). \tag{5}$$

Definition 4. *Any* $x \in [0, 1 - c(o_1) - c^*]$, *i is the smallest index such that* $c(D_g^i) > x$, *defines:*

$$g_1(x) = g(x) + f(o_1 \mid D_g^{i-1}). \tag{6}$$

Then $g_1(x) \leq g_+(x)$.

Lemma 1. *if* $i \leq j - 1$ *then*

$$\frac{f(d_g^{j+1} \mid D_g^i)}{c(d_g^{j+1} \mid D_g^i)} \geq \frac{f(d_g^{j+1} \mid D_g^j)}{c(d_g^{j+1} \mid D_g^j)}. \tag{7}$$

Proof. The following will prove from three cases.

If the generated intermediate solutions $D_g^j \backslash D_g^i$ do not add a disk to the sensor where d_g^{j+1} is located. Then $c(d_g^{j+1} \mid D_g^i) = c(d_g^{j+1} \mid D_g^j)$. The following holds:

$$\frac{f(d_g^{j+1} \mid D_g^i)}{c(d_g^{j+1} \mid D_g^i)} \geq \frac{f(d_g^{j+1} \mid D_g^j)}{c(d_g^{j+1} \mid D_g^j)}. \tag{8}$$

If $D_g^{j-1} \backslash D_g^i$ does not have the disk of the sensor where d_g^{j+1} is located and d_g^j and d_g^{j+1} on the same sensor. Then:

$$\frac{f(d_g^j \mid D_g^{j-1})}{c(d_g^j \mid D_g^{j-1})} \geq \frac{f(d_g^{j+1} \mid D_g^{j-1})}{c(d_g^{j+1} \mid D_g^{j-1})}. \tag{9}$$

The inequality above has been proved.

$$\frac{f(d_j \mid D_{j-1})}{c(d_j \mid D_{j-1})} \geq \frac{f(d_{j+1} \mid D_{j-1})}{c(d_{j+1} \mid D_{j-1})}. \tag{10}$$

The inequality due to greediness. At the same time, $f(d_g^{j+1} \mid D_g^{j-1}) = f(d_g^j \mid D_g^{j-1}) + f(d_g^{j+1} \mid D_g^j)$. Then there is the following inequality:

$$\begin{aligned} \frac{f(d_g^{j+1} \mid D_g^i)}{c(d_g^{j+1} \mid D_g^i)} &\geq \frac{f(d_g^{j+1} \mid D_g^{j-1})}{c(d_g^{j+1} \mid D_g^{j-1})} \\ &= \frac{c(d_g^j \mid D_g^{j-1})\frac{f(d_g^j \mid D_g^{j-1})}{c(d_g^j \mid D_g^{j-1})} + c(d_g^{j+1} \mid D_g^j)\frac{f(d_g^{j+1} \mid D_g^j)}{c(d_g^{j+1} \mid D_g^j)}}{c(d_g^{j+1} \mid D_g^{j-1})}. \end{aligned} \tag{11}$$

Then

$$\frac{f(d_g^{j+1} \mid D_g^i)}{c(d_g^{j+1} \mid D_g^i)} \geq \frac{f(d_g^{j+1} \mid D_g^j)}{c(d_g^{j+1} \mid D_g^j)}. \tag{12}$$

From D_g^i to D_g^j, if k disks are added to the sensor where d_g^{j+1} is located, the above proof ideas and results and the greediness can be used repeatedly. The Lemma 1 has been proven.

Lemma 2. *Any* $x \in [0, 1 - c(o_1) - c^*]$, *we have*

$$g_1(x) + (1 - c(o_1))g'(x) \geq 1. \tag{13}$$

Proof. When $x = c(D_g^{i-1})$, for $i \geq 1$, there is $g_1(x) = g(x) + f(o_1 \mid D_g^{i-1}) = f(o_1 \cup D_g^{i-1})$. Since $f(OPT) = 1$, we have

$$\begin{aligned}
1 = & f(D_g^{i-1} \cup o_1) + f(OPT \backslash (D_g^{i-1} \cup o_1) \mid D_g^{i-1} \cup o_1) \\
\leq & \; g_1(x) + \sum_{e \in OPT \backslash (D_g^{i-1} \cup o_1)} f(e \mid D_g^{i-1} \cup o_1) \\
= & \; g_1(x) + \sum_{e \in OPT \backslash (D_g^{i-1} \cup o_1)} \frac{f(e \mid D_g^{i-1} \cup o_1)}{c(e \mid D_g^{i-1})} c(e \mid D_g^{i-1}) \\
\leq & \; g_1(x) + \sum_{e \in OPT \backslash (D_g^{i-1} \cup o_1)} \frac{f(e \mid D_g^{i-1})}{c(e \mid D_g^{i-1})} c(e \mid D_g^{i-1}) \\
\leq & \; g_1(x) + g'(x) \sum_{e \in OPT \backslash (D_g^{i-1} \cup o_1)} c(e \mid D_g^{i-1}) \\
\leq & \; g_1(x) + g'(x)[1 - c(o_1)].
\end{aligned} \tag{14}$$

The first inequality is due to monotonicity. The second and third inequalities are due to submodularity. The fourth inequality is due to greediness.

Theorem 1. *Greedy+ algorithm gives a 1/2-approximation to the energy-constrained geometric coverage problems and runs in* $O(m^2n^2)$.

Proof. Taking $x = 1 - c(o_1) - c^*$, by the Lemma 2, we have

$$g_1(1 - c(o_1) - c^*) + (1 - c(o_1))g'(1 - c(o_1) - c^*) \geq 1. \tag{15}$$

If $g_1(1 - c(o_1) - c^*) \geq 1/2$ then the theorem holds. If $g_1(1 - c(o_1) - c^*) < 1/2$ then

$$g'(1 - c(o_1) - c^*) \geq \frac{1 - g_1(1 - c(o_1) - c^*)}{1 - c(o_1)} > \frac{1}{2(1 - c(o_1))}. \tag{16}$$

$g(0) = 0, g'$ is non-incremental. For $x \in [0, 1]$ there is

$$\begin{aligned}
g(x) = & f(D_g^{i-1}) + [x - c(D_g^{i-1})] \frac{f(d_g^i \mid D_g^{i-1})}{c(d_g^i \mid D_g^{i-1})} \\
= & \sum_{j=1}^{i-1} [c(D_g^j) - c(D_g^{j-1})] \frac{f(d_g^j \mid D_g^{j-1})}{c(d_g^j \mid D_g^{j-1})} + [x - c(D_g^{i-1})] \frac{f(d_g^i \mid D_g^{i-1})}{c(d_g^i \mid D_g^{i-1})} \\
\geq & \sum_{j=1}^{i-1} [c(D_g^j) - c(D_g^{j-1})] \frac{f(d_g^i \mid D_g^{j-1})}{c(d_g^i \mid D_g^{j-1})} + [x - c(D_g^{i-1})] \frac{f(d_g^i \mid D_g^{i-1})}{c(d_g^i \mid D_g^{i-1})} \\
\geq & \sum_{j=1}^{i-1} [c(D_g^j) - c(D_g^{j-1})] \frac{f(d_g^i \mid D_g^{i-1})}{c(d_g^i \mid D_g^{i-1})} + [x - c(D_g^{i-1})] \frac{f(d_g^i \mid D_g^{i-1})}{c(d_g^i \mid D_g^{i-1})} \\
= & \; g'(x)x.
\end{aligned} \tag{17}$$

The first inequality is due to greediness. The second inequality is due to Lemma 1. We have

$$g(1-c(o_1)-c^*) \geq (1-c(o_1)-c^*)g'(1-c(o_1)-c^*) \geq \frac{1-c(o_1)-c^*}{2(1-c(o_1))}. \quad (18)$$

Since $x = 1-c(o_1)-c^*$ is the lastest intermediate solutions of greedy such that solution can add o_1. x_n denote the next intermediate solutions of this item. We have

$$\begin{aligned} g(x_n) &= f(x_n) \\ &\geq f(1-c(o_1)-c^*) + c^* g'(1-c(o_1)-c^*) \\ &= g(1-c(o_1)-c^*) + c^* g'(1-c(o_1)-c^*) \\ &\geq \frac{1-c(o_1)-c^*}{2(1-c(o_1))} + \frac{c^*}{2(1-c(o_1))} \\ &= 1/2. \end{aligned} \quad (19)$$

□

Because there are at most mn candidate disks per iteration. There are at most mn iterations. So the time complexity is $O(m^2n^2)$.

Next we show that the approximation ratio of the algorithm is tight. The idea of proof is similar to [21]. There are three users $\{u_1, u_2, u_3\}$ and three sensors $\{s_1, s_2, s_3\}$ on the plane. So we have some radius $\{r_{11}, r_{12}, r_{13}, r_{21}, r_{22}, r_{23}, r_{31}, r_{32}, r_{33}\}$ and some disks $\{D_{11}, D_{12}, D_{13}, D_{21}, D_{22}, D_{23}, D_{31}, D_{32}, D_{33},\}$. Let $c(D_{11}) = 1/2$, $c(D_{22}) = 1/2$ and $c(D_{33}) = (1+\epsilon)/2$. Other disks cost more than 1. Let $f(D_{11}) = 1/2$, $f(D_{22}) = 1/2$ and $f(D_{33}) = (1+\epsilon)/2$. The payoffs for the other disks are random positive numbers. Given energy budget $P = 1$. The OPT for this instance is $\{D_{11}, D_{22}\}$, but the *Greedy+* algorithm output $\{D_{33}\}$ (Fig. 1).

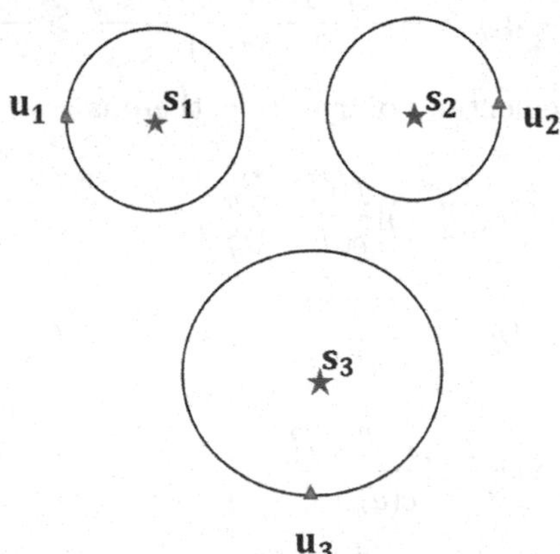

Fig. 1. Example of an energy-constrained geometric coverage problem.

4 Discussion

In this paper, the *Greedy+* algorithm for energy-constrained geometric coverage problems is proposed. The algorithm is improved based on the greedy algorithm. In each iteration of the greedy algorithm, the single element with the largest gain increment is added. *Greedy+* algorithm give a 1/2-approximation to the energy-constrained geometric coverage problems. The time complexity is $O(m^2n^2)$. We also show that the approximation ratio of the algorithm is tight.

Uncovered users are not considered in the energy-constrained geometric coverage problem. Giving corresponding penalties to uncovered users and maximizing the benefit function is a future research direction.

References

1. Zhang, Q., Li, W., Zhang, X., et al.: A local-ratio-based power control approach for capacitated access points in mobile edge computing (2022) https://doi.org/10.1145/3546000.3546027
2. Bilò, V., Caragiannis, I., Kaklamanis, C., Kanellopoulos, P.: Geometric clustering to minimize the sum of cluster sizes. In: Brodal, G.S., Leonardi, S. (eds.) ESA 2005. LNCS, vol. 3669, pp. 460–471. Springer, Heidelberg (2005). https://doi.org/10.1007/11561071_42
3. Alt, H., Arkin, E.M., Brönnimann, H., et al.: Minimum-cost coverage of point sets by disks. In: Amenta, N., Cheong, O. (eds.) Symposium on Computational Geometry, pp. 449–458. ACM, New York (2006)
4. Li, M., Ran, Y., Zhang, Z.: A primal-dual algorithm for the minimum power partial cover problem. J. Comb. Optim. **39**, 725–746 (2020)
5. Dai, H., Deng, B., Li, W., Liu, X.: A note on the minimum power partial cover problem on the plane. J. Comb. Optim. **44**(2), 970–978 (2022)
6. Abu-Affash, A.K., Carmi, P., Katz, M.J., Morgenstern, G.: Multi cover of a polygon minimizing the sum of areas. In: Katoh, N., Kumar, A. (eds.) WALCOM 2011. LNCS, vol. 6552, pp. 134–145. Springer, Heidelberg (2011). https://doi.org/10.1007/978-3-642-19094-0_15
7. Ran, Y., Huang, X., Zhang, Z., et al.: Approximation algorithm for minimum power partial multi-coverage in wireless sensor networks. J. Global Optim. **80**, 661–677 (2021)
8. Liu, X., Li, W., Xie, R.: A primal-dual approximation algorithm for the k-prize-collecting minimum power cover problem. Optim. Lett. 1–13 (2021). https://doi.org/10.1007/s11590-021-01831-z
9. Liu, X., Li, W., Dai, H.: Approximation algorithms for the minimum power cover problem with submodular/linear penalties. Theoret. Comput. Sci. **923**, 256–270 (2022)
10. Liu, X., Dai, H., Li, S., Li, W.: k-prize-collecting minimum power cover problem with submodular penalties on a plane. Chin. Sci.: Inf. Sci. **52**(6), 947–959 (2022)
11. Li, W., Liu, X., Cai, X., et al.: Approximation algorithm for the energy-aware profit maximizing problem in heterogeneous computing systems. J. Parallel Distrib. Comput. **124**, 70–77 (2019)
12. Lan, H.: Energy-constrained geometric coverage problem. In: Ni, Q., Wu, W. (eds.) AAIM 2022. LNCS, vol. 13513, pp. 268–277. Springer, Cham (2022). https://doi.org/10.1007/978-3-031-16081-3_23

13. Lev-Tov, N., Peleg, D.: Polynomial time approximation schemes for base station coverage with minimum total radii. Comput. Netw. **47**, 489–501 (2005)
14. de Rezende, P.J., Miyazawa, F.K., Sasaki, A.T.: A PTAS for the disk cover problem of geometric objects. Oper. Res. Lett. **41**(5), 552–555 (2013)
15. Logan, P., Haitao, W.: Algorithms for the line-constrained disk coverage and related problems. Comput. Geom. **105**, 101883 (2022)
16. Wolsey, L.: Maximising real-valued submodular functions: primal and dual heuristics for location problems. Math. Oper. Res. **7**(3), 410–425 (1982)
17. Khuller, S., Moss, A., Naor, J.: The budgeted maximum coverage problem. Inf. Process. Lett. **70**(1), 39–45 (1999)
18. Tang, J., Tang, X., Lim, A., Han, K., Li, C., Yuan, J.: Revisiting modified greedy algorithm for monotone submodular maximization with a knapsack constraint. Proc. ACM Meas. Anal. Comput. Syst. **5**(1), 1–22 (2021)
19. Kulik, A., Schwartz, R., Shachnai, H.: A refined analysis of submodular Greedy. Oper. Res. Lett. **49**, 507–514 (2021)
20. Feldman, M., Nutov, Z., Shoham, E.: Practical budgeted submodular maximization (2020). https://doi.org/10.48550/arXiv.2007.04937
21. Yaroslavtsev, G., Zhou, S., Avdiukhin, D.: "Bring Your Own Greedy"+ Max: near-optimal 1/2-approximations for submodular knapsack. In: Chiappa, S., Calandra, R. (eds.) International Conference on Artificial Intelligence and Statistics, pp. 3263–3274. Palermo, Sicily (2020)
22. Zhang, H., Vorobeychik, Y.: Submodular optimization with routing constraints. In: Schuurmans, D, Wellman, M. P., (eds.) Proceedings of the 30th AAAI Conference on Artificial Intelligence, Lake Tahoe, Nevada, pp. 819–826 (2016)
23. Chekuri, C., Kumar, A.: Maximum coverage problem with group budget constraints and applications. In: Jansen, K., Khanna, S., Rolim, J.D.P., Ron, D. (eds.) APPROX/RANDOM -2004. LNCS, vol. 3122, pp. 72–83. Springer, Heidelberg (2004). https://doi.org/10.1007/978-3-540-27821-4_7
24. Farbstein, B., Levin, A.: Maximum coverage problem with group budget constraints. J. Comb. Optim. **34**, 725–735 (2017). https://doi.org/10.1007/s10878-016-0102-0
25. Guo, L., Li, M., Xu, D.: Approximation algorithms for maximum coverage with group budget constraints. In: Gao, X., Du, H., Han, M. (eds.) COCOA 2017. LNCS, vol. 10628, pp. 362–376. Springer, Cham (2017). https://doi.org/10.1007/978-3-319-71147-8_25

Artificial Intelligence

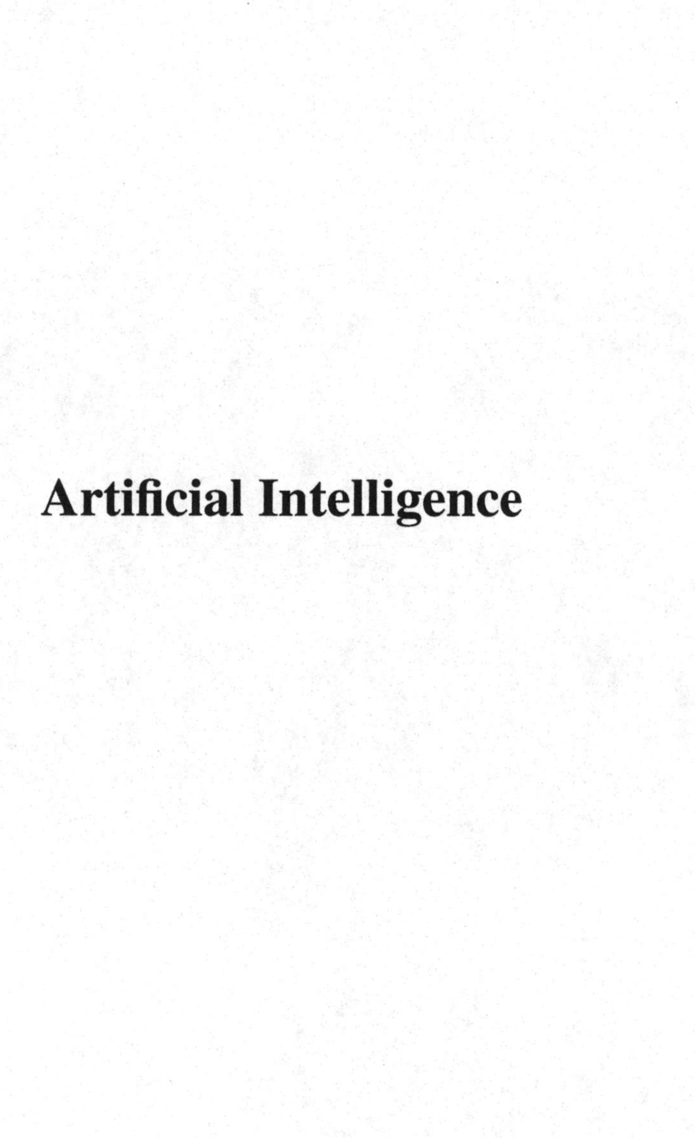

MixHop Graph WaveNet for Traffic Forecasting

Bing Ba, Qi Fu(✉), Chongjing Hang, and YunXia Jiang

Hunan University of Science and Technology, Xiangtan, China
fuqi@hnust.edu.cn

Abstract. Traffic forecasting is fundamental to realizing intelligent transportation systems (ITS) and challenging due to the complicated spatial dependencies of traffic data and nonlinear temporal trends. Graph convolutional networks (GCNs) have been employed in the latest studies to capture the intricate spatial relationships of roadways. However, due to the intrinsic restrictions of traditional GCNs, these methods cannot represent high-order or mixed neighborhood information. The MixHop Graph WaveNet (MH-GWN), a novel graph neural network architecture for traffic forecasting, is proposed in this research. In MH-GWN, a spatial-temporal convolutional layer that effectively integrates the MixHop graph convolutional layer and the dilated causal convolutional layer is designed, which can aggregate arbitrary-order neighborhood information and model the complex spatial-temporal dependencies of traffic data. Furthermore, via stacking spatial-temporal convolutional layers, the model's receptive field in the spatial-temporal domain can be exponentially improved. Extensive experiments on two real-world road network traffic datasets show that MH-GWN model is better than other baselines.

Keywords: Graph convolution neural network · Traffic forecasting · MixHop graph convolution · Spatial-temporal structure

1 Introduction

With rapid economic development, worldwide car ownership continues to rise, posing a challenge to many countries' transportation capacities. To address the traffic problem, an increasing number of countries are investing in the development of Intelligent Transportation Systems (ITS). The traffic forecasting problem is an important part of the realization of ITS. Given historical traffic data (recorded by sensors) and the basic road network, traffic forecasting is the process of projecting future road traffic circumstances (such as traffic flow). Accurate traffic forecasting can aid traffic management departments in better controlling traffic and reducing congestion [2, 3], as well as providing road users with better road options and guiding cars to their destinations more quickly.

Due to the complicated spatial correlations of traffic data and nonlinear temporal trends that change dynamically with road conditions, this task is extremely difficult. Early prediction methods were mostly based on statistical models or shallow machine learning models. However, these methods are generally designed for small datasets and are not suitable for dealing with complex and dynamic time-series data.

Z. Cai et al. (Eds.): NCTCS 2022, CCIS 1693, pp. 117–131, 2022.
https://doi.org/10.1007/978-981-19-8152-4_8

Recently, with the advancement of deep learning, it becomes possible to model the complex spatial-temporal dependencies of traffic forecasting. Current methods mostly use Recurrent Neural Networks (RNNs) or Causal Convolutional Networks for temporal dependency modeling; and Graph Convolutional Networks (GCNs) or their variants for spatial dependency modeling. These deep learning models utilize more features and more complex architectures than earlier methods, resulting in better performance. But these traditional GCN-based methods have two inherent limitations:

First, these methods mainly focus on the information of nodes' low-order neighborhoods and use it to model spatial dependencies. However, for the traffic forecasting problem, due to the characteristics of high-speed movement of vehicles, the information of low-order neighborhoods is not enough to model spatial dependencies well when predicting medium and long-term (more than 30 min) traffic conditions. In terms of message passing, traditional GCN needs to obtain high-order neighborhood information through stacking of GC layers. Too many GC layers will lead to a decrease in model efficiency and an increase in training difficulty, while too few GC layers will have a too-small receptive field. The higher-order neighborhood information that is more important for long-term traffic forecasting cannot be aggregated.

Second, traditional GCNs cannot model mixed neighborhood information. Even the simplest two-hop delta operator $f\left(\sigma\left(\hat{A}X\right)-\left(\sigma\left(\hat{A}^2X\right)\right)\right)$ cannot be learned by traditional GCNs. To address the above problems, a traffic forecasting model based on MixHop graph convolution is proposed, called MixHop Graph WaveNet (MH-GWN), which can not only aggregate arbitrary-order neighborhood information, but also model mixed neighborhood information. The contributions of this work are presented as follows:

- A new traffic forecasting model, MH-GWN, is proposed, which introduces MixHop graph convolution to solve the limitation of traditional graph convolution, which enables the model to aggregate arbitrary-order neighborhood information and enables the model to construct mixed neighborhood information.
- The importance of higher-order neighborhood information for modeling the spatial dependencies of long-term traffic forecasting is demonstrated.

Extensive experiments are conducted on two real-world urban traffic speed datasets, METR-LA and PEMSD8. It reached the advanced level within 15 min, 30 min, and 60 min.

2 Related Works

As an important part of ITS, researchers have proposed a large number of traffic forecasting methods in the past few decades. Most of the early methods were based on statistical learning methods or shallow machine learning methods. Ahmed and Cook [4] first proposed the use of Autoregressive Integrated Moving Average (ARIMA) to predict highway traffic data, and later some variants of ARIMA and other statistical learning methods [5–10] have also been widely used in this field. Traditional machine learning methods such as k-nearest neighbors (KNN), support vector machines (SVM), and neural networks (NN) are also used for traffic forecasting, which can achieve higher forecasting accuracy. However, these methods are generally designed for small data sets of a single node, limited by their ability to model nonlinearities, cannot effectively capture the dynamic nonlinear temporal trends in traffic data, and ignore or hardly consider the complex spatial dependencies.

Recent advances in deep learning have made it possible to model the complex spatial-temporal dependencies in traffic forecasting. Several studies [14–16] applied convolutional neural networks (CNNs) and recurrent neural networks (RNNs) to traffic forecasting. In these studies, CNNs are used to capture spatial correlations in transportation networks and RNNs are used to capture temporal correlations. But these CNN-based methods can only deal with traffic data with regular grid structure without considering the non-Euclidean correlations dominated by irregular road networks.

To address this issue, the researchers applied graph convolutions to model non-Euclidean correlations for traffic forecasting. Li et al. [1] proposed Diffusion Convolutional Recurrent Neural Networks (DCRNN), which replaced fully connected layers in Gated Recurrent Units (GRUs) with Diffusion Convolution Operators. Diffusion convolution performs graph convolution on a given graph, taking into account inflow and outflow relationships. Yu et al. [17] proposed Spatial-Temporal GCN (STGCN), which combines graph convolution and 1D causal convolution. In STGCN, graph convolutions are used to capture spatial correlations, while image convolutions are used on the time axis to capture temporal correlations. Due to the stronger parallelism of convolutions, the model is much more computationally efficient than RNNs.

The above GCN-based methods encode road network distances as a fixed weighted map representing spatial dependencies. To further model complex dependencies in traffic forecasting, Wu et al. [18] propose to use an adaptive adjacency matrix to capture hidden spatial dependencies that are not seen in a given graph. This adaptive adjacency matrix is achieved by computing the similarity of node embeddings. However, the hidden spatial dependencies are learned in a data-driven manner, and lacking the guidance of domain knowledge, overfitting problems may occur. In addition, existing graph convolution-based methods cannot model high-order neighborhood information and mixed neighborhood information.

3 Methodology

In this section, a formal definition of the traffic forecasting problem is given first, followed by a detailed introduction to MixHop graph convolution and temporal convolution, and finally, the general architecture of the MH-GWN model designed.

3.1 Traffic Forecasting Problem

The goal of traffic forecasting is to forecast future traffic on a road network based on historical data collected from N correlated sensors. A network of N related sensors is defined as a weighted directed graph $G = (V, E, A)$, where V is a set of $|V| = N$ nodes, E is the set of edges on the graph, representing the connectivity between nodes, and $A \in R^{N \times N}$ is a weighted adjacency matrix representing node proximities, where A_{v_i, v_j} denotes the proximity of node v_i to node v_j.

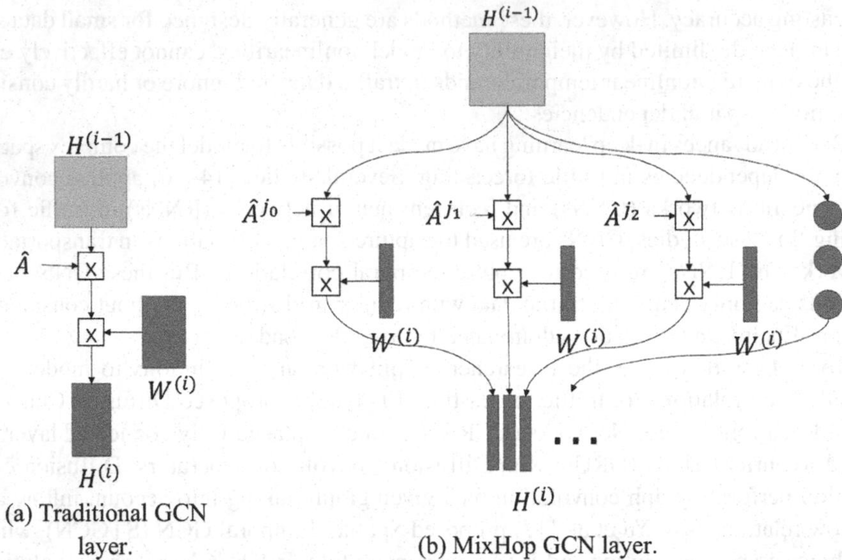

Fig. 1. Traditional GC layer (a), using adjacency $\hat{A}$, versus MixHop GC layer (b), using powers of $\hat{A}$.

The traffic forecasting problem can be described as a given graph G and the historical observation data of S time steps on it, predicting the feature information of the future T time steps on the graph G, $X^t \in R^{N\times D}$ represents the graph G feature information at time t. Therefore, the traffic forecasting problem can be formally defined as solving a mapping function f that satisfies the following conditions:

$$X^{t+1,\dots,t+T} = f\left(X^{t-S-1,\dots,t}, G\right), \tag{1}$$

where $X^{t+1,\dots,t+T} \in R^{N\times D\times T}$ and $X^{t-S-1,\dots,t} \in R^{N\times D\times S}$.

3.2 MixHop Graph Convolution Layer

Graph convolution has been proven useful in extracting spatial features. Kipf et al. [19] proposed a first approximation of Chebyshev spectral filter [20], which simplifies the definition of the convolution to become a simple neighborhood-averaging operator. In Kipf et al. [19] the graph convolution layer is written as:

$$Z = \hat{A}XW, \tag{2}$$

where $X \in R^{N\times D}$ and $Z \in R^{N\times M}$ are the input and output of this layer, $W \in R^{D\times M}$ is a parameter matrix, and $\hat{A} \in R^{N\times N}$ is a normalized adjacency matrix with self-loops.

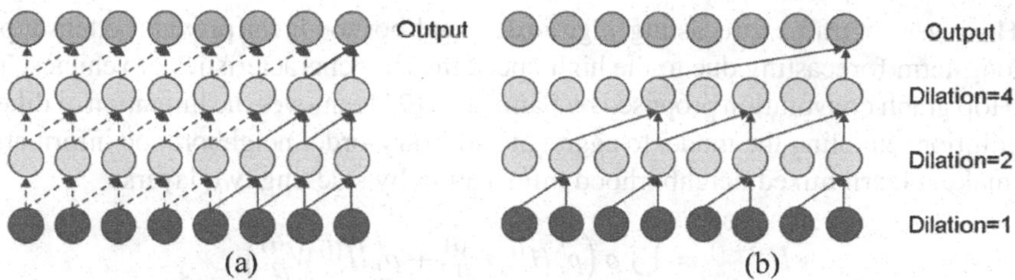

Fig. 2. Dilated casual convolution with kernel size 2. With a dilation factor k, it picks inputs every k step and applies the standard 1D convolution to the selected inputs.

Traditional graph convolution, as illustrated in Fig. 1(a), takes the feature matrix as input and collects the features of each node's first-order neighbors based on the weight information provided by the adjacency matrix. Finally, the internal characteristics of the nodes are linearly combined by multiplying the aggregated feature matrix by a trainable weight matrix. Convolution is defined more simply in traditional graph convolution. While this decreases computational cost, it also restricts the model's representation capabilities, leading to certain flaws in classic graph convolution:

- Traditional graph convolution has a limited receptive area because each layer can only gather information from its first-order neighbors.
- Traditional graph convolution, even with the simplest two-hop Delta operator $f\left(\sigma\left(\hat{A}X\right)-\sigma\left(\hat{A}^2X\right)\right)$, cannot model mixed neighborhood information.

In order to obtain a larger receptive field, Li et al. [1] developed a diffusion convolution layer for spatial-temporal modeling that proved to be effective. It combines information from consecutive K-order neighborhoods. Equation 1 is used to generalize its diffusion convolution layer, resulting in:

$$Z = \sum_{k=0}^{K} P^k X W_k, \tag{3}$$

The method aggregates the information of its k-hop nodes for each node by multiplying the feature matrix by the k-th power of its adjacency matrix. It is then multiplied by a learnable parameter matrix to perform a linear combination of node internal features. Finally, the per-hop information is added. P^k is separated into two cases among them. In the case of an undirected graph, $P^k = \hat{A}^k / ROWSUM\left(\hat{A}^k\right)$; in the case of a directed graph, the diffusion of the neighborhood can be separated into two directions, forward and backward, it contains forward transition matrix $p_f^k = \hat{A}^k / ROWSUM\left(\hat{A}^k\right)$ and backward transition matrix $p_b^k = \hat{A}^{k^T} / ROWSUM\left(\hat{A}^{k^T}\right)$. The diffusion convolution proposed by Li et al. [1] limits the range of neighborhood learning to a limited K-steps, and for conventional semi-supervised learning, the information of low-order neighborhoods is more important for model training.

However, for traffic forecasting, high-order neighborhoods can provide better support for long-term forecasting due to the high-speed moving characteristics of vehicles. The MixHop graph convolution proposed by Sami et al. [21] removes the limitation of dilated convolution, enabling the model to aggregate arbitrary-order neighborhood information and make it learn mixed neighborhood information by stacking two layers:

$$H^{(i+1)} = \bigcup_{j \in Q} \sigma\left(p_f^j H^{(i)} W_{j1}^{(i)} + p_f^j H^{(i)} W_{j2}^{(i)}\right), \tag{4}$$

where the hyperparameter Q represents a set of integers to specify the order of neighborhoods to be aggregated, $H^{(i)}$ represents the output of the i-th layer, σ is an element-wise activation function, and $\cup$ denotes column-wise concatenation. The difference between the MixHop graph convolution layer and the traditional graph convolution layer is shown in Fig. 1. When setting $Q = \{1\}$, MixHop degenerates to traditional graph convolution, and when $Q = \{0, 1, ..., K\}$, the model is equivalent to dilated convolution.

Finally, an adaptive adjacency matrix is used to understand spatial dependencies that are buried in the data but not visible in the graph. The adaptive adjacency matrix has the following definition:

$$\hat{A}_{adp} = SoftMax\left(ReLU\left(E_1 E_2^T\right)\right), \tag{5}$$

where $E_1 \in R^{N \times c}$ is the dynamic embedding matrix of source node information, and $E_2 \in R^{N \times c}$. The spatial dependency weight between the source and destination nodes can be derived by multiplying E_1 and E_2^T. The ReLU function is used to eliminate weak connections, and the SoftMax function is used to normalize the adaptive adjacency matrix.

Combining adaptive adjacency matrix with MixHop graph convolution, the following graph convolutional layers are proposed:

$$H^{(i+1)} = \bigcup_{j \in Q} \sigma\left(\begin{matrix} p_f^j H^{(i)} W_{j1}^{(i)} + p_f^j H^{(i)} W_{j2}^{(i)} \\ + \hat{A}_{adp}^j H^{(i)} W_{j3}^{(i)} \end{matrix}\right), \tag{6}$$

To learn mixed neighborhood information, stack two MixHop graph convolutional layers and add a fully connected layer as the final graph convolutional layer.

3.3 Temporal Convolution Layer

Dilated causal convolution [22] is used in temporal convolutional layers to extract temporal correlations within nodes. For traditional sequence processing methods such as RNN and LSTM, the output of the model depends on the state of the hidden layer at the previous moment, so the parallelization of the model cannot be realized. When compared to the standard sequence processing method, causal convolution does not require recursive processing of the sequence and has a considerable improvement in parallelism and reduction of gradient explosion.

However, causal convolution also has some problems, which need to expand the receptive field of convolution by stacking many layers, as shown in Fig. 2(a). The increase in the number of convolutional layers will lead to problems such as gradient disappearance, poor fitting effect, and complex training.

Dilated causal convolution, as a special case of causal convolution, controls the kernel to skip parts of the input through a stride factor. Assuming that at node v_i, given a 1-dimensional time series $x \in R^T$ and a convolution kernel $f \in R^K$, the dilated causal convolution can be written as:

$$x \star f(t) = \sum_{s=0}^{K-1} f(s)x(t - d \times s), \tag{7}$$

where d is the expansion factor that controls the skipping distance, that is, an input is obtained every d steps, and K is the size of the expanded causal convolution kernel. Compared with causal convolution, dilated causal convolution improves the receptive field exponentially through the stacking of layers, which can make the model have a very large receptive field when the number of layers is small, as shown in Fig. 2(b).

Finally, in order to enable the model to fully learn the nonlinear relationship in the time trend, a gating mechanism is introduced, which has been proved to be effective in the problem of sequential data modeling [23]. It is defined as follows:

$$Z = \delta(\Theta_1 \star \chi + b) \odot \sigma(\Theta_2 \star \chi + c), \tag{8}$$

where Θ_1, Θ_2, b, c are learnable model parameters, $\odot$ is element-wise multiplication, $\delta(\cdot)$ can be any activation function, $\sigma(\cdot)$ is a sigmoid function, which controls which information in $\delta(\cdot)$ can be transmitted into the next level.

3.4 Framework of Mixhop Graph WaveNet

The overall model architecture of MH-GWN is shown in Fig. 3. The architecture consists of a Mixhop graph convolutional layer and a gated temporal convolutional layer to form a spatial-temporal layer to model the spatial dependence and temporal correlation of the traffic forecasting problem. The gated temporal convolutional layer consists of two parallel dilated causal convolutional layers (TCN-a, TCN-b), and the graph convolutional layer consists of two Mixhop graph convolutional layers and a fully connected layer. The MH-GWN can handle spatial relationships at different temporal levels by stacking numerous spatial-temporal layers. For example, at the bottom layer, the GCN receives short-term temporal information, while at the top-level GCN processes long-term temporal information. Finally, the results of multiple spatiotemporal layers are added and passed to the output layer.

As the model's objective function, use the mean absolute error (MAE), which is defined as follows:

$$Loss = \frac{1}{TND} \sum_{i=1}^{T} \sum_{j=1}^{N} \sum_{k=1}^{D} \left| \hat{Y}_{jk}^{t+i} - Y_{jk}^{t+i} \right|, \tag{9}$$

where $\hat{Y} \in R^{T \times N \times D}$ is the predicted ground truth (GT).

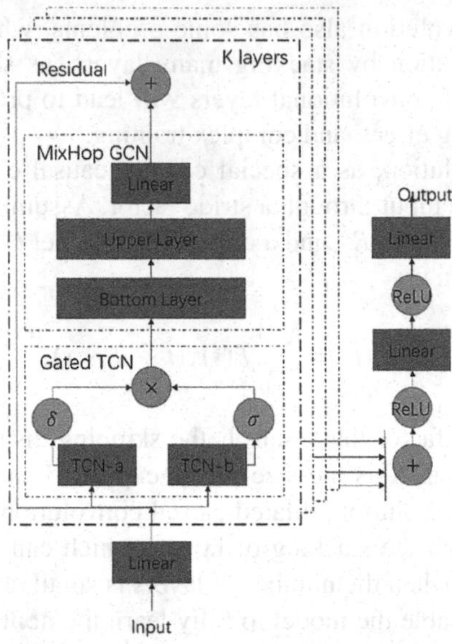

Fig. 3. The framework of MH-GWN.

4 Experiments

4.1 Datasets

Extensive experiments are conducted on two real-world urban traffic speed datasets, METR-LA and PEMSD8. The METR-LA [1] dataset collects 4 months of traffic speed statistics on 207 sensors on Los Angeles freeways; PEMSD8 contains traffic data for San Bernardino from July to August 2016, which installs 170 sensors on 8 roads. In the experimental data, the sampling interval of data records is 5 min, and the adjacency matrix of nodes is constructed by the road network distance and the threshold Gaussian kernel [24]. The data is divided in the order of sampling time. The first 70% is the training set, the middle 10% is the validation set, and the last 20% is the test set. During the training process, the data set is randomly shuffled and removed the Contextual relevance of the data using Z-score normalization. Detailed dataset statistics are provided in Table 1.

Table 1. The statistics of METR-LA and PEMSD8

Dataset	#Nodes	#Edges	#Time steps
METR-LA	207	1515	34272
PEMSD8	170	295	17856

4.2 Baselines

To test model performance, MH-GWN is compared with the following models:

- ARIMA [1]: Auto-regressive integrated moving average model with Kalman filter.
- FC-LSTM [1]: Recurrent neural network with fully connected LSTM hidden units.
- WaveNet [25]: A convolutional network architectures for Sequence Data.
- DCRNN [1]: Combining random walk-based graph convolutional networks with recurrent neural networks in an encoder-decoder fashion.
- Graph WaveNet [18]: Modeling hidden spatial dependencies in data using adaptive adjacency matrix.
- MRA-BGCN [26]: the bicomponent graph convolution is introduced to explicitly model node and edge dependencies.
- STGCN [17]: Combines gated temporal convolution with graph convolution.
- ASTGCN [27]: Attention-based Spatial-temporal Graph Convolutional Networks.
- LSGCN [28]: GLU processing time dependence is proposed.
- USTGCN [29]: Using Unified Spatial-temporal Graph Convolutional Networks.

4.3 Experimental Setups

Table 2. Performance comparison of MH-GWN model and other baseline models.

Data	Models	15 min			30 min			60 min		
		MAE	RMSE	MAPE	MAE	RMSE	MAPE	MAE	RMSE	MAPE
METR-LA	ARIMA	3.99	8.21	9.60%	5.15	10.45	12.70%	6.90	13.23	17.40%
	FC-LSTM	3.44	6.30	9.60%	3.77	7.23	10.90%	4.37	8.69	13.20%
	WaveNet	2.99	5.89	8.04%	3.59	7.28	10.25%	4.45	8.93	13.62%
	DCRNN	2.77	5.38	7.30%	3.15	6.45	8.80%	3.60	7.60	10.50%
	Graph WaveNet	2.69	5.15	6.90%	3.07	6.22	8.37%	3.53	7.37	10.01%
	MRA-BGCN	2.67	5.12	**6.8%**	3.06	6.17	8.3%	3.49	7.30	10.0%
	MH-GWN	**2.67**	**5.12**	6.9%	**3.03**	**6.10**	**8.2%**	**3.45**	**7.12**	**9.8%**
PEMS8	DCRNN	1.17	2.59	2.32%	1.49	3.56	3.21%	1.87	4.50	4.28%
	STGCN	1.19	2.62	2.34%	1.59	3.61	3.24%	2.25	4.68	4.54%
	ASTGCN	1.49	3.18	3.16%	1.67	3.69	3.59%	1.89	4.13	4.22%
	LSGCN	1.16	2.45	2.24%	1.46	3.28	3.02%	1.81	4.11	3.89%
	USTGCN	1.14	**2.15**	**2.07%**	**1.25**	**2.58**	**2.35%**	1.70	**3.27**	**3.22%**
	MH-GWN	**1.10**	2.48	2.18%	1.37	3.36	2.94%	**1.61**	4.13	3.73%

The operating environment of this experiment is Core(TM) i7-9750H CPU @ 2.60 GHz, NVIDIA GeForce GTX1660Ti GPU, and 6 GB video memory. An 8-layer MH-GWN with dilation factor sequences of 1, 2, 1, 2, 1, 2, 1, 2 is used to cover the input sequence length. This paper defines Q = {1, 2} in the bottom MixHop graph convolution layer and Q = {2, 4, 8, 16, 32} in the upper layer and randomly initializes node embeddings with a uniform distribution of size 10. The model is trained using the Adam optimizer with an initial learning rate of 0.001 that decays to 1/3 after every 10 iterations. Apply Dropout with p = 0.3 to the output of the graph convolutional layer. Selected evaluation metrics include mean absolute error (MAE), root mean square error (RMSE), and mean absolute percent error (MAPE). Missing values are excluded from training and testing.

4.4 Experimental Results

Based on the METR-LA and PEMS-BAY experimental data, Table 2 presents the performance statistics of MH-GWN model and the baseline model. The error values (or performances) for the 15-min, 30-min, and 60-min forecasts are listed in Table 2, respectively. On both datasets, it is obvious that the model suggested in this research generates better performance outcomes (Fig. 4).

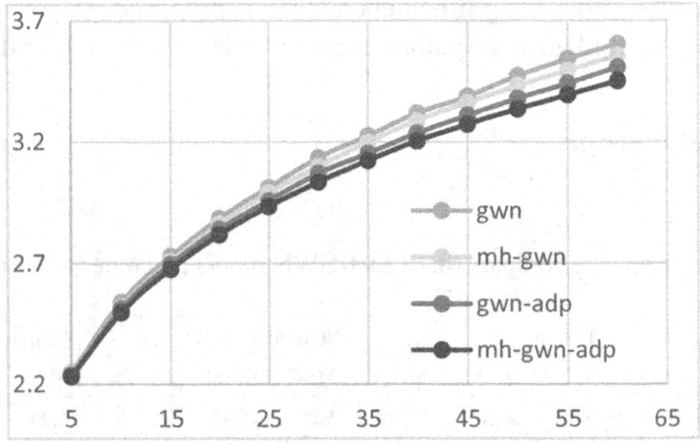

Fig. 4. Performance comparison between mh-gwn and gwn.

Specifically, the model proposed has huge advantages compared with the traditional time series model ARIMA. On the METR-LA dataset, MH-GWN model is 33.08%, 41.16%, and 50% lower than ARIMA in model-predicted MAE values at 15 min, 30 min, and 60 min, respectively. Compared with the best-performing DCRNN among RNN-based models, MH-GWN model is 3.61%, 3.8%, and 4.16% lower in predicted MAE values for the 15-min, 30-min, and 60-min models, respectively. Compared with Graph WaveNet based on spatiotemporal graph convolution, STGCN and ASTGCN with attention mechanism, MH-GWN model also has different degrees of improvement in performance. Comparing the best performing MRA-BGCN among the benchmark models, it can be seen that MH-GWN model performs about the same at 15-min predictions; but at 30-min and 60-min predictions, MH-GWN is 0.03 and 0.04 lower in MAE values, respectively. The MRA-BGCN method also introduces the idea of aggregating multi-neighborhood information, but its proposed method based on multi-range attention mechanism is weaker than this paper proposed method based on Mixhop graph convolution in terms of performance and efficiency. It can be seen that MH-GWN achieves better prediction results in terms of long-term prediction relative to other baseline methods.

In the graph convolution layer, in order to enable the model to have the ability to aggregate high-order neighborhood information and learn mixed neighborhood information, the MixHop graph convolution (mh-gwn) is introduced on the basis of Graph WaveNet, and the adaptive adjacency matrix is combined. (mh-gwn-adp). It can be seen from Fig. 5 that when the prediction window length of MH-GWN model is 5 min, the introduction of MixHop graph convolution and adaptive adjacency matrix does not bring significant improvement to the prediction performance. But as the prediction window increases, the difference between the performance of MH-GWN model and the Graph WaveNet model also increases, and MH-GWN model already has a clear performance advantage at 60-min predictions. This is because, in the short-term prediction, the low-order neighborhood information of the nodes in the road network is enough to provide effective support for the prediction. When MixHop graph convolution mixes the neighborhood information, it will weaken or even shield the high-order neighborhood information. At this time, MixHop graph convolution will degenerate into traditional graph convolution or dilated convolution.

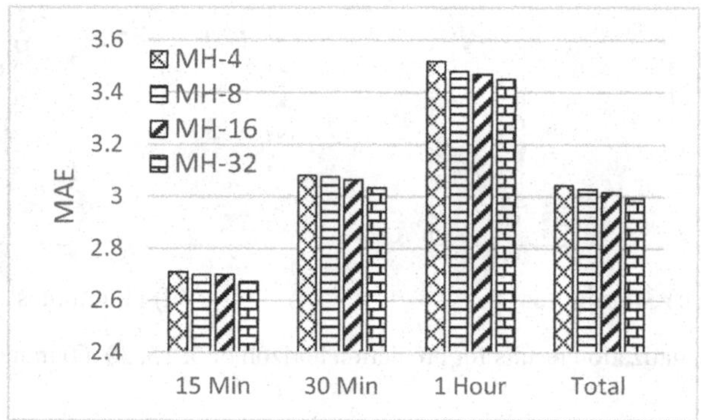

Fig. 5. Performance comparison for different MH-GWN variants.

However, when the prediction window continues to increase, the low-order neighborhood information can no longer provide sufficient support for the prediction, and the MixHop graph convolution will increase the weight of the high-order neighborhood information so that the model can obtain better prediction results.

In the MixHop graph convolutional layer, the hyperparameter Q controls which order of neighborhood information is aggregated by the convolutional layer. To evaluate the effect of higher-order neighborhood information on traffic forecasting, four different sets of integer adjacency powers are designed. Where MH-4, MH-8, MH-16, MH-32 indicate that Q is equal to {2, 4}, {2, 4, 8}, {2, 4, 8, 16} and {2, 4, 8, 16, 32}, respectively. Figure 5 shows the performance of the model constructed by these four sets of hyperparameters on the METR-LA dataset. It is observed that with the addition of high-order neighborhood information, the overall performance of the model continues to improve, especially in long-term forecasting, where the advantage is more pronounced. This suggests that higher-order neighborhood information can provide better support for long-term predictions.

The same hyperparameters as METR-LA are used on the PEMSD dataset. Compared with the best-performing USTGCN in the benchmark model, the obtained results are 0.04 and 0.09 lower in the 15-min and 60-min prediction on MAE evaluation metrics, respectively, but significantly weaker than the USTGCN in 30-min prediction. This is due to the fact that the intricacy of the road network and information on road conditions varies greatly between datasets. For different datasets, it is necessary to aggregate neighborhood information of different orders to build different MixHop architectures.

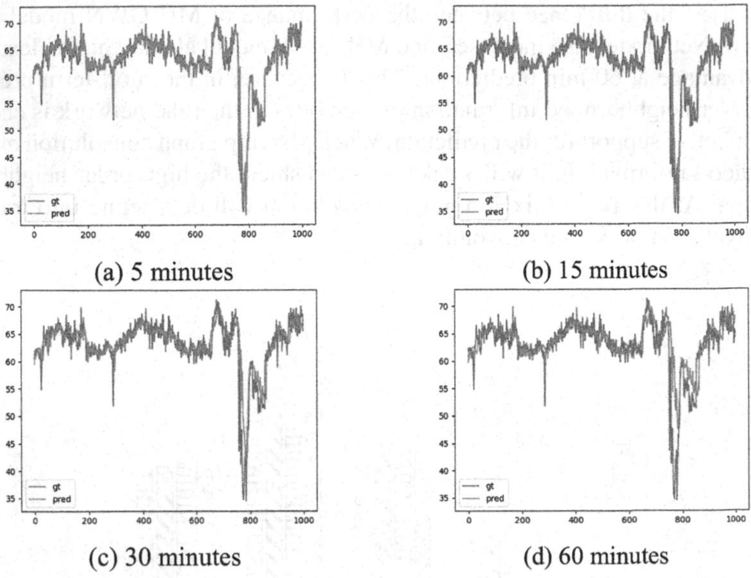

(a) 5 minutes (b) 15 minutes

(c) 30 minutes (d) 60 minutes

Fig. 6. The visualization results for prediction horizon of 5, 15, 30, 60 min on PEMSD8.

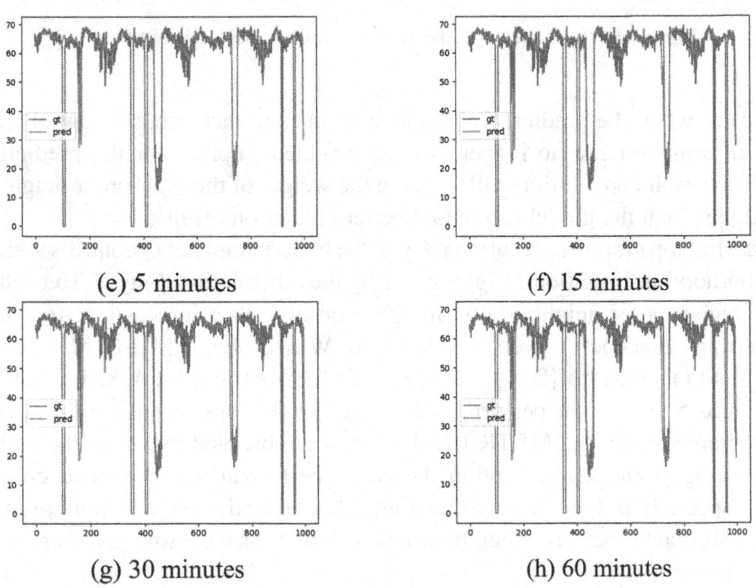

(e) 5 minutes (f) 15 minutes

(g) 30 minutes (h) 60 minutes

Fig. 7. The visualization results for prediction horizon of 5, 15, 30, 60 min on METR-LA.

4.5 Visualized Analysis

To better understand the model, visualize the MH-GWN model's prediction results based on two real datasets. A node was randomly selected in each of the two datasets and the prediction results were visualized. It can be seen from Fig. 6 and Fig. 7 that the predicted traffic speed has a similar trend to the actual traffic speed under different time series lengths, which proves its effectiveness in real-time traffic forecasting.

5 Conclusion

A new traffic prediction model based on MixHop graph convolution is proposed, which addresses the limitations of traditional graph convolution-based models. Specifically, MixHop graph convolutions are used to aggregate and model admixture neighborhood information of arbitrary order, and dilated causal convolutions are used to capture temporal dynamics. The effect of high-order neighborhood information on long-term prediction is further verified. MH-GWN model achieves better predictions than baselines when evaluated on two large real-world traffic datasets. For future work, the following two aspects will be investigated (1) applying the proposed model to other spatial-temporal prediction tasks; (2) further introducing L2 Group Lasso regularization to build different MixHop architectures for different datasets.

Acknowledgments. Research in this article is supported by the National Natural Science Foundation of China (No. 62177014), and Research Foundation of Hunan Provincial Education Department of China (No. 19A174, 20B222).

References

1. Li, Y., Yu, R., Shahabi, C., Liu, Y.: Diffusion convolutional recurrent neural network: data-driven traffic forecasting. In: ICLR (2018)
2. Lv, Z., Xu, J., Zheng, K., Yin, H., Zhao, P., Zhou, X.: LC-RNN: a deep learning model for traffic speed prediction. In: IJCAI-2018, pp. 3470–3476, July 2018. https://doi.org/10.24963/ijcai.2018/482
3. Zheng, C., Fan, X., Wen, C., Chen, L., Wang, C., Li, J.: DeepSTD: mining spatio-temporal disturbances of multiple context factors for citywide traffic flow prediction. IEEE Trans. Intell. Transp. Syst. **21**(9), 3744–3755 (2020). https://doi.org/10.1109/TITS.2019.2932785
4. Ahmed, M.S., Cook, A.R.: Analysis of freeway traffic time-series data by using Box-Jenkins techniques. Transp. Res. Rec. (1979). http://onlinepubs.trb.org/Onlinepubs/trr/1979/722/722-001.pdf
5. Williams, B.M., Hoel, L.A.: Modeling and forecasting vehicular traffic flow as a seasonal ARIMA process: theoretical basis and empirical results. J. Transp. Eng. **129**, 664–672 (2003). https://doi.org/10.1061/(ASCE)0733-947X(2003)129:6(664)
6. Shekhar, S.S.R., Williams, B.M.: Adaptive seasonal time series models for forecasting short-term traffic flow. Transp. Res. Rec. **2024**, 116–125 (2007). https://doi.org/10.3141/2024-14
7. Li, X., et al.: Prediction of urban human mobility using large-scale taxi traces and its applications. Front. Comput. Sci. **6**, 111–121 (2011). https://doi.org/10.1007/s11704-011-1192-6

8. Moreira-Matias, L., Gama, J., Ferreira, M., Mendes-Moreira, J., Damas, L.: Predicting taxi-passenger demand using streaming data. IEEE Trans. Intell. Transp. Syst. **14**, 1393–1402 (2013). https://doi.org/10.1109/TITS.2013.2262376
9. Lippi, M., Bertini, M., Frasconi, P.: Short-term traffic flow forecasting: an experimental comparison of time-series analysis and supervised learning. IEEE Trans. Intell. Transp. Syst. **14**, 871–882 (2013). https://doi.org/10.1109/TITS.2013.2247040
10. Wagner-Muns, I.M., Guardiola, I.G., Samaranayke, V.A., Kayani, W.I.: A functional data analysis approach to traffic volume forecasting. IEEE Trans. Intell. Transp. Syst. **19**, 878–888 (2018). https://doi.org/10.1109/TITS.2017.2706143
11. Li,Z., Sergin, N., Yan, H., Zhang, C., Tsung, F.: Tensor completion for weakly-dependent data on graph for metro passenger flow prediction. In: AAAI (2020). https://doi.org/10.1609/aaai.v34i04.5915
12. Duan, P., Mao, G., Liang, W., Zhang, D.: A unified spatio-temporal model for short-term traffic flow prediction. IEEE Trans. Intell. Transp. Syst. **20**, 3212–3223 (2019). https://doi.org/10.1109/TITS.2018.2873137
13. Shin, J., Sunwoo, M.: Vehicle speed prediction using a Markov chain with speed constraints. IEEE Trans. Intell. Transp. Syst. **20**, 3201–3211 (2019). https://doi.org/10.1109/TITS.2018.2877785
14. Ma, X., Dai, Z., He, Z., Ma, J., Wang, Y., Wang, Y.: Learning traffic as images: a deep convolutional neural network for large-scale transportation network speed prediction. Sensors **17** (2017). https://doi.org/10.3390/s17040818
15. Zhang, J., Zheng, Y., Qi, D., Li, R., Yi, X., Li, T.: Predicting citywide crowd flows using deep spatio-temporal residual networks. ArXiv, abs/1701.02543 (2018). https://doi.org/10.1016/j.artint.2018.03.002
16. Liu, H., Zhang, X., Yang, Y., Li, Y., Yu, C.: Hourly traffic flow forecasting using a new hybrid modelling method. J. Central South Univ. **29**(04), 1389–1402 (2022). https://doi.org/10.1007/s11771-022-5000-2
17. Yu, B., Yin, H., Zhu, Z.: Spatio-temporal graph convolutional networks: a deep learning framework for traffic forecasting. In: IJCAI-2018, pp. 3634–3640 (2018). https://doi.org/10.24963/ijcai.2018/505
18. Wu, Z., Pan, S., Long, G., Jiang, J., Zhang, C.: Graph wavenet for deep spatial-temporal graph modeling. In: IJCAI-2019, pp. 1907–1913. International Joint Conferences on Artificial Intelligence Organization, July 2019. https://doi.org/10.24963/ijcai.2019/264
19. Kipf, T., Welling, M.: Semi-supervised classification with graph convolutional networks. ArXiv, abs/1609.02907 (2017). https://doi.org/10.48550/arxiv.1609.02907
20. Defferrard, M., Bresson, X., Vandergheynst, P.: Convolutional neural networks on graphs with fast localized spectral filtering. In: NIPS (2016). https://doi.org/10.48550/arxiv.1606.09375
21. Abu-El-Haija, S., et al.: MixHop: higher-order graph convolutional architectures via sparsified neighborhood mixing. In: ICML (2019). https://doi.org/10.48550/ARXIV.1905.00067
22. Yu, F., Koltun, V.: Multi-scale context aggregation by dilated convolutions. CoRR, abs/1511.07122 (2016). https://doi.org/10.48550/arxiv.1511.07122
23. Ma, T., Kuang, P., Tian, W.: An improved recurrent neural networks for 3D object reconstruction. Appl. Intell. **50**(3), 905–923 (2019). https://doi.org/10.1007/s10489-019-01523-3
24. Shuman, D.I., Narang, S.K., Frossard, P., Ortega, A., Vandergheynst, P.: The emerging field of signal processing on graphs: extending high-dimensional data analysis to networks and other irregular domains. IEEE Sig. Process. Mag. **30**(3), 83–98 (2013). https://doi.org/10.1109/MSP.2012.2235192
25. van den Oord, A., et al.: WaveNet: a generative model for raw audio. ArXiv, abs/1609.03499 (2016). https://doi.org/10.48550/ARXIV.1609.03499

26. Chen, W., Chen, L., Xie, Y., Cao, W., Gao, Y., Feng, X.: Multi-range attentive bicomponent graph convolutional network for traffic forecasting. In: AAAI (2020). https://doi.org/10.1609/aaai.v34i04.5758
27. Guo, S., Lin, Y., Feng, N., Song, C., Wan, H.: Attention based spatial-temporal graph convolutional networks for traffic flow forecasting. In: AAAI (2019). https://doi.org/10.1609/aaai.v33i01.3301922
28. Huang, R., Huang, C., Liu, Y., Dai, G., Kong, W.: LSGCN: long short-term traffic prediction with graph convolutional networks. In: IJCAI (2020). https://doi.org/10.24963/ijcai.2020/326
29. Roy, A., Roy, K.K., Ali, A.A., Amin, M.A., Rahman, A.K.M.M.: Unified spatio-temporal modeling for traffic forecasting using graph neural network. In: 2021 International Joint Conference on Neural Networks (IJCNN), pp. 1–8 (2021). https://doi.org/10.1109/IJCNN52387.2021.9533319

A Brief Discussion on the Reform of Mathematics Teaching in Artificial Intelligence Majors - Taking Matrix Computation and Optimization as Examples

Miaomiao Li[1(✉)] and Bo Liu[2]

[1] College of Electronic Information and Electrical Engineering, Changsha University, Changsha, China
miaomiaolinudt@gmail.com

[2] College of Artificial Intelligence, Chongqing Technology and Business University, Chongqing, China

Abstract. The Artificial Intelligence program is an engineering application program but involves deeper mathematical theory. Matrix Computation and Optimization belong to the core theoretical courses of AI majors. This paper discusses the inner connection between the two courses and the current teaching problems. In order to enable students to connect theory with practice, this paper proposes the organic integration of the two courses and proposes classroom teaching reform methods and practical teaching reform methods for the integrated course in order to improve the teaching quality of the classroom, mobilize students' classroom enthusiasm, and cultivate students' innovative thinking and teamwork ability. These methods are also inspiring for the teaching of other courses in artificial intelligence.

Keywords: Artificial intelligence · Optimization · Matrix calculation · Teaching methods

1 Introduction

Artificial intelligence technology is currently attracting attention from countries around the world. The United States, the United Kingdom, and other countries have taken AI as an important strategic plan, aiming to use AI technology as an important driving force for their economic development. China follows the world trend and is also accelerating the deployment of AI strategy. on July 20, 2017, China launched the highest level of special planning in the field of artificial intelligence: the "new generation of artificial intelligence development

Supported by organization x.

Z. Cai et al. (Eds.): NCTCS 2022, CCIS 1693, pp. 132–141, 2022.
https://doi.org/10.1007/978-981-19-8152-4_9

plan", which clearly states that by 2020 the AI industry becomes a new important economic growth point, and by 2025 AI becomes the main driving force for China's industrial upgrading and economic transformation. In October 2017, General Secretary Xi Jinping clearly mentioned artificial intelligence as a development content in the report of the 19th National Congress of the Communist Party of China and the Government Work Report, which means that artificial intelligence has risen to the national strategic level. On October 31, 2018, the Political Bureau of the CPC Central Committee held the ninth collective study on the current situation and trends of artificial intelligence development. In this study, General Secretary Xi Jinping emphasized that artificial intelligence is an important driving force for the new round of scientific and technological revolution and industrial transformation and accelerating the development of a new generation of artificial intelligence is a strategic issue related to the opportunities of the new round of technological revolution and industrial transformation. In the Thirteenth Five-Year Plan for Scientific and Technological Innovation of Chongqing, the Chongqing Municipal Government proposed to build an artificial intelligence and innovation center, focusing on core devices such as processors and intelligent sensors optimized for artificial intelligence applications, artificial intelligence processing equipment, and mobile intelligent terminals, wearable devices, virtual reality/augmented reality hardware, etc., as well as research and application of artificial intelligence software technologies and artificial intelligence systems including theory and algorithms, basic software, and application software. Whether it is from the national strategic level or from the perspective of developing the local economy, there is an urgent need for artificial intelligence talent support, which requires colleges and universities to cultivate high-tech compound talents with innovative consciousness, proficiency in the core knowledge of artificial intelligence, and able to cope with future changes.

Artificial intelligence has not only a wide range of applications but also a deep theoretical foundation [1–3]. The theory of artificial intelligence covers a wide range of topics including calculus, linear algebra, matrix analysis, matrix computation, optimization, probability theory, statistics, discrete mathematics, and so on. These theories are important foundations for further study of AI-related courses (e.g., machine learning, computer vision, natural language processing, etc.). Therefore, how to design the corresponding mathematical teaching system according to the characteristics of AI is an important problem that must be solved in the current AI teaching. The relationship between artificial intelligence and various courses is shown in Fig. 1.

2 Problem

Artificial intelligence involves a lot of mathematical theory, there are many abstract concepts and knowledge points, and the update speed is faster. Artificial intelligence belongs to engineering, so the mathematics curriculum system is still set up according to engineering mathematics in its talent training plan. The main problems with this setup are:

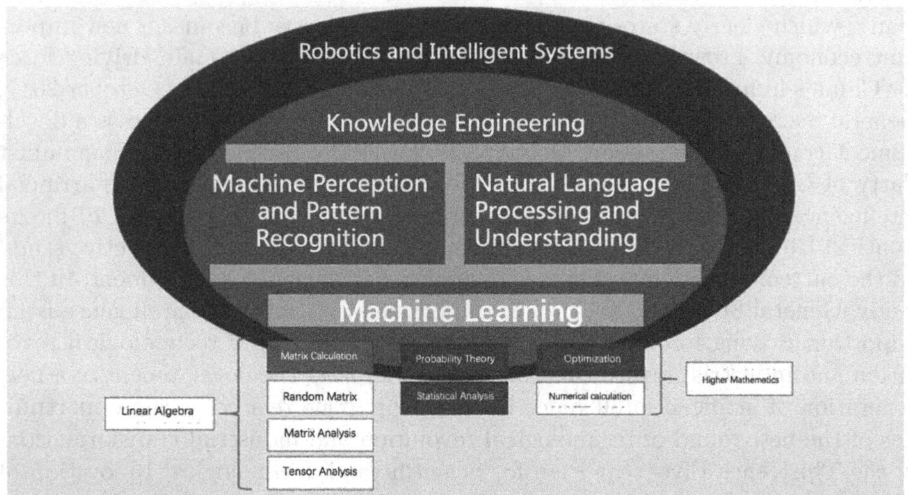

Fig. 1. Relationship between artificial intelligence and various courses.

(1) the traditional engineering mathematics class time quantity is less, and can not teach artificial intelligence to need the mathematics knowledge completely;
(2) the traditional teaching content of engineering mathematics does not cover all the mathematical theories needed by AI, for example, convex optimization (an important part of optimization course-RRB- is the core basic course of AI, but engineering mathematics can not be taught;
(3) the teaching materials for these mathematical theories are very theoretical, which is not conducive to students' understanding;
(4) engineering mathematics courses usually do not offer practical courses, or set the content of practical courses is thin, monotonous teaching methods;

3 The Optimization of the Curriculum System

Some of the courses in the mathematical theory of artificial intelligence (calculus, linear algebra, probability theory, etc.) will be taught in traditional engineering mathematics. However, optimization and matrix calculation are seldom involved in the course system of engineering mathematics, and they are important basic courses in artificial intelligence. So consider including these two courses in the curriculum of artificial intelligence. Mathematical optimization is used in a wide range of AI applications (for example, in deep learning), and the Stochastic gradient descent used to solve deep neural network models is an optimization method. In addition to calculus and linear algebra being the basis of optimization, matrix calculation is also the basis of it. Linear regression is used as an example to explain the relationship between matrix calculation and optimization.

The linear regression model is an important model of statistical machine learning, which can be solved by mathematical optimization. When we calculate the result according to the given data, we need to calculate the inverse of the matrix, which belongs to the content of the matrix calculation. QR decomposition and singular value analysis are also involved in solving large-scale least squares, while the Steepest Gradient Descent is used to solve quadratic programming problems, you must compute the eigenvalues of the matrix [4]. The curriculum for matrix calculation and optimization is shown in Fig. 2.

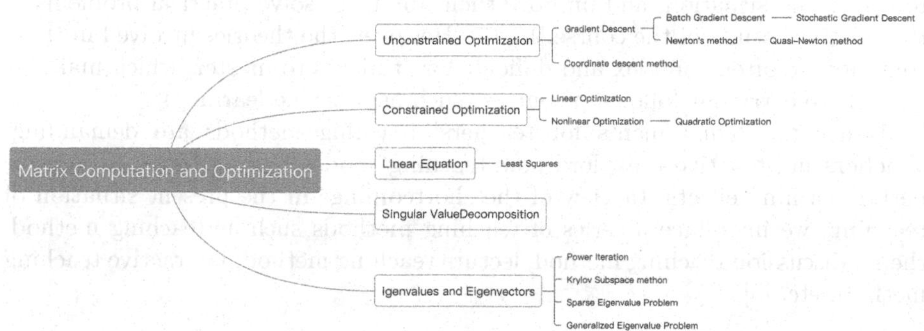

Fig. 2. Matrix calculation and optimization of course system.

The above examples fully illustrate that matrix computation plays an important role in optimization. Matrix calculation and optimization can be taught together. This course is called "Matrix calculation and optimization" in this paper. The advantages of this course are: (1) it can solve the problem of insufficient time in the mathematics course; (2) facilitate the integration of the two courses. In the use of artificial intelligence methods to solve practical problems, we need to calculate the results based on data. This involves mathematical modeling, model derivation, programming to calculate the results, and so on. If the two courses together, students can easily apply the theory to practical applications, thus improving students' ability to analyze and solve problems.

4 The Reform of Teaching Mode and Method

The teaching of Matrix Calculation or Optimization will involve abstract concepts. There are three basic problems in matrix calculation [7–9]: (1) the solution of linear equations and the linear least squares problem; (2) singular value decomposition; (3) matrix eigenvalue calculation. While emphasizing the theoretical structure and practical value of these contents, we should also emphasize its most challenging aspects at present, such as how to efficiently carry out large-scale matrix calculations. Due to the limitation of class hours, it is difficult to teach so many knowledge points at the same time. Optimization is a commonly used mathematical thought and method of artificial intelligence. From a mathematical perspective, it is one of the basic research objects of applied mathematics [13,14]. It studies the mathematical theory and method of optimal selection for different problems, including optimization problems and modeling, mathematical basis of optimization methods, linear programming, nonlinear programming, multi-objective programming, heuristic intelligent optimization algorithms, etc. [15]. Students majoring in artificial intelligence, can master some basic methods of optimization and have a comprehensive understanding of the development of current optimization methods through this course. They can choose and synthesize effective optimization methods to find solutions to problems according to the actual situation, and improve their ability to solve practical problems in the practical study of the course [16,17]. However, the theories involved in these contents are often complex and difficult for students to master, which makes it difficult to carry out follow-up courses (such as machine learning).

Hence the requirements for teachers' teaching methods are demanding. Teachers must actively explore new teaching modes and methods to achieve better teaching effects. In view of the shortcomings in the present situation of teaching, we introduce a series of teaching methods such as teaching method, theme discussion teaching method, lecture teaching method, interactive teaching method, etc. [5].

4.1 Design a New Curriculum System

From the perspective of computer science and technology, we plan and research the training objectives of the course, and take the basic knowledge and key technologies of matrix calculation and optimization as the teaching content [18], so that the teaching content is closely linked with the practical application, strengthening the students' practical application ability and improving their theoretical understanding ability while strengthening the theory of higher mathematics and linear algebra. In the course system, we should first strengthen the teaching content of advanced mathematics and linear algebra, and we can consider the experimental courses of advanced mathematics and linear algebra. These courses can be taken as the first required courses of our course. Determine the experimental topics closely related to the practical application, and design the applied curriculum based on the actual situation of students. For example, in the experimental class, we can carry out comprehensive experiments based on optimization, so that the entire teaching content includes basic knowledge and related applications, and also includes the content of improving students' software programming and system understanding ability.

4.2 Example Teaching Method

The content of Matrix Calculation and Optimization is abstract. Hence, specific applications and related program implementation can be introduced in teaching to explain these contents. For example, 1) we can introduce the solution method of the least squares model based on specific data, and then introduce the rotation, reflector, Gram-Schmidt orthogonalization, and QR decomposition [4,7] of the matrix in the process of programming and calculating the final result; 2) we can explain the optimization method with introducing spectral clustering principle. 3) in order to obtain the final numerical solution, we can introduce the eigenvector calculation method based on Power iteration; 4) when explaining the conjugate gradient method, we can introduce the Krylov subspace [6] used to calculate eigenvectors, give the specific implementation code, and then introduce its application in principal component analysis. This example teaching method can stimulate students' interest and expand their ideas [19,20].

4.3 Thematic Discussion Teaching Method

Some topic-oriented methods can be used for heuristic teaching and classroom discussion [21]. During the teaching process, we can carefully design some problems closely related to the content of this course, and let everyone discuss these problems in the classroom to encourage students to put forward their own opinions or solutions [22]. There are some topic examples, the advantages, and disadvantages of random gradient descent; how to balance the efficiency and accuracy of eigenvalue calculation according to the application. Students first select the questions for their own groups, and consult relevant materials, then discuss in groups. After the discussion, every group should organize the discussion results into a course essay, and the teacher will give corresponding scores according to the quality of the essay. The general steps of this teaching method are: ① the teacher designs the topic to be discussed; ② teachers and students jointly analyze the knowledge points involved in the topic; ③ the students consult relevant materials within the specified time; ④ class discussion; ⑤ compose essay; ⑥ the teacher gives the discussion results.

This teaching method can cultivate students' ability to find, analyze and solve problems. In the process of consulting materials and composing essays, it can improve students' innovation ability, and also cultivate team spirit.

4.4 Lecture-Based Teaching Method

In order to deepen students' understanding of the course content and keep abreast of the latest developments and developments in these fields, lecture teaching can be adopted in teaching [23]. Invite senior professors in relevant fields to give special lectures on their research fields and achievements. Students can understand the application and cutting-edge content of technology in these fields from an engineering perspective, so as to improve students enthusiasm and broaden their horizons. For example, when explaining the knowledge points of gradient decline, senior professors' in-depth learning can be invited to give special lectures for students [24].

These three teaching methods mentioned above can cultivate students' innovation ability and significantly improve teaching quality.

4.5 Interactive Teaching Method

Matrix Calculation and Optimization is a highly theoretical course. This course has fewer class hours but more content, a large knowledge system, low relevance of each chapter, and strong practice and application. If we follow the traditional teaching mode, we cannot deeply introduce important knowledge points. In order to solve this contradiction, the course team adopts the flipped classroom teaching mode that combines online platform learning with classroom teaching. Strengthen classroom questioning and discussion [25], and cultivate students' ability to learn independently, find problems, explore problems and solve problems [3,26].

In flipped classroom teaching [27], the class is divided into three stages: before class, in class, and after class, which are the online learning stage, flipped implementation stage, and summary stage [28], respectively. (1) Before class, teachers should design learning objectives and assign teaching tasks according to the teaching content. According to the tasks they have received, students should clarify the teaching objectives, conduct online learning, and answer the tasks assigned by teachers online. Students are required to learn knowledge points and record them, as well as difficult problems. (2) In class, students should have group discussions on online learning content, they will be randomly divided into different groups with 3–4 people in each group. The discussion time should be controlled at about 5 min, and the time for students to ask the teacher questions should be about 5 min. Compared with the traditional teaching mode, this discussion process makes students become passive and active, and teachers play a guiding role in this process. The teacher assesses the students' learning knowledge and answers the students' puzzles according to their specific conditions. Then the teacher explains the key points and difficulties. (3) After class, the teachers summarize the content and effect of classroom teaching, and make a questionnaire to understand the basic situation that students have mastered. The students will display the results according to the teaching content to improve their interest in learning and cultivate their learning ability.

5 Practice Teaching Reform

5.1 Start Practical Course

Practical teaching is an important part of the course, which can deepen students' understanding of theoretical knowledge and improve students' ability to solve practical problems. "Matrix Computation and Optimization" is not only highly theoretical but also closely related to various applications. Therefore, in addition to classroom teaching, practical teaching is of great significance to the realization of the course teaching objectives and the improvement of teaching quality, which plays an important role in guiding students to acquire more knowledge from practice [29]. The practical teaching content of this course is mainly divided into verification-driven and design-driven. In verification-driven experiments, students mainly verify some knowledge through programming to deepen their understanding of the theory. Design-driven experiments are comprehensive experiments. Students need to solve practical problems based on the knowledge they have learned, and design corresponding algorithms and application programs. Through the training of these experiments, students can improve their ability to analyze and solve problems, and deepen their understanding of knowledge. Design-driven experiments are comprehensive experiments. Students need to solve practical problems based on the knowledge they have learned, and design corresponding algorithms and application programs. Through the training of these experiments, students can improve their ability to analyze and solve problems, and deepen their understanding of knowledge. For example, while explaining singular value decomposition, the teaching goal is to grasp commonly used singular value decomposition algorithms. After finishing this part of the knowledge, the students should be able to choose a suitable singular value decomposition algorithm to solve the image compression problem and use a programming language to realize it. Design a series of practical teaching links that are closely related to practical applications, which would help students to construct a deep understanding of knowledge, improve students' collaboration ability, give full play to their unique insights, improve the ability of logical thinking, analyze and solve problems. It is more helpful to cultivate students' interest in learning [30].

5.2 Strengthen the Construction of Online Resources

In view of the lack of content and slow updating of the textbook "Cloud Computing", we have introduced online resources for some important chapters, exercises, and experimental projects of the textbook. Students can find linear resources such as how-to videos for related content, and online materials that introduce the theory [31] for further study while reading the relevant content through the course website. The advantages are:

1. It's very convenient to obtain relevant content. Students could obtain the corresponding extended content as long as through the course website [32];
2. Compared with paper-made textbooks, the online content is easy to update and expand. Specifically, the latest research progress and classic papers in related fields are put online for students to read. Some mathematical theories can also be shared online. The mathematical derivation of some machine learning models can also be put online for students to learn;
3. For some important content, it is convenient to communicate and discuss, which could improve the teaching interaction between teachers and students;
4. Students can give feedback on the content of online resources, and teachers can also grasp the learning situation of students in time, e.g. Whether students are concentrated on reviewing;
5. The number of visits to each question can be counted to determine the understanding situation of students of the knowledge taught.

6 Conclusion

"Matrix Computation" and "Optimization" are core theoretical courses of artificial intelligence. The teaching content and teaching purpose are self-particularly. Therefore, teaching activities should be carried out according to their characteristics in terms of teaching content and teaching methods. According to the inner connection of the two courses, we combine them to teach the content of the two courses better and discuss the methods of teaching and practical teaching after the combination. Teachers should always keep updating teaching content and diversifying teaching methods in order to stimulate students' interest in learning, improve their thinking innovation and technological innovation ability, and ultimately improve the teaching quality of this course.

References

1. Russell, S.J.: Artificial Intelligence a Modern Approach. Pearson Education Inc., New York (2010)
2. Chunjing Xiao, H.Y., Li, J.: Exploration and practice of teaching method reform of artificial intelligence. Modern Comput. (2013)
3. Wang, M.: Exploration and practice of artificial intelligence teaching methods. J. Heilongjiang Inst. Educ. (2013)
4. Watkins, D.S.: Fundamentals of Matrix Computations. Wiley, Hoboken (2015)
5. Aixiang Feng, X.L.: Exploration on teaching reform of undergraduate artificial intelligence course. China Electric Power Education (2011)
6. Nocedal, J., Wright, S.T.: Numerical Optimization. Springer, Heidelberg (2006)
7. Golub, G.H., Van Loan, C.F.: Matrix Computations, 4th edn. Johns Hopkins, Baltimore (2013)
8. Boyd, S., Vandenberghe, L.: Introduction to Applied Linear Algebra: Vectors, Matrices, and Least Squares. Cambridge University Press, Cambridge (2018)
9. Bubeck, S., et al.: Convex optimization: algorithms and complexity. Found. Trends® Mach. Learn. **8**(3–4), 231–357 (2015)
10. Jiaofen Li, X.Z., Li, C.: Teaching experience and reflection on the basic course "matrix computing" for postgraduates. Educ. Teach. Forum (2020)
11. Shuangbing Guo, X.W., Dong, R.: Discussion on the teaching of numerical algebra in the training of applied talents. Math. Learn. Res. (2018)
12. Xinlong Feng, Z.Z., Rexiti, A.: Some experiences on the teaching of matrix computation. College Math. (2011)
13. Wenru Fan, J.L.: Exploration of the teaching reform of the course optimization and optimal control. J. Electr. Electron. Educ. (2022)
14. Dong, L.: Discussion on the teaching reform of the optimization method course in colleges and universities. Sci. Educ. Lit. (Last Ten-Day Issue) (2020)
15. Li, D., Chen, S.: On the reform and practice of optimization method teaching. Educ. Inf. Forum (2019)
16. Ren, H.: Suggestions on teaching reform of optimization and optimal control course. Educ. Teach. Forum (2017)
17. Cailing Wang, Y.S.: Reform and practice of optimization method teaching. J. Jilin Radio Telev. Univ. (2016)
18. Hongjie Lv, X.G.: Some reflections on the teaching reform of the optimization method course for postgraduates. Sci. Educ. Guide (2016)

19. Xuexue Fan, Z.W., Dong, C.: Application of inquiry example teaching system in diagnostics teaching. China Higher Medical Education (2021)
20. He, Y.: Cloud storage for resource sharing across terminals and platforms - taking the teaching of "internet and its application examples" as an example. Shanghai Curriculum Teaching Research (2017)
21. Fu, W.: The application of the interactive thematic discussion teaching method in the teaching of nurse-patient communication skills. China Higher Medical Education (2020)
22. Li, Z.: Research on the application of discussion-based teaching method. Academic Theory (2015)
23. J. Q. S. L. S. C., Mu, L., Zhou, T.: Effects and problems of lecture-based teaching practice - take the course "new progress and research methods of geotechnical engineering research" as an example. J. Multimed. Netw. Teach. China (First Decade) (2021)
24. Jiang, N.: Preliminary study on lecture-based teaching mode - taking undergraduate environmental chemistry course as an example. Gansu Sci. Technol. (2020)
25. Cheng, Y.: Reflection and practice of interactive teaching design in smart classroom environment. J. Baise Univ. (2022)
26. Zhang, L.: Practice and reflection on the online interactive teaching mode of "spoc+qq group". J. China Multimed. Netw. Teach. (2022)
27. Z. W. W. L., Zhang, C., Chu, D.: On the reform of flipped classroom teaching - from connotation, and design to organization and implementation and key points analysis. Softw. Guide (2022)
28. Lu Zhao, J.L.: Exploring the teaching reform and practice of application-oriented colleges and universities under the mixed teaching mode of mooc+flipped classroom. Sci. Consult. (2022)
29. W. L. Z. S. J. L., Zhang, Q., Yue, D.: Research on the mixed teaching reform of practical courses under the framework of "gender once". Exp. Sci. Technol. (2022)
30. P. G., Tang, Y.: Research on the construction of practical curriculum of preschool education major in higher vocational colleges based on results-oriented education. Educ. Theory Practice (2022)
31. Dong, F.: Research on the innovation path of collaborative online resources for mixed courses in colleges and universities. Green Sci. Technol. (2022)
32. Gui, F.: Discussion on the construction of online and offline hybrid "golden course" curriculum resources - taking the course "interactive interface design" as an example. 2022 Collected Papers of Chongqing Forum on Education (2022)

Improved Spotted Hyena Optimizer Fused with Multiple Strategies

Chunhui Mo[1], Xiaofeng Wang[1,2](✉), and Lin Zhang[1]

[1] College of Computer Science and Engineering, North Minzu University, Yinchuan 750021, China
xfwang@nmu.edu.cn

[2] Ningxia Key Laboratory of Information and Big Data Processing, North Minzu University, Yinchuan 750021, China

Abstract. Aiming at the shortcomings of spotted hyena optimizer, such as slow convergence speed, low searching accuracy and easy to fall into local optimal, this paper proposes an improved spotted hyena optimization algorithm (OWSHO) integrating multiple strategies. The reverse population is constructed by using the Opposition-Based Learning strategy to increase the diversity of the population and further improve the convergence speed of the algorithm. At the same time, the spiral exploration mechanism of whale optimization algorithm is combined to enhance the ability of exploring unknown regions and improve the global search performance of the algorithm. Then adaptive weight strategy is introduced to balance and improve the global exploration and local development ability of the algorithm. In this paper, 8 benchmark functions of CEC test set are used for simulation experiments, and compared with 3 heuristic algorithms, the test results show that: The improved spotted hyena optimization algorithm based on the combination of reverse learning, spiral exploration mechanism and adaptive weight strategy has a great improvement in the search accuracy and convergence speed, and gets rid of the local optimal to a certain extent, which proves the effectiveness and advancement of the algorithm.

Keywords: Spotted Hyena Optimizer · Whale optimization algorithm · Opposition-based learning · Spiral exploration · Adaptive weight

1 Introduction

Spotted Hyena Optimizer (SHO) algorithm [1] is a swarm intelligence optimization algorithm proposed by Professor Dhiman et al. The algorithm is inspired by the fact that spotted hyenas are a group social animal that uses multiple senses to identify relatives and other individuals, and rank relationships within the same race, with high-status individuals in the group being given priority for trust [2]. It is due to this cohesive cluster characteristic that spotted hyenas have a high success rate in group hunting. Once this algorithm was proposed, Professor Dhiman tested it with 29 well-known benchmark functions, and used them to evaluate engineering problems, concluding that the algorithm can solve problems such as low computational complexity and low convergence,

Z. Cai et al. (Eds.): NCTCS 2022, CCIS 1693, pp. 142–159, 2022.
https://doi.org/10.1007/978-981-19-8152-4_10

with equally good applications in industry [3]. Literature [4] introduced an improved SHO algorithm with a nonlincar convergence factor for proportional-integral-derivative parameter optimization in automatic voltage regulators. Literature [5] uses the idea of hybrid algorithm to combine the concept of adversarial learning with mutation operators, and to deal with more complex real-world problems by improving the exploration intensity of SHO algorithm. Literature [6] improves the SHO algorithm by using the adaptive differential evolution (DE) algorithm [7], chaotic initialization and tournament selection strategy to enhance the local search ability, optimization efficiency and solution accuracy of the SHO algorithm, and achieves good results. Jia et al. [8] combined the simulated annealing algorithm with the spotted hyena optimization algorithm to solve the feature selection problem, which is also better than other optimization algorithms. Luo applied the spotted hyena optimizer to deep learning for the training of feedforward neural networks. In training the neural network, experimental results show that the SHO is able to obtain the optimal accuracy value with the best parameters [9]. Spotted hyena optimizer has been applied to train the pi-sigma neural network using 13 benchmark datasets from the UCI repository. The STS-SHO method proposed in the literature [10] is an effective and trustworthy algorithm to solve real-life optimization problems.

The above research methods have improved the convergence speed and accuracy of the SHO algorithm, but due to the short time to propose the SHO algorithm, there are still few researches on the SHO algorithm and its application, and some existing applications are limited to industrial applications. There are still few articles on the improvement of SHO algorithm, and further research on algorithm improvement needs to be developed. In order to further improve the convergence speed, convergence accuracy and population diversity of the basic spotted hyena optimizer and optimize the performance of the SHO algorithm, this paper proposes an improved spotted hyena optimization algorithm (OWSHO) that integrates multiple strategies. The idea is to use the Opposition-Based Learning (OBL) strategy [11], aiming at the problem that the population initialization is too random, the population diversity is reduced, and the population is initialized to reduce the search time, thereby enhancing the convergence accuracy of spotted hyenas. Combined with the spiral exploration mechanism in the whale optimization algorithm [12], by introducing the spiral exploration mechanism of the whale algorithm into the spotted hyena algorithm, the exploration ability of the spotted hyena is strengthened in more dimensions. An adaptive weight strategy is introduced to effectively balance the global search ability and local depth exploration ability of the spotted hyena optimization algorithm. This paper uses the OWSHO algorithm to conduct simulation experiments on 8 benchmark functions in the benchmark test set CEC. The experimental results show that the OWSHO algorithm has stronger optimization ability and faster convergence speed than the comparison algorithm.

2 Spotted Hyena Optimizer

The spotted hyena optimizer is inspired by the spotted hyenas that live in the African and Asian savannahs. Spotted hyenas are highly gregarious animals, and they often hunt in packs. This highly gregarious pattern allows them to cooperate efficiently when hunting, maximizing fitness. Therefore, Dhiman et al. [13] described the hunting behavior of spotted hyenas as four processes: Encircling prey, Hunting, Attacking prey (exploitation) and Search for prey (exploration). The mathematical modeling of SHO algorithm is discussed in detail.

2.1 Encircling Prey

Spotted hyenas track their prey by relying on their own three steps of seeing, hearing, and smelling, to make judgments about the location of the prey, so as to surround them. By analyzing the social hierarchy of spotted hyenas, the spotted hyena closest to the prey is defined as the current optimal solution, and the positions of other spotted hyenas will be updated according to the optimal solution to achieve the purpose of obtaining the global optimal solution. The mathematical model of this behavior is represented by the following equations:

$$\vec{D}_h = \left| \vec{B} \cdot \vec{P}_p(x) - \vec{P}(x) \right| \tag{1}$$

$$\vec{P}(x+1) = \vec{P}_p(x) - \vec{E} \cdot \vec{D}_h \tag{2}$$

where $\vec{D}_h$ define the distance between the prey and spotted hyena, x indicates the current iteration, $\vec{P}$ is the position vector of spotted hyena, $\vec{P}_p$ indicates the position vector of prey, $\vec{P}(x+1)$ define the next iteration position vector of spotted hyena, $\vec{B}$ and $\vec{E}$ are coefficient vectors.

Whereas, the vector $\vec{B}$ and $\vec{E}$ are calculated as follows:

$$\vec{B} = 2 \cdot \vec{rd}_1 \tag{3}$$

$$\vec{E} = 2\vec{h} \cdot \vec{rd}_2 - \vec{h} \tag{4}$$

$$\vec{h} = 5 - x * (5/Mt) \tag{5}$$

where $x = 1, 2, 3, \ldots, Mt$, Mt is the maximum number of iterations.

Where $\vec{h}$ is the control factor, which decreases linearly from 5 to 0 along with the increase in the number of iterations, and exists to balance the search and exploitation of the objective function; $\vec{rd_1}$ and $\vec{rd_2}$ are random numbers of [0, 1]. By varying the values of $\vec{B}$ and $\vec{E}$, the spotted hyena can reach any position in the search space.

2.2 Hunting

During hunting, spotted hyenas usually rely on a group of trusted partners to identify the location of prey. To define the behavior of spotted hyenas more precisely, it is assumed that the best searching individual is aware of the location of the prey regardless of which individual is optimal. And the other search individuals form a cluster of trusted partners to move closer to the best search individual and save to the currently obtained best hunting solution to update their position. The following mathematical model is developed.

$$\vec{D}_h = \left|\vec{B} \cdot \vec{P}_h - \vec{P}_k\right| \tag{6}$$

$$\vec{P}_{\mathrm{k}} = \vec{P}_h - \vec{E} \cdot \vec{D}_h \tag{7}$$

$$\vec{C}_h = \vec{P}_{\mathrm{k}} + \vec{P}_{\mathrm{k+1}} + \cdots + \vec{P}_{\mathrm{k+N}} \tag{8}$$

where $\vec{P}_h$ is the first best position of spotted hyena. $\vec{P}_k$ is the position of other spotted hyenas. N is the number of spotted hyenas and $\vec{C}_h$ is the cluster of N optimal solutions. Where N is obtained by Eq. (9).

$$N = count_{nos}\left(\vec{P}_h, \vec{P}_{h+1}, \vec{P}_{h+2}, \ldots, \left(\vec{P}_h + \vec{M}\right)\right) \tag{9}$$

M is a random vector of [0.5, 1]; nos is the number of feasible solutions and computes all candidate solutions, similar to the optimal solution in the given search space.

2.3 Attacking Prey(Exploitation)

Spotted hyenas launch their attacks at the final stage of the hunt, and to accurately describe this behavior, the following mathematical model is defined.

$$\vec{P}(x+1) = \vec{C}_h/N \tag{10}$$

where: $\vec{P}(x + 1)$ saves the optimal solution and updates the location of other search agents according to the location of the best search agent. The SHO algorithm allows its search agent to update its location and attack prey. $\vec{C}_h$ is the cluster of optimal solutions.

2.4 Search for Prey (Exploration)

Spotted hyenas generally search for prey based on the position of the spotted hyena group located in the optimal cluster $\vec{C}_h$. Spotted hyenas move away from each other to search or attack for prey. The author use vector $\vec{E}$ with random values which are greater than 1 or less than -1 to force the search agents to move far away from the prey. When the convergence factor $|E| > 1$, the spotted hyenas are in a dispersed state, away from the current prey, and search for a more suitable prey location. This mechanism enables the SHO algorithm to perform a global search. Another alternative search of SHO algorithm can be achieved by changing the value of vector $\vec{B}$. In Eq. (3), vector $\vec{B}$ contains the random value of the random weight of the prey. In order to show the more random behavior of SHO algorithm, assume that vector $\vec{B} > 1$ takes precedence over $\vec{B} < 1$, which will help to explore and avoid local optimization. Vector $\vec{B}$ provides random values for exploration during the initial iteration and the final iteration. This mechanism is very helpful to avoid local optimization problems and is more effective than ever in the final iteration. Finally, the SHO algorithm is terminated by satisfying the termination conditions.

2.5 Algorithm Pseudocode

The pseudo-code of SHO's algorithm is as follows.

Algorithm1 Spotted Hyena Optimizer

```
    Input: the spotted hyenas population P_i (i = 1,2,.., n)
    Output: the best search agent P_h
1.Procedure SHO
2.Initialize the parameters h,B,E , N=30 ,iteration x=1 , Mt=500
3.Calculate the fitness(i) of each search agent
4. P_h = the best search agent
5. C_h = the group or optimal solution cluster
6.  while ( x < Mt ) do
          for i :=1 to size( P_i ) do
            Update the position of current agent P(x+1) by equation (10)
          end for
7.        Update parameters h,B,E,N
8.        Check if any search agent goes beyond the given search space and then adjust it
9.        Calculate the fitness of each agent
10.       if (fitness( x +1)<fitness( x )) then
                    choose the better solution and then update P_h
             else
                    keep the same as before
          end if
11.       Update the optimal solution cluster C_h about the optimal location P_h by equations
           (8) and (9)
12.   x=x+1
13.   end while
14.return best search agent P_h
15.end Procedure
```

3 Improved Spotted Hyena Optimizer

3.1 Opposition-Based Learning

The traditional spotted hyena optimizer uses a pseudo-random initialization strategy to generate the initial population, which means that the upper and lower bounds of the function are known and the initialization is done by taking random values in the range between the upper and lower bounds to generate the initial population. A purely random strategy generates populations that are very unsatisfactory in terms of population quality and convergence speed, and the generated populations are not evenly distributed, which can reduce population diversity. To address this problem, a Opposition-Based Learning (OBL) strategy is added to improve the pseudo-random initialization of the population. The Opposition-Based Learning strategy was proposed by Tizhoosh in 2005, introducing the concept of pairwise points and replacing random search with adversarial search

[11]. Since the probability that an individual and a reverse individual are close to the optimal solution is fifty percent each, by considering the reverse individual of each individual, the closer individual is selected as the initial individual of the population, making each individual closer to the optimal solution, improving the population quality and convergence speed, and enhancing the algorithm's ability to find the best. This strategy has been used in many optimization algorithms, and in the literature [14] a Opposition-Based learning strategy is added to the whale algorithm to perform global optimization problems. He et al. [15] introduced an elite Opposition-Based learning mechanism to increase population diversity, which was shown through experiments to improve the original algorithm's merit-seeking ability and convergence speed. Dexin Yin et al. [16] similarly used Opposition-Based learning strategy to increase population diversity.

In this paper, we define the ith randomly generated initial population individual as X_i, then the reverse population individual corresponding to X_i as $\overline{X}_i$, and the mathematical model is as follows.

$$\overline{X}_i = rand * (LB + UB) - X_i \tag{11}$$

where *UB* is the upper bound of the feasible solution, *LB* is the lower bound of the feasible solution, and *rand* is the random number of [0, 1]. By solving the reverse population, the optimal individual is selected after the fitness comparison, and the random population and the reverse population are combined into a new population Y, as the initial population of the optimization algorithm. As shown in Eq. (12).

$$Y = \begin{cases} X_i, f(X_i) < f(\overline{X}_i) \\ \overline{X}_i, else \end{cases} \tag{12}$$

The steps of the initialization population algorithm are as follows.

Step 1: Generate an initial population by randomization.
Step 2: Generate a corresponding inverse population from the initial population according to Eq. (11).
Step 3: In order, individuals are taken out from the initial population and the corresponding inverse population respectively, and their fitness is calculated by the fitness function, from which the individuals with better fitness values are selected to be placed in the final population.

3.2 Spiral Exploration

Whale Optimization Algorithm (WOA) was published in 2016, as a heuristic optimization algorithm simulated by Prof. Mirjalili et al. by observing the feeding behavior of humpback whales. The algorithm has the features of simple principle, easy implementation, less parameters and better global search. The WOA algorithm abstracts into three phases: encircling prey, bubble-net attacking method, and search for prey. The humpback whale captures its prey in a spiraling and decreasing radius in the bubble net attack, which is described as a spiral exploration mechanism in the WOA algorithm.

The traditional spotted hyena optimizer updates its own position by the position of the spotted hyena pack. The exploration ability of the SHO algorithm depends mainly on the random vector $\vec{B}$ and $\vec{E}$ parameter values to assist, and to enhance the algorithm to better find the optimal solution that meets the conditions from the vicinity of the current location in the given search space, the spotted hyena is simulated to move toward the prey in a logarithmic spiral. Based on the spiral attack behavior model of the whale optimization algorithm, the scope of the original spiral exploration model is further improved according to the dispersion characteristics of the spotted hyena search to better fit the hunting behavior of the spotted hyena and further improve the global exploration capability of the spotted hyena algorithm. Equations (13) and (14) are the spiral exploration mathematical models used to update the position of the spotted hyena.

$$\vec{P}(x+1) = \vec{D_h} d \cos(k) + \vec{P}_h(x) \tag{13}$$

$$d = R \times e^{kb} \tag{14}$$

where: $k \in [0, 2\pi]$, d is the radius of the helix per turn. The shape of the helix is defined by the constants R and b, , respectively ($R = b = 1$).

3.3 Adaptive Weight

Considering the effect of the prey attack process on the relationship between individual spotted hyena updates and spotted hyena position updates improved by spiral exploration, an adaptive weighting strategy is proposed in this paper, i.e., by letting the weights vary nonlinearly as the number of iterations increases by Eq. (15). The change of weights is used to enhance the local development ability of the algorithm, so that the algorithm can find the optimal solution more quickly and accurately, and speed up the algorithm's search ability and convergence speed. The mathematical model of adaptive weights is shown in Eq. (15).

$$W = \tan(x/Mt) \times (2/\pi) \tag{15}$$

The improved weight change curve is shown in Fig. 1.

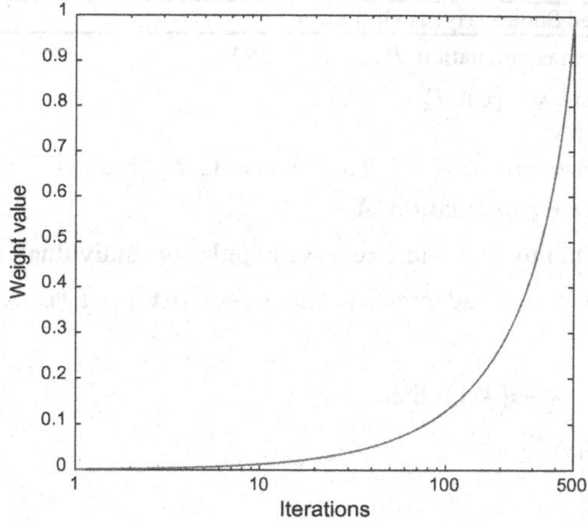

Fig. 1. Adaptive weighting curve

The algorithm search process is from global to local. At the beginning of the algorithm iteration, the algorithm conducts global search with small weights, when the target is unclear and has a small impact on the spotted hyena location update. In the middle and later stages of the algorithm iteration, the algorithm gradually enters the local search stage from the global search stage, when the target is gradually clear and the prey becomes more attractive to the individual, and the algorithm convergence speed and local exploitation capability are enhanced by gradually increasing the weights.

Therefore, using Eq. (15) to rewrite Eq. (13) and Eq. (10), Eq. (16) and (17) are derived.

$$\vec{P}(x+1) = (\vec{C}_h/N) \times (1 - W) \tag{16}$$

$$\vec{P}(x+1) = W \times \vec{P}_h(x) + \vec{D}_h d\cos(k) \tag{17}$$

where, Eq. (16) is the adaptive attack model. Equation (17) is the adaptive spiral exploration model.

3.4 Improved Pseudocode for the Spotted Hyena Optimizer

The pseudo-code of the spotted hyena optimizer incorporating the reverse learning strategy, the whale algorithm spiral exploration mechanism and adaptive weights is as follows.

Algorithm2 Improved Spotted Hyena Optimizer

Input: Spotted hyenas population P_i ($i = 1,2,.., n$)

Output: the best search agent P_h

1.**Procedure** OWSHO

2.Initialize the parameters h, B, E , N=30 ,iteration x=1 , Mt=500

3.Randomly generate a population X

4.Using equation(11) to generate a reverse population individual $\bar{X}_i$

5.Solve separately for the adaptation values $fitness(X_i)$ and $fitness(\bar{X}_i)$ corresponding to X_i 和 $\bar{X}_i$

6.**if** ($fitness(X_i) < fitness(\bar{X}_i)$) then

$Y_i = X_i$

else

$Y_i = \bar{X}_i$

end if

7.Calculate the $fitness$ of Y

8. P_h= the best search agent

9. C_h= the group or optimal solution cluster

10 **while** $x < Mt$ do

update the weights by equation (15)

if $|E| > 1$ then

Update the current position $P(x+1)$ according to equation (17)

else

Update the current position according to equation (16)

end if

11. Initialize the parameters h, B, E, N

12. Check if any search agent goes beyond the given search space and then adjust it

13. Calculate the fitness of P_h

14. **if** ($fitness(x+1) < fitness(x)$) then

choose the better solution and then update P_h

else

keep the same as before

end if

15.Update the optimal solution cluster C_h about the optimal location P_h by equations (8) and (9)

16. x=x+1

17. **end while**

18.return best search agent P_h

19.**end Procedure**

The improved algorithm flow chart is shown in Fig. 2.

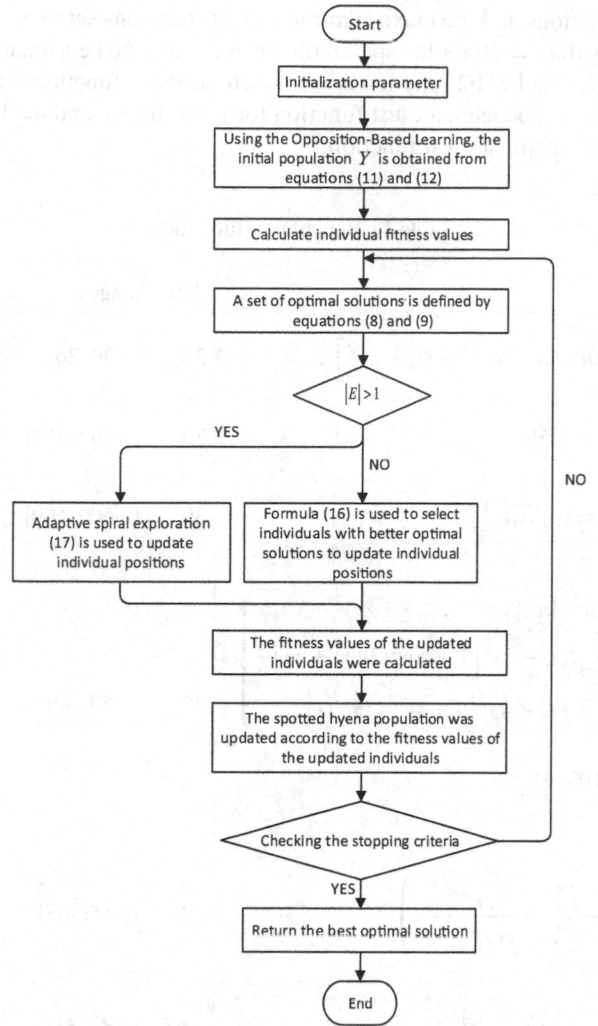

Fig. 2. Improved algorithm flow chart

4 Experiments and Performance Analysis

4.1 Experimental Environment and Parameter Settings

In this paper, a total of eight CEC test functions of three types are selected for simulation experiments from several swarm intelligence optimization algorithms literature [17–20].The experimental environment is MATLAB R2017b, 64-bit Windows 10, and the processor type is Intel Core(TM) m5-6Y54.In order to reduce the influence of random factors and to more reasonably determine the performance strength of different intelligent optimization algorithms, this paper conducts 30 independent experiments on the objective function using each algorithm in the same experimental environment, with the number of populations and the maximum number of iterations set to $N = 30$ and $Mt =$ 500,r espectively,d im $= 30$ for the spatial dimension. And the benchmark functions are shown in Table 1. The F1–F2 function is the benchmark test function for unimodal, the F3–F4 function is the benchmark test function for multimodal, and the F5–F8 function is the compound benchmark test function.

Table 1. Benchmark functions

Functions	dim	range	Optimal value
$F_1(x) = \sum_{i=1}^{n-1} \left[100(x_{i+1} - x_i^2)^2 + (x_i - 1)^2\right]$	30	[−30, 30]	0
$F_2(x) = \sum_{i=1}^{n} ([x_i + 0.5])^2$	30	[−100, 100]	0
$F_3(x) = \sum_{i=1}^{n} -x_i \sin(\sqrt{\lvert x_i \rvert})$	30	[−500, 500]	−12569.4
$F_4(x) = 0.1\left\{\begin{array}{l}\sin^2(3\pi x_1)+ \\ \sum_{i=1}^{n} (x_i - 1)^2\left[1 + \sin^2(3\pi x_i + 1)\right]+ \\ (x_n + 1)^2\left[1 + \sin^2(2\pi x_n)\right]\end{array}\right\} + \sum_{i=1}^{n} u(x_i, 5, 100, 4)$	30	[−50, 50]	0
$F_5(x) = \left(\frac{1}{500} + \sum_{j=1}^{25} \frac{1}{j+\sum_{i=1}^{2} (x_i - a_{ij})^6}\right)^{-1}$	2	[−65, -65]	1
$F_6(x) = \sum_{i=1}^{11} \left[a_i - \frac{x_1(b_i^2 + b_1 x_2)h}{b_i^2 + b_1 x_3 + x_4}\right]^2$	4	[−5, −5]	0.1484
$F_7(x) = \left(x_2 - \frac{5.1}{4\pi^2}x_1^2 + \frac{5}{\pi}x_1 - 6\right)^2 + 10\left(1 - \frac{1}{8\pi}\right)\cos x_1 + 10$	2	[−5, -5]	0.3
$F_8(x) = -\sum_{i=1}^{4} c_i \exp\left(-\sum_{j=1}^{3} a_{ij}(x_j - p_{ij})^2\right)$	3	[1, 3]	−3

4.2 Experimental Results and Analysis

For the eight benchmark test functions selected from the CEC test functions, the algorithm calculates the mean, standard deviation, best and worst values of the solution as the evaluation criteria of the algorithm. The mean value is used to reflect the accuracy of the optimization of the algorithm, the standard deviation reflects the stability and robustness of the algorithm, and the best and worst values reflect the quality of the solution. The data format is set to 0.0000E+00.

Experimental Accuracy. In order to verify the accuracy of the improved algorithm OWSHO, this paper starts from the idea of comparing with the basic algorithm, and the basic SHO algorithm is selected for comparison. The basic WOA algorithm is selected to compare the performance of the unimproved whale algorithm, and the classical heuristic algorithm particle swarm algorithm (PSO) [21, 22] is selected for comparison experiments. Thirty experiments were conducted on them under the same experimental environment, and the results of these 30 experiments were averaged, the standard deviation was obtained, and the best and worst values were recorded. The experimental results are shown in Table 2.

Table 2. Test results

Functions	Evaluation metrics	OWSHO	SHO	WOA	PSO
F1	mean	4.1577E−01	2.8780E+01	2.7856E+01	2.8445E+04
	std	6.9788E−01	1.1189E−01	5.1495E−01	2.5688E+04
	best	3.8429E−05	2.868E+01	2.6801E+01	1.9411E+03
	worst	2.7940E+0	2.8983E+01	2.8775E+01	1.0493E+05
F2	mean	4.1577E−01	4.8763E+00	4.4381E−01	4.8413E+02
	std	6.9788E−01	2.2967E+00	2.1135E−01	2.8480E+02
	best	3.8429E−05	5.0892E−02	1.1394E−01	6.5601E+01
	worst	2.7940E+0	7.0084E+00	9.9452E−01	1.3900E+03
F3	mean	−6.5584E+03	−2.7532E+03	−1.0724E+04	−7.5019E+03
	std	1.8230E+03	7.1165E+02	1.8634E+03	7.6968E+02
	best	−1.1334E+04	−5.1983E+03	−1.2568E+04	−8.7974E+03
	worst	−2.8164E+03	−1.5338E+03	−6.5733E+03	−6.0840E+03
F4	mean	6.0567E−02	2.9516E+00	4.7559E−01	3.0321E+01
	std	8.3547E−02	2.2197E−02	2.2469E−01	3.3006E+01
	best	5.6856E−04	2.9126E+00	1.4822E−01	6.8846E+00
	worst	3.1461E−01	2.9940E+00	9.9308E−01	1.9113E+02
F5	mean	2.7385E+00	1.0077E+01	2.8665E+00	9.9800E−01
	std	2.9400E+00	3.1977E+00	2.8693E+00	1.1616E−09
	best	9.9800E−01	2.9829E+00	9.9800E−01	9.9800E−01
	worst	1.2670E+01	1.2670E+01	1.0763E+01	9.9800E−01

(continued)

Table 2. (*continued*)

Functions	Evaluation metrics	OWSHO	SHO	WOA	PSO
F6	mean	1.5287E−03	3.2004E−04	7.4572E−04	9.9638E−03
	std	2.8994E−03	5.9447E−06	5.6326E−04	9.2555E−03
	best	1.6827E−02	3.4134E−04	2.2519E−03	2.2553E−02
	worst	4.5038E−04	3.1242E−04	3.1358E−04	9.0046E−04
F7	mean	4.2143E−01	5.4572E−01	3.9790E−01	6.0393E−01
	std	8.0641E−02	3.8946E−01	2.4220E−05	5.2528E−01
	best	3.9798E−01	3.9790E−01	3.9789E−01	3.9789E−01
	worst	8.5222E−01	2.2083E+00	3.9802E−01	1.9431E+00
F8	mean	−3.6721E+00	−3.7877E+00	−3.8547E+00	−3.8615E+00
	std	9.3504E−02	7.8892E−02	1.6366E−02	2.8049E−03
	best	−3.5072E+00	−3.4693E+00	−3.7863E+00	−3.8549E+00
	worst	−3.8507E+00	−3.8576E+00	−3.8628E+00	−3.8628E+00

The results in Table 2 show that for the unimodal benchmark test functions F1–F2, the solution accuracy of the OWSHO algorithm is closer to the optimal value than the other three algorithms, and the standard deviation of the OWSHO algorithm is also smaller, indicating that the OWSHO algorithm has better stability in solving the unimodal benchmark test functions. In solving the multimodal benchmark functions F3–F4, the OWSHO algorithm has better solution accuracy than the SHO algorithm in solving the F3 benchmark functions, but it is slightly deficient compared with the WOA algorithm and PSO algorithm. In solving the state benchmark function F4, OWSHO has the best solution accuracy compared to the other three algorithms, WOA is the next best, and SHO and PSO have the worst performance. Through the standard deviation comparison of the F4 function, OWSHO also performs quite well in terms of algorithm stability; in solving the composite modal benchmark test functions F5–F8, for solving the composite modal benchmark functions F5–F6, it can be seen through the average value that OWSHO is slightly inferior to the PSO algorithm in terms of solution accuracy, but is closer to the optimal value than SHO and WOA, especially compared with the SHO algorithm, the OWSHO algorithm has significantly improved solution accuracy. For solving the composite modal reference function F7, the average value shows that the OWSHO and WOA algorithms are closer to the optimal value and have better algorithm stability, while SHO and PSO are slightly worse in terms of solution accuracy and stability. For solving the composite modal reference function F8, the accuracy of the OWSHO algorithm is better than the other three algorithms. The above analysis shows that the improved algorithm OWSHO has obvious improvement over SHO algorithm in terms of solution accuracy and algorithm stability, and the OWSHO algorithm does not differ much from other algorithms in the individual test functions of multimodal benchmark test and composite modal benchmark test. In summary: OWSHO algorithm has good global search capability and stability.

Convergence Analysis. The stability of the OWSHO algorithm can be judged by the analysis of the above table, but its convergence cannot be compared. In order to understand the OWSHO algorithm more deeply, this paper uses each optimization algorithm to iteratively solve the optimal value of the same objective function under the same experimental environment, as shown in Fig. 3. Figure 3(a) and Fig. 3(b) show the convergence plots of the benchmark test functions F1 and F2 for the unimodal state. From Fig. 3(a), it can be seen that OWSHO converges with the highest accuracy and PSO comes second. Compared with the other three algorithms, OWSHO is the first to complete the convergence and obtain the optimal value. From Fig. 3(b), we can see that PSO has the highest convergence accuracy and OWSHO is the second, and compared with the other three algorithms, OWSHO is the first to complete convergence and obtain the optimal value. Figure 3(c) and Fig. 3(d) show the convergence curves of the benchmark test functions F3 and F4 for multimodal. The convergence accuracy of OWSHO in Fig. 3(c) is the smallest, and the convergence accuracy of OWSHO in Fig. 3(d) is slightly smaller than that of PSO, but OWSHO converges faster and completes the convergence first. Figure 3(e)–Fig. 3(h) shows the convergence curves of the composite modal benchmark

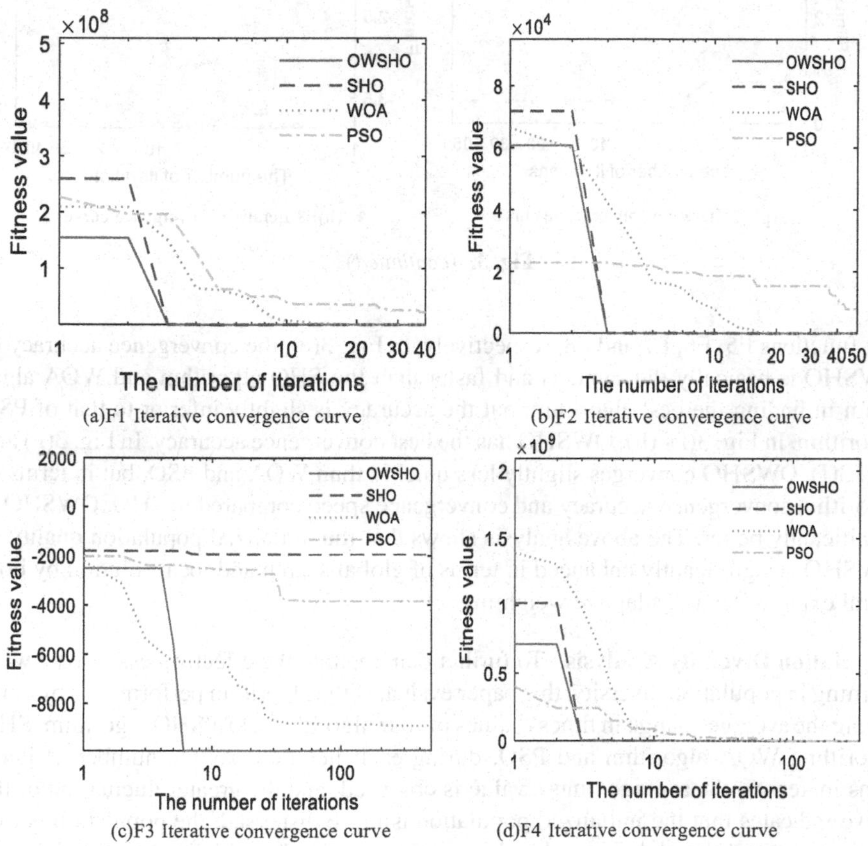

Fig. 3. Test function convergence curve

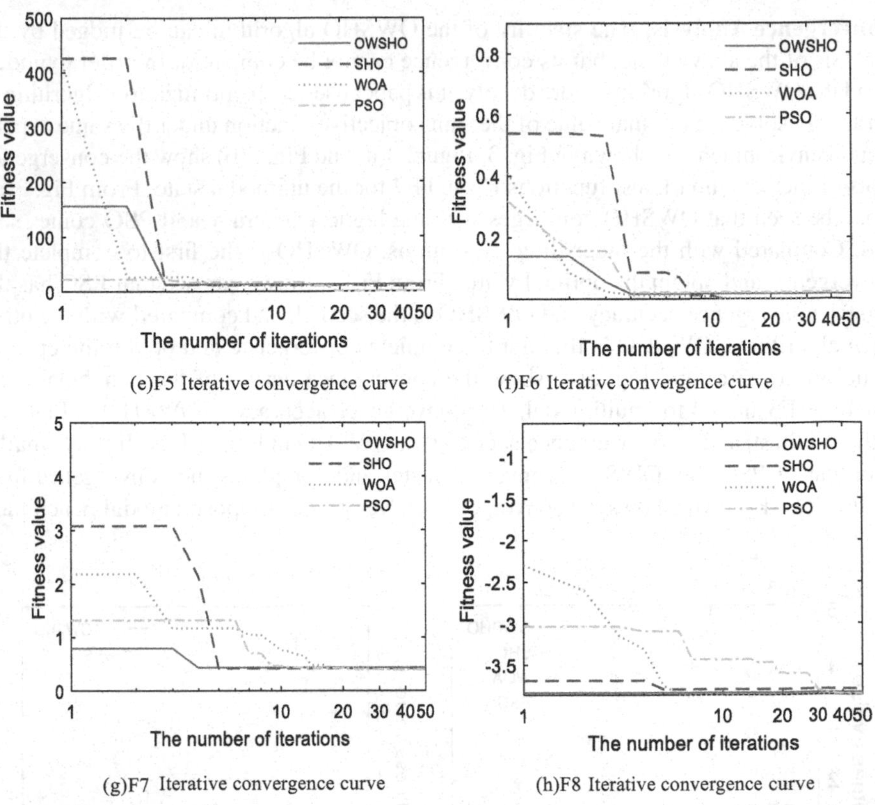

(e)F5 Iterative convergence curve

(f)F6 Iterative convergence curve

(g)F7 Iterative convergence curve

(h)F8 Iterative convergence curve

Fig. 3. (*continued*)

test functions F5, F6, F7 and F8, respectively. In Fig. 3(e), the convergence accuracy of OWSHO is basically the same as and faster than the SHO algorithm and WOA algorithm in finding the best algorithm, but the accuracy is slightly inferior to that of PSO algorithm. In Fig. 3(f)–(h), OWSHO has the best convergence accuracy. In Fig. 3(g) and Fig. 3(f), OWSHO converges slightly less quickly than WOA and PSO, but in terms of algorithm convergence accuracy and convergence speed compared to SHO, OWSHO is significantly better. The above analysis shows that the initialized population quality of OWSHO is significantly enhanced in terms of global search and local solution by both spiral exploration and adaptive weighting.

Population Diversity Analysis. To further demonstrate the effectiveness of backward learning in population diversity, this paper evaluates the algorithm performance by comparing the average change in fitness values of four algorithms, OWSHO algorithm, SHO algorithm, WOA algorithm and PSO, during each iteration. As the number of iterations increases, the average fitness value is observed, and the greater fluctuation of the curve indicates that the initialized population is more dispersed, the population is rich in diversity, and the global search is better. Conversely, the initialized populations are too concentrated, with poor population diversity and weak global search ability. Five

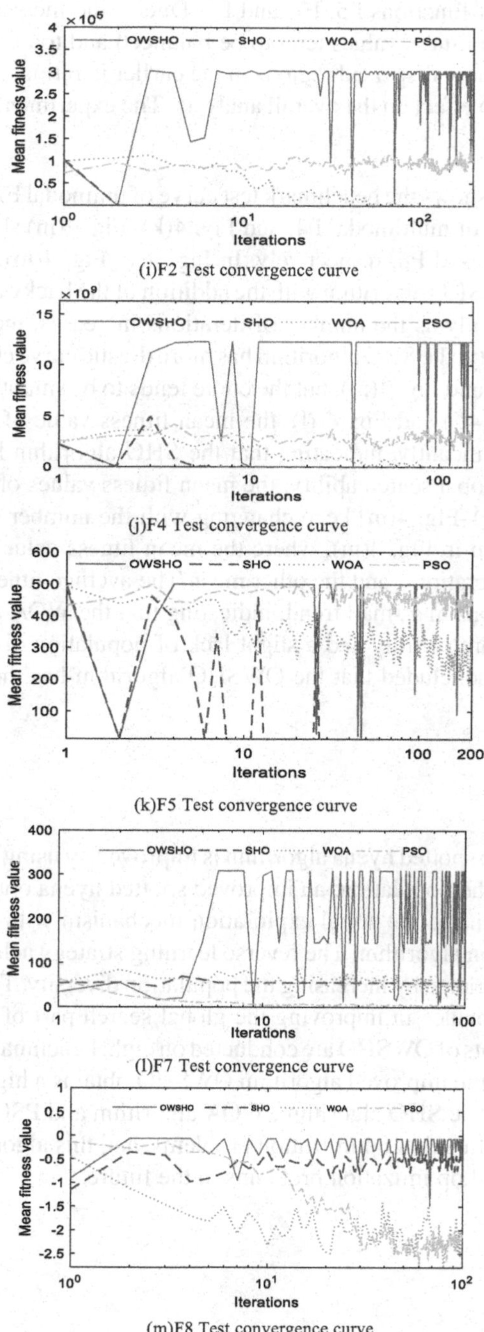

(i)F2 Test convergence curve

(j)F4 Test convergence curve

(k)F5 Test convergence curve

(l)F7 Test convergence curve

(m)F8 Test convergence curve

Fig. 4. Test function population diversity graph

benchmark test functions are selected here for illustration, namely, the unimodal benchmark test function F2, the multimodal benchmark test function F4, and the composite modal benchmark test functions F5, F7, and F8. Due to the increase in the number of iterations, the average fitness values tend to be balanced and too concentrated for poor visualization, so the more dispersed regions in the earlier iterations are selected here for analysis, which has no effect on the overall analysis. The experimental results are shown in Fig. 4.

In Fig. 4, Fig. 4(i) shows the benchmark test curve of unimodal F2, Fig. 4(j) shows the benchmark test curve of multimodal F4, and Fig. 4(k)–Fig. 4(m) shows the benchmark test curves of F5, F7, and F8, respectively. In Fig. 4(i)–Fig. 4(m), the average fitness value curve of the OWSHO algorithm with the addition of the backward learning strategy changes more drastically as the number of iterations increases, indicating its stronger global search capability; the SHO algorithm has more drastic curve changes in the first 20 iterations in Fig. 4(k) and Fig. 4(m), but the curve tends to be smooth after 20 iterations, and in Fig. 4(i), Fig. 4(j) and Fig. 4 (l), the mean fitness value of the SHO algorithm has not changed significantly, indicating that the SHO algorithm has poor population diversity and weak global search ability; the mean fitness values of the WOA and PSO algorithms in Fig. 4(i)–Fig. 4(m) keep changing with the number of iterations, except for the PSO algorithm in Fig. 4(m), where the mean fitness value changes drastically with the number of iterations, and the other mean The average fitness value varies with the number of iterations in a small trend, indicating that the WOA and PSO algorithms have weak global search ability and a slight lack of population diversity. Through the above analysis, it is concluded that the OWSHO algorithm has the best global search ability.

5 Conclusion

In this paper, the basic spotted hyena algorithm is improved by using a backward learning strategy to initialize the population; an improved spotted hyena optimization algorithm is proposed by combining the spiral exploration mechanism with adaptive weights in the whale optimization algorithm. The reverse learning strategy achieves the purpose of expanding the search range by increasing the population diversity. The spiral exploration part has good performance in improving the global search part of SHO. In this paper, simulation experiments of OWSHO are conducted on eight benchmark test functions, and the results show that the improved algorithm OWSHO obtains a higher search accuracy compared with the basic SHO algorithm, WOA algorithm and PSO algorithm, and can effectively deal with function optimization problems, and this algorithm can be applied to some combinatorial optimization problems in the future.

References

1. Dhiman, G., Kumar, V.: Spotted hyena optimizer: a novel bio-inspired based metaheuristic technique for engineering applications. Adv. Eng. Softw. **114**, 48–70 (2017)
2. Ilany, A., Booms, A.S., Holekamp, K.E.: Topological effects of network structure on long-term social network dynamics in a wild mammal. Ecol. Lett. **18**(7), 687–695 (2015)
3. Dhiman, G., Kumar, V.: Multi-objective spotted hyena optimizer: a multi-objective optimization algorithm for engineering problems. Knowl.-Based Syst. **150**, 175–197 (2018)
4. Zhou, G., Li, J., Tang, Z., et al.: An improved spotted hyena optimizer for PID parameters in an AVR system. Math. Biosci. Eng. **17**(4), 3767–3783 (2020)
5. Panda, N., Majhi, S.K., Singh, S., et al.: Oppositional spotted hyena optimizer with mutation operator for global optimization and application in training wavelet neural network. J. Intell. Fuzzy Syst. **38**(5), 6677–6690 (2020)
6. Jia, H., Jiang, Z., Li, Y., et al.: Simultaneous feature selection optimization based on improved spotted hyena optimizer algorithm. J. Comput. Appl. **41**(05), 1290–1298 (2021)
7. Storn, R., Price, K.: Differential evolution - a simple and efficient heuristic for global optimization over continuous spaces. J. Global Optim. **11**(4), 341–359 (1997)
8. Jia, H., Jiang, Z., Li, Y., et al.: Feature selection based on simulated annealing spotted hyena optimization algorithm. Appl. Sci. Technol. **47**(01), 74–79 (2020)
9. Luo, Q., Li, J., Zhou, Y.Q., et al.: Using spotted hyena optimizer for training feedforward neural networks. Cogn. Syst. Res. **65**, 1–16 (2020)
10. Panda, N., Majhi, S.K.: Improved spotted hyena optimizer with space transformational search for training pi-sigma higher order neural network. Comput. Intell. **36**(1), 320–350 (2020)
11. Tizhoosh, H.R.: Opposition-based learning: a new scheme for machine intelligence. In: International Conference on Computational Intelligence for Modelling, Control and Automation, 2005 and International Conference on Intelligent Agents, Web Technologies and Internet Commerce, vol. 1, pp. 695–701. IEEE (2005)
12. Mirjalili, S., Lewis, A.: The whale optimization algorithm. Adv. Eng. Softw. **95**, 51–67 (2016)
13. Dhiman, G., Kaur, A.: Spotted hyena optimizer for solving engineering design problems. In: 2017 International Conference on Machine Learning and Data Science (MLDS), pp. 114–119 (2017)
14. Chen, H., Li, W., Yang, X.: A whale optimization algorithm with chaos mechanism based on quasi-opposition for global optimization problems. Expert Syst. Appl. **158**, 113612 (2020)
15. Xiao-long, H., Gang, Z., Yue-hua, C., et al.: Multi-class algorithm of WOA-SVM using Levy flight and elite opposition-based learning. Appl. Res. Comput. **38**(12), 3640–3645 (2021)
16. Yin, D., Zhang, D., Cai, P., et al.: improved sparrows search optimization algorithm and its application. Comput. Eng. Sci. 1–8 (2022)
17. Yao, X., Liu, Y., Lin, G.: Evolutionary programming made faster. IEEE Trans. Evol. Comput. **3**(2), 82–102 (1999)
18. Kumar, V., Kaleka, K., Kaur, A.: Spiral-inspired spotted hyena optimizer and its application to constraint engineering problems. Wirel. Pers. Commun. **116**(1), 865–881 (2021)
19. Liu, L., Fu, S., Huang, H., et al.: A grey wolf optimization algorithm based on drunkard strolling and reverse learning. Comput. Eng. Sci. **43**(09), 1558–1566 (2021)
20. Zhang, X., Zhang, Y., Liu, L., et al.: Improved sparrow search algorithm fused with multiple strategies. Appl. Res. Comput. **39**(04), 1086–1091+1117 (2022)
21. Kennedy, J., Eberhart, R.: Particle swarm optimization. In: Proceedings of ICNN 1995-International Conference on Neural Networks, vol. 4, pp. 1942–1948. IEEE (1995)
22. Eberhart, R., Kennedy, J.: A new optimizer using particle swarm theory. In: MHS 1995. Proceedings of the Sixth International Symposium on Micro Machine and Human Science, pp. 39–43. IEEE (1995)

Regularized Framework on Heterogeneous Hypergraph Model for Personal Recommendation

Tingting Zhu[1,2], Jianrui Chen[1,2](✉), Zhihui Wang[1,2], and Di Wu[1,2]

[1] Key Laboratory of Intelligent Computing and Service Technology for Folk Song, Ministry of Culture and Tourism, Xian, China

[2] School of Computer Science, Shaanxi Normal University, Xi'an, China

{tingting_zhu,jianrui_chen,zhihui_wang,wudi2}@snnu.edu.cn

Abstract. Filtering-based recommendations are one of the most widely used recommendation algorithms in recent years. Most of which are based on simple graph to construct network model, and the nodes connected by edges are all pairwise relationships. In practice, some relationships are more complex than pairwise relationships. Moreover, collaborative filtering only focused on the relationships between users and users, items and items, users and items, without considering the relations between items and tags. To address these problems and improve the accuracy of the recommendation algorithms, we propose a regularized framework based on heterogeneous hypergraph, which integrates tag information into the recommendation system. Firstly, the hyperedges are built for each user and all items those are rated by the user, and then the similarity index between items in the hyperedge is calculated. Secondly, the relational graph between items and tags is constructed. Thirdly, we establish a regularization framework, and minimize the cost function for scoring prediction and recommendation. Finally, we verify the effectiveness of our proposed algorithm on Movielens-100k, Restaurant & consumer and Filmtrust datasets, and the diverse simulation results show that our proposed algorithm gains better recommendation performance.

Keywords: Hypergraph · Regularization framework · Collaborative filtering · Personal recommendation

1 Introduction

The advent of information era has changed people's lifestyle. Comparing with shopping in the store, people prefer online shopping because of its convenience.

Supported by National Natural Science Foundation of China (No. 62006149, 62003203, 62102239); Natural Science Foundation of Shaanxi Province (No. 2021JM-206, 2021JQ-314); Fundamental Research Funds For the Central Universities (No. 2021CSLY023, 2021TS035, GK202205038); Center for Applied Mathematics of Inner Mongolian (ZZYJZD2022003); the Shaanxi Key Science and Technology Innovation Team Project (No. 2022TD-26).

Z. Cai et al. (Eds.): NCTCS 2022, CCIS 1693, pp. 160–174, 2022.
https://doi.org/10.1007/978-981-19-8152-4_11

However, with more and more information appearing on the Internet, it is difficult and time-consuming for people to find their favorite items (products, movies, etc.) from a large number of items. The emergence of recommendation system is to address the "information overload" problem [1]. It can predict users' demands based on their historical information and provide recommendations [2], so as to reduce the difficulty of users' choices.

Collaborative filtering (CF) is a classic and widely used recommendation algorithm. Generally, it can be divided into two categories: memory-based CF and model-based CF, where memory-based CF also can be divided into user-based CF [3] and item-based CF [4]. User-based CF mainly applies the behavior information of user groups with similar interests to make recommendations, and its recommendation results are relatively social. Item-based CF is to recommend items related to the users' historical interests, and its recommendation results are personalized. Nevertheless, both of them have cold start and data sparsity problems. In order to address these problems, model-based CF algorithms are gradually concerned. In the model-based recommendation, the historical sparse data is applied to predict the rating relationship between users and items, and the items with higher scores are recommended to the target users. The model-based main methods can be divided into clustering-based algorithms [5,6], matrix decomposition algorithms [7], neural network algorithms [8] and so on. Among them, clustering-based CF algorithms divide users or items into different communities, and then calculate the similarity within the community for score prediction. Matrix factorization (MF) algorithms are popular CF technology in recommendation system. MF-based recommendations calculate the potential factors of users and items by decomposing the user-item rating matrix [9], which can improve the problem of data sparsity, and are widely used because of high speed and scalability. For instance, Wu *et al.* established a multi-objective low-rank sparse matrix decomposition model based on singular value coding [10], and the recommendation performance was greatly improved. Unlike matrix decomposition algorithms using the inner product of potential features for recommendation, neural networks are used to complete the complex interaction between features in CF [11], so as to alleviate the sparsity problem and enhance the interpretability of the model. Although the model-based algorithms improve memory-based algorithms to some extent, they are facing with the problems of speed and scalability. To address these problems, Su *et al.* proposed a parallel CF recommendation model based on the extended vector [12], which reduced the time complexity. Generally, in the previous recommendation algorithms, most of them are based on simple graph for network modeling. However, in the actual network, there are different types of objects and relationships, and some of the relationships are high-order [13]. If one simply casts a high-order relationship into a binary association relationship, one will lose a lot of useful information. To avoid these problems, hypergraphs were introduced into recommendation systems [14]. Zheng *et al.* leveraged hypergraph topology to describe and analyze the internal relationships of social networks [15], which took into account the higher-order information among nodes, and the results were significantly improved. The introduction of hypergraph into recommendation system works out the issue that simple graph can't express high-order relationship. Nevertheless, the existing hypergraph networks for recommendation only considered the relationship between users and users, items and items, users and items, and they did not consider adding tags information into hypergraph.

Based on the above work, in this article, we propose a regularized recommendation framework in view of heterogeneous hypergraph. It mainly addresses the problem of information loss caused by forcing high-order relationship into binary relationship in previous recommendation systems, and improves the performance of recommendation by establishing complex relationship among nodes. The main contributions are summarized as follows:

- **Constructing the heterogeneous hypergraph network.** In this article, we introduce the hypergraph model to better represent the higher-order relationships among nodes. We exploit a hyperedge to connect the user and all the items that he has rated, and then fully mine the relationship of nodes in the hypergraph, such as the relationship between items, the relationship between items and tags.
- **Adding tag information.** Although the previous recommendation system considered the relations between users and items, they ignored the relationship between items and tags. In this paper, we integrate tags information into the recommendation system to further measure some interactions by establishing the adjacency matrix between items and tags.
- **Modeling regularization framework.** In order to predict the score according to the degree of nodes, in this research, we propose a regularization framework for hypergraph. It makes a unified framework suitable for link prediction of complex data relationships, and achieves the better recommendation performance by optimizing the cost function.

The rest of this paper is organized as follows: Sect. 2 reviews the related work. In the Sect. 3, we mainly describe our proposed algorithm. The experimental results are presented in Sect. 4. Eventually, our work is summarized in Sect. 5.

2 Related Work

In this section, we briefly review the previous related work: hypergraph modeling, fusion tag recommendation, and regularization framework.

Hypergraph Modeling. Traditional recommendation systems typically used a simple graph to represent the interaction information between users and items. In practice, the relationship between objects is more complex. Hence, hypergraphs are introduced into the recommendation system [16,17]. Moreover, hypergraph was adopted in image retrieval to simulate the relationship between a group of objects [18,19]. Afterwards, higher-order relationships in hypergraph are also widely applied in machine learning, such as classification [20–22], and link prediction [23].

Fusion Tag Recommendation. In reality, tags information has a crucial role in improving recommendation performance. Tags were first popular in social networks, but now they are gradually applied to recommendation systems [24]. Due to the interation between items and tags, users may miss some information if they only focus on item or tag during recommendation [25]. The above work shows that integrating tags into the recommendation system can better mine nodes information and improve the recommendation performance.

Regularization Framework. At first, regularization is to avoid overfitting of complex models, and then it is gradually applied to various models to improve algorithms performance [26]. In addition, a unified alternating direction method of multiplier optimization framework was proposed [27] by combining the adaptive manifold regularization. Moreover, the regularization framework was applied to many fields of machine learning, such as manifold regularization [28], graph embedding [29], image processing [30,31], clustering [32,33], etc.

3 Proposed Algorithm

In this paper, we present an algorithm based on **R**egularized framework on **H**eterogeneous **H**ypergraph model for personal recommendation, denoted as *RHH*. We begin with an overview, and the overall framework is shown in Fig. 1. As can be seen clearly from Fig. 1, first of all, users, items and tags are input as nodes, then, a hypergraph network, relation graph of items and tags are established through these nodes. In addition, the hypergraph regularization framework is built based on the hypergraph network and relation graph. Finally, based on the regularization model, recommendation list is generated for each user.

RHH is described in detail and the organization is as follows. Subsection 3.1 introduces the construction of heterogeneous hypergraph network in detail. Then, Subsect. 3.2 shows the hypergraph regularization framework for rating prediction and recommendation. Subsection 3.3 gives the calculation method of items similarity and prediction score.

3.1 Construction of Heterogeneous Hypergraph Network

Network construction is significantly important in the recommendation algorithm. It can fully dig out the connections between nodes to improve the recommendation performance. In this article, we consider the following surroundings: m users, n items, and r tags exist in the recommendation system. In our network model, $G(V, E, w)$ denotes a hypergraph, where V is the set of nodes (i.e., users, items and tags), E is the set of hyperedges, and w is the the set of hyperedges weights. Each hyperedge $e \in E$ is a subset of V. The degree of a hyperedge e is defined by $\delta(e) = |e|$, that is the number of nodes in hyperedge e. If each hyperedge has a degree of 2, the hypergraph is simplified to a simple graph. H is the node-hyperedge incidence matrix, and its element $h(i, e)$ is 1 if $i \in e$, otherwise it is 0. If each hyperedge has the same degree, the hypergraph called

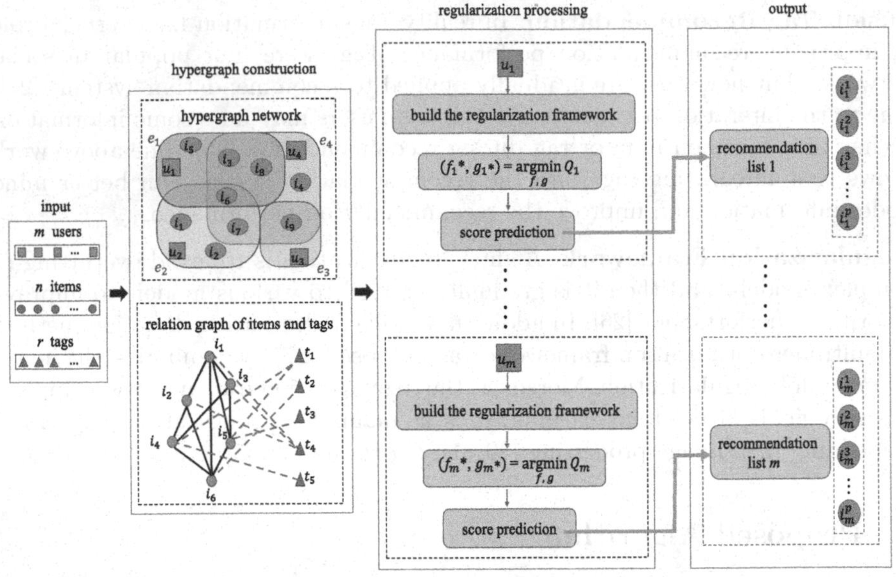

Fig. 1. The framework of the proposed method *RHH*.

be a uniform hypergraph. Based on the incidence matrix, the degree of node d_i and the degree of hyperedge $\delta(e)$ are defined as follows:

$$d_i = \sum_{e \in E} w(e) h(i, e), \tag{1}$$

$$\delta(e) = \sum_{i \in V} h(i, e), \tag{2}$$

where $w(e)$ is the weight of the hyperedge e, and its weight is 1. D is a diagonal matrix and its diagonal elements are d_i, i.e., $D^{ii} = d_i$. Thus, D_v is degree diagonal matrix of item, and D_u is degree diagonal matrix of user.

In the following, for each user, we create a hyperedge, which contains the user and all the items those rated by the user. That means, m users in the system correspond to m hyperedges in the hypergraph network. A simple hypergraph model is shown in Fig. 1.

According to Fig. 1, we find node set $V = \{u_1, u_2, u_3, u_4, i_1, i_2, i_3, i_4, i_5, i_6, i_7, i_8, i_9\}$, hyperedge set $E = \{e_1, e_2, e_3, e_4\}$. There are four hyperedges, among which hyperedges e_1, e_2, e_3 and e_4 are represented by blue area, lavender area, green area and yellow area, respectively. Beside, $\{u_1, i_3, i_5, i_6, i_8\} = e_1$, $\{u_2, i_1, i_2, i_6, i_7\} = e_2$, $\{u_3, i_9\} = e_3$, and $\{u_4, i_3, i_4, i_6, i_7, i_8, i_9\} = e_4$.

By applying these information, we establish the incidence matrix H of nodes and hyperedges. From the incidence matrix H, it can be easily seen which hyperedge each node belongs to and the degree of hyperedge is row sum in H.

In our network model, we have three types of nodes: users, items, and tags, which are represented as U, I, and T, respectively. To describe the relationship between tags and items, we apply a relation graph, which is shown in Fig. 1. In the relation graph of items and tags, solid lines are the relationship between items, which can be calculated by *Cosine* similarity or *Pearson* similarity, etc. In this research, we utilize *Cosine* similarity to calculate the edge weight between items. The dashed lines indicate the relationship between items and tags, and we exploit the number of times that an item is labeled by the corresponding tag to denote the weight of the edge. For example, in Fig. 1, if item i_4 is labeled 3 times using tag t_1, then the weight of this edge is set to 3. If an item has a strong association with a tag, that is, it is always marked by the same tag, then the item is likely to have the same score as the tag.

There are three types of information nodes in the heterogeneous hypergraph: users, items and tags.

Users (**U**) are the viewers of items, and they are encouraged to rate the items they have seen, which is an explicit means to obtain user preferences. Items (**I**) are the recommendation objects, and the ultimate goal is to recommend some items according to users' requests. Tags (**T**) are leveraged to mark items.

On account of our analysis of real datasets, the possible second-order or higher-order relations can be divided into the following four forms:

- E^1 represents the pairwise friendship relationships between users.
- E^2 is the pairwise relationships between items, and items may have different strength of connection depending on the genre.
- E^3 shows the relationships between users and items. Personalized ratings of items are the most explicit preferences of users. In addition, if there are no explicit ratings, the visiting or watching history can be regarded as implicit acceptance of users to items. It is worth noting that some connections are multi-to-multi or one-to-multi.
- E^4 denotes the markup relationships between items and tags.

3.2 Regularization Framework Based on Hypergraph

In this paper, we mainly discuss the score predictions and recommendations on hypergraph. Firstly, for each user, the regularization framework is established step by step.

If two pieces of musics are popular to many common users, they likely have similar scores, and if two people always join the same interest group, there have a high probability that they obtain similar scores. Both of the above two examples show that different items may have similar scores, if they are included in many common hyperedges. In order to express this case, the following equation is established:

$$\frac{1}{2}\alpha\sum_{i=1}^{n}\sum_{j=1}^{n}W_{ij}\left(\frac{f_i}{\sqrt{d_{ii}}}-\frac{f_j}{\sqrt{d_{jj}}}\right)^2, \tag{3}$$

where f is the item score vector, and W is a symmetric weight matrix. D_v is the degree matrix of items, which is a diagonal matrix, d_{ii} and d_{jj} are its diagonal elements.

Equation (3) mines items information from two aspects of similarity and degree. In fact, it's very similar to CF recommendation, where you can look for similar items based on historical information, and then predict score, i.e., similar items, similar scores.

In addition, there is a relation between items and tags. If an item has a strong correlation with a tag, that is, the item is always marked with this tag, and then the tag and the item have a similar score. For this issue, we define the following equation:

$$\beta \sum_{i=1}^{n} \sum_{t=1}^{r} A_{it} \left(\frac{f_i}{\sqrt{z_{ii}}} - \frac{g_t}{\sqrt{z_{tt}}}\right)^2, \tag{4}$$

where g is tag vector and A is the adjacency matrix of items and tags. Z_i is the diagonal matrix, and its diagonal elements are z_{ii}, i.e., the number of times that the item i is marked. Z_t is a diagonal matrix with diagonal elements of z_{tt}, i.e., the number of times that the tag t marks items.

Equation (4) further explores the correlation between nodes by establishing the relationship between items and tags.

Moreover, in order to prevent overfitting, the following two regularization terms are established:

$$\mu \sum_{i=1}^{n} \|P_{\Omega_i}(f_i - y_i)\|^2 + \sigma \sum_{t=1}^{r} \|g_t - s_t\|^2, \tag{5}$$

where y is the score vector of items. If an item has been rated, y_i is user's rating to the item i, otherwise y_i is the average score of the rated items similar to item i. Ω_i is the set of the items that the user i has rated, and P_{Ω_i} is the projection of vector $(f_i - y_i)$. In fact, $P_{\Omega_i}(f_i - y_i)$ is to find the errors between prediction scores and real scores for the items they have been rated. s is the original score vector of tag, and s_t is its element.

Finally, $Q_u(f, g)$ denotes the loss of user u in the system, and it is defined as follows:

$$\begin{aligned} Q_u(f,g) = \frac{1}{2}\alpha \sum_{i=1}^{n} \sum_{j=1}^{n} W_{ij} \left(\frac{f_i}{\sqrt{d_{ii}}} - \frac{f_j}{\sqrt{d_{jj}}}\right)^2 + \beta \sum_{i=1}^{n} \sum_{t=1}^{r} A_{it} \left(\frac{f_i}{\sqrt{z_{ii}}} - \frac{g_t}{\sqrt{z_{tt}}}\right)^2 \\ + \mu \sum_{i=1}^{n} \|P_{\Omega_i}(f_i - y_i)\|^2 + \sigma \sum_{t=1}^{r} \|g_t - s_t\|^2. \end{aligned}$$

Here, α, β, μ, and σ are four parameters, which control the relative importance of each part. They satisfy $\alpha + \beta + \mu + \sigma = 1$, and $0 < \alpha, \beta, \mu, \sigma < 1$. Our ultimate goal is to minimize $Q_u(f, g)$, i.e., $(f_u^*, g_u^*) = \operatorname*{argmin}_{f,g} Q_u(f, g)$. Meantime, to minimize $Q_u(f, g)$, the differences of Eq. (3) and Eq. (4) are as small as possible.

Lemma 1. *The matrix form of Eq. (6) can be represented as:*

$$Q_u(f,g) = \alpha f^T(I-B)f + \beta(f^T f + g^T g - 2f^T Cg) \\ + \mu(f-y)^T(f-y) + \sigma(g-s)^T(g-s). \tag{6}$$

$Q_u(f,g)$ can be minimized, the optimal result is denoted as:

$$(f_u^*, g_u^*) = \underset{f,g}{\operatorname{argmin}}\, Q_u(f,g). \tag{7}$$

In the following, we adopt analytic and iterative methods to obtain the optimal value f_u^*.

Theorem 1. *The analytical solution of Eq. (6) is*

$$g_u = \frac{\beta C^T f + \sigma s}{\beta + \sigma}, \tag{8}$$

$$f_u^* = [(1-\sigma)I - \alpha B - \frac{\beta^2 CC^T}{\beta+\sigma}]^{-1}(\frac{\sigma\beta Cs}{\sigma+\beta} + \mu y). \tag{9}$$

Although it is feasible to calculate f_u^* by analytic method, it involves a process of inversion in the method. As the dataset scale is large, it will be very time-consuming. In order to shorten the running time of the algorithm, we introduce the iterative method.

Theorem 2. *The iterative method to find the optimal solution of Eq.(6) is*

$$g_u(k+1) = \frac{\beta}{\beta+\sigma} C^T f_u(k) + \frac{\sigma}{\beta+\sigma} s, \tag{8'}$$

$$f_u(k+1) = \frac{\alpha}{1-\sigma} B f_u(k) + \frac{\beta}{1-\sigma} C g_u(k+1) + \frac{\mu}{1-\sigma} y. \tag{9'}$$

The iteration sequence $\{Q(f(k), g(k))\}$, generated by Eqs. (8′)–(9′), is nonincreasing.

Through simulation experiments, we find that when the number of iterations reaches 20, f_u^* obtained by iterative method Eq. (8′) is very close to that obtained by analytic method Eq. (6). When the dataset is small, the two methods are both feasible, and the difference is not big in speed. However, once the dataset is relatively large, the analytic method is very time-consuming because of matrix inverse calculation cost.

Since our datasets are not particularly large, the results of the two methods are very similar. In the following, we adopt the analytical method to find f_u^* to prove the efficiency of our method.

3.3 Score Prediction and Recommendation

In the following, we will predict the scores in the test set and recommend the first several items to the target users. In this article, *Cosine* method is used to calculate the similarity between items:

$$S_{ij} = \frac{\sum_{u\in L_{ij}} R_{ui}R_{uj}}{\sqrt{\sum_{u\in L_{ij}} R_{ui}^2}\sqrt{\sum_{u\in L_{ij}} R_{uj}^2}}, \tag{10}$$

where L_{ij} represents the set of users who have rated items i and j, and R_{ui} is the rating of the item i by user u.

In addition to the similarity calculation, the choice of the target item's nearest neighbor is also important. In the following comparison experiments, we analyze the influence of different neighbor numbers on the experimental results. Moreover, the possible scores for the unrated items based on proximity and similarity are predicted, and the prediction method is as follows:

$$P_{ui} = \overline{R}_i + \frac{\sum_{j\in N_i} S_{ij}(R_{uj} - \overline{f}_u^*)}{\sum_{j\in N_i} S_{ij}}, \tag{11}$$

where N_i represents the nearest neighbor of item i, $\overline{R}_i$ is the average score of item i, S_{ij} means the similarity between items i and j, $\overline{f}_u^*$ denotes the average score of user u, and P_{ui} represents the predicted score of user u for item i.

4 Experiments and Results

This section presents the details of our diverse experiments. To test the validity of our proposed algorithm, Movielens-100k[1], Restaurant & consumer[2] and Filmtrust-1[3]are tested in this paper.

Besides, in order to verify the effectiveness of *RHH*, we leverage the following seven indicators. First, the accuracy of the prediction score is tested by Mean Absolute Error (*MAE*) and Root Mean Square Error (*RMSE*). *Recall*, *Precision*, F_1 and ACC are applied to test the recommended accuracy. On this basis, we also leverage AUC to evaluate the system model.

4.1 Parameter Influence on Our Proposed Method

RHH has four parameters, i.e., α, β, μ, and σ, which respectively control the relative importance of each part in Eq. (6). To explore the influence of different parameters on the results of our algorithm, we conduct an experiment on the Movielens-100k dataset. Figure 2 shows the variation of *MAE* and *RMSE* values with parameters. The smaller *MAE* and *RMSE* values are, the better prediction.

[1] https://grouplens.org/datasets/movielens/100k/.
[2] https://archive.ics.uci.edu/ml/datasets/Restaurant.
[3] http://www.public.asu.edu/jtang20/datasetcode/truststudy.htm.

As can be seen from the Fig. 2(a), *MAE* values first decrease and then increase with the augment of α. With the rise of β, *MAE* value first increases, and begins to decrease when it is larger than 0.05. It is obvious from Fig. 2(b) that the larger the μ value is, the lower the *MAE* value is. However, with the rise of σ, the *MAE* value presents a trend of first increasing and then decreasing, which indicates that although the effect of tags on the prediction results is not as great as that of items in the hyperedge, it is still not to be underestimated. Since $\alpha+\beta+\mu+\sigma=1$, these parameters constrain each other. In order to keep the *MAE* lower, we take a comprehensive look at the four values. Figure 2(c), (d) show *RMSE* values change with parameters that are similar to *MAE*. In this paper, we set $\alpha=0.25$, $\beta=0.07$, $\mu=0.65$, and $\sigma=0.03$.

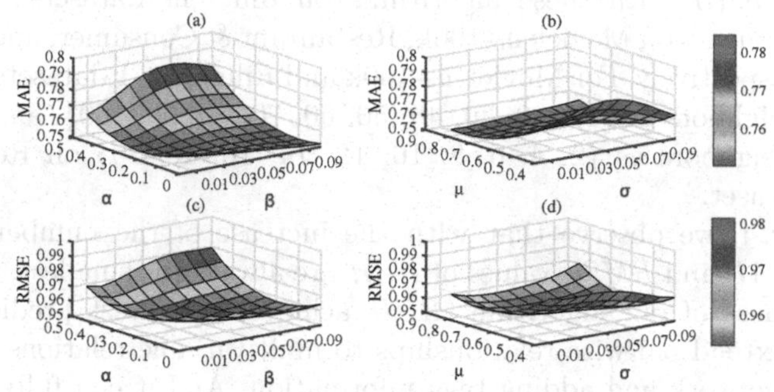

Fig. 2. Movielens-100k. Exploring the influence of different parameter settings on the performance of *MAE* and *RMSE*.

4.2 Tags Influence on Our Proposed Method

In this paper, we add tag information to the recommender system, and further measure several connections by establishing the adjacency matrix between items and tags. In order to verify that adding tags can improve the prediction accuracy, we compare the *MAE* values with and without tags on Movielens-100k, Restaurant & Consumer and Filmtrust-1 datasets. In Fig. 3, the red line represents the *MAE* values of *RHH*, and the green line denotes the *MAE* values of *RHH-without tag*. From Fig. 3, we observe that the *MAE* values of *RHH* are always lower than *RHH-without tag*, which also verifies the effectiveness of adding the tag information. In other words, *RHH* with tags is necessary and meaningful.

4.3 Comparing Results of Different Algorithms

In this article, we compare *RHH* with two classical algorithms (*CF-global* [2], *Kmeans-CF* [34]) and two state-of-the-art algorithms (*EHC-CF* [35], *BCDSVD++* [36]). Among them, *CF-global* is the *CF* without clustering, *BCDSVD++* is a recommendation algorithm based on matrix decomposition, *Kmeans-CF* and *EHC-CF* are both based on different clustering methods.

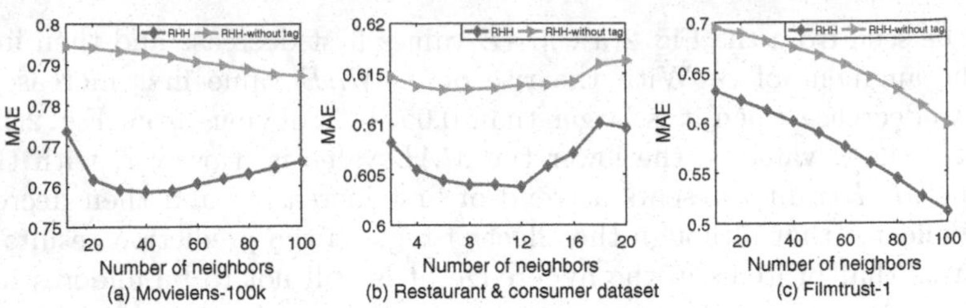

Fig. 3. Comparison of *MAE* values with and without tags on Movielens-100k, Restaurant & consumer and Filmtrust-1 datasets. (Color figure online)

To compare *RHH* with these algorithms on different datasets, we perform diverse experiments on Movielens-100k, Restaurant & Consumer, and Filmtrust-1 datasets, respectively. For Movielens-100k and Filmtrust-1 datasets, we set the number of neighbors as {10, 20, 30, 40, 50, 60, 70, 80, 90, 100}, and we set the number of neighbors as {2, 4, 6, 8, 10, 12, 14, 16, 18, 20} on Restaurant & consumer dataset.

From Fig. 4, we observe that with the increase of the number of nearest neighbors, *MAE* and *RMSE* values of *RHH* are always the smallest, which prove the effectiveness of our algorithm. *RHH* achieve the lowest prediction errors because we extend pairwise relationships to multivariable relations by building hypergraph network and adding tags information. And it can fully exploit the relations among nodes in the hyperedges.

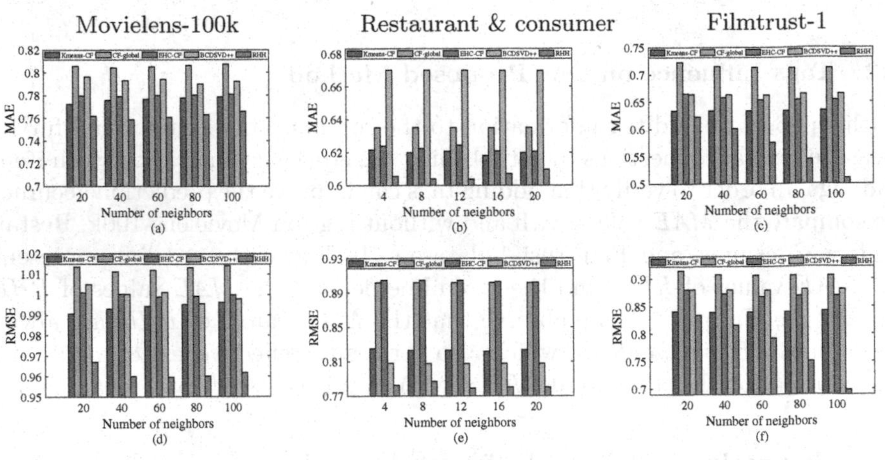

Fig. 4. Comparing results for three different datasets. (a)–(c) Comparison results of *MAE* for five algorithms. (d)–(f) Comparison results of *RMSE* for five algorithms.

Besides, to verify the effectiveness of the hypergraph model, we compare *RHH* with the other compared algorithms by *ACC* and *AUC*. As can be seen from Fig. 5(a), when the number of neighbors is more than 10, *ACC* and *AUC* values of *RHH* are significantly higher than the other compared algorithms, and increases with the number of neighbors. When the number of neighbors is 50, the *AUC* of *RHH* reaches the maximum value of 0.7765, which is greater than the maximum value of other algorithms. *ACC* and *AUC* values also demonstrate the effectiveness of *RHH*.

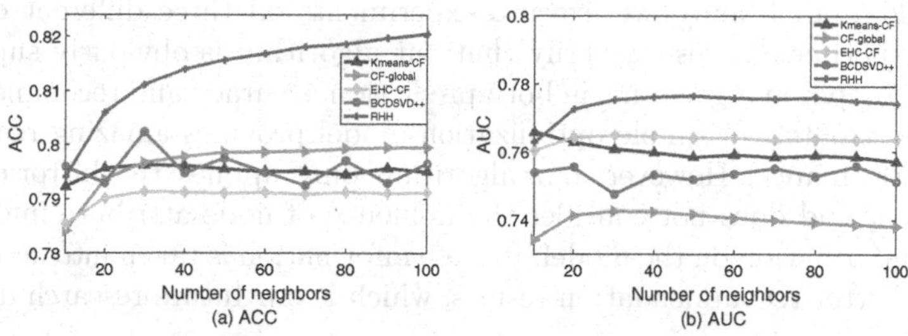

Fig. 5. Movielens-100k. (a) Comparison results of *ACC* of five algorithms. (b) Comparison results of *AUC* of five algorithms.

It can be seen from Table 1, the values of these three recommended indicators of *RHH* reach the optimal values. Since we consider the complex high-order relationship, we can achieve the best performance than these compared algorithm.

Table 1. *Precision*, *Recall* and F_1 values of *Kmeans-CF*, *CF-global*, *EHC-CF*, *BCDSVD++* and *RHH* on three different datasets.

Algorithm	Metrics (%)	Movielens-100k	Restaurant & consumer	Filmtrust-1
Kmeans-CF	*Precision*	86.1756	78.0560	84.8090
	Recall	71.1011	28.5300	75.7880
	F_1	77.9111	41.7330	83.8410
CF-global	*Precision*	88.3478	60.2400	96.6040
	Recall	72.9033	21.8860	65.8890
	F_1	79.8867	32.0740	78.3410
EHC-CF	*Precision*	81.9444	62.6620	92.9640
	Recall	67.6189	22.9090	75.1060
	F_1	74.0956	33.5110	83.0850
BCDSVD++	*Precision*	77.3211	53.6430	89.1030
	Recall	63.8022	24.1180	71.9880
	F_1	69.9133	33.2640	79.6350
RHH	*Precision*	**89.3956**	**80.7860**	**94.8360**
	Recall	**73.7689**	**29.5540**	**76.6180**
	F_1	**80.8367**	**43.2230**	**84.7570**

5 Conclusion

In this paper, a novel regularization framework based on heterogeneous hypergraph network is proposed. First of all, each user and all items rated by the user are represented as a hyperedge, and the similarity between items within the hyperedge is calculated. Secondly, we integrate tags information into the recommendation system and further explore the relationship between nodes by establishing a relation graph of items and tags. Then, a regularization framework is constructed to optimize the objective function for scoring prediction and recommendation. Finally, we execute experiments on three different datasets, and the experimental results verify that our algorithm is obviously superior to the other compared algorithms in both prediction accuracy and recommendation results. Fortunately, a simple optimization model provides amazing recommendation performance. However, our algorithm only applies the historical score information, and does not consider the influence of node attribute information and time information on the model. If these information is taken into account, we may gain better recommendation results, which is our future research direction.

References

1. Borchers, A., Herlocker, J.: Ganging up on information overload. Computer **31**(4), 106–108 (1998)
2. Wei, G., Wu, Q., Zhou, M.: A hybrid probabilistic multiobjective evolutionary algorithm for commercial recommendation systems. IEEE Trans. Comput. Soc. Syst. **8**(3), 589–598 (2021)
3. Zhao, Z., Shang, M.: User-based collaborative-filtering recommendation algorithms on Hadoop. In: IEEE International Conference on Knowledge Discovery and Data Mining, pp. 478–481 (2010)
4. Lv, Y., Zheng, Y., Wei, F., et al.: AICF: attention-based item collaborative filtering. Adv. Eng. Inform. **44**(101090), 1–11 (2020)
5. Chen, J., Wang, Z., Zhu, T., Rosas, F.E.: Recommendation algorithm in double-layer network based on vector dynamic evolution clustering and attention mechanism. Complexity **2020**(3), 1–19 (2020)
6. Chen, J., Wang, B., Ouyang, Z., Wang, Z.: Dynamic clustering collaborative filtering recommendation algorithm based on double-layer network. Int. J. Mach. Learn. Cybern. **12**(1), 1–17 (2021)
7. Ma, X., Dong, D., Wang, Q.: Community detection in multi-layer networks using joint nonnegative matrix factorization. IEEE Trans. Knowl. Data Eng. **31**(2), 273–286 (2019)
8. Xiao, T., Shen, H.: Neural variational matrix factorization for collaborative filtering in recommendation systems. Appl. Intell. **49**(6), 3558–3569 (2019)
9. Lee, P., Long, D., Ye, B., et al.: Dynamic BIM component recommendation method based on probabilistic matrix factorization and grey model. Adv. Eng. Inform. **43**(101024), 1–7 (2020)
10. Wu, T., Shi, J., Jiang, X., Zhou, D., Gong, M.: A multi-objective memetic algorithm for low rank and sparse matrix decomposition. Inf. Sci. **468**, 172–192 (2018)
11. He, X., Liao, L., Zhang, H., Nie, L., Hu, X., Chua, T.: Neural collaborative filtering. In: The 26th International Conference, pp. 173–182 (2017)

12. Su, H., Zhu, Y., Wang, C., Yan, B., Zheng, H.: Parallel collaborative filtering recommendation model based on expand-vector. In: International Conference on Multisensor Fusion and Information Integration for Intelligent Systems, pp. 1–6 (2014)
13. Bu, J., Tan, S., Chen, C., Wang, C., Wu, H., et al.: Music recommendation by unified hypergraph: combining social media information and music content. In: ACM International Conference on Multimedia, pp. 391–400 (2010)
14. Wu, W., Sam, K., Zhou, Y., Jia, Y., Gao, W.: Nonnegative matrix factorization with mixed hypergraph regularization for community detection. Inf. Sci. **435**, 263–281 (2018)
15. Zheng, X., Luo, Y., Sun, L., Ding, X., Zhang, J.: A novel social network hybrid recommender system based on hypergraph topologic structure. World Wide Web-Internet Web Inform. Syst. **21**, 985–1013 (2018)
16. Yu, N., Wu, M., Liu, J., Zheng, C., Xu, Y.: Correntropy-based hypergraph regularized NMF for clustering and feature selection on multi-cancer integrated data. IEEE Trans. Cybern. **99**(8), 1–12 (2020)
17. Du, W., Qiang, W., Lv, M., Hou, Q., Zhen, L., Jing, L.: Semi-supervised dimension reduction based on hypergraph embedding for hyperspectral images. Int. J. Remote Sens. **39**, 1696–1712 (2017)
18. Pedronette, D., Valem, L., Almeida, J., Torre, R.: Multimedia retrieval through unsupervised hypergraph-based manifold ranking. IEEE Trans. Image Process. **28**(12), 5824–5838 (2019)
19. Wang, Y., Zhu, L., Qian, X., Han, J.: Joint hypergraph learning for tag-Based image retrieval. IEEE Trans. Image Process. **27**(9), 4437–4451 (2018)
20. Wang, M., Liu, X., Wu, X.: Visual classification by ℓ_1-hypergraph modeling. IEEE Trans. Knowl. Data Eng. **27**(9), 2564–2574 (2015)
21. Yu, J., Rui, Y., Tang, Y., Tao, D.: High-order distance-based multiview stochastic learning in image classification. IEEE Trans. Cybern. **44**(12), 2431–2442 (2014)
22. Yu, J., Tao, D., Wang, M.: Adaptive hypergraph learning and its application in image classification. IEEE Trans. Image Process. **21**(7), 3262–3272 (2012)
23. Derdeyn, P., Douglas, K.C., Schneider, D., Yoo, C.: In silico discovery of ACC cancer biomarkers: applying link prediction to a purpose-built hypergraph. In: Big Data in Precision Health. https://doi.org/10.13140/RG.2.2.18721.35685
24. Guan, Z., Bu, J., Mei, Q., Chen, C., Wang, C.: Personalized tag recommendation using graph-based ranking on multi-type interrelated objects. In: Proceedings of the 32nd International ACM SIGIR Conference on Research and Development in Information Retrieval, pp. 540–547 (2009)
25. Zheng, X., Wang, M., Chen, C., Wang, Y., Cheng, Z.: Explore: explainable item-tag co-recommendation. Inf. Sci. **474**, 170–186 (2019)
26. Zhou, D., Huang, J., Scholkopf, B.: Learning with hypergraphs: clustering, classification, and embedding. Adv. Neural. Inf. Process. Syst. **19**, 1601–1608 (2006)
27. Liu, X., Zhai, D., Chen, R., Ji, X., Zhao, D., Gao, W.: Depth restoration from RGB-D data via joint adaptive regularization and thresholding on manifolds. IEEE Trans. Image Process. **28**(99), 1068–1079 (2018)
28. Meng, M., Zhan, X.: Zero-shot learning via low-rank-representation based manifold regularization. IEEE Signal Process. Lett. **25**(9), 1379–1383 (2018)
29. Zhang, Y., Sun, F., Yang, X., Xu, C., Ou, W., Zhang, Y.: Graph-based regularization on embedding layers for recommendation. ACM Trans. Inform. Syst. **39**(1), 1–27 (2020)
30. He, L., Wang, Y., Xiang, Z.: Support driven wavelet frame-based image deblurring. Inf. Sci. **479**, 250–269 (2019)

31. Shi, J., Liu, X., Zong, Y., Qi, C., Zhao, G.: Hallucinating face image by regularization models in high-resolution feature space. IEEE Trans. Image Process. **27**(6), 2980–2995 (2018)
32. Toli, D., Antulov-Fantulin, N., Kopriva, I.: A nonlinear orthogonal non-negative matrix factorization approach to subspace clustering. Pattern Recogn. **82**, 40–55 (2018)
33. Huang, X., Yang, X., Zhao, J., Xiong, L., Ye, Y.: A new weighting k-means type clustering framework with an l-norm regularization. Knowl.-Based Syst. **151**, 165–179 (2018)
34. Dakhel, G., Mahdavi, M.: A new collaborative filtering algorithm using K-means clustering and neighbors voting. In: 11th International Conference on Hybrid Intelligent Systems, pp. 179–184 (2011)
35. Chen, J., Wang, H., Yan, Z.: Evolutionary heterogeneous clustering for rating prediction based on user collaborative filtering. Swarm Evol. Comput. **38**, 35–41 (2018)
36. Cai, J., Lei, Y., Chen, M.: Efficient solution of the SVD recommendation model with implicit feedback. Sci. Sin. Inform. **10**, 1544–1558 (2019)

Hybrid Pre-training Based on Masked Autoencoders for Medical Image Segmentation

Yufei Han, Haoyuan Chen, Pin Xu, Yanyi Li, Kuan Li(✉), and Jianping Yin

Dongguan University of Technology, Dongguan, China
likuan@dgut.edu.cn

Abstract. The application of deep learning in the field of medical images has been gaining attention in recent years. However, due to the small number of medical images, the inability to generate them manually, and the high cost of annotation, it is difficult to train them. Masked Autoencoders (MAE), a recent hot new approach in the field of self-supervision, is based on Vision Transformer (ViT) architecture coding to improve the learning difficulty by adding masking to the cut non-overlapping image patches to obtain deeper image representations. In this paper, we employ three different small-scale pre-training datasets using MAE's pre-training method to pre-train and select the medical segmentation task as its performance test task. We experimentally find that the new hybrid dataset pre-trained with the training set of the hybrid downstream task and other datasets has good performance, and the results are improved compared to those without pre-training, and better than those obtained with a single dataset, showing the potential of the self-supervised method hybrid pre-training for medical segmentation tasks.

Keywords: Masked autoencoders · Hybrid pre-training · Medical image segmentation

1 Introduction

In recent years, there has been increasing interest in the application of deep learning to medical image tasks as it has yielded exciting results in many application areas such as radiology [14] and dermatology [12]. However, since deep learning tasks often rely on a large amount of annotation data, the sample data of medical images are small and cannot be generated manually; the sample annotation of medical images will in turn involve more expertise, and the annotators need to make accurate judgments on information such as the size, shape, and edges of lesions, or even more than two reviews by experienced experts. This increases the difficulty of applying deep learning in the medical field. Therefore loading pre-trained network parameters first and then fine-tuning them in specific downstream tasks is a commonly adopted approach for medical image tasks [13].

Z. Cai et al. (Eds.): NCTCS 2022, CCIS 1693, pp. 175–182, 2022.
https://doi.org/10.1007/978-981-19-8152-4_12

Self-supervised learning can learn representations using unlabeled data and then fine-tune the parameters on a specific downstream task. The mainstream self-supervised methods are generally divided into two categories: Contrastive-based methods and Generative-based methods [11]. Contrastive-based methods do not require the model to be able to reconstruct the original input, but rather expect the model to discriminate between different inputs in the feature space, e.g., SimCLR [2], MoCo [8]; Generative-based methods are mainly concerned with reconstruction errors, e.g., BERT [3] in the field of natural language processing: by capping a sentence's token for the model to predict, so that the error between the obtained prediction and the real token is taken as the loss. With the expansion of the Transformer framework from the field of natural language processing to the field of computer vision, the birth of Vision Transformer (ViT) [4] has brought a lot of attention to self-supervised learning methods based on Masked Image Modeling (MIM) [16], and recent advances in self-supervised learning have shown that the use of MIM methods in ViT as the backbone network of the model is very effective to maintain a large diversity in the attention heads of each layer [5]. Among the current MIM frameworks, Masked Autoencoders (MAE) [7] is one of the most effective ones.

Usually, due to the lack of large volume of medical image data, the datasets used in the pre-training process are mostly natural image datasets, such as ImageNet, but they are more different from natural images for medical images, and it is not appropriate to use models pre-trained on natural images for medical image tasks. It has been shown [10,17] that the architectural improvements of ImageNet do not lead to improvements in medical image tasks. And the emergence of MIM-based self-supervised pre-training methods gives us an idea: can the performance of medical image tasks be improved by using small-scale medical image datasets for pre-training and making them migrate to downstream tasks by means of self-supervised learning?

In this paper, we selected the multi-organ segmentation task on Synapse [6] as the downstream task, and used (1) the multi-organ segmentation dataset consistent with the downstream task, (2) the kidney cell carcinoma image dataset, (3) the 1:1 hybrid dataset of both as the pre-training dataset based on the MAE model, respectively. To ensure the consistency of variables, the selected data volume is 2211 for dataset (1) multi-organ segmentation dataset, dataset (2) is composed of 2211 randomly selected from the original dataset of renal cell carcinoma images with the data volume of 28040, and dataset (3) is a mixture of 1105 randomly selected from the original dataset of dataset (2) and 1106 randomly selected from the multi-organ segmentation dataset. ViT-B/16 was used as the backbone network for all pre-training tasks. TransUnet [1], which has the advantages of both Transformers and U-Net and is a strong and effective scheme for medical image segmentation, so we uniformly select it for fine-tuning and testing of downstream tasks.

Our study shows that the pre-trained model with MAE pre-training loaded with a dataset consistent with the downstream task achieves an improvement compared to the pre-trained model without any pre-training, while the pre-trained model with MAE pre-training loaded with a hybrid dataset not only achieves an improvement but also outperforms the pre-trained model with any single dataset, which demonstrates the effectiveness of MAE pre-training in small-scale data scenarios. This not only demonstrates the effectiveness of MAE pre-training in small-scale data scenarios, but also shows the potential of hybrid pre-trained datasets to improve the effectiveness of the task. Interestingly, we added a set of official MAE-supplied ViT-B/16 pre-trained with ImageNet1K for comparison, and found that the actual results were not as good as the first two (Fig. 1).

2 Methodology

2.1 Pre-training with Masked Autoencoders

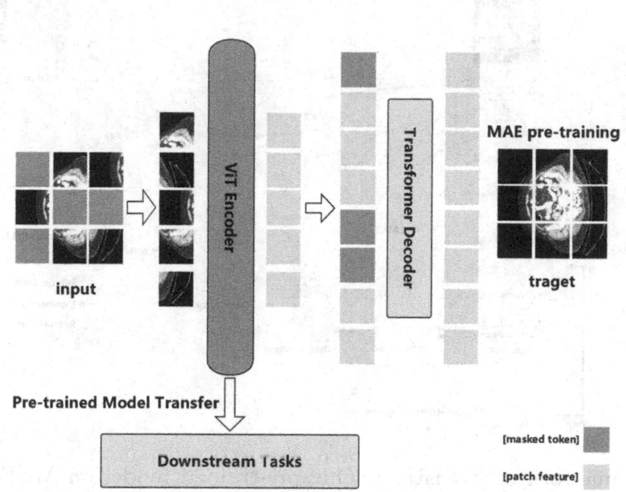

Fig. 1. MAE pre-training process. The initial stage divides the input image into non-overlapping patches, randomly masks some of them, and puts the other part into the ViT encoder to extract representations. And a Transformer decoder is added to reconstruct the image. If the pre-trained model is transferred to a downstream task, only the encoder part is needed.

MAE consists of two main components, an encoder for extracting features of the ViT architecture the other is a Transformer-based encoder for reconstructing images and acting on specific downstream tasks.

MAE Encoder. The MAE encoder uses the ViT architecture, but only works on unmasked images; like ViT, the input image is first divided into non-overlapping patches, and then the patches are randomly divided into visible and hidden groups. The MAE Encoder first encodes the image by Linear Projection, then by positional encoding, and then sends it to a bunch of consecutive Transformer

Blocks. But the encoder only operates on a small subset (e.g., 25%) of the entire set of image patches, and removes masked patches.

MAE Decoder. The MAE decoder uses Transformer architecture to input all patches of the image into the decoder, not only visible patches but also those tokens that are masked out, and all tokens are added with positional embedding in order to record the information of the position of the masked token in the image. Each masked token is a shared, learned vector indicating the presence of a missing patches to be predicted (Fig. 2).

2.2 TransUnet Architecture for Image Segmentation Tasks

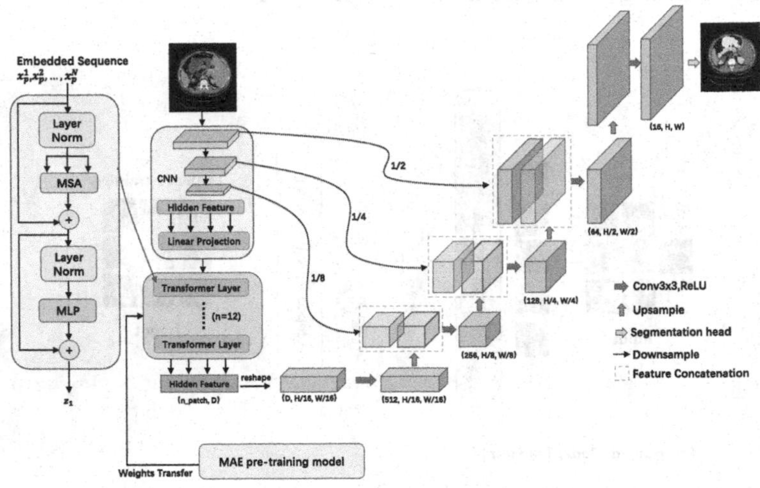

Fig. 2. The framework of TransUnet. Our pre-trained model on MAE transfers its weights directly to the Transformer block.

After completing the MAE pre-training, we migrate the pre-trained model to TransUnet for fine-tuning to perform the segmentation task.

CNN-Transformer Hybrid as Encoder. TransUnet uses a hybrid CNN-Transformer model to compensate for the loss caused by the Transformer encoder. The CNN is first used as a feature extractor to generate a feature map for the input. Then Transformer uses a self-attention mechanism to encode the tokenized image blocks from the CNN feature map for extracting the global context of the input sequence.

Cascaded Upsampler. In the same idea as the architecture of U-Net [15], cascaded upsampling (CUP) together with a hybrid encoder forms a U-shaped architecture. To decode the final segmentation mask of the hidden feature output, the CUP uses multiple upsampling steps, each upsampling block consists of a 2 upsampling operator, a 33 convolutional layer and a ReLU layer in turn, where the hidden feature sequence $\mathbf{z}_L \in \mathbb{R}^{\frac{HW}{P^2} \times D}$ is reshaped into $\frac{H}{P} \times \frac{W}{P} \times D$, and the cascade achieves full resolution from $\frac{H}{P} \times \frac{W}{P}$ to $H \times W$.

3 Experiments and Results

The segmentation task used in our experiments is the Synapse multi-organ segmentation dataset used by TransUnet, and we emailed the authors of TransUnet to obtain the processed dataset. The dataset was obtained by the authors from a total of 3779 axially enhanced abdominal clinical CT images (images of 512 × 512 pixels) using 30 abdominal CT scans from the MICCAI 2015 Multi-Atlas Abdomen Labeling Challenge, from which the authors randomly selected 18 CTs (2212 images) as the training cases and 12 CTs were used for validation.

3.1 Implementation Details

For all experiments, we did not perform additional data augmentation. For the MAE pre-training part, we uniformly used ViT-B/16 as the encoder for arithmetic considerations. For the downstream task, we use "R50-ViT" from TransUnet, a hybrid encoder combining ResNet-50 [9] and ViT. The input resolution is the default 224 × 224, the patch size is 16, the learning rate is 0.01, the momentum is 0.9, and the weight decay is 1e−4. The default batch size is 24, and the number of training iterations is 14k.

We mainly used three different datasets for the pre-training experiments, namely (1) the training set itself (Synapse) used for the downstream task, (2) the renal cell carcinoma (Rcc) dataset, and (3) a new dataset formed by hybridizing the Synapse dataset and the Rcc dataset in a 1:1 ratio, and the dataset information is presented next.

Synapse Dataset. The dataset is a direct processed dataset by the authors of TransUnet, with 2211 images in total, where the images have been transformed into grayscale maps with a size of 512 × 512 pixels.

Rcc Dataset. The Rcc dataset comes from the hospital with which our group collaborated. The original dataset contains 28040 images, and in order to maintain the consistency of the data volume with the Synapse dataset, we randomly selected 2211 images to form the Rcc dataset. The images are RGB three-channel images with a size of 512 × 512 pixels, which we grayed out.

Hybrid Dataset. The dataset consists of a mixture of Synapse dataset and Rcc dataset, which contains 2211 images, randomly selected from Synapse dataset and Rcc dataset respectively in the ratio of 1:1. 1106 images were extracted from Synapse dataset and 1105 images were extracted from Rcc dataset, all of which are grayscale images, and all of which are 512 × 512 pixels in size (Fig. 3).

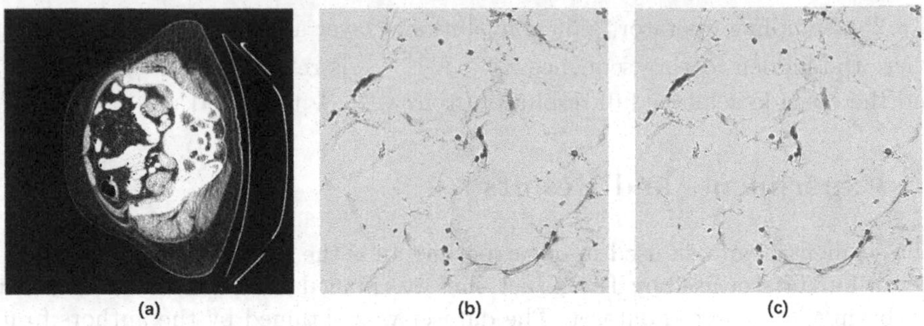

Fig. 3. (a) Image in the Synapse dataset (b) Image of the Rcc dataset extracted from the Original dataset (c) Grayed-out image in the Rcc dataset.

3.2 Results

To verify the performance of pre-training with different parameter settings, we conducted several sets of experiments in terms of epoch rounds, batch size, and dataset type. From the results of the experiments, the Rcc dataset achieves the best result of 76.28% DSC after increasing the number of epochs to 600 epochs, while the effect of batch size on the results is more prominent in the Synapse dataset, and after training 400 epochs with a batch size of 16 The Hybrid dataset was trained with the parameters of the best training results for the Synapse and Rcc datasets respectively, and the results were not satisfactory at 75.42% DSC, and 75.04% DSC respectively. After trying to train 400 epochs with a batch size of 16 using the next best parameter configuration, the results obtained completely surpassed the results obtained from any single dataset and were 0.06% higher than the optimal results obtained from the Synapse dataset (Table 1).

Table 1. Segmentation results with different parameter configurations.

Architectures	Method	Dataset	Epochs	Batch size	DSC↑
ViT-B/16	MAE	Hybrid	600	14	75.04%
ViT-B/16	MAE	Hybrid	400	12	75.42%
ViT-B/16	MAE	ImageNet-1K	None	None	75.53%
ViT-B/16	MAE	Rcc	400	16	76.01%
ViT-B/16	MAE	Synapse	400	16	76.02%
ViT-B/16	MAE	Rcc	600	14	76.28%
ViT-B/16	MAE	Synapse	400	8	76.30%
None	None	None	None	None	**76.40%**
ViT-B/16	MAE	Synapse	400	12	76.47%
ViT-B/16	MAE	Hybrid	400	16	76.53%

4 Discussion and Conclusion

We found that the MAE pre-training method is effective in migrating to the segmentation task after pre-training with a small sample of medical image datasets, and pre-training with a hybrid of datasets from the downstream task itself and other datasets is better than any single dataset.

In our comparison experiments, it can be found that the difference in the type of dataset has a significant effect on the task completion, and the best results achieved with a single training using the Synapse dataset composed of the downstream task itself are higher than the results without any pre-training and other types of datasets, which we believe may be since the MAE self-supervised pre-training method gives a more challenging task that allows The model can learn deeper features from itself, allowing it to perform better in the segmentation task, after all, it belongs to the same class of images. When the type of data changes, we can see a significant change in the results, with a more or less degraded performance from other types of datasets. The most obvious is that the model trained by a large-scale dataset like ImageNet-1K, on the contrary, does not give good results, while the best case of the Rcc dataset does not exceed the case of not using a pre-trained model. But a certain ratio of blending seems to solve this problem, and it can be seen that the Hybrid dataset obtained by 1:1 blending achieves the best results in the experiments, surpassing in one fell swoop the dataset pre-trained using the training set of the downstream task itself. This gives us an insight to train in the face of the lack of samples in the medical image domain: using a part of the training set from the downstream task itself and a hybrid dataset obtained from the homogeneous dataset may be the solution. And what is the optimal ratio of this mixture? What is the best image type for the blend? It remains for us to continue our research in the future.

References

1. Chen, J., et al.: TransUNet: transformers make strong encoders for medical image segmentation. arXiv preprint arXiv:2102.04306 (2021)
2. Chen, T., Kornblith, S., Norouzi, M., Hinton, G.: A simple framework for contrastive learning of visual representations. In: International Conference on Machine Learning, pp. 1597–1607. PMLR (2020)
3. Devlin, J., Chang, M.W., Lee, K., Toutanova, K.: BERT: pre-training of deep bidirectional transformers for language understanding. arXiv preprint arXiv:1810.04805 (2018)
4. Dosovitskiy, A., et al.: An image is worth 16×16 words: transformers for image recognition at scale. arXiv preprint arXiv:2010.11929 (2020)
5. El-Nouby, A., Izacard, G., Touvron, H., Laptev, I., Jegou, H., Grave, E.: Are large-scale datasets necessary for self-supervised pre-training? arXiv preprint arXiv:2112.10740 (2021)
6. Fu, S., et al.: Domain adaptive relational reasoning for 3D multi-organ segmentation. In: Martel, A.L., et al. (eds.) MICCAI 2020. LNCS, vol. 12261, pp. 656–666. Springer, Cham (2020). https://doi.org/10.1007/978-3-030-59710-8_64

7. He, K., Chen, X., Xie, S., Li, Y., Dollár, P., Girshick, R.: Masked autoencoders are scalable vision learners. In: Proceedings of the IEEE/CVF Conference on Computer Vision and Pattern Recognition, pp. 16000–16009 (2022)
8. He, K., Fan, H., Wu, Y., Xie, S., Girshick, R.: Momentum contrast for unsupervised visual representation learning. In: Proceedings of the IEEE/CVF Conference on Computer Vision and Pattern Recognition, pp. 9729–9738 (2020)
9. He, K., Zhang, X., Ren, S., Sun, J.: Deep residual learning for image recognition. In: Proceedings of the IEEE Conference on Computer Vision and Pattern Recognition, pp. 770–778 (2016)
10. Ke, A., Ellsworth, W., Banerjee, O., Ng, A.Y., Rajpurkar, P.: CheXtransfer. In: Proceedings of the Conference on Health, Inference, and Learning. ACM (2021). https://doi.org/10.1145/3450439.3451867
11. Liu, X., et al.: Self-supervised learning: generative or contrastive. IEEE Trans. Knowl. Data Eng. (2021)
12. Liu, Y., et al.: A deep learning system for differential diagnosis of skin diseases. Nat. Med. **26**(6), 900–908 (2020)
13. Matsoukas, C., Haslum, J.F., Söderberg, M., Smith, K.: Is it time to replace CNNs with transformers for medical images? arXiv preprint arXiv:2108.09038 (2021)
14. Nabulsi, Z., et al.: Deep learning for distinguishing normal versus abnormal chest radiographs and generalization to two unseen diseases tuberculosis and COVID-19. Sci. Rep. **11**(1), 1–15 (2021). https://doi.org/10.1038/s41598-021-93967-2. Funding Information: This study was funded by Google LLC and/or a subsidiary thereof ('Google'. Z. N., A. S., S. J., E. S., A. P. K., W. Y., J. Yang, R.P., S. K., J. Yu, G. S. C., L. P., K. E., D. T., N. B., Y. L., P.-H. C. C., and S. S. are employees of Google and own stock as part of the standard compensation package. C. L. is a paid consultant of Google. R. K., M. E., F. G. V., and D. M. received funding from Google to support the research collaboration
15. Ronneberger, O., Fischer, P., Brox, T.: U-Net: convolutional networks for biomedical image segmentation. In: Navab, N., Hornegger, J., Wells, W.M., Frangi, A.F. (eds.) MICCAI 2015. LNCS, vol. 9351, pp. 234–241. Springer, Cham (2015). https://doi.org/10.1007/978-3-319-24574-4_28
16. Xie, Z., Geng, Z., Hu, J., Zhang, Z., Hu, H., Cao, Y.: Revealing the dark secrets of masked image modeling (2022). https://doi.org/10.48550/ARXIV.2205.13543, https://arxiv.org/abs/2205.13543
17. Zhou, H.Y., Yu, S., Bian, C., Hu, Y., Ma, K., Zheng, Y.: Comparing to learn: surpassing ImageNet pretraining on radiographs by comparing image representations (2020). https://doi.org/10.48550/ARXIV.2007.07423, https://arxiv.org/abs/2007.07423

Deep Transfer Learning Based Risk Prediction Model for Infectious Disease

Youshen Jiang, Zhiping Cai, Kaiyu Cai, Jing Xia(✉), and Lizhen Yan(✉)

College of Computer, National University of Defense Technology, Changsha 410073, China

jingxia@nudt.edu.cn, 419542577@qq.com

Abstract. In recent years various epidemics have posed a serious threat to human health and there is an urgent need for intelligent infectious disease risk prediction methods. Advance prediction of the share of suffering from infectious diseases is essential to curb the spread of infectious diseases and the deterioration of patient conditions. Most existing work investigates the diagnosis of diseases, but these methods often require large datasets. In this paper, we propose a transfer learning-based multilayer perceptron approach (TLMLP). To meet the challenge in the real world, some newly established hospitals or small clinics do not have a sufficient amount of data themselves. In the model framework, the student model is trained by knowledge distillation. The idea of transfer learning is used to give the target model a better predictive performance. We compare the proposed approach with the most commonly used statistical methods and deep learning models. Also, we conduct comparative experiments on three models used for transfer learning to observe the prediction performance of the models under the transfer learning framework. We conducted extensive experiments on a real-world epidemic dataset. The method has strong predictive performance and can be easily used for infectious disease prediction.

Keywords: Transfer learning · Infectious diseases · Knowledge distillation

1 Introduction

Infectious diseases have so far been a health problem for humans [17]. In particular, recent years have seen the emergence of various new infectious diseases, such as coronavirus disease 2019 (neo-coronavirus pneumonia) [6], SARS, avian influenza [7], and simian foamy viruses [13]. Therefore, effective control of infectious diseases is essential for public health, which also relies on the ability to make advanced predictions and intervention decisions about infectious diseases.

In practice, however, some challenges make it difficult for doctors to fully assess a patient's health and accurately identify key factors with the limited data available. One reason is the early stages of infectious disease when deterioration is often not obvious and therefore requires extensive clinical experience

Z. Cai et al. (Eds.): NCTCS 2022, CCIS 1693, pp. 183–193, 2022.
https://doi.org/10.1007/978-981-19-8152-4_13

to diagnose [1]. Another reason is that medical records are not shared between different hospitals, creating silos of data and preventing access to comprehensive information for diagnosis [3]. As can be seen, accurate disease prediction is time-consuming and challenging for medical staff to gain experience, in addition to the security of medical data sharing.

Therefore, there is an urgent need to construct an intelligent prediction method for infectious diseases [1]. Early prediction of infectious diseases helps patients to be treated earlier and, for society, also facilitates more effective control measures for targeting the early transmission dynamics of infectious diseases [16]. In addition, an intelligent approach reduces the reliance on the clinical experience of medical staff and can assist doctors in determining the likely illness of a patient and making a more comprehensive diagnosis.

However, most existing models [7,16]rely on information-rich datasets, which are often inadequate across hospitals. In some fledgling hospitals and small clinics, this is difficult to achieve. Current prediction methods rarely take this into account and are inevitable in practical applications. Due to the privacy of patient records, data cannot usually be shared between hospitals. In addition, existing deep learning models need to be trained from scratch, which has limitations.

Recently, some researchers [8,12,15,18] have attempted to use migration learning methods for prediction. For example, Gupt [5] applied to source and target datasets that have exactly the same features by means of a migration learning approach. However, each hospital dataset usually has different features.

Therefore, such a research challenge remains: how can datasets with different characteristics be used to predict whether an enquirer has an infectious disease or not? In this paper, we present transfer learning Multilayer Perceptron (TLMLP). In summary, contributes to the community in the following aspects:

- We propose a depth learning framework that is combined with transfer learning ideas. Based on features extracted from physical health conditions, the model was used to predict whether the enquirer had an infectious disease or not.
- We conduct disease risk prediction experiments in patients with infectious diseases such as hepatitis and hand-foot-mouth disease (HFMD). The experimental results showed that the method outperformed the baseline method in prediction under the evaluation index. We simultaneously completed risk prediction for diseases including HFMD and various types of hepatitis and analyzed the effectiveness of the method when different diseases are predicted together. A large number of experiments have shown that the prediction of disease risk is useful to assist physicians in diagnosing patients' disease conditions.
- To validate that the method has strong predictive performance and can be used to aid in the prediction of infectious diseases. We use real-world datasets from two hospitals.

The rest of this paper is organized as follows. Section 2 reviews the work related to infectious disease prediction and transfer learning in recent years. In the third section, the problems studied in this paper and the prediction objectives of the model are presented. In Sect. 4, the methods of the prediction model and the transfer learning framework is outlined. Thc experimental results are presented and discussed in Sect. 5. Section 6 summarizes this article.

2 Related Work

2.1 Infectious Disease Prediction

In many studies, infectious disease risk prediction is expressed as a multi-label classification problem, wherein the self-return model is widely used. Zhang et al. [21] describe an evaluation and comparison of ARIMA and support vector machines. In addition, seasonal time characteristics are also considered. Song et al. [15] used time series analysis to predict the incidence of influenza method. Xuan et al. [19] proposed a prediction technique based on gradient boosting decision trees. The model uses the extracted information to determine multiple decision tree features and, therefore, helps to reduce the effect of rank imbalance.

2.2 Deep Transfer Learning

Transfer Learning is a term used in machine learning to refer to the influence of one type of learning on another or the influence of an acquired experience on the completion of other activities [14,18]. The transfer learning is widely found in the learning of various knowledge, skills, and social norms. To achieve this training using a small number of its own features yields models that work much better [8]. Transfer learning addresses this problem as a new learning framework. Currently, migration learning has been applied very successfully in the field of CV and NLP, but it has been applied less in medical disease prediction. In [12], transfer learning is a very valuable method used to infer general laws for feature-specific samples of artificial systems, assuming that multiple tasks are available simultaneously.

3 Problem Formulation

In the early stage of infectious diseases, the symptoms are not obvious, and it is difficult for human doctors to comprehensively assess the health of patients. This also led to the discovery of infectious diseases after a large number of transmissions and missed the best containment time. We take the patient's health status as the variable input and the probability of suffering from various diseases as the output. We officially define our research issues and provide a list of symbols used in TLMLP in Table 1.

We obtained EMR medical records of infectious disease patients from two hospitals in Changsha. Extract the health indicators related to infectious diseases from the medical records, and use the vector $x_{i,j}$ to represent the j th indicator of patient i. The trained model can output Y $\{y_{i,1}, y_{i,1}, \ldots, y_{i,k}\}$ corresponding to the input X_i, and $y_{i,k}$ represents the disease probability of patient i with the disease k.

Table 1. Notations Used in TLMLP.

Notation	Definition
$x_{i,j}$	The corresponding value of indicator j for patient i
$y_{i,j}$	Corresponding values of disease j for patient i
L	The number of categories of features in the source dataset
l_1	The number of categories of shared features in the source dataset
l_2	The number of categories of private features in the source dataset
k	Number of predicted disease categories
D	A vector representing all indicators
s, t	The sample representation features of teacher and student model
W	Weight parameters for intermediate states and hidden layers
h	Super parameter of hidden layer state
b	Bias corresponding to each layer of the neural network
f_{tea}	The features extracted by MLP in the teacher model
f_{stu}	The features extracted by MLP in the student model
f_{trans}	The features extracted by MLP in the target model

4 Method

TLMLP is based on the source dataset and target dataset that use different characteristics to improve the performance in the target domain. In order to solve the cold start problem of the prediction model on the target dataset, a transfer learning framework is used. Figure 1 shows the TLMLP framework designed, which contains three key steps:

- The model framework initializes the dataset by embedding.
- The model framework extracts the health features of the patients by special Multilayer Perceptron (MLP) [11], which extracts personalized features and common features respectively.
- The teacher model is obtained from the source dataset training. The student model is trained using a specific loss through distillation learning idea. The student model is used to assist in the prediction of the target model.

4.1 Dataset Preprocessing

The dataset preprocessing [2] before performing the prediction task. The information such as all health indicators were integrated. and designed as a list $D\{d_1, d_2, \dots\}$, such as gender, age, and headache degree, corresponding to $d1$, $d2$, and $d3$, respectively. Then the negatives were extracted from the patient's medical records, and some of the negatives are shown in Table 2. When the d_j description in D has negatives, the value x_j corresponding to d_j is set to -1 and no negatives to 1. In addition, if d_j has a missing value, it is set to 0.

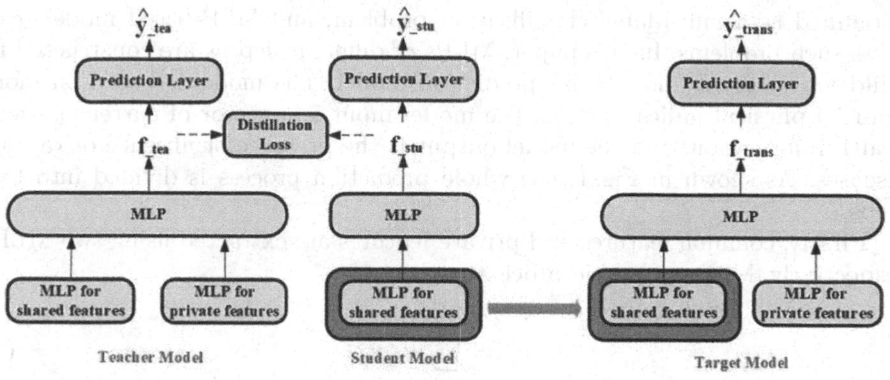

Fig. 1. TLMLP model frame map.

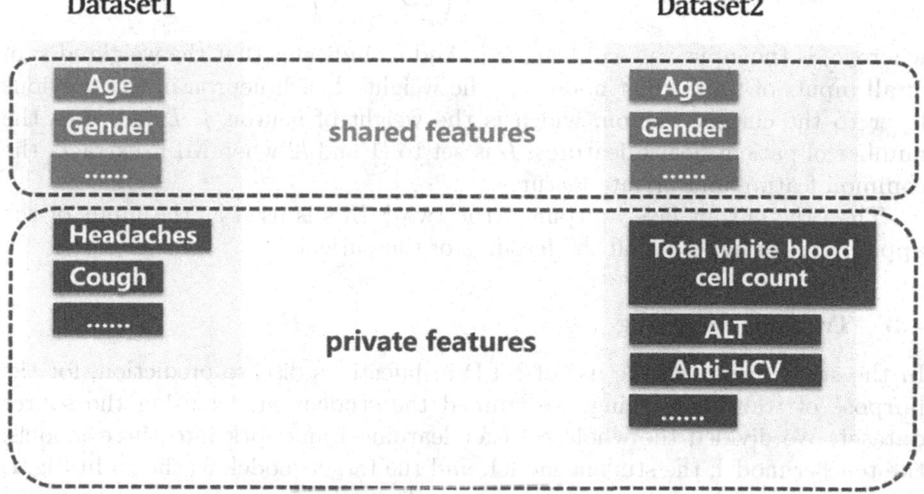

Fig. 2. Shared features and private features.

In addition, the missing values (eigenvalues of 0) are converted into trainable vectors. In order to make X as input to the supervised learning task, TLMLP uses embedding for feature encoding.

Finally, as shown in Fig. 2, the features of two real data sets are divided into two categories to facilitate TLMLP to distill knowledge. One is the shared feature, that is, the feature of two datasets at the same time. The second type is private features, that is, features other than the same features.

4.2 MLP Feature Learning

MLP is often used for classification, where each output corresponds to different binary classification. In this paper, the infectious disease risk prediction problem is defined as a multi-label classification problem, and MLP-based models can solve such problems. In this paper, MLPs of different depths are constructed to build an infectious disease risk prediction model. The model is based on more than 50 physical indicators, i.e., the model input is a vector of current patient health information, and the model output is the presence or absence of various diseases. As shown in Fig. 1, the whole prediction process is divided into two steps.

Firstly, common features and private features are extracted using two MLPs respectively. MLP extraction process:

$$\mathrm{h}_j = \sum_{i=1}^{L} \mathbf{w}_{ij}\mathbf{x}_j \tag{1}$$

$$y = \mathrm{a}_j = relu\left(\sum_{i=1}^{L} \mathbf{w}_{ij}\mathbf{x}_j\right) \tag{2}$$

where x_j is the input value of feature j. And h_j indicates that the weighted sum of all inputs of the current node, w_{ij} the weight of each neuron in the previous layer to the current neuron, which is the weight of neuron j. L indicates the number of patient health features. L is set to $l1$ and $l2$ when MLP extracts the common feature and private features.

Then the output layer output of the two MLPs is used as the input of the upper MLP to integrate all the features of the patient.

4.3 Transfer Learning

In the study, based on the use of MLP in infectious disease prediction, for the purpose of transfer learning, we trained the student model using the source dataset. We divided the whole transfer learning framework into three models: the teacher model, the student model, and the target model, as shown in Fig. 1. the teacher model is trained on the source dataset to learn the complete source dataset features. The features extracted from the last layer of the MLP hidden layer, f_{tea}, are used in the calculation of distillation loss values. f_{tea} is extracted from the knowledge of the teacher model to assist in the training of the student model.

$$f_{tea} = relu\left(W_i^T x + b_i\right) \tag{3}$$

where x is the vector representing the patient's health characteristics, W_i, b represents the super parameters of this iterative hidden layer, $relu$ is an activation function.

The student model is trained on shared features. And the features f_{stu}, extracted from the last layer of the MLP hidden layer, is used for distillation loss value calculation. And the weights of the hidden layer parameters of the teacher model are learned by knowledge distillation.

$$L_{dist} = \sum_{(x_1,\ldots,x_n)\in X} l\left(\varphi\left(t_1,\ldots,t_n\right)\varphi\left(s_1,\ldots,s_n\right)\right) \tag{4}$$

where t and s are the sample representation features of teacher and student, respectively. φ denote the relation between features. And l denotes the distance function between the relation.

We transfer the MLP from the student model to the target model. and combine it with the MLP for private feature of the target model. The two MLPs jointly extract features to predict the risk of infectious diseases in the target dataset. Implementing the student model helps the target model to start quickly and the target model does not need to be trained from scratch.

5 Experimental Evaluation

In this section of experiments, we use EMR medical record data from The First Affiliated Hospital of Zhengzhou University (Dataset1) and Hunan Provincial People's Hospital (Dataset2) for experiments. We conducted extensive experiments on more than a dozen infectious disease datasets from the two hospitals to evaluate the method's performance. We answer the following questions:

- Q1. Is the transfer learning scheme effective in alleviating the cold start problem of models with few data sets?
- Q2. Can TLMLP be applied to a wider range of infectious disease risk prediction tasks and have superior performance compared to the most commonly used networks?
- Q3. How does the number of MLP hidden layers in TLMLP architecture affect the prediction?

5.1 Experiment Setting

Data Set. The data sets of the two hospitals are shown in Table 2:

Table 2. Features Recorded in Dataset.

Dataset	Dataset 1	Dataset 2
Size	2424	3311
Feature	21	60
Ave_feature	5	8
Disease	13	14
Gender (Male: Female)	65%:35%	64%:36%
Age (years)	(1,94)	(1,96)

We keep the data set in the same proportion according to the ratio of various infectious diseases in the data set and divide it into a training set, validation set, and test set in the ratio of 5:2:3. In the experiments, the neural structures were learned using the training set. The validation set is used to determine when the model is optimal. Finally, the prediction effectiveness of the model is evaluated by the test set.

The details of the dataset are as follows: Dataset1 has 2424 medical records with 21 features, with an average of 5 features per patient that are not missing values. The sample included 13 infectious diseases including HFMD. The male-to-female ratio of cases was 65%:35%, with an age range of 1 to 94 years. Dataset2 was also as described above, and was all real-world data.

Evaluation Indicators. Four accuracy metrics are used to evaluate the performance of the model: F1-score, recall, precision, and accuracy.

$$F1 - score = \frac{2Precision * Recall}{Precision + Recall} \tag{5}$$

$$Recall = \frac{tp}{tp + fn} \tag{6}$$

$$Precision = \frac{tp}{tp + fp} \tag{7}$$

$$Accuracy = \frac{tp + tn}{tp + tn + fp + fn} \tag{8}$$

In this experiment, Precision indicates how many of the samples predicted to be sick were predicted correctly. Recall indicates how many of the sick patients were predicted correctly. Accuracy indicates what percentage of the samples were predicted correctly. F1-score is used to combine precision and Recall as an evaluation index [20].

Baseline. We introduce several practical commonly used models as baseline methods, as shown below.

- **Decision Tree (DT)** [9] is a very versatile algorithm in machine learning algorithms, which can perform classification and regression tasks, and even multiple output tasks. The decision tree algorithm is very powerful and can fit complex data sets well even for some complex problems. Decision trees are one of the most powerful machine learning algorithms at the moment.
- **Support Vector Machine (SVM)** [10] is a linear classifier with a maximum interval defined in the feature space. SVM is suitable for small and medium data samples, nonlinear and high-dimensional classification problems.
- **Long Short-term Memory (LSTM)** [4] is a kind of time cycle neural network, which is specially designed to solve the long-term dependence problem of general cyclic neural network(RNN). All RNNs have a chain form of repetitive neural network modules.

Experimental Environment. Experiments were performed on a machine installed in the Intel Core i7-10700F eight-core, 32G memory, and GPU: NVIDIA GeForce RTX3070. The code is implemented based on pytorch1.5.0. In order to train the model, the learning rate is set to 0.005.

5.2 Experiment Results

Table 3. Comparison performances with baselines on the dataset1.

Method	F1-score	Accuracy	Recall	Precision
DT	0.464	0.431	0.431	0.508
SVM	0.466	0.481	0.481	0.507
MLP	**0.539**	**0.603**	**0.603**	**0.514**
% relative gain	0.157	0.254	0.254	0.012

The predictive performance of TLMLP was tested individually, with experiments on dataset1 and dataset2, respectively. The whole experiments were cross-validated using ten-fold to derive performance evaluation metrics. As shown in Table 3, overall, the special MLP used in this paper can correctly predict more than 60% of the patients. Based on the Recall not exceeding 50%, it can be seen that the probability that DT and SVM can detect the real sick people is not high. Meanwhile, the prediction performance of TLMLP is better than several baseline methods. In comparison, MLP improved accuracy by 25.4%.

Table 4. Comparison performances with baselines on the dataset2.

Method	F1-score	Accuracy	Recall	Precision
DT	0.431	0.429	0.429	0.436
SVM	0.532	0.565	0.565	0.533
LSTM	0.420	0.441	0.441	0.425
MLP	**0.595**	**0.633**	**0.633**	**0.629**
% relative gain	0.118	0.120	0.120	0.180

Table 4 shows the performance of all models in dataset2. MLP always outperformed other prediction models, which also reflects the higher applicability of TLMLP to assist physicians in correctly determining the risk of disease in 60% of patients. Comparing Table 3 and Table 4, we can find that the performance of the baseline method decreases on dataset2, while the MLP prediction is superior. We speculate that it is because the MLP is better with richer data and higher dimensionality of variables.

5.3 Ablation Experiment

In this experiment, as shown in Table 5, it is necessary to test the performance of the migration method of TLMLP for evaluation. teacher_model is the teacher model. student_model_notea is the model that does not perform knowledge distillation with the help of the teacher model. Conversely, student_model_tea is the model that uses knowledge distillation, while target_model_notrans is the target model that does not use the student model for auxiliary prediction. Finally target_model_trans is the migration prediction model used in the TLMLP proposed in this paper. We verify whether the transfer learning approach is effective by comparing the prediction performance of several models mentioned above.

Table 5. The accuracy of each module, when dataset2 is the source data, dataset1 is the target dataset.

Method	Accuracy
teacher_model	0.604
student_model_notea	0.215
student_model_tea	0.472
target_model_notrans	0.518
target_model_trans	**0.568**
% relative gain	0.0965

As shown in Table 5, the student model improved its predictions by 119.5% after using knowledge distillation. It can be seen that the use of distillation loss values is effective for the construction of the student model. The effect is improved so much, on the one hand, because there are not many common features, which lead to poor prediction of student_model_notea. On the other hand, the distillation loss values help.

In addition, target_model_trans improves the prediction performance by 9.65% over target_model_notrans on dataset2. It is verified that the transfer learning method, on both real-world datasets, helps the model to improve the prediction performance on the new dataset. Thus, TLMLP's relocation transfer learning framework is effective.

6 Conclusion

In this paper, we propose a framework for infectious disease risk prediction based on MLP's TLMLP. To cope with the challenge of the cold start of the model on new datasets, TLMLP consists of knowledge distillation ideas to obtain the student model. The transfer learning framework is then used to make the student model assist the target model prediction. Experimental results on real-world datasets from two hospitals show that TLMLP outperforms several baseline approaches and helps in the prediction of patient infectious disease risk.

Acknowledgements. This work is supported by the National Key Research and Development Program of China (2020YFC2003400).

References

1. Chae, S., Kwon, S., Lee, D.: Predicting infectious disease using deep learning and big data. Int. J. Environ. Res. Public Health **15**(8), 1596 (2018)
2. Gao, J.: Data preprocessing (2012)
3. Gkoulalas-Divanis, A., Loukides, G.: Medical Data Privacy Handbook. Springer, Heidelberg (2015). https://doi.org/10.1007/978-3-319-23633-9
4. Graves, A.: Long short-term memory. In: Supervised Sequence Labelling with Recurrent Neural Networks, pp. 37–45 (2012)
5. Gupta, P., Malhotra, P., Vig, L., Shroff, G.: Transfer learning for clinical time series analysis using recurrent neural networks. arXiv preprint arXiv:1807.01705 (2018)
6. Lauer, S.A., et al.: The incubation period of coronavirus disease 2019 (covid-19) from publicly reported confirmed cases: estimation and application. Ann. Internal Med. **172**(9), 577–582 (2020)
7. Liu, S., et al.: Control of avian influenza in china: strategies and lessons. Transbound. Emerg. Dis. **67**(4), 1463–1471 (2020)
8. Lu, J., Behbood, V., Hao, P., Zuo, H., Xue, S., Zhang, G.: Transfer learning using computational intelligence: a survey. Knowl.-Based Syst. **80**, 14–23 (2015)
9. Myles, A.J., Feudale, R.N., Liu, Y., Woody, N.A., Brown, S.D.: An introduction to decision tree modeling. J. Chem.: J. Chemometrics Soc. **18**(6), 275–285 (2004)
10. Noble, W.S.: What is a support vector machine? Nat. Biotechnol. **24**(12), 1565–1567 (2006)
11. Noriega, L.: Multilayer perceptron tutorial. School of Computing, Staffordshire University (2005)
12. Parisi, G.I., Kemker, R., Part, J.L., Kanan, C., Wermter, S.: Continual lifelong learning with neural networks: a review. Neural Netw. **113**, 54–71 (2019)
13. Santos, A.F., Cavalcante, L.T., Muniz, C.P., Switzer, W.M., Soares, M.A.: Simian foamy viruses in central and South America: a new world of discovery. Viruses **11**(10), 967 (2019)
14. Song, Q., Zheng, Y.J., Sheng, W.G., Yang, J.: Tridirectional transfer learning for predicting gastric cancer morbidity. IEEE Trans. Neural Netw. Learn. Syst. **32**(2), 561–574 (2020)
15. Song, X., Xiao, J., Deng, J., Kang, Q., Zhang, Y., Xu, J.: Time series analysis of influenza incidence in Chinese provinces from 2004 to 2011. Medicine **95**(26) (2016)
16. Sun, W., Liu, F., Cai, Z., Fang, S., Wang, G.: A survey of data processing of emr (electronic medical record) based on data mining (2017)
17. Wang, L., et al.: Systematic review: national notifiable infectious disease surveillance system in china. Online J. Public Health Inf. **11**(1) (2019)
18. Weiss, K., Khoshgoftaar, T.M., Wang, D.: A survey of transfer learning. J. Big Data **3**(1), 1–40 (2016)
19. Xuan, P., Sun, C., Zhang, T., Ye, Y., Shen, T., Dong, Y.: Gradient boosting decision tree-based method for predicting interactions between target genes and drugs. Front. Genet. **10**, 459 (2019)
20. Yacouby, R., Axman, D.: Probabilistic extension of precision, recall, and f1 score for more thorough evaluation of classification models. In: Proceedings of the First Workshop on Evaluation and Comparison of NLP Systems, pp. 79–91 (2020)
21. Zhang, X., Zhang, T., Young, A.A., Li, X.: Applications and comparisons of four time series models in epidemiological surveillance data. Plos One **9**(2), e88075 (2014)

A Data-Driven Framework for Crack Paths Propagation

Xichen Tan, Jiaping Yu(✉), and Jing Xia

College of Computer, National University of Defense Technology, Changsha, Hunan 410073, China
{yujiaping19,jingxia}@nudt.edu.cn

Abstract. The random material system is often complex and presents a high level of stochasticity, making it difficult to study the geometrical information and the dynamics process of fracture propagation. Thus, traditional simulation models of crack behaviors achieve a relatively low accuracy of fracture growth prediction and are computationally prohibitive when the scale of the material is large. Since the detection scenario in the security mechanisms of the smart grid is similar to the material system where data have different underlying distributions and no class labels, in this paper, we adapt an unsupervised machine learning model, which is initially used for detecting covert data integrity assault in smart grid networks. Additionally, to reduce the computational cost of the model, we employ principal component analysis(PCA) for dimensionality reduction. PCA is also adapted when the size of power systems in the smart grid increases. To summarize, we propose a hybrid method combining material modeling and a machine learning algorithm, which can generate new crack paths only by numerical simulation. The consistency of microstructure and dynamic properties is maintained in the meanwhile.

Keywords: Crack propagation prediction · Manifold learning · Deep learning

1 Introduction

With the rapid development of deep learning and artificial intelligence, many crossover kinds of research have emerged. Since these deep learning models are suitable for dealing with nonlinear mappings, they have been widely used in manifold learning, computational mechanics, and many other interdisciplinary. For instance, in [1–5], many data-driven analysis based on machine learning tools are proposed to enrich data set and characterize materials properties. In [6,7], neural networks are applied to make the dimensionality reduction for complex materials to discover the underlying geometric features.

Speaking of microstructure reconstruction, we can refer to [8]. It claims there are three main approaches to characterize the microstructure, which are essential for microstructure reconstruction, i.e., approaches based on visual-feature,

Z. Cai et al. (Eds.): NCTCS 2022, CCIS 1693, pp. 194–205, 2022.
https://doi.org/10.1007/978-981-19-8152-4_14

statistical modeling, and deep learning. Visual-feature is terminology borrowed from computer vision, mainly used for face recognition. In the last decade, many material scientists have taken advantage of it to study structure property. In [9], it adapts concepts from Never Ending Image Learner(NEIL), which keeps analyzing images in our daily lives to build an extensive database and find common sense relationships from it. Inspired by NEIL, it develops a quantitive microstructure descriptor to classify a massive set of microstructural image data and uses underlying features computed to study relationships between different microstructures. Following this logic, multiple approaches used in feature extraction, feature selection, and classification are presented [10]. Although a priori knowledge of microstructural features is not required when computer vision methods are introduced, visual-feature based models are still roughly estimations for a micrograph compared with the objective measure. Meanwhile, the number of images required for model training of computer vision is often enormous in order to ensure the effectiveness of results. However, compared to vast amounts of data collected from the internet, the number of microstructure data is relatively small and may increase the difficulty of model training as a result.

To improve the richness and accuracy of data analysis, we consider involving statistical models. For instance, a descriptor-based model is proposed in [11] to quantitatively depict a heterogeneous microstructure system with just a small set of variables, and a statistical microstructural reconstruction is performed for finite element analysis(FEA). Furthermore, Gaussian random field [12] is used to guarantee the accuracy of FEA and a Markov Random Field (MRF) [13] reduces the computing cost.

Nevertheless, there are some limitations associated with statistical models which is the assumption that the local properties should be invariant throughout microstructure. In order to develop a more general methodology that can be applied to more classes of microstructures, a deep learning framework is considered. Because of its powerful simulation capability and versatility, many deep learning frameworks have been designed, and a number of interdisciplinary applications [14–16] have been spawned. In the material science field, a feature learning methodology involves a deep brief network [6] is presented to achieve dimension reduction while sustaining statistical equivalence between original complex material systems and lower-dimensional feature space. In [17], generative adversarial networks(GAN) are trained to overcome limitations during microstructural designing when available variables are not enough, which may result in losing important information during the microstructure reconstruction procedure. However, the input image data for these networks are of fixed size and not scalable, and different parameter choices can lead to unpredictable performance. As a result, these models are constrained to the systems that have already been demonstrated in the paper. Transfer learning [18–20] thus provides us with a new point of view, which can adopt knowledge from a learned method and then apply it to a new task. In [21], it combines modified CNN-based representations and traditional bag-of-words models, taking advantage of their respective strengths to analyze primary microconstituent and annealing conditions of complex and hierarchical microstructure systems. Likewise, a pre-trained CNN(VGG-19 [22]) network is adapted in [23]. It uses the texture vectors generated from VGG-19 to capture correlations visible in microstructure images based on a small data set. However, the limitation of the transfer learning approaches is that a well-trained CNN is required in advance, which is a challenging problem that should be addressed further.

Inspired by these papers, we aim to combine the stochastic models and ML (Machine Learning) techniques to mitigate some side effects mentioned above. First, using a stochastic model to generate numerical samples that concentrate on a specific subset and the probability distribution of which is unknown. Based on these given raw samples, we can then apply unsupervised machine learning tools to reveal the patterns and consistency in these samples and reconstruct crack paths based on the output data. So the rest of the paper will be organized as follows: Sect. 2 presents some related works that we are mainly based on. Section 3 is composed of data processing and model training. Section 4 provides an experiment to numerically show the performance of our model, and we conclude in Sect. 5.

2 Related Works

In [24], it proposes a phase-field model for cohesive fracture, and Lagrange multipliers are employed to simulate the actual physical constraints by which the evolution of damage is restricted. The governing equations are derived, and the robustness of the model is demonstrated by solving problems in multi-dimensional quasi-static and dynamic fractures. Based on [24], a data-driven framework is presented in [25] to explore the geometrical structure exhibited by crack patterns and reconstruct a posteriori crack path through Markovianization. It applies the phase-field/gradient damage formulation on a monodisperse random medium while assuming that the damage field would only reduce the tensile strength of materials and have no effect on compression resistance. After that, a molecular-dynamics-based algorithm [26] is used to generate the reference data samples. Finally, a probabilistic learning approach is used to generate a new data set based on the reference data samples. Also, in [27], we find a methodology that can generate realizations of a random vector, which can be taken into account to enrich the original data set and thus make the data set to fit our machine learning model better.

When it comes to machine learning, many applications regarding fracture prediction have already been investigated over the years. Such as [28], to conquer computational burden and the loss of crucial structural information when increasing material dimension, it develops a reduced order model to derive upscaled relationships and quantities to be used in the high-fidelity model. The chosen high-fidelity model is the Hybrid Optimization Software Suite(HOSS) which allows diverse initial conditions and fracture properties(fracture interaction, fracture coalescence, fracture nucleation, etc.)to be considered in advance. And then, an ML approach is developed to circumvent computationally intractable problem cost by HOSS. This paper compares three ML approaches(Decision Tree, Random Forests, Artificial Neural Network) based on the percent error of predicting fracture coalescence. The reader interested in the ML framework is referred to [29–31], more reduced-order models, graph-theoretic, and machine learning algorithms are presented for predicting fracture evolution.

3 Methodology

3.1 Filter Data

Our data set comes from [25], we get the diffuse crack path with phase-field/gradient damage formulation [24]. We assume that the random materials are statistical isotropy, and the crack propagation is completely random in consequence (Fig. 1).

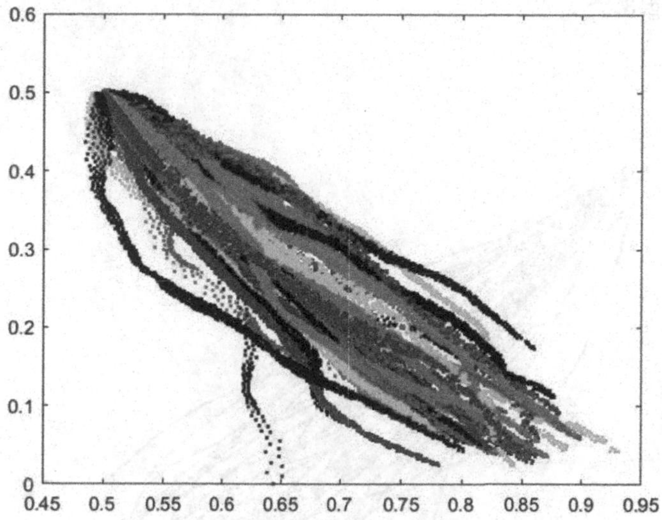

Fig. 1. Raw crack data samples.

However, the samples we get from the formulation are so scattered that we need to find a way to reconstruct a crack path from the original data set. There have been so many works that focus on it, and we follow [32], which is based on an optimization-based approach called non-maximum suppression. First, we need to identify an initial set of knots, partition them into subsets and identify the crack with the set of points with the highest density of surrounding damage. In the end, we can optimize the crack path with spline interpolation (Fig. 2).

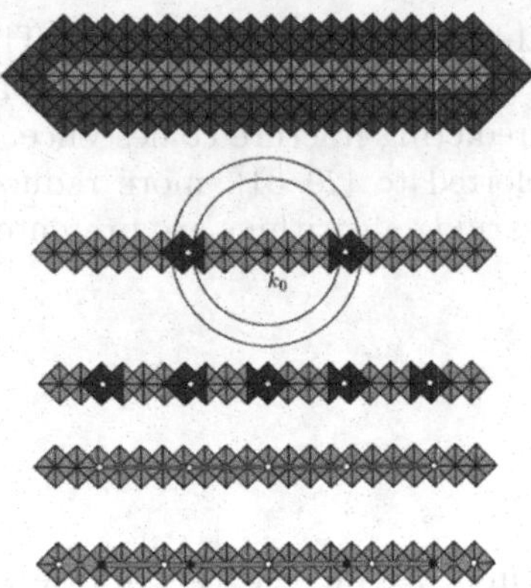

Fig. 2. Non-maximum suppression.

Through this algorithm, we can generate all the filtered crack paths, which are shown in Fig. 3.

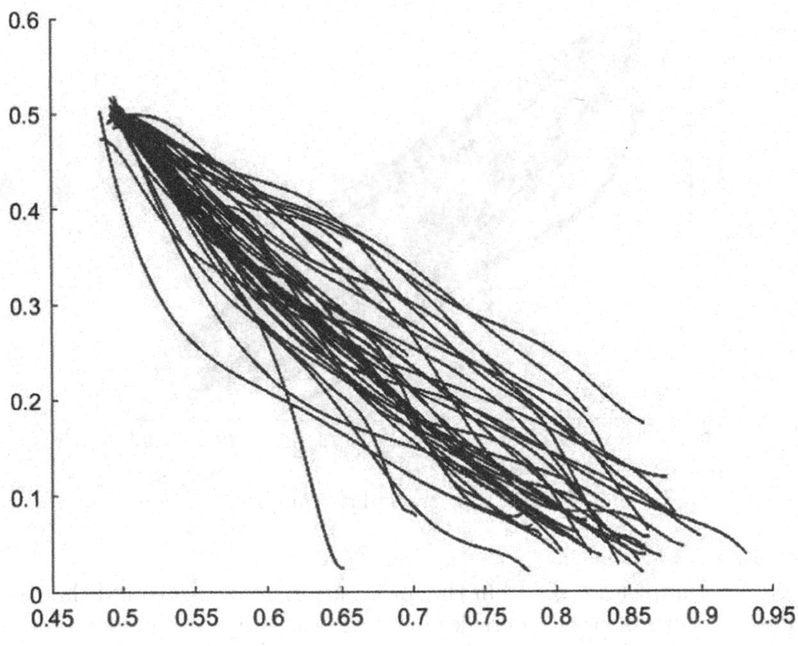

Fig. 3. Filtered crack paths.

3.2 New Data Sampling

Following [25], these paths can be interpreted as realizations of a space-time random field $d(x,t), x \in \Omega, t \in [0,T]$, and when t=T, the entire crack path is generated. Furthermore, for all x in Ω, each damage point belonging to x can be turned into a 2-dimensional coordinate point, and the whole crack paths can be gathered in a $2 \times N_D$ matrix.

$$[D] = [[D^{(1)}, ..., D^{(N)}]] \tag{1}$$

Here, $D^{(i)}$ is the vector of the ith crack points. To make the crack points fit our training model better, we need a larger data set. Employing the sampling method on manifold [27], we need to normalize the given data set first by using the principal component analysis(PCA). The random matrix $[\mathbf{D}]$ can be written as:

$$[\mathbf{D}] = [\underline{D}] + [\phi][\mu]^{1/2}[\mathbf{H}] \tag{2}$$

in which $[\underline{D}] = [\mathbf{d}, ..., \mathbf{d}]$, while $d = \frac{1}{N}\sum_{i=1}^{N} D(i)$. Let $[c] = \frac{1}{N-1}\sum_{i=1}^{N}(D(i) - d)(D(i)-d)^T$ be the empirical estimate of the covariance matrix, $[\phi]$ is the matrix whose columns are consist of the orthonormal eigenvectors associated with $[c]$, and μ is a diagonal matrix which is composed by the eigenvalue of $[c]$. Adopting $D^{(i)}$ as the realization of $[\mathbf{D}]$, then $[\mathbf{H}]$ can be computed as:

$$[\mathbf{H}] = [\mu]^{-1/2}[\phi]^T([\mathbf{D}] - [\underline{D}]) \tag{3}$$

It's easily to see that the mean vector $E[\mathbf{H}]$ is $\mathbf{0}$ and the covariance matrix of $[\mathbf{H}]$ is $[I_v]$, while v is the rank of matrix $[c]$, and thus we get the normalized realization of the given data.

Following [27], we need to construct a nonparametric estimate p_H of pdf of $[\mathbf{H}]$ and use it to construct an Itô stochastic differential equation(ISDE) to generate realization of the random matrix $[\mathbf{H}]$. Since the ISDE, which belongs to the Markov chain Monte Carlo (MCMC) procedures, does not allow the restriction of new samples to the subset S_v on which the probability is concentrated, we continue to introduce the diffusion maps to characterize the subset S_v. Following [33], let Gaussian kernel defined as:

$$k_\epsilon(\eta, \eta') = exp(-\frac{1}{4\epsilon}||\eta - \eta'||^2) \tag{4}$$

Let [K] be the symmetric matrix in M_N such that:

$$[K]_{ij} = k_\epsilon(\eta^i, \eta^j), i, j \in 1, ..., N \tag{5}$$

and [b] be the diagonal real matrix in M_N with entries $[b]_{ij} = \delta_{ij}\sum_{j'=1}^{N}[K]_{ij'}$ (δ_{ij} is the Kronecker's symbol). We can construct matrix $[P]$ as $[P] = [b]^{-1}[K]$ and let $[P_s]$ be the symmetric matrix in M_N such that:

$$[P_s] = [b]^{1/2}[P][b]^{-1/2} = [b]^{-1/2}[K][b]^{-1/2} \tag{6}$$

Considering λ_α and ϕ^α as the set of eigenvalues and eigenvectors of P_s, and we pick up the m most significant of them to construct the diffusion maps basis, which can be defined as $[G] = [g^1, ...g^m] \in M_{N,m}$, where:

$$g^\alpha = \lambda_\alpha^k [b]^{-1/2} \phi^\alpha, \alpha = 1, ..., m \tag{7}$$

In which k is a parameter chosen for exploring the underlying geometrical structure. Introducing the random matrix $[Z] \in M_{v,m}$, we can construct the following reduced-order representation of $[H]$.

$$[H] = [Z][g]^T \tag{8}$$

In [27], a reduced-order ISDE is given to generate matrix $[Z]$:

$$d[\mathcal{Z}(r)] = [\mathcal{Y}(r)]d(r) \tag{9}$$

$$d[\mathcal{Y}(r)] = [\mathcal{L}(\mathcal{Z}(r))]dr - \frac{1}{2} f_0 [\mathcal{Y}(r)]dr + \sqrt{f_0}[d\mathcal{W}(r)] \tag{10}$$

with the initial condition

$$[\mathcal{Z}(0)] = [H][g]([g]^T[g])^{-1}, [\mathcal{Y}(0)] = [\mathcal{N}][g]([g]^T[g])^{-1} \tag{11}$$

where $[\mathcal{N}]$ is a random matrix $M_{2,N}$ whose columns are independent copies of the normalized Gaussian random vector in R^2, and f_0 is a parameter. Function $[\mathcal{L}]$ is defined as

$$[\mathcal{L}(\mathcal{Z}(r))] = [L(\mathcal{Z}(r)[g]^T)][g]([g]^T[g])^{-1} \tag{12}$$

$$[L([U])]_{ij} = \frac{1}{f(\mathbf{u}^j)} \{\nabla_{u^j} f(u^j)\}_i \tag{13}$$

where $[U] \in M_{2,N}$, f is the kernel density estimator constructed with the normalized data [34] and $[d\mathcal{W}(r)] = [dW(r)][g]([g]^T[g])^{-1}$, where $[dW(r)] = [dW^1(r), ...dW^N(r)]$ and $\{W^i\}_{i=1}^N$ are independent copies of normalized Wiener process in R^2.

For numerically solving the reduced-order ISDE above, the Störmer-Verlet scheme is introduced. Using the filtered data we get from Fig. 3, we need to compute the eigenvalues of $[\mathbf{H}]$ first, which is needed for determining the parameter m and constructing the diffusion maps $[g]$ (Fig. 4).

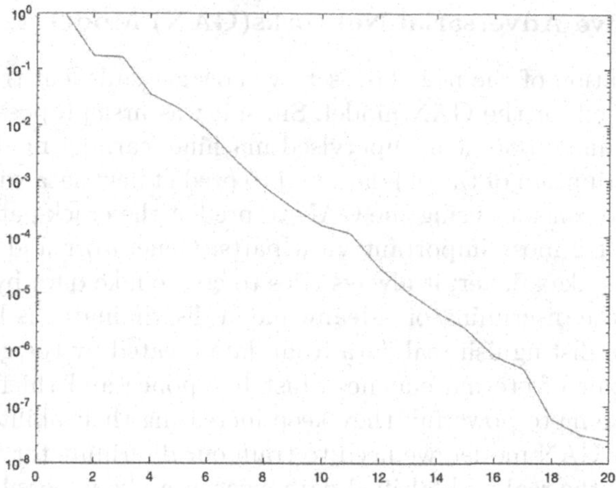

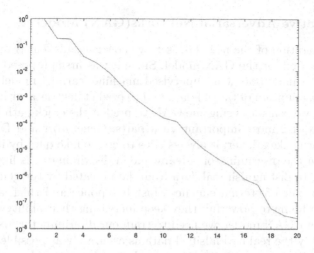

Fig. 4. Eigenvalues rank top 20.

With empirical estimation, we take $m = 3$, while the eigenvalue is small enough to ensure that reasonable convergence is reached and the geometric structure is maintained as well. In the end, the samples generated through reduced-order ISDE are shown in Fig. 5.

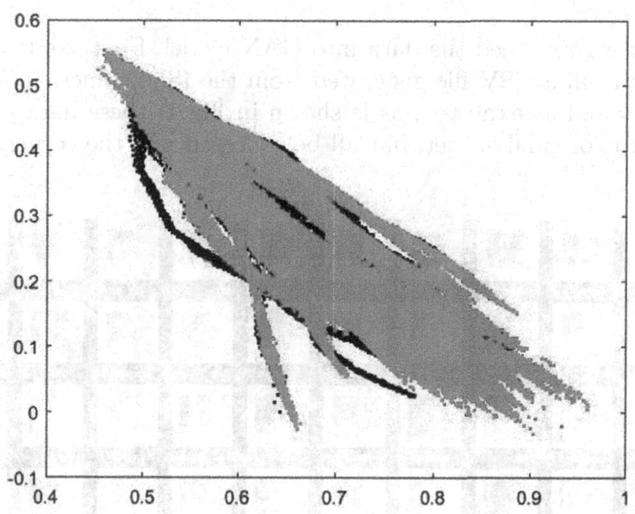

Fig. 5. Given data (black) and New data (red). (Color figure online)

Obviously, most of the new data generated from our formulation concentrate on the given data, which means our method and implementation live up to the expectations.

3.3 Generative Adversarial Networks(GAN) Model

After the generation of the new data set, we now get sufficient training data set which can be used for the GAN model. Since it was first proposed in 2014 [35], it has been the most potent unsupervised machine learning model to learn the probability distribution of the old data and to predict new data with a generative model. Thus, we consider using the GAN to predict the crack path propagation. GAN consists of 2 most important vital parts: Generatorr and Discriminator. The generator is like a faker; it always tries to create fake data by incorporating feedback from the discriminator. Meanwhile, a discriminator is like a classifier, always trying to distinguish real data from data created by the generator. They behave like a pair of eternal enemies. Just like police and thief, since both of them want to be more powerful, they keep increasing their ability all the time.

To train our GAN model, we need to train our discriminator first in order to make it identify the real and falsified data as accurately as possible. Meanwhile, we need to make the generator create data that is closer to real data. Specifically, it is achieved by the value function:

$$\min_{G}\max_{D} V(G,D) = E_{x\ P_{data}(x)}[logD(x)] + E_{z\ P_{data}(z)}[log(1-D(G(z)))] \quad (14)$$

where G and D are generator and discriminator respectively.

4 Experiment

We tried two ways to feed the data into GAN model. First, we tried to import data directly from a CSV file generated from the ISDE function, but the data was not generated as expected; as is shown in Fig. 6, these data points do not converge to the original subset, but all be squeezed into the corner.

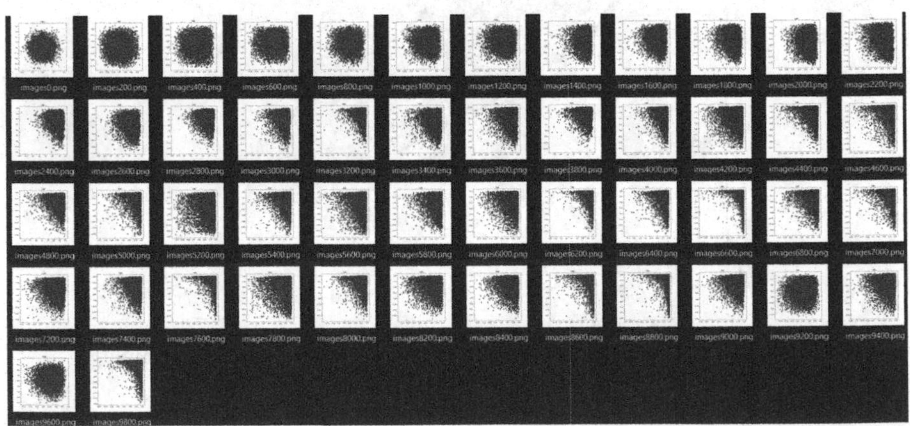

Fig. 6. Failed result.

Then we convert the data into grayscale images and apply binary cross-entropy as our loss function. As is shown in Fig. 7, after 4000 epochs of training, the discriminator accuracy approaches 0.5 in the end, which means it does not really know which image is true and which one is generated from the model.

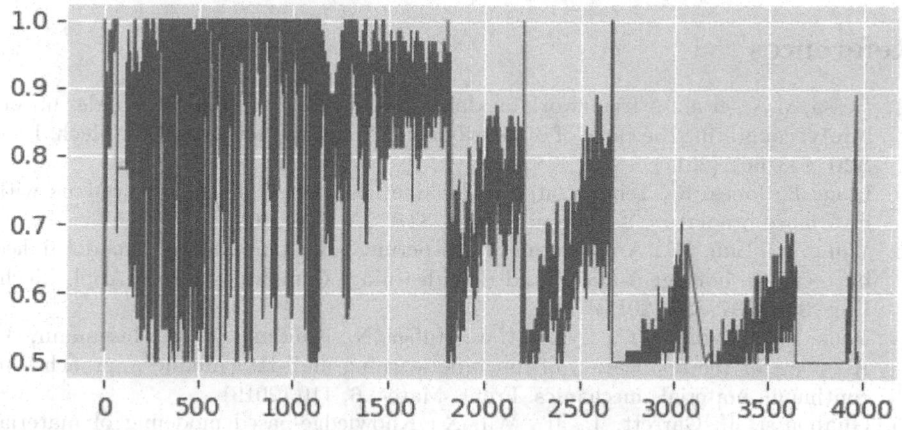

Fig. 7. Discriminator accuracy.

When the model reaches the point where $D(x) = 0.5$, then we enter some completely randomly generated grayscale images, and the result is as follows (Fig. 8):

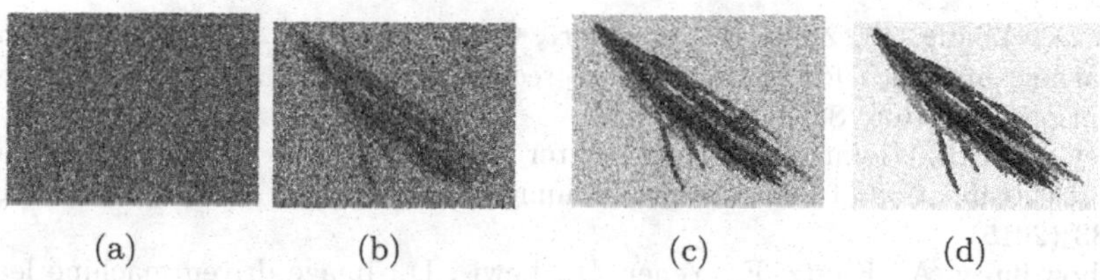

Fig. 8. New crack points generated by GAN.

The input data set is the random grayscale image, which means our model does not know the sample distribution beforehand. Through the generation process (a-d), the GAN model converges very well, and the geometrical structure is maintained.

5 Conclusion

A mixed framework is proposed in this paper for enriching the crack samples and predicting additional samples without further physical experiments. We take an experiment where the data set is generated from a damage formulation combined with a reduced-order ISDE and GAN model to verify the effectiveness of our framework. In the future, we can advance this research further by replacing some of these steps, like substituting reduced-order ISDE for ISDE, GAN model for DCGAN, BigGAN(or other GAN versions) or stochastic process (Markovianization), and design a uniform criterion to compare the convergence of these models.

References

1. Bessa, M.A., et al.: A framework for data-driven analysis of materials under uncertainty: countering the curse of dimensionality. Comput. Methods Appl. Mech. Eng. **320**, 633–667 (2017)
2. Ling, J., Jones, R., Templeton, J.: Machine learning strategies for systems with invariance properties. J. Comput. Phys. **318**, 22–35 (2016)
3. Wang, K., Sun, W.: A multiscale multi-permeability poroplasticity model linked by recursive homogenizations and deep learning. Comput. Methods Appl. Mech. Eng. **334**, 337–380 (2018)
4. Bock, F.E., Aydin, R.C., Cyron, C.J., Huber, N., Kalidindi, S.R., Klusemann, B.: A review of the application of machine learning and data mining approaches in continuum materials mechanics. Front. Mater. **6**, 110 (2019)
5. Ghaboussi, J., Garrett, J., Jr., Wu, X.: Knowledge-based modeling of material behavior with neural networks. J. Eng. Mech. **117**(1), 132–153 (1991)
6. Cang, R., Xu, Y., Chen, S., Liu, Y., Jiao, Y., Yi Ren, M.: Microstructure representation and reconstruction of heterogeneous materials via deep belief network for computational material design. J. Mech. Des. **139**(7), 071404 (2017)
7. Tripathy, R.K., Bilionis, I.: Deep uq: Learning deep neural network surrogate models for high dimensional uncertainty quantification. J. Comput. Phys. **375**, 565–588 (2018)
8. Li, X., Zhang, Y., Zhao, H., Burkhart, C., Brinson, L.C., Chen, W.: A transfer learning approach for microstructure reconstruction and structure-property predictions. Sci. Rep. **8**(1), 1–13 (2018)
9. DeCost, B.L., Holm, E.A.: A computer vision approach for automated analysis and classification of microstructural image data. Comput. Mater. Sci. **110**, 126–133 (2015)
10. Chowdhury, A., Kautz, E., Yener, B., Lewis, D.: Image driven machine learning methods for microstructure recognition. Comput. Mater. Sci. **123**, 176–187 (2016)
11. Xu, H., Li, Y., Brinson, C., Chen, W.: A descriptor-based design methodology for developing heterogeneous microstructural materials system. J. Mech. Des. **136**(5), 051007 (2014)
12. Jiang, Z., Chen, W., Burkhart, C.: Efficient 3d porous microstructure reconstruction via gaussian random field and hybrid optimization. J. Microscopy **252**(2), 135–148 (2013)
13. Liu, X., Shapiro, V.: Random heterogeneous materials via texture synthesis. Comput. Mater. Sci. **99**, 177–189 (2015)
14. Litjens, G., et al.: Deep learning as a tool for increased accuracy and efficiency of histopathological diagnosis. Sci. Rep. **6**(1), 1–11 (2016)
15. Pinaya, W.H.: Using deep belief network modelling to characterize differences in brain morphometry in schizophrenia. Sci. Rep. **6**(1), 1–9 (2016)
16. Socher, R., Huang, E., Pennin, J., Manning, C.D., Ng, A.: Dynamic pooling and unfolding recursive autoencoders for paraphrase detection. Adv. Neural Inf. Process. Syst. **24** (2011)

17. Li, X., Yang, Z., Brinson, L.C., Choudhary, A., Agrawal, A., Chen, W.: A deep adversarial learning methodology for designing microstructural material systems. In: International Design Engineering Technical Conferences and Computers and Information in Engineering Conference, vol. 51760, p. V02BT03A008. American Society of Mechanical Engineers (2018)
18. Bengio, Y.: Deep learning of representations for unsupervised and transfer learning. In: Proceedings of ICML Workshop on Unsupervised and Transfer Learning, pp. 17–36. JMLR Workshop and Conference Proceedings (2012)
19. Glorot, X., Bordes, A., Bengio, Y.: Domain adaptation for large-scale sentiment classification: a deep learning approach. In: ICML (2011)
20. Goodfellow, I., Mirza, M., Courville, A., Bengio, Y.: Multi-prediction deep boltzmann machines. Adv. Neural Inf. Process. Syst. **26** (2013)
21. DeCost, B.L., Francis, T., Holm, E.A.: Exploring the microstructure manifold: image texture representations applied to ultrahigh carbon steel microstructures. Acta Materialia **133**, 30–40 (2017)
22. Simonyan, K., Zisserman, A.: Very deep convolutional networks for large-scale image recognition. arXiv preprint arXiv:1409.1556 (2014)
23. Lubbers, N., Lookman, T., Barros, K.: Inferring low-dimensional microstructure representations using convolutional neural networks. Phys. Rev. E **96**(5), 052111 (2017)
24. Geelen, R.J., Liu, Y., Hu, T., Tupek, M.R., Dolbow, J.E.: A phase-field formulation for dynamic cohesive fracture. Comput. Methods Appl. Mech. Eng. **348**, 680–711 (2019)
25. Guilleminot, J., Dolbow, J.E.: Data-driven enhancement of fracture paths in random composites. Mech. Res. Commun. **103**, 103443 (2020)
26. Skoge, M., Donev, A., Stillinger, F.H., Torquato, S.: Packing hyperspheres in high-dimensional euclidean spaces. Phys. Rev. E **74**(4), 041127 (2006)
27. Soize, C., Ghanem, R.: Data-driven probability concentration and sampling on manifold. J. Comput. Phys. **321**, 242–258 (2016)
28. Moore, B.A., Rougier, E., O'Malley, D., Srinivasan, G., Hunter, A., Viswanathan, H.: Predictive modeling of dynamic fracture growth in brittle materials with machine learning. Comput. Mater. Sci. **148**, 46–53 (2018)
29. Hunter, A.: Reduced-order modeling through machine learning and graph-theoretic approaches for brittle fracture applications. Comput. Mater. Sci. **157**, 87–98 (2019)
30. Schwarzer, M., et al.: Learning to fail: predicting fracture evolution in brittle material models using recurrent graph convolutional neural networks. Comput. Mater. Sci. **162**, 322–332 (2019)
31. Pierson, K., Rahman, A., Spear, A.D.: Predicting microstructure-sensitive fatigue-crack path in 3D using a machine learning framework. JOM **71**(8), 2680–2694 (2019)
32. Ziaei-Rad, V., Shen, L., Jiang, J., Shen, Y.: Identifying the crack path for the phase field approach to fracture with non-maximum suppression. Comput. Methods Appl. Mech. Eng. **312**, 304–321 (2016)
33. Coifman, R.R., et al.: Geometric diffusions as a tool for harmonic analysis and structure definition of data: Diffusion maps. Proc. Natl. Acad. Sci. **102**(21), 7426–7431 (2005)
34. Soize, C.: Polynomial chaos expansion of a multimodal random vector. SIAM/ASA J. Uncertainty Quant. **3**(1), 34–60 (2015)
35. Goodfellow, I., et al.: Generative adversarial networks. Commun. ACM **63**(11), 139–144 (2020)

System and Resource Scheduling

A Modified List Scheduling Algorithm for the Online Hierarchical Load Balancing Problem with Bounded Processing Times

Man Xiao and Weidong Li(✉)

School of Mathematics and Statistics, Yunnan University, Kunming 650504, China
weidongmath@126.com

Abstract. For the online hierarchical scheduling problem on two parallel machines, the objective is to maximize the minimum machine load. When the processing times are bounded by an interval $[1, \alpha]$, Luo and Xu [8] designed an optimal algorithm with a competitive ratio of $1 + \alpha$ based on the threshold method. In this paper, we propose a simpler optimal online algorithm based on modified list scheduling.

Keywords: Semi-online · Hierarchical scheduling · Competitive ratio

1 Introduction

In the hierarchical scheduling problem, there are m machines with two hierarchies and a job set $\mathcal{J} = \{J_1, J_2, \cdots, J_n\}$. Some machines can process all jobs, and the remaining machines can only process partial jobs. The jobs arrive one by one, and each job can only be allocated using the information of the currently arrived jobs. The performance of the online algorithm is measured by the competitive ratio. For any instance I, let $C^A(I)$ (C^A, for short) denote the output value of online algorithm A, and $C^{OPT}(I)$ (C^{OPT}, for short) denote the offline optimal value. For a maximization (minimization) problem, the competitive ratio of algorithm A is defined as the minimum ρ that satisfies the $C^{OPT} \leq \rho C^A$ ($C^A \leq \rho C^{OPT}$) for any instance.

For the off-line problem, the information of all jobs is known in advance. When the goal is to minimize the makespan, Hwang et al. [19] considered the off-line model, and designed an approximation algorithm with approximate ratio no more than $\frac{5}{4}$ for $m = 2$, and the approximate ratio no more than $2 - \frac{1}{m-1}$ for $m \geq 3$. Ou et al. [21] designed an approximation algorithm with approximate ratio $\frac{4}{3}$, they also proposed a polynomial time approximation scheme (PTAS, for short) for this problem. Li et al. [20] designed an efficient PTAS for a special case, and presented a simpler fully PTAS. When the goal is to maximize the total early work, Chen et al. [17] proved this problem is NP-hard, even if $m = 2$. When the goal is to maximize the minimum machine completion time, Li et al. [22] presented a PTAS.

Z. Cai et al. (Eds.): NCTCS 2022, CCIS 1693, pp. 209–215, 2022.
https://doi.org/10.1007/978-981-19-8152-4_15

For the online makespan minimization problem on two machines, Park et al. [9] and Jang et al. [6] independently gave an optimal online algorithm with a competitive ratio of $\frac{5}{3}$. Meanwhile, Park et al. [9] also proposed an optimal algorithm with a competitive ratio of $\frac{3}{2}$ when the total job processing time is known in advance. Wu et al. [12] considered two semi-online versions where the offline optimal value or the largest processing time of all jobs is known, and proposed the optimal algorithms with competitive ratios of $\frac{3}{2}$ and $\frac{\sqrt{5}+1}{2}$ respectively. Chen et al. [4] studied several semi-online versions with the total processing time of low-hierarchy jobs is known, and designed several optimal online algorithms. If the processing times of all jobs are in $[1, \alpha]$ with $\alpha \geq 1$, Liu et al. [7] first considered this model in hierarchical scheduling on two machines. Zhang et al. [14] improved their result by giving an optimal online algorithm. Cao et al. [2] considered a combinatorial model where the maximum job processing time is known. Cao et al. [1] considered a combinatorial model with a buffer of size 1. Xiao et al. [15] also studied two semi-online models on three machines with a buffer of size 1. Zhao et al. [23] considered semi-online model with reassignment on three hierarchical machines.

For the online early work maximization problem on two machines, if two machines are identical, Chen et al. [17] designed an optimal online algorithm with a competitive ratio of $\sqrt{5}-1$. Chen et al. [16] also considered several semi-online cases. If two machines have different hierarchies, Xiao et al. [18] proposed three optimal online algorithms when the total size of low-hierarchy jobs, the total size of high-hierarchy jobs, and both the total size of low-hierarchy and high-hierarchy jobs are known in advance, respectively. Xiao et al. [25] considered two semi-online models, they designed two optimal online algorithms with competitive ratio of $\frac{4}{3}$ for the buffer model and rearrangement model, respectively.

For the online machine covering problem on two machines, i.e., the objective is to maximize the minimum machine completion time, Chassid and Epstein [3] showed that the competitive ratio of any online algorithm on the two hierarchical machines is infinite. When the number of machines is 2, He [24] considered several semi-online problems, and presented several different optimal semi-online algorithms, respectively. When the total sum of the processing times or the largest processing time is known, they proposed a optimal algorithm with a competitive ratio of $\frac{3}{2}$. Epstein et al. [5] considered the restricted assignment version with a buffer of size 1 on two machines. Wu et al. [11] considered several semi-online versions on two hierarchical machines. Wu and Li [10] considered a semi-online model with the processing times are discrete by $\{1, 2, 2^2, ..., 2^k\}$ with $k \geq 2$, and proposed an optimal online algorithm with a competitive ratio of 2^k. Xiao et al. [13] designed several optimal online algorithms for semi-online situation with known total processing time of low-hierarchy jobs.

Luo and Xu [8] studied a semi-online version with bounded processing times on two identical hierarchical machines, where the processing times of all jobs are in $[1, \alpha]$, $\alpha \geq 1$. The goal is to maximize the minimum machine completion time. They designed an optimal online algorithm with a competitive ratio of $1 + \alpha$. In this paper, we design a simpler modified list scheduling algorithm for the same problem. The rest of the paper is organized as follows. In Sect. 2, give problem statement and symbol description. In Sect. 3, give a modified list scheduling algorithm. In Sect. 4, give the discussion.

2 Preliminaries

We are given two hierarchical machines M_1 and M_2, and a series of jobs arriving online which are to be scheduled irrevocably at the time of their arrivals. The arrival of a new job occurs only after the current job is scheduled. Let $J = \{J_1, J_2, ..., J_n\}$ be the set of all jobs arranged in the order of arrival. We denote the j-th job as $J_j = (p_j, g_j)$, where the $p_j \in [1, \alpha]$ is the processing time of job J_j, and $g_j \in \{1, 2\}$ is the hierarchy of job J_j. If $g_j \geq g(M_i)$, job J_j could be processed by machine M_i, where $g(M_i) \in \{1, 2\}$ is the hierarchy of machine M_i. If $g_j = k$, we call J_j as a job of hierarchy $k \in \{1, 2\}$.

A feasible schedule is actually a partition (S_1, S_2) of the job set J, where $J_j \in S_i$ only if $g_j \geq g(M_i)$, $S_1 \cup S_2 = J$ and $S_1 \cap S_2 = \emptyset$. For $i = 1, 2$, let $L_i = \sum_{J_j \in S_i} p_j$ be the load of machine M_i. The online hierarchical scheduling problem [8], denoted by $P2|GoS, bounded|C_{min}$, is to find a schedule such that $\min_{i \in \{1,2\}} L_i$ is maximized.

For any i, j, k, let T_k^j be the total processing time of the first j jobs of hierarchy k, L_i^j be the load of M_i after job J_j is allocated, and T_k be the total processing time of the jobs with hierarchy k. Let T be the total size of the jobs. Clearly, we have

$$T_k^n = T_k, \ L_i^n = L_i,$$

and

$$T_1 + T_2 = L_1 + L_2 = T.$$

Luo and Xu [8] designed an optimal online algorithm with a competitive ratio of $1 + \alpha$ based on the threshold method. In this paper, we propose a modified list scheduling algorithm with the same competitive ratio. Our method is simpler, and it is possible to be extended to more general case.

3 A Modified List Scheduling Algorithm

Lemma 1 [8]. *The optimal minimum machine load C^{OPT} is at most $\min\{\frac{T}{2}, T_2\}$.*

The main idea of our method is to assign the jobs to machine M_2 preferentially. For convenience, let $L_{1,2}^j$ be the total processing time of jobs of hierarchy 2 assigned on M_1 after job J_j is scheduled. Clearly, we have

$$L_1 = L_{1,2}^n + T_1, \ T_2 = L_{1,2}^n + L_2.$$

The details of our algorithm is described in Algorithm 1.

Algorithm 1:

1 Initially, let $L_1^0 = L_{1,2}^0 = L_2^0 = 0$, let $n_2 = 0$ be the number of jobs of hierarchy 2 arrived.
2 When a new job $J_j = (p_j, g_j)$ arrives,
3 **if** $g_j = 1$ **then**
4 　Assign job J_j to M_1.
5 **else**
6 　Set $n_2 \leftarrow n_2 + 1$.
7 　**if** $n_2 = 1$ **then**
8 　　Assign job J_j to M_2.
9 　**if** $n_2 = 2$ **then**
10 　　Assign job J_j to M_1.
11 　**else**
12 　　**if** $L_2^{j-1} \leq L_{1,2}^{j-1} + \alpha$ **then**
13 　　　Assign job J_j to M_2.
14 　　**else**
15 　　　Assign J_j to M_1.
16 Update $L_1^j, L_{1,2}^j$ *and* L_2^j.
17 If there is another job, $j \leftarrow j+1$, go to **step 2.** Otherwise, stop.

Theorem 1. The competitive ratio of Algorithm 1 is at most $1 + \alpha$.

Proof. We distinguish the following two cases.

Case 1. There are at most two jobs of hierarchy 2.

Clearly, if there is at most one jobs of hierarchy 2, Algorithm 1 produces an optimal solution. If there are two jobs of hierarchy 2, by the choice of Algorithm 1, the first job of hierarchy 2 is assigned to M_2, and the second job of hierarchy 2 is assigned to M_1, which implies that

$$1 \leq L_2 \leq \alpha \text{ and } 1 \leq L_{1,2}^n \leq \alpha.$$

By Lemma 1, we have

$$\frac{C^{OPT}}{L_1} \leq \frac{T}{2L_1} = \frac{L_1 + L_2}{2L_1} \leq \frac{1}{2} + \frac{\alpha}{L_1} \leq 1 + \alpha,$$

and

$$\frac{C^{OPT}}{L_2} \leq \frac{T_2}{L_2} = \frac{L_{1,2}^n + L_2}{L_2} \leq 1 + \frac{\alpha}{L_2} \leq 1 + \alpha.$$

Case 2. There are at least three jobs of hierarchy 2.

By the choice of Algorithm 1, the first job of hierarchy 2 is assigned to M_2, and the second job of hierarchy 2 is assigned to M_1. Therefore, we have

$$L_1 \geq L_{1,2}^n \geq 1 \text{ and } L_2 \geq 1.$$

Let $J_l = (p_l, 2)$ be the last job of hierarchy 2 assigned to M_2. Therefore, we have

$$L_2^{l-1} \leq L_{1,2}^{l-1} + \alpha, \text{ and } L_2 = L_2^l = L_2^{l-1} + p_l \leq L_{1,2}^{l-1} + 2\alpha \leq L_{1,2}^n + 2\alpha.$$

By Lemma 1, we have

$$\begin{aligned}\frac{C^{OPT}}{L_1} &\leq \frac{T}{2L_1} = \frac{T_1 + T_2}{2(T_1 + L_{1,2}^n)}\\ &= \frac{T_1 + L_{1,2}^n + L_2}{2(T_1 + L_{1,2}^n)}\\ &\leq \frac{T_1 + 2L_{1,2}^n + 2\alpha}{2(T_1 + L_{1,2}^n)}\\ &\leq 1 + \alpha.\end{aligned}$$

If all jobs after the second job of hierarchy 2 are assigned to M_2, we have $L_{1,2}^n \leq \alpha$, implying that

$$\frac{C^{OPT}}{L_2} \leq \frac{T_2}{L_2} = \frac{L_{1,2}^n + L_2}{L_2} \leq \frac{L_2 + \alpha}{L_2} \leq 1 + \alpha.$$

Else, let $J_t = (p_t, 2)$ the last job of hierarchy 2 job assigned to M_1. By the choice of Algorithm 1, we have $L_2^{t-1} > L_{1,2}^{t-1} + \alpha$. Moreover, we have

$$L_2 \geq L_2^{t-1} > L_{1,2}^{t-1} + \alpha \geq L_{1,2}^{t-1} + p_t = L_{1,2}^t = L_{1,2}^n.$$

Thus,

$$\frac{C^{OPT}}{L_2} \leq \frac{T_2}{L_2} = \frac{L_{1,2}^n + L_2}{L_2} \leq \frac{2L_2}{L_2} \leq 2 \leq 1 + \alpha.$$

Therefore, in any case, we have

$$\frac{C^{OPT}}{C^A} = \frac{C^{OPT}}{\min\{L_1, L_2\}} = \max_{i=1,2} \frac{C^{OPT}}{L_i} \leq 1 + \alpha,$$

implying that the theorem holds. □

4 Discussion

In this paper, we gave a modified list scheduling algorithm with a competitive ratio of $1 + \alpha$ for the online hierarchical load balancing problem with bounded processing times on two machines [8]. It is interesting to extend our method to more general case with m hierarchical machines.

Acknowledgement. The work is supported in part by the National Natural Science Foundation of China [No. 12071417].

References

1. Cao, Q., Cheng, T.C.E., Wan, G., Li, Y.: Several semi-online scheduling problems on two identical machines with combined information. Theor. Comput. Sci. **457**, 35–44 (2012)
2. Cao, Q., Liu, Z., Cheng, T.C.E.: Semi-online scheduling with known partial information about job sizes on two identical machines. Theor. Comput. Sci. **412**, 3731–3737 (2011)
3. Chassid, O., Epstein, L.: The hierarchical model for load balancing on two machines. J. Comb. Optim. **15**(4), 305–314 (2008)
4. Chen, X., Ding, N., Dosa, G., Han, X., Jiang, H.: Online hierarchical scheduling on two machines with known total size of low-hierarchy jobs. Int. J. Comput. Math. **92**(5–6), 873–881 (2015)
5. Epstein, L., Levin, A., Stee, R.: Max-min online allocations with a reordering buffer. SIAM J. Disc. Math. **25**(3–4), 1230–1250 (2011)
6. Jiang, Y., He, Y., Tang, C.: Optimal online algorithms for scheduling on two identical machines under a grade of service. J. Zhejiang Univ. Sci. A. **7**, 309–314 (2006)
7. Liu, M., Chu, C., Xu, Y., Zheng, F.: Semi-online scheduling on 2 machines under a grade of service provision with bounded processing times. J. Comb. Optim. **21**, 138–149 (2011)
8. Luo, T., Xu, Y.: Semi-online hierarchical load balancing problem with bounded processing times. Theor. Comput. Sci. **607**, 75–82 (2015)
9. Park, J., Chang, S., Lee, K.: Online and semi-online scheduling of two machines under a grade of service provision. Oper. Res. Lett. **34**(6), 692–696 (2006)
10. Wu, G., Li, W.: Semi-online machine covering on two hierarchical machines with discrete processing times. In: Li, L., Lu, P., He, K. (eds.) NCTCS 2018. CCIS, vol. 882, pp. 1–7. Springer, Singapore (2018). https://doi.org/10.1007/978-981-13-2712-4_1
11. Wu, Y., Cheng, T.C.E., Ji, M.: Optimal algorithms for semi-online machine covering on two hierarchical machines. Theor. Comput. Sci. **531**(6), 37–46 (2014)
12. Wu, Y., Ji, M., Yang, Q.: Optimal semi-online scheduling algorithms on two parallel identical machines under a grade of service provision. Int. J. Prod. Econ. **135**(1), 367–371 (2012)
13. Xiao, M., Wu, G., Li, W.: Semi-online machine covering on two hierarchical machines with known total size of low-hierarchy jobs. In: Sun, X., He, K., Chen, X. (eds.) NCTCS 2019. CCIS, vol. 1069, pp. 95–108. Springer, Singapore (2019). https://doi.org/10.1007/978-981-15-0105-0_7
14. Zhang, A., Jiang, Y., Fan, L., Hu, J.: Optimal online algorithms on two hierarchical machines with tightly-grouped processing times. J. Comb. Optim. **29**(4), 781–795 (2015)
15. Xiao, M., Ding, L., Zhao, S., Li, W.: Semi-online algorithms for hierarchical scheduling on three parallel machines with a buffer size of 1. In: He, K., Zhong, C., Cai, Z., Yin, Y. (eds.) NCTCS 2020. CCIS, vol. 1352, pp. 47–56. Springer, Singapore (2021). https://doi.org/10.1007/978-981-16-1877-2_4
16. Chen, X., Kovalev, S., Liu, Y.Q., Sterna, M., Chalamon, I., Błażewicz, J.: Semi-online scheduling on two identical machines with a common due date to maximize total early work. Disc. Appl. Math. **290**, 71–78 (2021)
17. Chen, X., Sterna, M., Han, X., Błażewicz, J.: Scheduling on parallel identical machines with late work criterion: offline and online cases. J. Schedul. **19**(6), 729–736 (2016)

18. Xiao, M., Liu, X., Li, W.: Semi-online early work maximization problem on two hierarchical machines with partial information of processing time. In: Wu, W., Du, H. (eds.) AAIM 2021. LNCS, vol. 13153, pp. 146–156. Springer, Cham (2021). https://doi.org/10.1007/978-3-030-93176-6_13
19. Hwang, H.C., Chang, S.Y., Lee, K.: Parallel machine scheduling under a grade of service provision. Comput. Oper. Res. **31**(12), 2055–2061 (2004)
20. Li, W., Li, J., Zhang, T.: Two approximation schemes for scheduling on parallel machines under a grade of service provision. Asia-Pac. J. Oper. Res. **29**(5), Article 1250029 (2012)
21. Ou, J., Leung, J.Y.T., Li, C.: Scheduling parallel machines with inclusive processing set restrictions. Naval Res. Logist. **55**(4), 328–338 (2008)
22. Li, J., Li, W., Li, J.: Polynomial approximation schemes for the max-min allocation problem under a grade of service provision. Disc. Math. Algor. Appl. **1**(3), 355–368 (2009)
23. Zhao, S., Xiao, M., Li, W.: Semi-online algorithms for hierarchical scheduling on three machines with reassignment. Comput. Eng. Sci. **44**(6), 1126–1132 (2022)
24. He, Y.: Semi-on-line scheduling problems for maximizing the minimum machine completion time. Acta Mathematicae Applicatae Sinica **17**, 107–113 (2001)
25. Xiao, M., Bai, X., Li, W.: Online early work maximization problem on two hierarchical machines with buffer or rearrangements. In: Ni, Q., Wu, W. (eds) Algorithmic Aspects in Information and Management. AAIM 2022. Lecture Notes in Computer Science, vol. 13513. Springer, Cham (2022). https://doi.org/10.1007/978-3-031-16081-3_5

An Improved ACS Algorithm by CA for Task Scheduling in Heterogeneous Multiprocessing Environments

Ningbo Liu[1(✉)], Liangli Ma[1], Wei Ren[2,3,4], and Muyuan Wang[1]

[1] School of Electronic Engineering, Navy University of Engineering, Wuhan, China
ningboliucs@sina.com

[2] School of Computer Science, China University of Geosciences, Wuhan, China

[3] Key Laboratory of Network Assessment Technology CAS Institute of Information Engineering, Chinese Academy of Sciences, Beijing 100093, China

[4] Henan Key Laboratory of Network Cryptography Technology, Zhengzhou, China

Abstract. In heterogeneous multi-core architecture, to improve the running efficiency of the program is of critical importance. However, it depends on whether the subtasks of the program can be efficiently scheduled to the heterogeneous processing units, which is unfortunately a NP-complete problem. List scheduling algorithms are currently considered to be promising, which can approach suboptimal solutions in terms of low time consumption, but the overall quality of their solutions is often lower than those of ant colony algorithms. On the contrary, ant colony algorithms can obtain better solutions, but the convergence speed of the algorithms is worse. Especially when the number of nodes increases, this shortcoming is remarkably unacceptable. To tackle above observations, we propose a new ant colony optimization method for DAG task scheduling in heterogeneous multi-core environments, by combining culture algorithm and ant colony system (ACS) algorithm (namely, CACS). The group space of CACS is redesigned based on the ACS. Under the DAG tasks model, the heuristic function is improved by using the increase value of the scheduling length as the visibility of the ant colony, in order to improve the ants to obtain the local optimal nodes more effectively. To avoid the algorithm falling into the local optimum and improving the convergence speed, CACS adopts the critical tasks optimization algorithm in the belief space to mutate the local optimum individuals introduced in the group space, probabilistically generate elite individuals, and guide the group space evolution through the dynamic pheromone enhancement mechanism. Experiments with sufficient amount and randomness demonstrate that the CACS algorithm outperforms list scheduling algorithms and ant colony algorithms in terms of scheduling length and convergence speed.

Keywords: Ant colony algorithm · Cultural algorithm · Heterogeneous multi-core architecture · Parallel computing

Z. Cai et al. (Eds.): NCTCS 2022, CCIS 1693, pp. 216–235, 2022.
https://doi.org/10.1007/978-981-19-8152-4_16

1 Introduction

Heterogeneous multi-core processors [1] are designed for specific application scenarios, especially in the field of industrial control. Each program is composed of multiple subtasks. Due to the different operational logics of the subtasks, they have different affinity within each heterogeneous core, resulting in different running efficiency. Moreover, the order of execution of subtasks is related to their dependencies, which are commonly described by directed acyclic graph (DAG). It is a NP-complete [2] combinatorial optimization problem in that how to efficiently schedule subtasks in parallel under heterogeneous multi-core architecture.

Ant colony optimization (ACO) algorithm [3] is envisioned as a candidate among the effective algorithms to solve the problem of DAG task scheduling in heterogeneous multiprocessing environments. Recently, ACO algorithm has attract more and more attentions, and a series of efficient ant colony algorithms [4–6] with improved performances are proposed.

Although these improved algorithms have many advantages in solving combinatorial optimization problems, such as global optimization, positive and negative feedback mechanism, parallelism, and distributed computing, etc. Nonetheless, some difficulties still remain. For example, due to the even distribution of pheromone at the beginning, the ant colony's tracking is blind. Because of this blindness, it takes longer for the ant colony to accumulate pheromone on the optimal path. In the later of the iteration, the search space shrinks sharply and the probability of algorithm stagnation increases greatly due to the effect of the positive feedback mechanism.

In order to further improve the convergence speed and quality of the algorithm, we propose a new ant colony optimization method for DAG tasks scheduling in heterogeneous multi-core environments, by combining culture algorithm (CA) and ant colony system (ACS) algorithm (namely, CACS). The major contributions of the paper are listed as follows:

1) For the task scheduling problem over heterogeneous multi-core architecture, we redesign the heuristic function by using the increase value of the scheduling length as the visibility of the ant colony in order to make ant colony search for local optimal nodes more effectively.
2) We also propose a critical tasks optimization algorithm in belief space, in order to improve the quality of solutions and avoid a local optimum.
3) In order to improve the convergence speed of the algorithm, a dynamic pheromone enhancement mechanism is proposed.

The rest of the paper will be organized as follows: Sect. 3 presents research work in the relevant literature. In Sect. 3, we describe the application model in detail. In Sect. 4, we clarify the proposed algorithms. The experimental and analysis are presented in Sect. 5. Section 6, concludes the paper.

2 Related Work

At present, DAG task scheduling algorithms in heterogeneous multi-core architecture mainly include three types, namely list scheduling algorithms, task replication-based scheduling algorithms and swarm intelligence optimization algorithms.

2.1 List Scheduling Algorithms

The basic idea of list scheduling algorithms [7] is to construct a scheduling list statically or dynamically by sorting the priority of nodes according to a certain strategy.Then, according to the order of the scheduling list the task is assigned to the processing unit that enables it to start or finish earliest. List scheduling algorithms include heterogeneous earliest finish time (HEFT) algorithm [8] and critical path on a processor (CPOP) algorithm [9] commonly. In 2021,Zhang et al. proposed an improved HEFT algorithm [10] for task scheduling and got a desired results. In 2016, Yuan et al. proposed a novel CPOP algorithm [11] based on Pi calculus to improve programming efficiency. Experiments show that the list scheduling algorithms can approach suboptimal solutions in terms of low time cost.

2.2 Replication-Based Scheduling Algorithms

The scheduling algorithms based on task duplication [12] make full use of the unbalanced load of the processing unit caused by the decrease in the parallel performance of the program due to the dependency between the subtasks, and copy the executed subtask to the idle processing unit for running again. In this method, the communication overhead between subtasks effectively reduces. In 2021, Yao et al. proposed a task duplication-based scheduling algorithm [13] for budget-constrained workflows in cloud computing. This algorithm improves resource utilization effectively.

2.3 Swarm Intelligence Optimization Algorithms

Inspired by the regular behavior of biological communities, swarm intelligence optimization algorithms [14] are developed to solve complex optimization problems. In 1992, Dr. Dorigo proposed ACO [3] algorithm, which was inspired by the behavior of ants in finding the path during food search, and in 1997, based on ACO algorithm, he proposed ACS algorithm with positive feedback mechanism, distributed computing, and greedy heuristic. In 1995, Eberhart et al. proposed the particle swarm optimization algorithm (PSO) [15], the concept of which was derived from the study of birds foraging behavior. In 2021, Qamar combined PSO with ant system to put forward an improved algorithm [16] for traveling salesman problem(TSP) [17]. Zhao et al. proposed a model [18] by combining PSO algorithm and artificial swarm algorithm to solve the problem of crowd evacuation in 2020.

Cultural algorithm (CA) [19] is a double-layer evolution mechanism inspired by the conceptual models of the human cultural evolution process. Acquiring, preserving, and integrating problem-solving experience through a belief space independent of the group space guides the group to evolve faster than simply relying on genetic inheritance or natural characteristics. In 2014, Xianmin Wei et al. incorporated ACO algorithm into CA framework and adopted multi-population spatial parallel evolution strategy to solve TSP. Mojab et al. design a deadline-constrained big data workflow scheduling algorithm [20] for task scheduling. Numerous studies have shown that CA is effective in improving the convergence speed and solution quality of swarm intelligence optimization algorithm.

3 Model Selection

Suppose the heterogeneous multi-core processing architecture is composed of m heterogeneous cores, all of which are interconnected and can be described by a directed complete graph $DCG = (P, B)$, as shown in Fig. 1, where P is the set of processor cores, and B is the edge set of the graph which indicating that communication between different cores is enabled. We assume that the application consists of n different tasks, and the dependencies between the subtasks are represented by a DAG model, defined as $DAG = (T, E, D_e)$, where $T = \{T_i \mid i = 1, 2 \cdots, n\}$ is the set of subtasks.

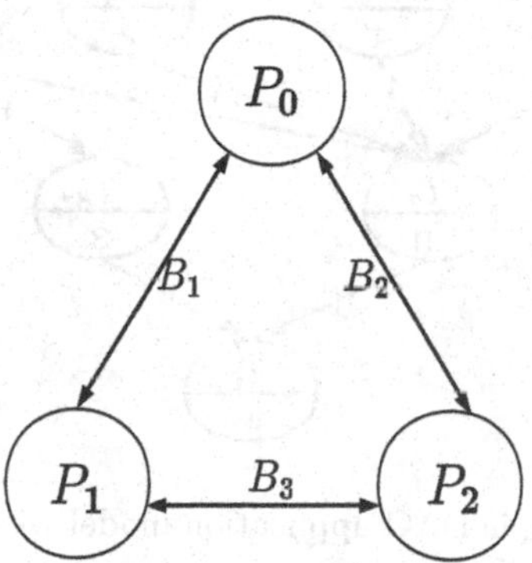

Fig. 1. A DCG model with 3 processors.

As displayed in Fig. 2, the upper part of the subtask node is the task number, and the lower part represents the execution time on a certain heterogeneous core.The execution time of a subtask is denoted by $W_{P_i}(T_i)$, which is present in Table 1. E is the edge set of the graph, which indicates the dependency between subtasks, As shown in Table 2, D is the weight of edge e, which represents the amount of communication data between subtasks. The set of subtasks scheduling strategies is denoted by S, and $s \in S$ is a scheme that schedules n subtasks to m heterogeneous cores for execution on the premise of satisfying inter-task dependencies. The task scheduling problem can be formally described as:

$$s : T \rightarrow P, s \in S$$

Let RT be the running time of the application, the optimization objective function of task scheduling can be described as:

$$\min_{s \in S} RT(s)$$

where

$$RT(s) = \max_{1 \leq i \leq m} \{makespan(P_i)_s\}$$

Here, $makespan(P_i)_s$ represents the completion time of the last task on the processor P_i under the scheduling strategy s.

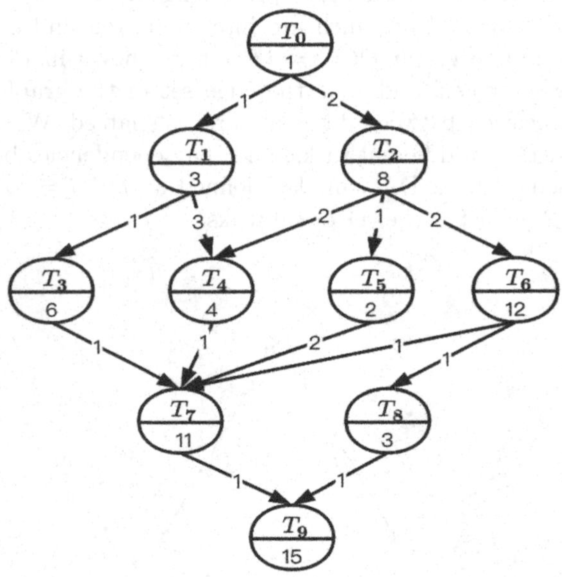

Fig. 2. A simple DAG application model with 10 subtasks.

To clarify our research, we give the following three definitions:

1) Tasks are not allowed to migrate or replicate on different heterogeneous cores, and task preemption is not supported;
2) The communication overhead $c_{T_iT_k}$ between subtasks is defined as the product of the path length (PL) between the two processors and the amount of communication data $D_{T_iT_k}$. If the two subtasks are executed in the same core, the communication overhead is 0, that is:

$$c_{T_iT_j} = \begin{cases} 0 & if\ s(T_i) = s(T_j) \\ D_{T_iT_j} \times PL & else \end{cases} \quad (1)$$

Table 1. The cost of a task running in different processors.

Task	W_{P_0}	W_{P_1}	W_{P_2}	$\overline{W}$
T_0	1	4	7	4
T_1	2	4	2	3
T_2	9	7	8	7
T_3	5	3	4	4
T_4	4	2	3	3
T_5	2	4	3	3
T_6	12	23	11	12
T_7	11	23	13	12
T_8	4	6	5	5
T_9	5	6	7	6

Table 2. Dependency matrix.

Task	T_0	T_1	T_2	T_3	T_4	T_5	T_6	T_7	T_8	T_9
T_0	0	1	2	∞	∞	∞	∞	∞	∞	∞
T_1	∞	0	∞	1	3	∞	∞	∞	∞	∞
T_2	∞	∞	0	∞	2	1	2	∞	∞	∞
T_3	∞	∞	∞	0	∞	∞	∞	1	∞	∞
T_4	∞	∞	∞	∞	0	∞	∞	1	∞	∞
T_5	∞	∞	∞	∞	∞	0	∞	2	∞	∞
T_6	∞	∞	∞	∞	∞	∞	0	1	1	∞
T_7	∞	∞	∞	∞	∞	∞	∞	0	∞	1
T_8	∞	∞	∞	∞	∞	∞	∞	∞	0	1
T_9	∞	∞	∞	∞	∞	∞	∞	∞	∞	0

The function $s(T_i)$ represents the heterogeneous core assigned to task T_i under the scheduling strategy s. In order to simplify the model, we ignores the impact of processor location on communication overhead, that is, $PL = 1$.

3) The earliest finish time (EFT) of T_i running on processor P_j is defined as follows:

$$EFT_{T_i} = \max\left\{avail(P_j), \max_{T_k \in pred_{T_i}} (EFT_{T_k} + c_{T_k T_i})\right\} + W_{P_j}(T_i) \tag{2}$$

Here, $avail(P_j)$ is the earliest available time of the processor P_j. The $c_{T_k T_i}$ is the communication overhead between subtasks T_k and T_i.$W_{P_j}(T_i)$ shows the execution time of subtask T_i on the heterogeneous core P_j. The $pred_{T_i}$ is the predecessor set of task T_i and $succd_{T_i}$ represents the successor set of task T_i. If the predecessor set is empty, it means that the task is the starting point and if the successor set is empty, it means that the task is the meeting point.

4 Proposed Algorithms

ACS is an improved algorithm of the basic ACO algorithm. Compared with ACO algorithm, ACS algorithm introduces real-time local pheromone update to reduce the concentration of pheromone on the tracked path, so as to increase the chance of other paths being selected by other ants, and expand the search space of the colony. Based on the ACS algorithm, in this paper we improve the definition of heuristic function for heterogeneous multi-core DAG tasks scheduling model, so that it can motivate individual ants to select local optimal nodes more effectively. Then the improved ACS is incorporated into the CA framework and a new algorithm is proposed, namely CACS. The CACS architecture is composed of two independent evolution spaces, namely group space and belief space, as shown in Fig. 3. Communication protocols *accept*() and $influence()$ are adopted for communication between the two parallel evolution spaces. The group space contains a series of possible solutions to the problem. The improved ACS is used as the group evolution algorithm, and the local optimal individuals are transmitted to the belief space regularly by calling *accept*(). As well as, the belief space uses prior knowledge to initialize the pheromone nonuniform distribution, thus expanding the ant colony search space effectively at the beginning of the algorithm. At the same time, the critical task optimization algorithm is used to mutate the local optimal individuals introduced in the group space to form experience for solving the problem. And the belief space uses the experience to guide the evolution of group space through calling $influence()$ with opening the pheromone enhancement mechanism. CACS can effectively improve the convergence speed and the quality of the solution through the co-evolution of two independent spaces.

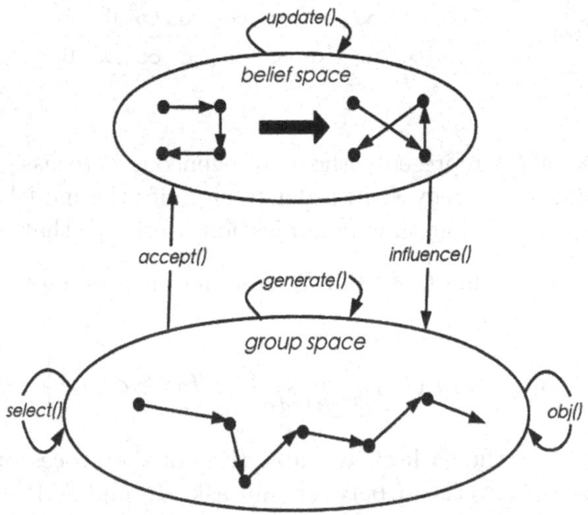

Fig. 3. Cultural algorithm architecture.

In the activity on edge (AOE) network [21], the length of the critical path [22] determines the shortest completion time of the engineering activity. In topological sorting, it is often used to advance the start time of activities on the critical path to shorten the completion time of the entire project activity. So the critical task optimization algorithm is proposed by moving the critical tasks positions forward in the scheduling list carried by ant individuals from the group space, which is shown in Fig. 4. In this way, critical tasks can be executed as early as possible to reduce the scheduling length. And it's important to obtain the critical tasks. We transform a DAG model into an AOE network by taking the average communication cost of tasks as the weight of edges and the average running time of tasks as the execution time of activities. And the critical tasks are obtained from the AOE network. The CACS algorithm is described in detail in Algorithm 1.

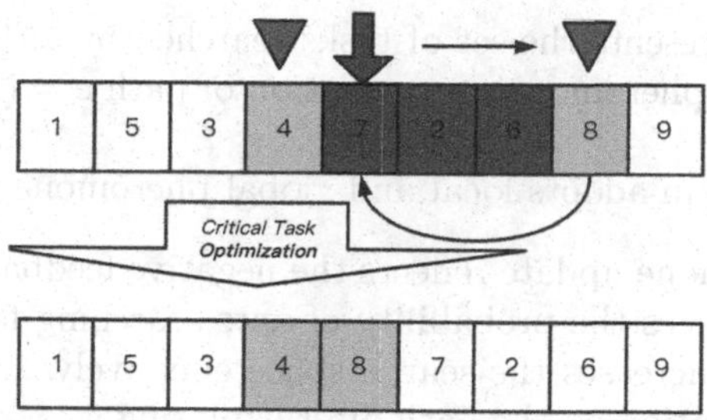

Fig. 4. Critical task optimization.

Input: *DAG* and *DCG* graph, the running time matrix of the subtasks on each heterogeneous core
Output: Optimal scheduling length

$DAG \rightarrow AOE$ *network*
To obtain funlly ordered set $task_{key}$ of cirtical tasks from AOE
Initialize the group space
Initialize the belief space
while $iter < iter_{max}$ **do**
  Initialize the colony $ant_k, k-1, 2, \cdots, l$
  Call Algorithm 2 to guide the evolution of the group space
  if $iter \ \% \ AStep = 0$ **then**
    Call *accept*() to pass the locally optimal individual into the belief space
    Call Algorithm 4 to guide individual variation in belief space
  end
  if $iter \ \% \ IStep = 0$ **then**
    Call *influence*() to affect the evolution of the population space
  end
end
return The minimum $RT(s)$

Algorithm 1: CACS algorithm

4.1 Designing Group Space

In order to solve practical problems, We indicate that the initialized ant colony is an artificial colony. Compared to natural ant colony, the ants domesticated have the ability to memorize the searched task as well as the assignment plan of the task. In addition, the ant does not repeatedly search for the route that has been tracked and stop until all the nodes are traversed. Compared with the list scheduling algorithms, ACS algorithm, which is shown in Algorithm 2, adopts the strategy of topology sorting and task scheduling simultaneously, which is that, every time the ant selects a task node, it will call Algorithm3 for task scheduling. In each iteration, after the ant traverses all nodes, it will carry the topological sort top_{ant_k} and the scheduling plan s_{ant_k} of the subtasks. In order to facilitate the description of the improved ACS algorithm, the following definitions are given:

1) $finished_{ant_k}$ represents the set of tasks searched by ant_k;
2) τ_e represents the pheromone concentration of path $e = (T_i, T_j)$, initialized to a constant τ_0;
3) The ACS algorithm adopts local and global pheromone update modes:

The local pheromone update reflects the negative feedback mechanism of the ACS algorithm, reduces the probability of ants searching for the path that has been traveled, and increases the search space effectively. Each ant updates the pheromone concentration on the path after exploring a task node. The rules are as follows:

$$\tau_e = (1-\theta)\tau_e + \theta\tau_{tiny} \tag{3}$$

$$\Delta\tau_{T_iT_j} = \begin{cases} TL_{gb}^{-1} & if\ (T_i, T_j) \in T_{gb} \\ 0 & else \end{cases} \tag{4}$$

where $\rho(0 < \rho < 1)$ is the global volatile factor of pheromone, and T_{gb} is the global optimal path. Through the global pheromone update, the optimal path can be retained to affect the pathfinding process of the next generation of ants.

4) $Avail_{T_i}^{ant_k}$ represents the set of tasks that ant_k can search in the next step at the current node. It can be known from the inter-task dependency and the search characteristics of artificial ant colonies:

$$Avail_{T_i}^{ant_k} = \left\{x | x \in \eth_T^{finished_{ant_k}} \wedge pred_x \subseteq finished_{ant_k}\right\} \tag{5}$$

5) The rule for ant_k to transfer from node T_i to T_j is:

$$T_j = \begin{cases} \max\limits_{T_l \in Avail_{T_i}^{ant_k}} \left\{(\tau_{T_iT_l})^\alpha (\eta_{T_iT_l})^\beta\right\} & if\ r < r_0 \\ V & else \end{cases} \tag{6}$$

where V represents that the ant explores the next task node T_j from task node T_i by using pseudo-random proportion rules, and the probability formula is as follows:

$$P_{T_iT_j} = \begin{cases} \frac{(\tau_{T_iT_j})^{\alpha}(\eta_{T_iT_j})\beta}{\sum_{T_l \in Avail_{T_i}^{ant_k}} (\tau_{T_iT_j})^{\alpha}(\eta_{T_iT_j})\beta} & if\ T_j \in Avail_{T_i}^{ant_k} \\ 0 & else \end{cases} \tag{7}$$

r is a random number evenly distributed in the interval [0, 1], and r_0 is a constant given in the interval [0, 1]. The smaller r_0 is, the greater the probability that the ant selects the next task by the random method, which leads to the expansion of the group search space and the higher the quality of solutions, but the slower the convergence speed of the algorithm.

$\eta_{T_iT_j}$ is the improved heuristic information function, which is defined as follows:

$$\eta_{T_iT_j} = \begin{cases} \frac{1}{(EFT_{T_j} - EFT_{T_i})} & if\ EFT_{T_j} > EFT_{T_j} \\ 1 & else \end{cases} \tag{8}$$

We choose the difference between the earliest finish time of the next node and the earliest finish time of the current node as the visibility of the ant colony, and take into full consideration that the scheduling of the next node, without increasing the total scheduling length, is given the maximum visibility. And maximum visibility of the node means that the ants are most inclined to choose this task. Heuristic information indicates that the ant selects the task node with the minimum increase in scheduling length. α and β are two parameters representing the relative importance of pheromone and heuristic information.

Input: $ant_k, k = 1, 2, \cdots, l$
Output: The average scheduling length of the ant colony

for *each* ant_k **do**
  Add the starting point to the list $finished_{ant_k}$
  Call algorithm 3 to get the starting point allocation scheme
  while $finished_{ant_k} \subsetneqq T$ **do**
    Select the next task node according to formula (6) and (7)
    Local pheromone updates
    Call algorithm 3 to get the allocation scheme of the node
    Update the completed task list $finished_{ant_k}$
  end
  $RT_{sum} = RT_{sum} + RT(s_{ant_k})$
  Update the global optimal solution TL_{gb} and global optimal path T_{gb}
end
Global pheromone update
Determine whether to call *accept*() to communicate with the belief space
return The minimum RT_{sum}/l

Algorithm 2: The improved ACS algorithm

4.2 Designing Belief Space

The design of the belief space is the biggest difference from the previous ant colony algorithm optimization schemes. The design of the space is mainly divided into two parts, as shown in Algorithm 4. First, at the beginning of the algorithm

Input: $ant_k, k = 1, 2, \cdots, l$ and T_i
Output: The processing unit assigned to T_i and earliest finish time EFT_{T_i} of T_i

for *each* $p_k \in P$ **do**
  Calculate EFT_{T_i} according to formula (2)
end
return The minimum EFT_{T_i} and the corresponding processing unit P

Algorithm 3: The task assignment scheme

iteration, the pheromone is initialized non-uniformly by following formula. In this method, the search space of the ant colony can be effectively expanded, and the belief space can be provided with more abundant individuals, thus increasing the probability of better mutation. Second, the belief space accepts the local optimal solution from the group space according to the *accept*() function as the object, and then makes full use of the critical task optimization algorithm to guide its mutation. Comparing the solutions between the mutated individual and the elite individual, the smaller one is regarded as the next elite individual in belief space.

$$\tau_{T_{entry}T_j} = \begin{cases} \frac{EFT_{T_j}}{\sum_{T_j \in succd_{T_{entry}}} EFT_{T_j}} & if\ T_j \in succd_{T_{entry}} \\ \tau_0 & else \end{cases} \tag{9}$$

4.3 Communication Protocol

During the ant colony evolution in the colony space, local optimal individuals are input into the belief space at a certain frequency by calling the *accept*() function, for example, every $AStep = 10$ iterations.

The independent evolution of belief space affects the evolution of the group space by calling the $influence()$ function when it passes through the every $Istep$ generation. The $influence()$ mainly includes two parts. First, the global optimal solution may be updated by comparing the solution of the elite individual with the current optimal solution in the group space. Second, when the number of iterations is greater than C, the pheromone enhancement mechanism will be turned on, given by $formula$ (11). The pheromone enhancement mechanism is proposed in order to achieve the purpose of guiding the evolution of the ant colony and increasing the speed of convergence. The value of $Istep$ is related to the number of iterations, as shown in Eq. (10).

$$IStep = \begin{cases} BaseStep & if\ iter < C \\ BaseStep \times \frac{EndStep - iter}{EndStep - C} & else \end{cases} \tag{10}$$

$$\tau_{T_iT_j} = \begin{cases} (1-\rho)\tau_{T_iT_j} + \rho\tau_0 & if\ (T_i, T_j) \in top_{ant_{elite}} \\ \tau_{T_iT_j} & else \end{cases} \tag{11}$$

Among them, *EndStep* is the maximum number of iterations, *BaseStep* and C are constants, which are related to the volatilization speed of pheromone. In general, the smaller the value of *BaseStep* and C is, the faster the algorithm converges, and the solution quality of the algorithm decreases accordingly.

Input: The set $task_{key}$ of critical tasks and the local optimal individual ant_k in group space

Output: The elite individual ant_elite in belief space

```
Let RT = +∞
while |task_key| > 1 do
    Take the first two tasks as T_i, T_j
    Let ant_tmp = ant_k, ant_best = ant_k
    Take the tasks before T_i in top_{ant_tmp} as the total order set finished_tmp;
    for Take each task T_t from T_i to T_j in top_{ant_tmp} do
        Add T_t to finished_tmp
        if pred_{T_j} ⊂ finished_tmp then
            Change the top_{ant_tmp} order to put T_j after T_t, leaving the other
            tasks in the same relative order
            break
        end
    end
    for Each task T_i in top_{ant_tmp} from T_j to the end do
        Call Algorithm 3 to update the assignment scheme s_{ant_tmp} of the task
    end
    if RT > RT(S_{ant_tmp}) then
        RT = RT(s_{ant_tmp})
        ant_best = ant_tmp
    end
    Delete the first task T_i in task_key;
end
if RT(s_{ant_elite}) > RT(s_{ant_best}) then
    ant_elite=ant_best
end
return ant_elite
```

Algorithm 4: Individual mutation based on critical task optimization algorithm

5 Experimental Results and Analysis

We carry out experiments on a single machine. And, the specification for PC hardware and software is depicted in Table 3.

Using randomly generated DAG models, simulation experiments are performed on the algorithms HEFT, CPOP, ACS, MMAS, and CACS. For the ant colony algorithms, the parameters are set as: ant colony size $l = \frac{|T|}{4}$, $\theta = 0.01$, $\rho = 0.02$, $\tau_0 = 0.8$, $\alpha = 1$, $\beta = 1$, $EndStep = 1000$, $AStep = 1$, $BaseStep = 10$, $C = 320$. In particular, under the research model of this paper, after many experiments, the MMAS algorithm adopts the pheromone updating rules of local optimal and global optimal mixed strategies, which can approach the optimal performance on the whole. The convergence statistics of MMAS are modified slightly due to the influence of the minimum pheromone mechanism. If the difference between the mean value of the solutions is less than one percent of the

Table 3. Experimental specification.

PC	Version
CPU	Intel(R) i5 @ 2.1 GHz
Memory	2 GB
OS	Debian 7
Programming language	C STD99

global optimal solution for two consecutive iterations, the solutions of the two iterations are considered to be the same. If the solutions of iteration 30 are the same, the algorithm is considered to converge and the convergence time is marked (Table 4).

Table 4. Algorithm scheduling performance comparison.

Algorithm		HEFT	CPOP	ACS	MMAS
CACS	*Better*	2724	3120	1182	2026
	Equal	382	32	1303	853
	Worse	134	88	755	361
Combine(%)	*Better*	84.1%	96.2%	36.5%	62.5%
	Equal	11.8%	1%	40.2%	26.3%
	Worse	4.1%	2.8%	23.3%	11.2 %

5.1 Comparative Metrics

Algorithm performance comparison is based on the following three metrics:

- *makespan*: The main performance metrics of the algorithm, the smaller the value, the better the solution of the algorithm.
- *speedup*: The calculation method is shown in the following formula. Under the same number of heterogeneous computing cores, the larger the value, the better the algorithm performance.

$$speedup = \frac{\min\limits_{P_j \in P}\{\sum_{T_i \in T} W_{P_j}(T_i)\}}{makespan} \tag{12}$$

- *convergence time*: Since HEFT, CPOP and other table scheduling algorithms do not have an iterative process, this metric is only used for ant colony algorithm analysis.

5.2 Randomly Generated Model

By referring to the idea of the paper [23], we design a DAG model random generator based on the OpenSSL random number algorithm. During the experiment, we take parameter values from the following values to generate different DAG and DPG models. Due to the random generation of the execution time of subtasks, out-degree, in-degree, and communication data volume between subtasks, the same parameter settings produce different DAG models. In order to avoid the influence of accidental factors on the results of the algorithms, each set of parameters is adopted to generate 5 DAG models for algorithms comparison.

- $SET_T = \{20, 30, 40, 50, 60, 70\}$,
- $SET_P = \{4, 8, 16\}$,
- $SET_{CCR} = \{0.1, 1.0, 5.0\}$,
- $SET_\alpha = \{0.4, 0.6, 0.8, 1.0\}$,
- $SET_\beta = \{0.8, 1.4, 1.8\}$.

The combination of these parameters produces a total of 3240 different types of test models. Sufficient and random testing schemes ensure the fairness of algorithms comparison.

5.3 Algorithm Performance Evaluation

It can be seen from Table 3 that in the random test environment, the CACS scheduling length is significantly better than the list scheduling algorithms HEFT and CPOP, and the ratio of *better* reaches more than 80%. Compared to MMAS, the times of *better* of CACS algorithm reaches 2026, accounting for 62.5%. Compared with the ACS algorithm whose performance is closest to CACS, the ratio of *better* of CACS exceeds 36.5%, and the ratio of *not worse* is about 76.7%.

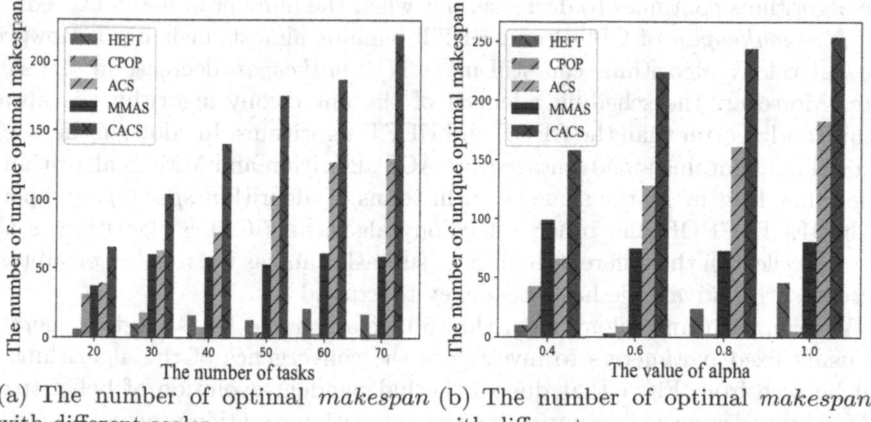

(a) The number of optimal *makespan* with different scales (b) The number of optimal *makespan* with different α

Fig. 5. The number of optimal *makespan*.

We count the number of optimal solutions. If the same solutions appear in the algorithms, no statistics are made in this test. Figure 5 depicts that with the increase of the graph parameter α and the scheduling scale, the performance of HEFT and CPOP becomes worse and worse. On the contrary, the scheduling performance of the ant colony algorithms is significantly better than that of HEFT and CPOP algorithms. In addition, compared with the MMAS algorithm and ACS algorithm, the CACS algorithm has a greater growth rate of *better* as the α and scheduling scale increase. It completely explains the performance of CACS algorithm is better When the program parallelism is higher and the number of subtasks is more.

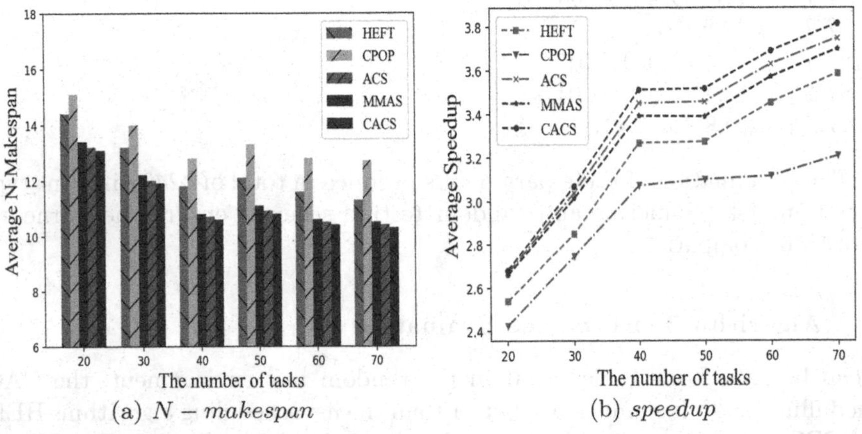

Fig. 6. The number of *makespan* and *speedup* with different scales.

$N - makespan$ is *makespan* divided by the number of task nodes, as shown in Fig. 6. As the number of nodes increases, in general the $N - makespan$ of the algorithms continues to decrease, but when the number of nodes exceeds 50, the $N - makespan$ of CPOP and HEFT remains almost unchanged. However, the ant colony algorithms can still make $N - makespan$ decrease at the same rate. Moreover, the scheduling length of the ant colony algorithms is always significantly better than the CPOP and HEFT algorithms. In addition the CACS algorithm maintains an advantage over ACS algorithm and MMAS algorithm in scheduling length. At the same time, in terms of algorithm *speedup*, compared with HEFT, CPOP and other ant colony algorithms CACS algorithm is also more excellent in the different number of subtasks, and as the number of subtasks increases, this advantage has a tendency to expand.

We run each ant colony algorithm 50 times on the DAG model generated by using fixed parameters to investigate the convergence of the algorithms. It can be seen from Fig. 7 that due to the independent evolution of belief space, CACS bring dramatic fluctuations to the population iteration process, effectively expanding the search space of the ant colony and reducing the possibility of algorithm stagnation. And the dynamic pheromone enhancement mechanism can make the pheromone quickly converge on the global optimal path in the later

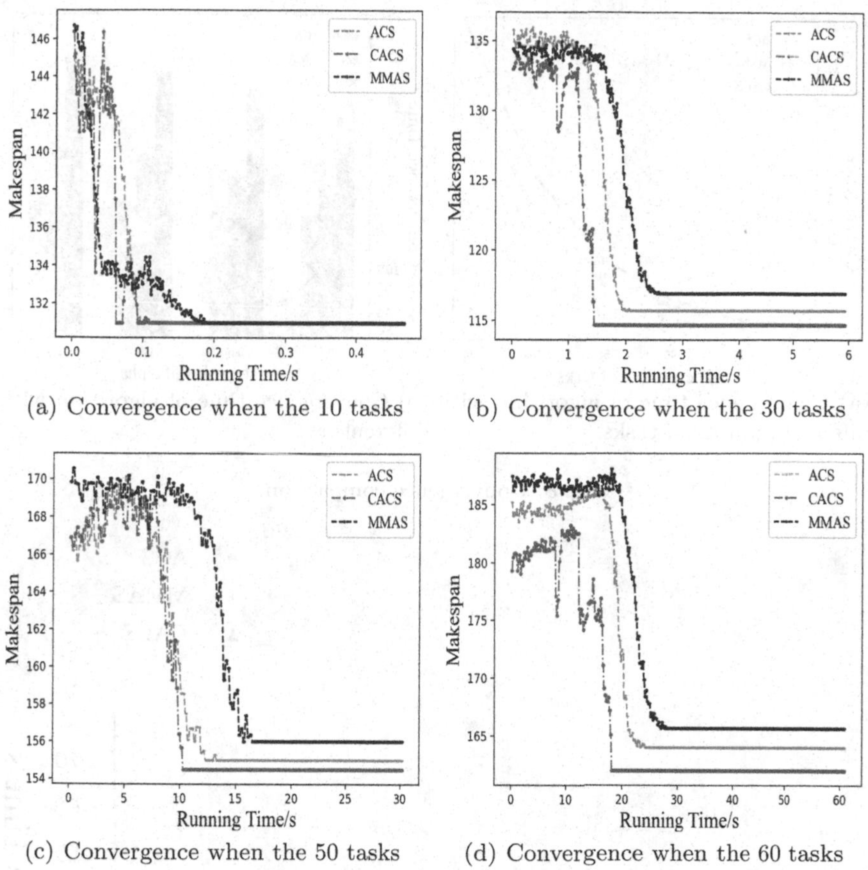

(a) Convergence when the 10 tasks (b) Convergence when the 30 tasks

(c) Convergence when the 50 tasks (d) Convergence when the 60 tasks

Fig. 7. Convergence of algorithm with different number of tasks.

stage of the algorithm, which greatly improves the convergence speed of CACS. When the number of task nodes is relatively small, the ant colony algorithm performs almost the same scheduling performance. But as the number of tasks exceeds 30, CACS has shorter convergence time than ACS algorithm and MMAS algorithm while maintaining the scheduling length shortest.

Figure 8(a) demonstrates that as the increase of the number of subtasks, the convergence time of the algorithms increase sharply, but compared with the ACS algorithm and MMAS algorithm, the convergence time of the CACS algorithm increases significantly more slowly. When the number of nodes reaches 70, the convergence time of CACS algorithm is reduced by 18.2% and 32.2% respectively compared with ACS algorithm and MMAS algorithm. When taking different values of α, the same conclusion can be obtained, which is shown in Fig. 8(b), with the increase of α, the convergence time of ACS and MMAS algorithms increases markedly, while the convergence time of CACS is almost unchanged. Meanwhile, when the α is 1.0 the convergence time of CACS algorithm is reduced by 22.5% and 33.8% respectively compared with ACS algorithm and MMAS algorithm.

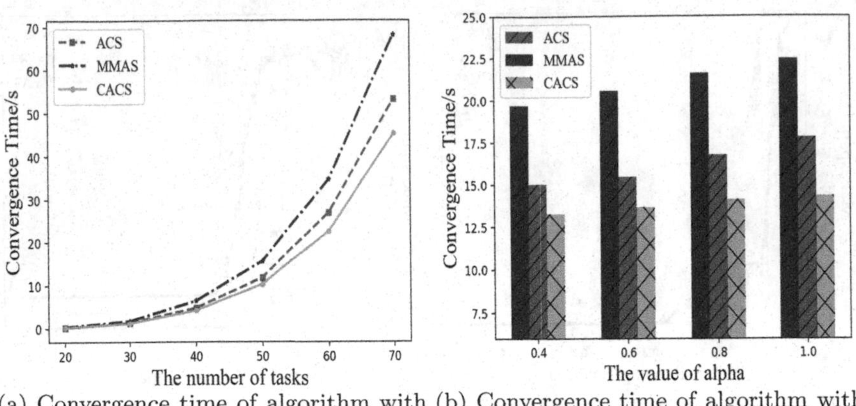

(a) Convergence time of algorithm with different number of tasks

(b) Convergence time of algorithm with different α

Fig. 8. Convergence comparison.

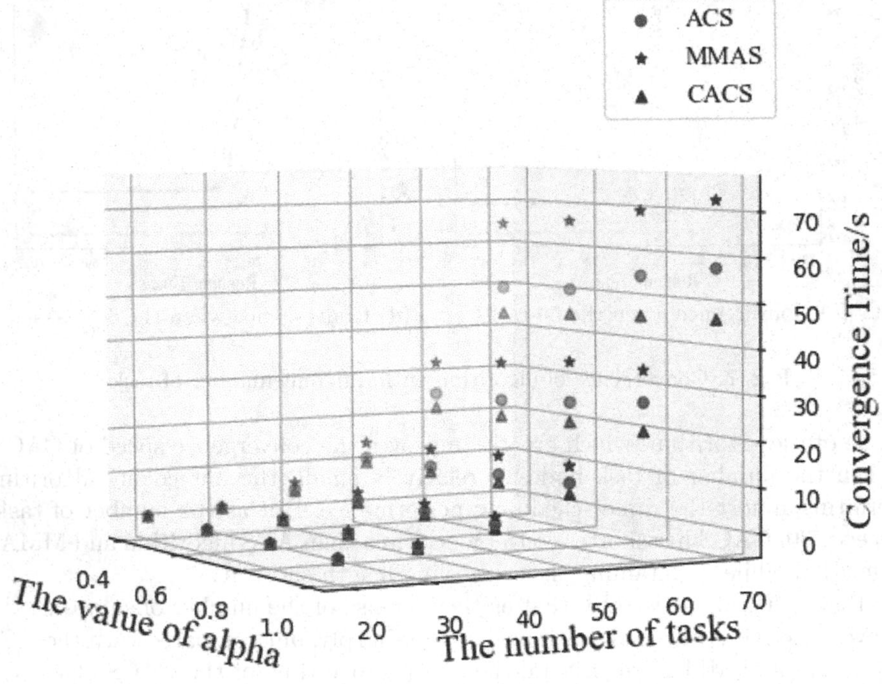

Fig. 9. Convergence comparison with different number of tasks and α.

Figure 9 displays more intuitively that with the increase of the number of nodes and the value of the α, the increase speed of the convergence time of the CACS algorithm is significantly less than that of the MMAS and ACS algorithms.

The experimental results point out using the CA framework to optimize the ACS algorithm is effective, especially in terms of suppressing the increase in the running time of the algorithm.

6 Conclusion

In this paper, we propose a novel ant colony algorithm called CACS to solve the DAG tasks scheduling in heterogeneous multiprocessing environments. Compared with the previous ant colony algorithm optimization schemes, CACS makes full use of the CA architecture.In the group space, CACS improves the heuristic function by taking the increased value of the scheduling length as the visibility of the ant colony, so that the ant colony selects the local optimal nodes more efficiently. CACS also adopts critical task optimization algorithm and dynamic pheromone enhancement mechanism to improve the solution quality and convergence speed of algorithm. The performance of CACS is evaluated extensively on different DAG testing schemes obtained from DAG model random generator. The experiment results illustrates that compared ACS and MMAS algorithms, CACS faster convergence and better accuracy. Also, CACS outperforms when the application has a higher degree of parallelism and a larger number of subtasks. And when the number of subtasks reaches 70 and the value of α is 1.0, compared with the MMAS and ACS algorithms, the CACS algorithm makespan's dominant ratio reaches 76% and 48% respectively, far exceeding the 13% of the MMAS algorithm and 29% of the ACS algorithm, in addition the convergence time of CACS algorithm is reduced by 23.2% and 34% respectively. Future work could be that CACS algorithm is combined with replication technology to further shorten the algorithm scheduling length.

Acknowledgement. The research was financially supported by National Natural Science The research was financially supported by National Natural Science Foundation of China (No. 61972366), the Provincial Key Research and Development Program of Hubei (No. 2020BAB105), the Foundation of Henan Key Laboratory of Network Cryptography Technology (No. LNCT2020-A01), the Foundation of Key Laboratory of Network Assessment Technology, Chinese Academy of Sciences (No. KFKT2019-003), and the Foundation of State Key Laboratory of Public Big Data (No.PBD2021-02, No. 2019BDKFJJ003, No. 2019BDKFJJ011).

References

1. Chang, S., Zhao, X., Liu, Z., Deng, Q.: Real-Time scheduling and analysis of parallel tasks on heterogeneous multi-cores. J. Syst. Arch. **105**, 101704 (2020). https://doi.org/10.1016/j.sysarc.2019.101704
2. Wegener, I.: The Theory of NP-Completeness. Springer, Heidelberg (2005). https://doi.org/10.1007/3-540-27477-4_5
3. Dorigo, M.E.: Ant colony optimization and swarm intelligence. In: International Workshop (2006)

4. Dorigo, M., Gambardella, L.M.: Ant colony system: a cooperative learning approach to the traveling salesman problem. IEEE Trans. Evol. Comput. **1**(1), 53–66 (1997)
5. Jangra, R., Kait, R.: Analysis and comparison among ant system; ant colony system and max-min ant system with different parameters setting. In: International Conference on Computational Intelligence & Communication Technology. IEEE (2017)
6. Stutzle, T., Hoos, H.H.: Max-min ant system. Future Gener. Comput. Syst. **16**(8), 889–914 (2000)
7. Dorostkar, F., Mirzakuchaki, S.: List scheduling for heterogeneous computing systems introducing a performance-effective definition for critical path. In: 2019 9TH International Conference on Computer and Knowledge Engineering (ICCKE 2019), Ferdowsi Univ Mashhad, Dept Comp Engn, 2019, 9th International Conference on Computer and Knowledge Engineering(ICCKE), Ferdowsi Univ Mashhad, Mashhad, Iran, 24–25 October 2019, pp. 356–362 (2019)
8. Topcuoglu, H., Hariri, S., Wu, M.Y.: Task scheduling algorithms for heterogeneous processors, In: Heterogeneous Computing Workshop, 1999, (HCW 1999) Proceedings, Eighth (1999)
9. Topcuoglu, H., Hariri, S., Wu, M.Y.: Performance-effective and low-complex task scheduling for heterogeneous computing. IEEE Trans. Parallel Distrib. Syst. **13**(3), 260–260 (2002)
10. Zhang, H., Wu, Y., Sun, Z.: EHEFT-R: multi-objective task scheduling scheme in cloud computing. Complex Intell. Syst. **8**(6), 4475–4482 (2022). https://doi.org/10.1007/s40747-021-00479-7
11. Yuan, H., Zhao, Y., Kang, H.: The research and implementation of the criticalpath on a processor (cpop) algorithm based on pi calculus. In: Ma, Z.L., Fang, Z.G., Ke, J.F. (eds.) Proceedings of the 2016 International Conference on Computer Engineering, Information Science & Application Technology (ICCIA 2016), Vol. 56 of ACSR-Advances in Computer Science Research, 2016, International Conference on Computer Engineering, Information Science & Application Technology (ICCIA), Guilin, Peoples R China, 24–25 September 2016, pp. 337–345 (2016)
12. Tang, Q., Zhu, L.-H., Zhou, L., Xiong, J., Wei, J.-B.: Scheduling directed acyclic graphs with optimal duplication strategy on homogeneous multiprocessor systems. J. Parallel Distrib. Comput. **138**, 115–127 (2020). https://doi.org/10.1016/j.jpdc.2019.12.012
13. Yao, F., Pu, C., Zhang, Z.: Task duplication-based scheduling algorithm for budget-constrained workflows in cloud computing. IEEE Access **9**, 37262–37272 (2021). https://doi.org/10.1109/ACCESS.2021.3063456
14. Tang, J., Liu, G., Pan, Q.: A review on representative swarm intelligence algorithms for solving optimization problems: applications and trends. IEEE-CAA J. Automatica Sinica **8**(10), 1627–1643 (2021). https://doi.org/10.1109/JAS.2021.1004129
15. Kashan, A.H., Karimi, B., Noktehdan, A.: A novel discrete particle swarm optimization algorithm for the manufacturing cell formation problem. Int. J. Adv. Manuf. Technol. **73**(9–12), 1543–1556 (2014)
16. Qamar, M.S., et al.: Improvement of traveling salesman problem solution using hybrid algorithm based on best-worst ant system and particle swarm optimization. Appl. Sci.-Basel **11**(11) (2021). https://doi.org/10.3390/app11114780
17. Wei, X., Han, L., Hong, L.: A modified ant colony algorithm for traveling salesman problem. Int. J. Comput. Commun. Control **9**(5), 633–643 (2014)

18. Zhao, R., Liu, Q., Li, C., Wang, Y., Dong, D.: Performance comparison and application of swarm intelligence algorithms in crowd evacuation. In: 2020 the 4th International Conference on Management Engineering, Software Engineering and Service Sciences (ICMSS 2020), pp. 47–51, 4th International Conference on Management Engineering, Software Engineering and Service Sciences (ICMSS), Wuhan, Peoples R China, 17–19 January 2020 (2020). https://doi.org/10.1145/3380625.3380646
19. Maheri, A., Jalili, S., Hosseinzadeh, Y., Khani, R., Miryahyavi, M.: A comprehensive survey on cultural algorithms. Swarm Evol. Comput. **62**, 100846 (2021). https://doi.org/10.1016/j.swevo.2021.100846
20. Mojab, S.Z.M., Ebrahimi, M., Reynolds, R.G., Lu, S.: iCATS: scheduling big data workflows in the cloud using cultural algorithms. In: 2019 IEEE Fifth International Conference on Big Data Computing Service and Applications (IEEE Big Data Service 2019). IEEE; IEEE Comp Soc, 2019, 5th IEEE International Conference on Big Data Computing Service and Applications (IEEE BigDataService)/Workshop on Big Data in Water Resources, Environment, and Hydraulic Engineering/Workshop on Medical, Healthcare, Using Big Data Technologies, San Francisco, CA, 04–09 April 2019, pp. 99–106 (2019). https://doi.org/10.1109/BigDataService.2019.00020
21. Ying, W., Yan, T.: Research on network course setting based on the topological sort and activity on edge network. In: 2013 Fourth International Conference on Intelligent Systems Design and Engineering Applications, Cent S Univ; St Johns Univ; Hunan Univ Technol, Dept Elect Sci & Technol; Natl Univ Defense Technol; Intelligent Computat Technol & Automat Soci, 2013, 4th International Conference on Intelligent Systems Design and Engineering Applications (ISDEA), Zhangjiajie, Peoples R China, 06–07 November 2013, pp. 507–510. https://doi.org/10.1109/ISDEA.2013.520
22. Lang, C.G.: Research on expanded critical path algorithm and its application. In: Wunsch, D.C., Tan, H.H., Zeng, D.H., Luo, Q. (eds.) Nanotechnology and Computer Engineering, vol. 121–122 of Advanced Materials Research, Intelligent Informat Technol Applicat Res Assoc; Int Ind Elect Ctr; Wuhan Inst Technol, 2010, International Conference on Advances in Computer Science and Engineering, Qingdao, Peoples R China, 20–21 July 2010, pp. 300–303 (2010). https://doi.org/10.4028/www.scientific.net/AMR.121-122.300
23. Akbari, M., Rashidi, H., Alizadeh, S.H.: An enhanced genetic algorithm with new operators for task scheduling in heterogeneous computing systems. In: Engineering Applications of Artificial Intelligence (2017)

On the Parameterized Tractability of Single Machine Scheduling with Rejection to Minimize the Weighted Makespan

Ruiqing Sun(✉)

School of Mathematics and Statistics, Yunnan University, Kunming, China
ruiqing2020@126.com

Abstract. In this paper, we consider the single machine scheduling problem with rejection to minimize the weighted makespan. In such problem, a job is either accepted and processed on the machine, or rejected and paid a rejection penalty. The objective is to minimize the weighted makespan of accepted jobs plus the overall rejection cost of rejected jobs, conditional on the number of accepted jobs no great than a given threshold. The problem is NP-hard even if the number of accepted jobs is unbounded, which was proved by Lu et al. [20]. We show that this problem is W[1]-hard where parameterized by the maximum number of jobs to be accepted, that is, k. Furthermore, we show that the problem is fixed-parameter tractable with respect to the following parameters: (1) the number of different weights and processing times, (2) the number of different weights and rejection costs, and (3) the number of different processing times and rejection costs.

Keywords: Scheduling with rejection · Weighted makespan · Parameterized complexity · Fixed-parameter tractability

1 Introduction

Scheduling problems are usually analyzed in terms of classical computational complexity, i.e. one of the main problems is whether it is NP-hard. A recent research trend in parameterized complexity is to analyze scheduling problems from the perspective of parameterized complexity which can be found in the surveys [1,3,8,14].

1.1 Scheduling with Rejection

Scheduling with job rejection was first proposed by Bartal et al. [2]. The objective is to minimize the makespan of the accepted jobs plus the total penalty of the rejected jobs. For the off-line problem, they presented a $(2 - \frac{1}{m})$-approximation algorithm in time $O(n \log n)$ and a polynomial-time approximation scheme

Z. Cai et al. (Eds.): NCTCS 2022, CCIS 1693, pp. 236–247, 2022.
https://doi.org/10.1007/978-981-19-8152-4_17

(PTAS). Later, Ou et al. [22] improved a $(3/2+\varepsilon)$-approximation algorithm in time $O(n\log n+\frac{n}{\varepsilon})$, where $\varepsilon>0$ can be any small given constant. Zhang et al. [25] studied single machine scheduling with release dates and rejection. They proved that this problem is NP-hard and presented a fully polynomial time approximation scheme (FPTAS). For more problems and results on scheduling with rejection, we refer the reader to a survey on off-line scheduling with rejection by Shabtay et al. [23]. More scheduling with rejection results can be found in the surveys [6,16–19,24].

1.2 Parameterized Complexity

Definition 1. A problem is fixed-parameter tractable (FPT) with respect to some parameter if there is an algorithm that solves any instance of the problem in $f(k)n^{O(1)}$ time, where n is the size of the instance, k is the value of the parameter, and $f(k)$ is some computable function that solely depends on k.

There are two concepts in parameterized complexity that are relevant to this paper. The first is W[t]-hardness for fixed $t\geq 1$, where W[t] is a complexity class that includes all FPT problems, and it is conjectured that FPT $\neq$ W[t]. The second concept is that of para-NP-hardness where the problem is NP-hard even for constant values of the parameter (see, e.g., [5,10]).

In 2015, Mnich and Wiese [21] studied the single machine scheduling problem with rejection, conditional on the number of rejected jobs can not exceed a given bound k. The objective is to minimize the sum of the total weighted completion time of the accepted jobs and the total rejection penalty of the rejected jobs. They proved that the problem is W[1]-hard with respect to the maximum number k of accepted jobs, and FPT for $k+\upsilon_w$, $k+\upsilon_p$, and $\upsilon_w+\upsilon_p$ where υ_w and υ_p are the number of different weights and processing times, respectively. In 2022, Hermelin et al. [13] proposed that a general scheme for solving a large set of scheduling problems with rejection in FPT time.

1.3 Scheduling to Minimize the Weighted Makespan

When job rejection is not allowed, Feng and Yuan [9] introduced the weighted makespan $WC_{\max}$ on a single machine and they proved that this problem is strongly NP-hard. Li [15] studied the online single machine scheduling problem to minimize the weighted makespan, where jobs arrive over time. When the number of machine is 1, they proved a lower bound 2, and then provided an online algorithm with a competitive ratio of 3. Chai et al. [4] provided the best-possible competitive ratio of 2 for this problem on single machine. Recently, Lu et al. [20] considered the single machine scheduling problem with rejection to minimize the weighted makespan. They showed that this problem is NP-hard and propose an FPTAS for this problem.

The remainder of this paper is structured as follows. In Sect. 2, we provide the problem formulation on our problems and present some useful results which is inspired by the work of Hermelin et al. [13]. In Sect. 3, we show that our scheduling problem is W[1]-hard where parameterized by the maximum number of jobs to be accepted, that is, k. Then, in Sects. 4, we show that the problem is fixed-parameter tractable with respect to the following parameters: the number of different weights and processing times, the number of different weights and rejection costs, the number of different processing times and rejection costs.

2 Preliminaries

Single machine scheduling with rejection to minimize the weighted makespan can be described as follows. We are given a set $\mathcal{J} = \{J_1, J_2, \cdots, J_n\}$ of n jobs and a single machine. Each job J_j is associated with three parameters: a weight w_j, a processing time p_j and a rejection cost e_j. Without loss of generality, we assume that all p_j, w_j and e_j values are positive integers. J_j is either rejected where the rejection cost e_j has to be paid, or accepted and processed on the machine. Let A and R be the set of the accepted jobs and the set of the rejected jobs, respectively. Furthermore, for each job J_j with $J_j \in A$, let C_j be the completion time of job J_j. We define $WC_{\max} = \max\{w_j C_j : J_j \in A\}$ and $\sum_{J_j \in R} e_j$ by the weighted makespan (the maximum weighted completion time) and rejection cost, respectively. The objective is to minimize the sum of the weighted makespan of the accepted jobs and the total rejection cost of the rejected jobs, conditional on the number of accepted jobs no great than a given threshold k, i.e., $|A| \leq k$. Using the general notation introduced by Graham et al. [12], the corresponding problem can be denoted by $1||A| \leq k|WC_{\max} + \sum_{J_j \in R} e_j$.

When job rejection is not allowed and the number of accepted jobs is unbounded, Li [15] proved that the Largest Weight first (LW) rule minimizes the weighted makespan. Thus, in optimal schedule for problem $1||WC_{\max} + \sum_{J_j \in R} e_j$ such that all accepted jobs are processed in the LW rule. Meanwhile, Lu et al. [20] obtain the following theorem by a reduction from the Partition problem:

Theorem 1 ([20]). *Problem* $1||WC_{\max} + \sum_{J_j \in R} e_j$ *is binary NP-hard.*

Thus, our problem is also NP-hard. In this paper, we consider the parameterized tractability of problem $1||A| \leq k|WC_{\max} + \sum_{J_j \in R} e_j$ with respect to the following parameters:

- k: the maximum number of jobs to be accepted.
- $v_w \cdot v_p$: The number of different weights and processing times.
- $v_w \cdot v_e$: The number of different weights and rejection costs.
- $v_p \cdot v_e$: The number of different processing times and rejection costs.

In real life, the above parameters are indeed very natural. For example, the number of job types (v_p) produced by the manufacturer is limited. If there are few customer types, and all customers in each type are of equal importance, limited weighting and rejection costs may arise.

We next present a few lemmas that will be useful for our problem which is proposed by Hermelin et al. [13].

Lemma 1 [13]. *If* $\varphi_{i1} \leq \varphi_{i2} \leq \cdots \leq \varphi_{in_i}$, *then the constraint* $y_i \geq \sum_{j=1}^{x_i} \varphi_{ij}$ *is equivalent to the set of linear constraints*

$$y_i \geq (x_i - j + 1)\varphi_{ij} + \sum_{\ell=1}^{j-1} \varphi_{i\ell} \text{ for all } j = 1 \cdots, n_i.$$

Lemma 2 [13]. *If* $\varphi_{i1} \geq \varphi_{i2} \geq \cdots \geq \varphi_{in_i}$, *then the constraint* $y_i \geq \sum_{j=x_i+1}^{n_i} \varphi_{ij}$ *is equivalent to the set of linear constraints*

$$y_i \geq (j - x_i)\varphi_{ij} + \sum_{\ell=j+1}^{n_i} \varphi_{i\ell} \text{ for all } j = 1 \cdots, n_i.$$

3 W[1]-hardness with Respect to *k*

In this section, we show that problem $1||A| \leq k|WC_{\max} + \sum_{J_j \in R} e_j$ is W[1]-hard for parameter the maximum number k of accepted jobs. Our reduction modify the reduction from Partition problem in [20] that shows that $1||WC_{\max} + \sum_{J_j \in R} e_j$ is NP-hard.

Theorem 2. *Problem* $1||A| \leq k|WC_{\max} + \sum_{J_j \in R} e_j$ *is W[1]-hard for parameter the maximum number* k *of accepted jobs.*

Proof. We use the k - Subset Sum problem for the reduction. It is known to be W[1]-hard, parameterized by k (see Fellows et al. [7]). □

***k* - Subset Sum:** Given a set of n integers $S = \{a_1, a_2, \cdots, a_n\}$ and three values $B, k, q \in \mathbb{N}$ with $\sum_{i=1}^{n} a_i = B$. The goal is to select a subset S_1 of k of the given integers a_i that sum up to q.

For a given instance of the k - Subset Sum, we construct an instance of the decision version of $1||A| \leq k|WC_{\max} + \sum_{J_j \in R} e_j$ as follows.

- $n + 1$ jobs.
- $w_j = 4, p_j = e_j = a_j$ for $1 \leq j \leq n$.
- $w_j = B + q + 4, p_j = 2, e_j = 3B + q + 9$ for $j = n + 1$.
- The threshold value is defined by $Y = 3B + q + 8$.
- $|A \setminus J_{n+1}| \leq k$.
- The decision version asks whether there is a schedule π such that

$$WC_{\max} + \sum_{J_j \in R} e_j \leq Y.$$

If the instance of k-Subset Sum is "yes", then we construct a schedule in the following way: Schedule the job J_{n+1} as the first processed job on the machine, and then schedule all jobs J_j with $j \in S_1$ consecutively after J_{n+1} on the machine. It can be seen that, for the job J_{t+1}, we have $w_{n+1}C_{n+1} = (B + q + 4) \times 2 = 2B + 2q + 8$; for the job J_j with $j \in S_1$, we have $w_jC_j \le (q+2)\times 4 \le 4q+8 < 2B+2q+8$. Thus, we have $WC_{\max} = 2B+2q+8$ and $|A \setminus J_{n+1}| \le k$. We further reject all jobs J_j with $j \in S \setminus S_1$. Thus, we have $\sum_{J_j\in R} e_j = \sum_{j\in S\setminus S_1} a_j = B-q$. It follows that $WC_{\max} + \sum_{J_j\in R} e_j = 3B+q+8 = Y$.

Next, we assume there exists a schedule π such that $WC_{\max} + \sum_{J_j\in R} e_j \le Y$ and $|A \setminus J_{n+1}| \le k$. We will prove that the instance of k-Subset Sum is a "yes"-instance. Let A and R be the set of accepted jobs and the set of rejected jobs in π, respectively. We have the following two claims.

Claim 1. Job J_{n+1} must be accepted and J_{n+1} is the first processed job in π.

Proof. If job J_{n+1} is rejected, then we have $WC_{\max} + \sum_{J_j\in R} e_j \ge e_{n+1} = 3B+q+9 > Y$, a contradiction. Furthermore, if job J_{n+1} is not the first processed job in π, then we have $C_{n+1}(\pi) \ge 3$. Thus, we have $WC_{\max} + \sum_{J_j\in R} e_j \ge (B+q+4)\times 3 = 3B+3q+12 > Y$, a contradiction again. Claim 1 follows. □

Claim 2. $\sum_{J_j\in R} a_j = B-q$.

Proof. By Claim 1, we have $WC_{\max} \ge w_{t+1}C_{t+1} = 2B+2q+8$. Furthermore, we have $\sum_{J_j\in R} a_j = \sum_{J_j\in R} e_j \le B-q$ since $WC_{\max} + \sum_{J_j\in R} e_j \le Y = 3B+q+8$. Next, we assume that $\sum_{J_j\in R} a_j < B-q$. Thus, we have

$$\begin{aligned}
WC_{\max} + \sum_{J_j\in R} e_j &\ge 4(\sum_{J_j\in A\setminus J_{n+1}} p_j + 2) + \sum_{J_j\in R} e_j \\
&= 4(\sum_{J_j\in A\setminus J_{n+1}} a_j + 2) + \sum_{J_j\in R} a_j \\
&= 8 + 4(\sum_{J_j\in A} a_j + \sum_{J_j\in R} a_j) - \sum_{J_j\in R} a_j \\
&= 8 + 4B - \sum_{J_j\in R} a_j \\
&> 4B + 8 - (B-q) \\
&= 3B + q + 8 \\
&= Y
\end{aligned}$$

a contradiction. Thus, we have $\sum_{J_j\in R} a_j = B-q$. Clearly, $\sum_{i\in S_1} a_i = q$. Theorem 2 follows. □

4 Weighted Makespan with Rejection

In this section, we will prove that this problem is FPT when we combine either parameters v_w and v_p, or parameters v_w and v_e . We then use a slightly complicated method to show that this problem is also FPT when we combine parameters v_e and v_p.

Lu et al. [20] proved that $1||WC_{\max}+\sum_{J_j\in R}e_j$ is NP-hard when there are only two distinct weights. Therefore, the following holds:

Lemma 3. *Problem* $1||A|\le k|WC_{\max}+\sum_{J_j\in R}e_j$ *is NP-hard when there are* $\upsilon_w\ge 2$.

4.1 Parameter $\upsilon_w\cdot\upsilon_p$

We partition $\mathcal{J}$ into k_1 subsets $\mathcal{J}_1,\cdots,\mathcal{J}_{k_1}$ such that all jobs in $\mathcal{J}_i$ have the same processing time p_i and the same weight w_i , for $i=1,\cdots,k_1(k_1=\upsilon_w\cdot\upsilon_p)$. We number the sets according to the LW rule, that is, $w_1\ge w_2\ge\cdots\ge w_{k_1}$. We use $n_i=|\mathcal{J}_i|$ to denote the number of jobs in $\mathcal{J}_i$. Note that $\sum_{i=1}^{k_1}n_i=n$. We sort the jobs in each $\mathcal{J}_i$ in nonincreasing order of rejection cost, such that $e_{i1}\ge e_{i2}\ge\cdots\ge e_{in_i}$ for each $i=1,2,\cdots,k_1$. We first present the following lemma:

Lemma 4. *If* x_i *is the optimal number of accepted jobs in* $\mathcal{J}_i$ *then there exists an optimal solution in which the* x_i *jobs with the biggest rejection cost in* $\mathcal{J}_i$ *are accepted, that is, accepts the first* x_i *jobs in* $\mathcal{J}_i$.

Since $n_i=|\mathcal{J}_i|$, we have

$$0\le x_i\le n_i \text{ for each } i=1,\cdots,k_1, \tag{1}$$

$$\sum_{i=1}^{k_1}x_i\le k. \tag{2}$$

As all jobs in $\mathcal{J}_\ell$ have a same weight, the last scheduled job in $\mathcal{J}_\ell$ has the maximal weighted makespan among all jobs in the set. The completion time of the last scheduled job from $\mathcal{J}_\ell$ is at time $\sum_{i=1}^{\ell}p_ix_i$. Therefore, we have

$$WC_{\max}=\max_{\ell=1,\cdots,k_1}\{w_\ell\sum_{i=1}^{\ell}p_ix_i\}. \tag{3}$$

Since the rejection costs are nonincreasing in each $\mathcal{J}_i$, we can represent the total rejection cost by adding integer variables $y_1,\cdots,y_k$ and n additional linear constraints. By Lemma 2 and Lemma 4, we have

$$\sum_{J_j\in R}e_j=\sum_{i=1}^{k_1}\sum_{j=x_i+1}^{n_i}e_{ij}=\sum_{i=1}^{k_1}y_i, \tag{4}$$

$$y_i\ge(j-x_i)e_{ij}+\sum_{\ell=j+1}^{n_i}e_{i\ell} \quad \text{for all } i=1,\cdots,k_1 \text{ and all } j=1,\cdots,n_i. \tag{5}$$

Finally, we can replace (3) by adding a new additional integer variable y_0, and the constraints:

$$y_0\ge w_\ell\sum_{i=1}^{\ell}p_ix_i \text{ for all } \ell=1,\cdots,k_1. \tag{6}$$

Thus, objective function can be rewritten as $\min \sum_{i=0}^{k_1} y_i$ and constrained to (1), (2), (5) and (6).

In summary, this problem can be formulated as a mixed integer linear program (MILP) with $O(k_1)$ integer variables, we can use the [11] to solve this problem in FPT time.

Theorem 3. *Problem* $1||A| \leq k|WC_{\max} + \sum_{J_j \in R} e_j$ *can be solved in* $k_1^{O(k_1)} \cdot n^{O(1)}$ *time, where* $k_1 = v_w \cdot v_p$.

4.2 Parameter $v_w \cdot v_e$

We partition $\mathcal{J}$ into k_1 subsets $\mathcal{J}_1, \cdots, \mathcal{J}_{k_1}$ such that all jobs in $\mathcal{J}_i$ have the same rejection cost e_i and the same weight w_i , for $i = 1, \cdots, k_1 (k_1 = v_w \cdot v_e)$. We number the sets according to the LW rule so that $w_1 \geq w_2 \geq \cdots \geq w_{k_1}$. We use $n_i = |\mathcal{J}_i|$ to denote the number of jobs in $\mathcal{J}_i$. Note that $\sum_{i=1}^{k_1} n_i = n$. We sort the jobs in each $\mathcal{J}_i$ in nondecreasing order of processing time, such that $p_{i1} \leq p_{i2} \leq \cdots \leq p_{in_i}$ for each $i = 1, 2, \cdots, k_1$. We first present the following lemma:

Lemma 5. *If x_i is the optimal number of accepted jobs in $\mathcal{J}_i$ then there exists an optimal solution in which the x_i jobs with the smallest processing time in $\mathcal{J}_i$ are accepted, that is, accepts the first x_i jobs in $\mathcal{J}_i$.*

Since $n_i = |\mathcal{J}_i|$, we have

$$0 \leq x_i \leq n_i \text{ for each } i = 1, \cdots, k_1, \tag{7}$$

$$\sum_{i=1}^{k_1} x_i \leq k. \tag{8}$$

Note that as all jobs in each $\mathcal{J}_i$ have the same rejection cost e_i , the total rejection cost is given by the linear function:

$$\sum_{J_j \in R} e_j = \sum_{i=1}^{k_1} (n_i - x_i) e_i. \tag{9}$$

We also note that all jobs in $\mathcal{J}_\ell$ have a same weight, the last scheduled job in $\mathcal{J}_\ell$ has the maximal weighted makespan among all jobs in the set. The completion time of the last scheduled job from $\mathcal{J}_\ell$ is at time $\sum_{i=1}^{\ell} \sum_{j=1}^{x_i} p_{ij}$. Therefore,

$$WC_{\max} = \max_{\ell=1,\cdots,k_1} \{w_\ell \sum_{i=1}^{\ell} \sum_{j=1}^{x_i} p_{ij}\}. \tag{10}$$

According to Lemma 1, we can replace (10) with

$$WC_{\max} = \max_{\ell=1,\cdots,k_1} \{w_\ell \sum_{i=1}^{\ell} y_i\} \tag{11}$$

where $y_1, \cdots, y_{k_1}$ are new integer variables satisfying the following set of linear constraints:

$$y_i \geq (x_i - j + 1)p_{ij} + \sum_{\ell=1}^{j-1} p_{i\ell}$$
$$\text{for all } i = 1, \cdots, k_1 \text{ and all } j = 1, \cdots, n_i. \tag{12}$$

Moreover, we can replace (11) by adding a new additional integer variable y_0, and the constraints:

$$y_0 \geq w_\ell \sum_{i=1}^{\ell} y_i \text{ for all } \ell = 1, \cdots, k_1. \tag{13}$$

Thus, objective function can be rewritten as $\min y_0 + \sum_{i=1}^{k_1}(n_i - x_i)e_i$ and constrained to (7), (8), (12) and (13).

In summary, this problem can be formulated as a MILP with $O(k_1)$ integer variables, by using the [11] to solve this problem in FPT time.

Theorem 4. *Problem* $1||A| \leq k|WC_{\max} + \sum_{J_j \in R} e_j$ *can be solved in* $k_1^{O(k_1)} \cdot n^{O(1)}$ *time, where* $k_1 = \upsilon_w \cdot \upsilon_e$.

4.3 Parameter $\upsilon_p \cdot \upsilon_e$

We next provide an FPT algorithm for problem $1||A| \leq k|WC_{\max} + \sum_{J_j \in R} e_j$ when we combine parameters υ_p and υ_e. First we formulate the problem as an integer linear program (ILP) for this problem, denote by Γ that has $O(n + k_1)$ integer variables. Then, by relaxing the integer variables, we obtain Γ', which is a MILP relaxation of Γ with only $O(k_1)$ integer variables. According to [11] Γ' is fixed-parameter tractable. Finally, we prove that in an optimal solution for Γ' all the variables have an integer value, meaning that the optimal solution for Γ' is also an optimal solution for Γ.

We partition $\mathcal{J}$ into k_1 subsets $\mathcal{J}_1, \cdots, \mathcal{J}_{k_1}$ such that all jobs in $\mathcal{J}_i$ have the same processing time p_i and rejection cost e_i, for $i = 1, \cdots, k_1 (k_1 = \upsilon_p \cdot \upsilon_e)$. Moreover, let $w_1, \cdots, w_{\upsilon_w}$ be the set of $O(n)$ different weights in our input job set $\mathcal{J}$ and assume without loss of generality that $w_1 \geq w_2 \geq \cdots \geq w_{\upsilon_w}$. We use $n_i = |\mathcal{J}_i|$ to denote the number of jobs in $\mathcal{J}_i$. Note that $\sum_{i=1}^{k_1} n_i = n$. Finally, let δ_{ij} be the number of jobs in $\mathcal{J}_i$ with weight of w_j, for $i = 1, \cdots, k_1$ and $j = 1, \cdots, \upsilon_w$.

We let x_{ij} be an integer variable representing the number of accepted jobs in $\mathcal{J}_i$ having a weight of w_j for $i = 1, \cdots, k_1$ and $j = 1, \cdots, \upsilon_w$. By definition, we have the following constraints:

$$x_{ij} \leq \delta_{ij} \text{ for } i = 1, \cdots, k_1 \text{ and } j = 1, \cdots, \upsilon_w, \tag{14}$$
$$x_i = \sum_{j=1}^{\upsilon_w} x_{ij} \text{ for } i = 1, \cdots, k_1, \tag{15}$$
$$0 \leq x_i \leq n_i \text{ foreach } i = 1, \cdots, k_1, \tag{16}$$

and

$$\sum_{i=1}^{k_1} x_i \leq k. \tag{17}$$

The total rejection cost is then given by the linear function (9) since all job in set $\mathcal{J}_i$ have same rejection cost e_i. Furthermore, by LW rule the maximal weighted makespan value can be represented as follows:

$$WC_{\max} = \max_{\ell=1,\cdots,\upsilon_w} \{w_\ell \sum_{i=1}^{k_1}\sum_{j=1}^{\ell} p_i x_{ij}\}. \tag{18}$$

We can therefore express $WC_{\max}$ value by adding a new integer variable y_0, and adding the following set of υ_w linear constraints:

$$y_0 \geq w_\ell \sum_{i=1}^{k_1}\sum_{j=1}^{\ell} p_i x_{ij} \text{ forall } \ell = 1,\cdots,\upsilon_w. \tag{19}$$

Note that Γ is indeed an ILP formulation for the $1||A| \leq k|WC_{\max}+\sum_{j\in R} e_j$ problem with $O(n+k_1)$ integer variables. We next define Γ' by relaxing the constraint that only require the integer variables have to be nonnegative and we can use the [11] to solve Γ' in FPT time.

Lemma 6. *Γ' can be solved in $k_1^{O(k_1)} \cdot n^{O(1)}$ time, where $k_1 = \upsilon_p \cdot \upsilon_e$.*

We next present our rounding procedure for Γ'. It relies on the following lemma.

Lemma 7. *If there is a feasible schedule for the $1||A| \leq k|WC_{\max} + \sum_{J_j\in R} e_j$ problem with x_i accepted jobs from each $\mathcal{J}_i$, then there exists a feasible schedule where we accept the x_i jobs with the smallest weight among all jobs in $\mathcal{J}_i$ for each $1 \leq i \leq k_1$.*

Below, we apply a rounding procedure to obtain integer variables x^*_{ij} by using the integer variables $x_1,\cdots,x_k$ for Γ'. The rounding procedure is based on the result in Lemma 7. Thus, if there exists a variable $x_{ij}(j=1,\cdots,\upsilon_w)$ that has a value that is not integer then, we simply set $x_{ij}=1$ for the x_i jobs in $\mathcal{J}_i$ having the smallest weight among all jobs in the set, and set all other x_{ij} variables to zero.

Rounding procedure
For $i=1,\cdots,k_1$, if there exists a variable $x_{ij}(j=1,\cdots,\upsilon_w)$ that has a value that is not integer, then, we let r_i be the unique index that satisfies the condition $\sum_{j=r_i+1}^{\upsilon_w} \delta_{ij} \leq x_i \leq \sum_{j=r_i}^{\upsilon_w} \delta_{ij}$. We set

$$x^*_{ij} = \begin{cases} 0, & \text{for } j=1,\cdots,r_i-1 \\ x_i - \sum\limits_{i=r_i+1}^{\upsilon_w} \delta_{ij}, & \text{for } j=r_i \\ \delta_{ij}, & \text{for } j=r_i+1,\cdots,\upsilon_w. \end{cases} \tag{20}$$

Otherwise, we set $x^*_{ij} = x_{ij}$ for $j=1,\cdots,\upsilon_w$.

Lemma 8. *If $\boldsymbol{x}$ is a feasible solution to Γ, then $\boldsymbol{x}^*$ is a feasible solution to Γ' where $\boldsymbol{x} = \{x_{ij} : i = 1, \cdots, k_1 \text{ and } j = 1, \cdots, v_w\} \cup \{x_i : i = 1, \cdots, k_1\}$ and $\boldsymbol{x}^* = \{x^*_{ij} : i = 1, \cdots, k_1 \text{ and } j = 1, \cdots, v_w\} \cup \{x^*_i : i = 1, \cdots, k_1\}$.*

Proof. The fact that all x_i and δ_{ij} are integer, implies that all x^*_{ij} are integer values as well. Let us check that the solution remains feasible. From (20) and Lemma 7, we have that (i) $x^*_i = \sum_{j=1}^{v_w} x^*_{ij} = x_i$, and that (ii) $\sum_{\ell=1}^{j} x^*_{i\ell} \leq \sum_{\ell=1}^{j} x_{i\ell}$ for $i = 1, \cdots, k_1$ and $j = 1, \cdots, v_w$. Based on (i), we have that $\sum_{i=1}^{k_1}(n_i - x^*_i)e_i = \sum_{i=1}^{k_1}(n_i - x_i)e_i$ and $\sum_{i=1}^{k_1} x^*_i = \sum_{i=1}^{k_1} x_i \leq k$. Clearly, $\boldsymbol{x}^*$ satisfies constraints (14) and (16) for $j = 1, \cdots, v_w$, and the vector of variables $(x^*_{i1}, x^*_{i2}, \cdots, x^*_{iv_w})$ minimizes the value of $\sum_{j=1}^{\ell} x_{ij}$ for each $\ell = 1, \cdots, v_w$. Thus, we also have that

$$w_\ell \sum_{i=1}^{k_1} \sum_{j=1}^{\ell} p_i x^*_{ij} \leq w_\ell \sum_{i=1}^{k_1} \sum_{j=1}^{\ell} p_i x_{ij}$$

for $\ell = 1, \cdots, v_w$. Thus

$$\begin{aligned} WC_{\max}(\boldsymbol{x}^*) &= \max_{\ell=1,\cdots,v_w} \{w_\ell \sum_{i=1}^{k_1} \sum_{j=1}^{\ell} p_i x^*_{ij}\} \leq WC_{\max}(\boldsymbol{x}) \\ &= \max_{\ell=1,\cdots,v_w} \{w_\ell \sum_{i=1}^{k_1} \sum_{j=1}^{\ell} p_i x_{ij}\}. \end{aligned}$$

□

Therefore $\boldsymbol{x}^*$ is also an optimal solution for Γ. Finally, combining Lemma 8 with Lemma 6, we have the following theorem:

Theorem 5. *Problem $1||A| \leq k|WC_{\max} + \sum_{J_j \in R} e_j$ can be solved in $k_1^{O(k_1)} \cdot n^{O(1)}$ time, where $k_1 = v_p \cdot v_e$.*

5 Conclusions and Future Research

We analyze the parameterized tractability of single machine scheduling problem with rejection to minimize the weighted makespan. In this problem the objective is to minimize the sum of the weighted makespan of accepted jobs and the total rejection cost of rejected jobs, conditional on the number of accepted jobs no great than a given threshold. Our results are summarized in Table 1.

Table 1. Parameterized complexity results for scheduling problem with rejection to minimize the weighted makespan.

Scheduling problem	Parameter	Complexity
$1\|\|A\| \leq k\|WC_{\max} + \sum_{J_j \in R} e_j$	k	W[1]-hard
$1\|\|A\| \leq k\|WC_{\max} + \sum_{J_j \in R} e_j$	$v_w \cdot v_p$	FPT
$1\|\|A\| \leq k\|WC_{\max} + \sum_{J_j \in R} e_j$	$v_w \cdot v_e$	FPT
$1\|\|A\| \leq k\|WC_{\max} + \sum_{J_j \in R} e_j$	$v_p \cdot v_e$	FPT

Note that it is still open for future research whether problem $1||A| \leq k|WC_{\max} + \sum_{J_j \in R} e_j$ can be solved in FPT time with respect to the number of different processing time v_p or rejection cost v_e. Finally, we will extend this problem to parallel machine setting in the future.

References

1. Alix, M.K.: A fixed-parameter algorithm for scheduling unit dependent tasks on parallel machines with time windows. Disc. Appl. Math. **290**, 1–6 (2021)
2. Bartal, Y., Leonardi, S., Spaccamela, A.M., Stougie, J.: Multi-processor scheduling with rejection. SIAM J. Disc. Math. **13**, 64–78 (2000)
3. Bodlaender, H.L., Fellows, M.R.: W[2]-hardness of precedence constrained k-processor scheduling. Oper. Res. Lett. **18**(2), 93–97 (1995)
4. Chai, X., Lu, L., Li, W., Zhang, L.: Best-possible online algorithms for single machine scheduling to minimize the maximum weighted completion time. Asia-Pacific J. Oper. Res. **35**, 1850048 (2018)
5. Cygan, M., Fomin, F.V., Kowalik, Ł, Lokshtanov, D., Marx, D., Pilipczuk, M., Pilipczuk, M., Saurabh, S.: Parameterized Algorithms. Springer, Cham (2015). https://doi.org/10.1007/978-3-319-21275-3
6. Dai, B., Li, W.: Vector scheduling with rejection on two machines. Int. J. Comput. Math. **97**(12), 2507–2515 (2020)
7. Fellows, M.R., Koblitz, N.: Fixed-parameter complexity and cryptography. In: Cohen, G., Mora, T., Moreno, O. (eds.) AAECC 1993. LNCS, vol. 673, pp. 121–131. Springer, Heidelberg (1993). https://doi.org/10.1007/3-540-56686-4_38
8. Fellows, M.R., McCartin, C.: On the parametric complexity of schedules to minimize tardy tasks. Theor. Comput. Sci. **298**(2), 317–324 (2003)
9. Feng, Q., Yuan, J.: NP-hardness of a multicriteria scheduling on two families of jobs. OR Trans. **11**, 121–126 (2007)
10. Flum, J., Grohe, M.: Parameterized Complexity Theory. Springer, Heidelberg (2006). https://doi.org/10.1007/3-540-29953-X
11. Frank, A., Tardos, E.: An application of simultaneous diophantine approximation in combinatorial optimization. Combinatorica **1**(7), 49–66 (1987)
12. Graham, R.L., Lawler, E.L., Lenstra, J.K., Kan, A.H.G.R.: Optimization and approximation in deterministic sequencing and scheduling: a survey. Ann. Disc. Math. **5**, 287–326 (1979)
13. Hermelin, D., Shabtay, D., Zelig, C., Pinedo, M.: A general scheme for solving a large set of scheduling problems with rejection in FPT time. J. Sched. **25**(2), 229–255 (2022)

14. Knop, D., Koutecký, M.: Scheduling meets n-fold integer programming. J. Sched. **21**, 493–503 (2018). https://doi.org/10.1007/s10951-017-0550-0
15. Li, W.: A best possible online algorithm for the parallel-machine scheduling to minimize the maximum weighted completed time. Asia-Pacific J. Oper. Res. **32**, 1550030 (2015)
16. Li, W., Li, J., Zhang, X., Chen, Z.: Penalty cost constrained identical parallel machine scheduling problem. Theor. Comput. Sci. **607**, 181–192 (2015)
17. Li, W., Cui, Q.: Vector scheduling with rejection on a single machine. 4OR-Q. J. Oper. Res. **16**(1), 95–104 (2018)
18. Liu, X., Xing, P., Li, W.: Approximation algorithms for the submodular load balancing with submodular penalties. Mathematics **8**(10), 1785 (2020)
19. Liu, X., Li, W.: Approximation algorithms for the multiprocessor scheduling with submodular penalties. Optim. Lett. **15**, 2165–2180 (2021)
20. Lu, L., Zhang, L., Ou, J.: Single machine scheduling with rejection to minimize the weighted makespan. In: Wu, W., Du, H. (eds.) AAIM 2021. LNCS, vol. 13153, pp. 96–110. Springer, Cham (2021). https://doi.org/10.1007/978-3-030-93176-6_9
21. Mnich, M., Wiese, A.: Scheduling and fixed-parameter tractability. Math. Program. **154**(1), 533–562 (2015)
22. Ou, J., Zhong, X., Wang, G.: An improved heuristic for parallel machine scheduling with rejection. Eur. J. Oper. Res. **241**(3), 653–661 (2015)
23. Shabtay, D., Gaspar, N., Kaspi, M.: A survey on off-line scheduling with rejection. J. Sched. **16**, 3–28 (2013)
24. Sun, R., Liu, X.: Approximation scheme for single-machine rescheduling with job delay and rejection. In: Ni, Q., Wu, W. (eds) AAIM 2022. LNCS, vol. 13513, pp. 35–45. Springer, Cham (2022). https://doi.org/10.1007/978-3-031-16081-3_4
25. Zhang, L., Lu, L., Yuan, J.: Single machine scheduling with release dates and rejection. Eur. J. Oper. Res. **198**, 975–978 (2009)

Multi-resource Allocation in Mobile Edge Computing Systems: A Trade-Off on Fairness and Efficiency

Xingxing Li[1], Weidong Li[2], and Xuejie Zhang[1](✉)

[1] School of Information Science and Engineering, Yunnan University, Kunming 650500, People's Republic of China
lixingxing@mail.ynu.edu.cn, xjzhang@ynu.edu.cn

[2] School of Mathematics and Statistics, Yunnan University, Kunming 650500, People's Republic of China
weidongmath@126.com

Abstract. Fairness and efficiency are two important goals of multi-resource allocation in mobile edge computing systems. We model the system as a shared computing system consisting of multiple servers, where user tasks have placement constraints and link bandwidth resources are independent of servers. For this model, we propose a mechanism, soft task share fairness - max-min efficiency (TSF-MME), to capture the trade-off between efficiency and fairness in multi-resource allocation. TSF-MME consists of α task share fairness mechanism (α-TSF) and max-min efficiency mechanism (MME). Compared with absolute fairness, TSF-MME can guarantee soft fairness of no less than α times. The lower bound of α is an adjustable value that can be set according to the fairness threshold that managers want to guarantee. Meanwhile, TSF-MME can maximize and directly display the overall efficiency of the system. Then, we design an algorithm to find the allocation of TSF-MME. Rigorous proof shows that TSF-MME satisfies soft fairness, soft sharing incentive, Pareto optimality and envy-freeness.

Keywords: Mobile edge computing · Multi-resource allocation · Task share fairness · Max-min efficiency · Placement constraint

1 Introduction

Multi-resource allocation in computing systems is fundamental to network and service management tasks [1–4]. Fair multi-resource allocation increasingly received attention in computer science in the past few decades [5–7]. In multi-resource allocation, the system must package and allocate various resources to users in proportion to their demands [5,8]. If we simply pursue fair allocation, it will inevitably lead to low utilization of some resources in the system [9,10]. The diversity of user requirements and the heterogeneity of server configurations in

Z. Cai et al. (Eds.): NCTCS 2022, CCIS 1693, pp. 248–262, 2022.
https://doi.org/10.1007/978-981-19-8152-4_18

mobile edge computing systems far exceed those of traditional computing systems [11]. Therefore, the system efficiency corresponding to fair multi-resource allocation in edge computing systems will be lower than that of general systems. There is now an extensive literature devoted to achieve a balance between fairness and efficiency [12–14].

But none of these mechanisms can be well applied directly to mobile edge computing systems. Mobile edge computing systems are different from traditional shared computing systems because performing tasks in edge systems requires not only traditional computing resources, but also bandwidth resources [15]. Users must offload tasks over the network to servers provided by other users. This feature brings new challenges to fair and efficient multi-resource allocation.

In addition, servers in mobile edge computing systems are usually provided by users, and machine differences naturally arise [16]. This difference can lead to machine configuration incompatibility with the prerequisites for task execution, namely user task deployment constraints. This incompatibility also poses a significant obstacle to achieving fair and efficient multi-resource allocation [17].

Task share fairness (TSF) proposed in [17] is an excellent way to achieve multi-resource fair allocation, when users' tasks have deployment constraints. TSF can satisfy various desirable properties such as sharing incentive, strategy-proofness, envy-freeness and Pareto optimality at the same time.

In this paper, we study the problem of fair and efficient multi-resource allocation in mobile edge computing systems. We model the system as a shared computing system consisting of multiple servers, where user tasks have placement constraints and link bandwidth resources are independent of servers. To achieve the trade-off between fairness and efficiency of multi-resource allocation in our model, we propose a mechanism, soft task share fairness - max-min efficiency (TSF-MME), which is a generalization of TSF. TSF-MME is composed of α task share fairness mechanism (α-TSF) and max-min efficiency mechanism (MME). In the process of resource allocation, α-TSF is executed first, and then MME is executed. α-TSF fairly allocates the ρ portion of system resources. Then, MME allocates the remaining resources after the α-TSF allocation with the goal of maximizing the minimum resource utilization.

Specifically, TSF-MME satisfies soft fairness: that is, compared with TSF, TSF-MME can ensure that the fairness of all users is not less than α times. In addition, TSF-MME satisfies soft sharing incentive: that is, TSF-MME can guarantee that the number of tasks that each user can perform is no less than ρ times the number of tasks that each user can perform using only the server provided by himself. More importantly, TSF-MME satisfies Pareto optimality: that is, there is no user' allocation can be improved without strictly decreasing the allocation of some other user. Finally, TSF-MME satisfies envy-freeness: that is, there is no user strictly prefers the allocation of some other user.

The remainder of this paper is organized as follows. In Sect. 2, we introduce our model and describe TSF-MME allocation mechanism. In Sect. 3, we design an algorithm for TSF-MME and show its pseudocode. In Sect. 4, we prove the properties that TSF-MME satisfies. Finally, we draw conclusions in Sect. 5.

2 System Model and Allocation Strategy

In this section, we model multi-resource allocation in a mobile edge computing system and propose a mechanism, TSF-MME, to capture the trade-off between efficiency and fairness.

2.1 System Model

There are n users sharing a mobile edge computing system consisting of m (possibly) heterogeneous edge computing servers, where each server has l types of resources (e.g., CPU, memory, storage) and users access servers through a shared communication channel [15]. Let $S = \{1, 2, \ldots, m\}$ and $U = \{1, 2, \ldots, n\}$ be the set of servers and users in the system, respectively. Let $R = R_S \bigcup R_{BW} = \{1, 2, \ldots, l, l+1\}$ be the set of $l+1$ resource types in the system, where $R_S = \{1, 2, \ldots, l\}$ denotes the set of l resources provided by servers and $R_{BW} = \{l+1\}$ denotes the set of link bandwidth resource. In subsequent expressions in this paper, both BW and $l+1$ refer to bandwidth resources.

Similar to the approach used in [15], we treat the wireless communication link as an external resource and differentiate it from resources provided by servers. Let $\mathbf{C}_s = (C_{s,1}, C_{s,2}, \ldots, C_{s,l})$ be the resource capacity vector of server $s \in S$, where $C_{s,r}$ denotes the total amount of resource $r \in R_S$ available in server s. Let C_{BW} be the total amount of available link bandwidth resource in the system.

For each user $u \in U$, let $\mathbf{D}_u = (D_{u,1}, D_{u,2}, \ldots, D_{u,l}, D_{u,BW})$ be the demand vector of user u, where $D_{u,r}$ denotes the amount of resource $r \in R$ consumed by executing a task for user u. It is worth noting that the consumed resources $r \in R_S$ comes from a specific server, while the consumed resource $r \in R_{BW}$ comes from the system. In addition, as the assumption in [18–20], we assume that each user u has an arbitrary positive demand for each resource r, i.e., $D_{u,r} > 0, u \in U, r \in R$.

2.2 Resource Allocation

Let $\mathbf{A} = (\mathbf{A}_1, \mathbf{A}_2, \ldots, \mathbf{A}_n)$ be the allocation matrix of all users in the entire computing system, where $\mathbf{A}_u$ denotes the allocation matrix of user $u \in U$. Let $\mathbf{A}_u = (\mathbf{A}_{u,1}, \mathbf{A}_{u,2}, \ldots, \mathbf{A}_{u,m}, \mathbf{A}_{u,BW})$, where $\mathbf{A}_{u,s}$ denotes the allocation vector of user u in server $s \in S$ and $\mathbf{A}_{u,BW}$ denotes the link bandwidth resource allocation of user u. Let $\mathbf{A}_{u,s} = (A_{u,s,1}, A_{u,s,2}, \ldots, A_{u,s,l})$ and $\mathbf{A}_{u,BW} = A_{u,BW}$, where $A_{u,s,r}$ denotes the amount of resource $r \in R_S$ allocated to user u in server s and $A_{u,BW}$ denotes the amount of link bandwidth resource allocated to user u.

Without accounting for the limit on link bandwidth resources, given user u's allocation $\mathbf{A}_{u,s}$ in server s, let $N_{u,s}^s(\mathbf{A}_{u,s})$ be the maximum number of tasks that user u can perform in server s and we have

$$N_{u,s}^s(\mathbf{A}_{u,s}) = \min_{1 \le r \le R_S} \{A_{u,s,r}/D_{u,r}\}.$$

In the presence of only link bandwidth resource constraints, given user u's bandwidth resource allocation $\mathbf{A}_{u,BW}$, let $N_u^{BW}(\mathbf{A}_{u,BW})$ be the maximum number of tasks that user u can perform and we have

$$N_u^{BW}(\mathbf{A}_{u,BW}) = A_{u,BW}/D_{u,BW}.$$

Let $\mathbf{N}(\mathbf{A}) = (N_1(\mathbf{A}_1), N_2(\mathbf{A}_2), \ldots, N_n(\mathbf{A}_n))$ be the vector of the number of tasks that all users can perform under allocation $\mathbf{A}$, where $N_u(\mathbf{A}_u)$ denotes the total number of tasks that user $u \in U$ can schedule under the allocation $\mathbf{A}_u$. We define $N_u(\mathbf{A}_u) = N_{u,1}(\mathbf{A}_{u,1}) + N_{u,2}(\mathbf{A}_{u,2}) + \ldots + N_{u,m}(\mathbf{A}_{u,m})$, where $N_{u,s}(\mathbf{A}_{u,s})$ denotes the number of tasks that user $u \in U$ can schedule on server $s \in S$. Then, we stipulate that

$$N_{u,s}(\mathbf{A}_{u,s}) = N_{u,s}^s(\mathbf{A}_{u,s}) \cdot min\{1, \frac{\sum_{s \in S} N_{u,s}^s(\mathbf{A}_{u,s})}{N_u^{BW}(\mathbf{A}_{u,BW})}\}.$$

More and more data processing tasks specify placement constraints [21,22], and these constraints restrict these tasks from running on certain classes of machines that meet specific requirements (e.g., specific type of CPU, GPU and SSD). The heterogeneity of servers coupled with the diversity of users demands make us have to account for tasks' practical placement constraint when allocating resources. Formally, let $\mathbf{P}_u = (P_{u,1}, P_{u,2}, \cdots, P_{u,m})$ be the boolean constraint vector of user $u \in U$ that indicates on which servers user $u's$ tasks can be executed. Specifically, $P_{u,s} = 1$ means user $u \in U$ can run tasks on machine $s \in S$, and $P_{u,s} = 0$ otherwise.

To maximize the system efficiency, we stipulate that each allocation produced by our mechanism is non-wasteful [18,23], i.e.,

$$\begin{aligned} A_{u,s,r} &= N_{u,s}(\mathbf{A}_{u,s}) \cdot D_{u,r} \cdot P_{u,s}, u \in U, s \in S, r \in R_S, \\ A_{u,BW} &= N_u(\mathbf{A}_u) \cdot D_{u,BW} = \sum\nolimits_{s \in S} N_{u,s}(\mathbf{A}_{u,s}) \cdot D_{u,BW}. \end{aligned} \tag{1}$$

We believe that the allocation $\mathbf{A}$ is feasible [24,25] if and only if it holds that

$$\begin{aligned} &\sum\nolimits_{u \in U} A_{u,s,r} \leq C_{s,r}, s \in S, r \in R_S, (a) \\ &\sum\nolimits_{u \in U} A_{u,BW} \leq C_{s,BW}. \ (b) \end{aligned} \tag{2}$$

From each server's perspective, the constraint (2.a) requires that the total amount of each resource allocated to all users do not exceed the capacity of that resource on each server. From the system perspective, the constraint (2.b) requires that the total amount of bandwidth resources allocated to all users do not exceed the capacity of the bandwidth resources in the system. Combining formulas (1) and (2), the allocation feasibility constraint can be expressed as

$$\begin{aligned} &\sum\nolimits_{u \in U} N_{u,s}(\mathbf{A}_{u,s}) \cdot D_{u,r} \cdot P_{u,s} \leq C_{s,r}, s \in S, r \in R_S, \ (a) \\ &\sum\nolimits_{s \in S} N_{u,s}(\mathbf{A}_{u,s}) \cdot D_{u,BW} \leq C_{s,BW}. \ (b) \end{aligned} \tag{3}$$

Additionally, we take into account the fact that different users have different weights due to their different contributions to the system [17,26]. Let $\mathbf{w} = (w_1, w_2, \ldots, w_n)$ be the vector of all users' weights, where w_u denotes the weight of user u and w_u is a positive real number. Intuitively, user u's weight is related to his contribution to the system, therefore we have

$$w_u = h_u / H_u, u \in U, \tag{4}$$

where h_u denotes the number of tasks that user u can schedule when he exclusively uses the server provided by himself, and H_u denotes the number of tasks that user u can schedule when he monopolizes the whole system and does not consider task placement constraints (i.e., $P_{u,s} = 1, s \in S$). Let $S_u = \{s_1, s_2, \ldots, s_u\}$ be the set of servers provided by user $u \in U$, then we have

$$\begin{aligned} h_u &= \sum\nolimits_{s \in S_u} N^s_{u,s}(\mathbf{C}_s) \cdot min\{1, \frac{\sum_{s \in S_u} N^s_{u,s}(\mathbf{C}_s)}{N^{BW}_u(\mathbf{A}_{u,BW})}\}, \\ H_u &= \sum\nolimits_{s \in S} N^s_{u,s}(\mathbf{C}_s) \cdot min\{1, \frac{\sum_{s \in S} N^s_{u,s}(\mathbf{C}_s)}{N^{BW}_u(\mathbf{A}_{u,BW})}\}. \end{aligned} \tag{5}$$

2.3 TSF

TSF proposed in [17,27] is a compelling multi-resource fair allocation mechanism for users with task placement constraints. TSF measures fairness among users based on users' task shares [1], where the task share of user u is defined as the ratio of the number of tasks u currently runs and the total number of tasks u can run, when user u uses the whole system alone and has no placement constraints.

Let $\mathbf{TS} = (TS_1, TS_2, \ldots, TS_n)$ be the vector of all users' task shares under allocation $\mathbf{A}$, where TS_u denotes the task share of user $u \in U$ with allocation $\mathbf{A}_u$. In the presence of users' weights, TS_u can be represented as

$$TS_u = N_u(\mathbf{A}_u) / (w_u \cdot H_u), u \in U. \tag{6}$$

Since the deployment of tasks needs to follow the task placement constraints, it is often impossible for all users to have the same task share. This means that the traditional way of measuring fairness where all users have absolutely consistent specific values (e.g. dominance share, number of tasks, etc.) is not suitable for our model. In our model, we call such a task share vector $\mathbf{TS} = (TS_1, TS_2, \ldots, TS_n)$ is the optimal task share fairness (TSF-optimal) vector:

Definition 1. $\mathbf{TS} = (TS_1, TS_2, \ldots, TS_n)$ *is TSF-optimal, if and only if* $\mathbf{TS}_\tau$ *is lexicographically greater than any other task share vector* $\mathbf{TS}'_\tau$, *where* $\mathbf{TS}_\tau$ *and* $\mathbf{TS}'_\tau$ *are obtained by arranging* $\mathbf{TS}$ *and* $\mathbf{TS}' = (TS'_1, TS'_2, \ldots, TS'_n)$ *in non-decreasing order of magnitude, respectively.*

As an example, there are two task share vectors $\mathbf{TS} = (0.5, 0.7, 0.6)$ and $\mathbf{TS}' = (0.8, 0.5, 0.5)$. $\mathbf{TS}$ is the TSF-optimal vector, because $\mathbf{TS}_\tau = (0.5, 0.6, 0.7)$ is lexicographically greater than $\mathbf{TS}'_\tau = (0.5, 0.5, 0.8)$.

We generalize TSF to multi-resource fair allocation with placement constraints in mobile edge computing systems where we treat bandwidth resources as external resources independent of servers. Specifically, TSF in our model is:

$$
\begin{aligned}
& \underset{\mathbf{N(A)},\mathbf{TS}}{TSF-optimal} \ (TS_1, TS_2, \ldots, TS_n) \\
s.t. \ & \sum_{u \in U} N_{u,s}(\mathbf{A}_{u,s}) \cdot D_{u,r} \cdot P_{u,s} \leq C_{s,r}, s \in S, r \in R_S, \quad (a) \\
& \sum_{s \in S} N_{u,s}(\mathbf{A}_{u,s}) \cdot D_{u,BW} \leq C_{BW}, \quad (b) \\
& TS_u = \sum_{s \in S} N_{u,s}(\mathbf{A}_{u,s})/(w_u \cdot H_u), u \in U, \quad (c) \\
& N_{u,s}(\mathbf{A}_{u,s}) \geq 0, u \in U, s \in S. \quad (d)
\end{aligned}
\tag{7}
$$

The objective function for the linear programming (7) is to find the TSF-optimal vector and the corresponding allocation. Note that constraints (7.a) and (7.b) guarantee the feasibility of the allocation from the perspectives of servers' resources capacities and the system's bandwidth resource capacity, respectively. Constraint (7.c) associates TS_u with $N_{u,s}(\mathbf{A}_{u,s})$. Constraint (7.d) restricts $N_{u,s}(\mathbf{A}_{u,s})$ to non-negative values.

For the allocation of TSF, let $\mathbf{TS}^* = (TS_1^*, TS_2^*, \ldots, TS_n^*)$ be the TSF-optimal solution of the linear programming (7). Let $\mathbf{A}_{u,s}^*$ and $N_{u,s}(\mathbf{A}_{u,s}^*)$ represent the allocation of user u and the number of tasks user u can schedule in server s, respectively.

It is worth noting that the TSF in our model retains many of the original excellent properties of the TSF, such as sharing incentive, strategy-proofness, envy-freeness and Pareto optimality. Due to space limitations, we omit the specific proof.

2.4 TSF-MME

In this subsection, we propose a new allocation mechanism, TSF-MME, to achieve a tradeoff between fairness and efficiency.

TSF-MME consists of α task share fairness mechanism (α-TSF) and max-min efficiency mechanism (MME). TSF-MME executes α-TSF first, and then executes MME. α-TSF focuses on ensuring fairness, and it allocates ρ part of resources fairly. MME focuses on ensuring efficiency, and it efficiently allocates the remaining resources after α-TSF allocation. Meanwhile, MME can intuitively reflect the resource utilization of the entire system by giving the minimum resource utilization.

For the allocation of α-TSF, let $\overline{\mathbf{A}}_{u,s}$ and $N_{u,s}(\overline{\mathbf{A}}_{u,s})$ be the allocation of user u and the number of tasks user u can schedule in server s, respectively. For the allocation of MME, let $\hat{\mathbf{A}}_{u,s}$ and $N_{u,s}(\hat{\mathbf{A}}_{u,s})$ be the allocation of user u and the number of tasks user u can schedule in server s, respectively. Meanwhile, let $\overline{\mathbf{TS}} = (\overline{TS}_1, \overline{TS}_2, \ldots, \overline{TS}_n)$ and $\hat{\mathbf{TS}} = (\hat{TS}_1, \hat{TS}_2, \ldots, \hat{TS}_n)$ represent the vector of task shares of all users $u \in U$ in the allocation of α-TSF and MME, respectively.

Combining the allocation of α-TSF and MME, we can get the allocation of TSF-MME. Specifically,

$$\begin{aligned} &\mathbf{A}_{u,s} = \overline{\mathbf{A}}_{u,s} + \hat{\mathbf{A}}_{u,s}, u \in U, s \in S, \\ &N_{u,s}(\mathbf{A}_{u,s}) = N_{u,s}(\overline{\mathbf{A}}_{u,s}) + N_{u,s}(\hat{\mathbf{A}}_{u,s}), u \in U, s \in S, \\ &TS_u = \overline{TS}_u + \hat{TS}_u, u \in U. \end{aligned} \tag{8}$$

Notably, when $\rho = 1$, TSF-MME is equivalent to TSF and we have $TS_u = \overline{TS}_u, \hat{TS}_u = 0$. In this condition, TSF-MME strictly seeks fairness. When $\rho = 0$, TSF-MME is equivalent to MME and we have $TS_u = \hat{TS}_u, \overline{TS}_u = 0$. In this condition, TSF-MME aims to seek absolute efficiency.

α-TSF. α-TSF aims to ensure no less than α degree of fairness relative to TSF's allocation for all users. α-TSF allocates the ρ portion of resources across all users via TSF. $\rho \in [0, 1]$ is an adjustable value. Formally, α-TSF is equivalent to the following linear programming:

$$\begin{aligned} &\underset{\mathbf{N}(\overline{\mathbf{A}}),\overline{\mathbf{TS}}}{TSF - optimal} \ (\overline{TS}_1, \overline{TS}_2, \ldots, \overline{TS}_n) \\ s.t. \ &\sum_{u \in U} N_{u,s}(\overline{\mathbf{A}}_{u,s}) \cdot D_{u,r} \cdot P_{u,s} \le \rho \cdot C_{s,r}, s \in S, r \in R_S, \quad (a) \\ &\sum_{u \in U} \sum_{s \in S} N_{u,s}(\overline{\mathbf{A}}_{u,s}) \cdot D_{u,BW} \le \rho \cdot C_{BW}, \quad (b) \\ &\overline{TS}_u = \sum_{s \in S} N_{u,s}(\overline{\mathbf{A}}_{u,s}) / (w_u \cdot H_u), u \in U, \quad (c) \\ &N_{u,s}(\overline{\mathbf{A}}_{u,s}) \ge 0, u \in U, s \in S. \quad (d) \end{aligned} \tag{9}$$

The objective of (9) and constraints (9.a–9.d) have the similar meaning as the objective of (7) and constraints (7.a–7.d), respectively. Solving the linear programming (9), we can get its TSF-optimal solution $\overline{\mathbf{TS}} = (\overline{TS}_1, \overline{TS}_2, \ldots, \overline{TS}_n)$. It is intuitive that we have

$$\begin{aligned} &\overline{TS}_u = \rho \cdot TS_u^*, u \in U, \\ &N_{u,s}(\overline{\mathbf{A}}_{u,s}) = \rho \cdot N_{u,s}(\mathbf{A}_{u,s}^*), u \in U, s \in S. \end{aligned} \tag{10}$$

MME. MME aims to improve the efficiency of system via maximizing the minimum resource utilization among all resources. At the same time, MME can directly reflect the efficiency of the system by returning the minimum resource utilization.

For each server $s \in S$, let $\mathbf{C_s}' = (C'_{s,1}, C'_{s,2}, \ldots, C'_{s,l})^T$ be the vector of remanent resources quantity after α-TSF allocation, where $C'_{s,r}$ denotes the amount of resource $r \in R_S$ available during MME allocation. Let C'_{BW} be the amount of available link bandwidth resource during MME allocation. Then, we have

$$
\begin{aligned}
C'_{s,r} &= C_{s,r} - \sum_{u \in U} N_{u,s}(\overline{\mathbf{A}}_{u,s}) \cdot D_{u,r} \cdot P_{u,s}, s \in S, r \in R_S, \\
C'_{BW} &= C_{BW} - \sum_{u \in U} \sum_{s \in S} N_{u,s}(\overline{\mathbf{A}}_{u,s}) \cdot D_{u,BW}.
\end{aligned} \tag{11}
$$

Definition 2. *For each user $u \in U$, we have $D'_{u,r} = D_{u,r} / \sum_{s \in S} C_{s,r}, s \in S, r \in R_S$, and $D'_{u,BW} = D_{u,BW}/C_{BW}$, then we find $r^*_u = arg\ max_{r \in R} D'_{u,r}$. Formally, we define the normalized demand vector of each user $u \in U$ as $\mathbf{d}_u = (d_{u,1}, d_{u,2}, \ldots, d_{u,BW})$, where $d_{u,r} = D'_{u,r}/D'_{u,r^*_u}, r \in R$.*

As an example, there are three users u_1, u_2, u_3, where $\mathbf{D}_1 = (0.1, 0.2, 0.3), \mathbf{D}_2 = (0.2, 0.4, 0.6), \mathbf{D}_3 = (0.3, 0.6, 0.9)$, $\sum_{s \in S} C_{s,r} = 1, r \in R$, then we can conclude that u_1, u_2, u_3 have the same normalized demand vector, i.e., $\mathbf{d}_1 = \mathbf{d}_2 = \mathbf{d}_3 = (1/3, 2/3, 1)$.

In order to maximize the task share fairness among users while improving the system efficiency, we stipulate that: MME will guarantee the TSF-optimality of the task share vector $(\hat{TS}_{u_1}, \hat{TS}_{u_2}, \ldots, \hat{TS}_{u_k})$, where users in $\{u_1, u_2, \ldots, u_k\}$ have the same normalized demand vector, i.e., $\mathbf{d}_{u_1} = \mathbf{d}_{u_2} = \ldots = \mathbf{d}_{u_k}$. This is because if these users are allocated different task shares, it will not affect the efficiency of the system, but it will affect the task share fairness between users. Specifically, we divide the set of all users U into $K \in N^+$ subsets $\{U_1, U_2, \ldots, U_K\}$ based on whether they have the same normalized demand vector. For each subset $U_k \in \{U_1, U_2, \ldots, U_K\}$, we have $\mathbf{d}_i = \mathbf{d}_j, \forall i, j \in U_k$.

Formally, MME is equivalent to the following linear programming:

$$
\begin{aligned}
\max_{\theta, \mathbf{N}(\hat{\mathbf{A}}), \hat{\mathbf{TS}}} \quad & \theta = \min_{r \in R} \frac{\sum_{u=1}^{n} D_{u,r} \cdot N_u(\overline{\mathbf{A}}_u) + \sum_{u=1}^{n} D_{u,r} \cdot N_u(\hat{\mathbf{A}}_u)}{C_r} \\
s.t. \quad & \sum_{u \in U} N_{u,s}(\hat{\mathbf{A}}_{u,s}) \cdot D_{u,r} \cdot P_{u,s} \le C'_{s,r}, s \in S, r \in R_S, && (a) \\
& \sum_{u \in U} \sum_{s \in S} N_{u,s}(\hat{\mathbf{A}}_{u,s}) \cdot D_{u,BW} \le C'_{BW}, && (b) \\
& \hat{TS}_u = \sum_{s \in S} N_{u,s}(\hat{\mathbf{A}}_{u,s}) / (w_u \cdot H_u), u \in U, && (c) \\
& N_{u,s}(\hat{\mathbf{A}}_{u,s}) \ge 0, u \in U, s \in S, && (d) \\
& TSF - optimal(\hat{TS}_{u_1}, \hat{TS}_{u_2}, \ldots, \hat{TS}_{u_k}), \\
& \mathbf{d}_{u_1} = \mathbf{d}_{u_2} = \ldots = \mathbf{d}_{u_k}, \{u_1, u_2, \ldots, u_k\} = U_k. && (e)
\end{aligned} \tag{12}
$$

We introduce θ to represent the minimum resource utilization among all resources. The objective of (12) aims to maximizes θ to increase the efficiency of the system. Constraints (12.a–12.d) have the similar meaning as constraints (7.a–7.d), respectively. Constraint (12.e) ensures the TSF-optimality of the task share vector $(\hat{TS}_{u_1}, \hat{TS}_{u_2}, \ldots, \hat{TS}_{u_k})$, where users in $\{u_1, u_2, \ldots, u_k\} = U_k$ have the same normalized demand vector, and $\forall U_k \in \{U_1, U_2, \ldots, U_K\}$.

3 The Pseudocode of TSF-MME

In this section, we propose the algorithm, TSF-MME, to achieve the allocation of TSF-MME. As shown in Algorithm 1, we give the pseudocode of TSF-MME. Symbols in the pseudocode have the same meaning as the corresponding symbols in Sect. 2.

Algorithm 1. TSF-MME

Input: $S, U, R, \mathbf{C_s}, C_{BW}, \mathbf{D}_u, \mathbf{P}_u, \rho$.

for $u \in U$ **do** ▷ User u provides the set of servers S_u.

$h_u = \sum_{s\in S_u} N^s_{u,s}(\mathbf{C}_s) \cdot min\{1, \frac{\sum_{s\in S_u} N^s_{u,s}(\mathbf{C}_s)}{N^{BW}_u(\mathbf{A}_{u,BW})}\}$

$H_u = \sum_{s\in S} N^s_{u,s}(\mathbf{C}_s) \cdot min\{1, \frac{\sum_{s\in S} N^s_{u,s}(\mathbf{C}_s)}{N^{BW}_u(\mathbf{A}_{u,BW})}\}$

$w_u = h_u / H_u$

$TS_u = \overline{TS}_u = \hat{TS}_u = 0, u \in U.$ ▷Initialize the allocation of each stage to 0.

$N_{u,s}(\mathbf{A}_{u,s}) = N_{u,s}(\overline{\mathbf{A}}_{u,s}) = N_{u,s}(\hat{\mathbf{A}}_{u,s}) = 0, u \in U, s \in S.$

Program: α-TSF $(S, U, R, \mathbf{C_s}, C_{BW}, \mathbf{D}_u, \mathbf{P}_u, \mathbf{w}, \rho)$

return: $\{N_{u,s}(\overline{\mathbf{A}}_{u,s}), \overline{TS}_u\}, u \in U, s \in S$

▷ Calculating the allocation of α-TSF.

Program: MME $(S, U, R, \mathbf{C_s}, C_{BW}, \mathbf{D}_u, \mathbf{P}_u, \mathbf{w}, \{N_{u,s}(\overline{\mathbf{A}}_{u,s})\})$

return: $\theta, \{N_{u,s}(\hat{\mathbf{A}}_{u,s}), \hat{TS}_u\}, u \in U, s \in S$

▷ Calculating the allocation of MME.

$TS_u = \overline{TS}_u + \hat{TS}_u, u \in U$

$N_{u,s}(\mathbf{A}_{u,s}) = N_{u,s}(\overline{\mathbf{A}}_{u,s}) + N_{u,s}(\hat{\mathbf{A}}_{u,s}), u \in U, s \in S$

$\mathbf{A}_{u,s} = \overline{\mathbf{A}}_{u,s} + \hat{\mathbf{A}}_{u,s} = D_{u,r} \cdot N_{u,s}(\overline{\mathbf{A}}_{u,s}) + D_{u,r} \cdot N_{u,s}(\hat{\mathbf{A}}_{u,s}), u \in U, s \in S$

Output: $\theta, \{\mathbf{A}_{u,s}, N_{u,s}(\mathbf{A}_{u,s}), TS_u\}, u \in U, s \in S$

TSF-MME receives input: $S, U, R, \mathbf{C_s}, C_{BW}, \mathbf{D}_u, \mathbf{P}_u, \rho$. According to formulas (4) and (5), the algorithm solves for $h_u, H_u, w_u, u \in U$. The algorithm initializes the allocation of TSF-MME, i.e. $TS_u = \overline{TS}_u = \hat{TS}_u = 0, N_{u,s}(\mathbf{A}_{u,s}) = N_{u,s}(\overline{\mathbf{A}}_{u,s}) = N_{u,s}(\hat{\mathbf{A}}_{u,s}) = 0, u \in U, s \in S$. The algorithm first executes program α-TSF to obtain $\{N_{u,s}(\overline{\mathbf{A}}_{u,s}), \overline{TS}_u\}, u \in U, s \in S$, and then executes program MME to obtain $\theta, \{N_{u,s}(\hat{\mathbf{A}}_{u,s}), \hat{TS}_u\}, u \in U, s \in S$. Finally, the results of the programs α-TSF and MME are combined to obtain the allocation of TSF-MME.

As shown in Algorithm 2, program α-TSF progressively determines $\overline{TS}_u$ and $N_{u,s}(\overline{\mathbf{A}}_{u,s}), u \in U, s \in S$ by alternately executing programs MMTS and IDTS. α-TSF maintains a dynamic set U_p. For user u in U_p, the task share of user u can be further increased compared to the current maximum task share. In each cycle t, the program MMTS determines the maximum task share TS^t_u that can be achieved simultaneously by all users in the current U_p. Then, the program IDTS checks whether the task share of each user in the U_p can be further increased. Specifically, it is to determine whether each user u in the

Algorithm 2. α-TSF

Program: α-TSF $(S, U, R, \mathbf{C_s}, C_{BW}, \mathbf{D}_u, \mathbf{P}_u, \mathbf{w}, \rho)$
$U_p = U$ ▷ The set of users whose task shares can be improved.
$r = 1$ ▷ Number of rounds.
while $U_p \neq \varnothing$ **do**
Program: MMTS$(S, U, R, \mathbf{C_s}, C_{BW}, \mathbf{D}_u, \mathbf{P}_u, \mathbf{w}, \rho, U_p, N_{u,s}(\overline{\mathbf{A}}_{u,s}))$
$\max_{N_{u,s}(A^t_{u,s})} \quad TS^t_u$
$s.t.$
$\sum_{u \in U_p} N_{u,s}(\mathbf{A}^t_{u,s}) \cdot D_{u,r} \cdot P_{u,s} + \sum_{u' \in U \backslash U_p} N_{u,s}(\overline{\mathbf{A}}_{u,s}) \cdot D_{u',r} \cdot P_{u',s}$
$\leq \rho \cdot C_{s,r}, s \in S, r \in R_S, \quad (a)$
$\sum_{s \in S} \sum_{u \in U_p} N_{u,s}(\mathbf{A}^t_{u,s}) \cdot D_{u,BW} + \sum_{s \in S} \sum_{u' \in U \backslash U_p} N_{u,s}(\overline{\mathbf{A}}_{u,s}) \cdot D_{u',BW}$
$\leq \rho \cdot C_{BW}, \quad (b)$
$TS^t_u = \sum_{s \in S} N_{u,s}(\mathbf{A}^t_{u,s})/(w_u \cdot H_u), u \in U_p, \quad (c)$
$N_{u,s}(\mathbf{A}^t_{u,s}) \geq 0, u \in U_p, s \in S, \quad (d)$
return: $TS^t_u, \{N_{u,s}(\mathbf{A}^t_{u,s}), u \in U, s \in S\}$
Program:
IDTS $(S, U, R, \mathbf{C_s}, C_{BW}, \mathbf{D}_u, \mathbf{P}_u, \mathbf{w}, \rho, U_p, N_{u,s}(\overline{\mathbf{A}}_{u,s}), TS^t_u, N_{u,s}(\mathbf{A}^t_{u,s}))$
for $u \in U_p$ **do**
$N_{u_1,s}(\mathbf{A}'_{u_1,s}) = N_{u_1,s}(\overline{\mathbf{A}}_{u_1,s}), u_1 \in U \backslash U_p,$
$N_{u_2,s}(\mathbf{A}'_{u_2,s}) = N_{u_2,s}(\mathbf{A}^t_{u_2,s}), u_2 \in U_p \backslash u,$
$TS'^t_u, \{N_{u,s}(\mathbf{A}'^t_{u,s}), s \in S\}$
$\Leftarrow$ MMTS$(S, U, R, \mathbf{C_s}, C_{BW}, \mathbf{D}_u, \mathbf{P}_u, \mathbf{w}, \rho, u, N_{u,s}(\mathbf{A}'_{u,s}))$
if $TS'^t_u = TS^t_u$ **do**
$\overline{TS}_u = TS^t_u$
$N_{u,s}(\overline{\mathbf{A}}_{u,s}) = N_{u,s}(\mathbf{A}^t_{u,s}), s \in S$
$U_p = U_p \backslash u$
return: $N_p, \{\overline{TS}_u, N_{u,s}(\overline{\mathbf{A}}_{u,s}), u \in U, s \in S\}$
r=r+1
return: $\{N_{u,s}(\overline{\mathbf{A}}_{u,s}), \overline{TS}_u\}, u \in U, s \in S$

U_p can use the remaining resources in the system after the current round of allocation. If the user u can utilize the remaining resources, the user u is kept in U_p and its allocation is temporarily uncertain. Otherwise, move the user u out of U_p and determine its assignment, i.e., $U_p = U_p \backslash u$, $\overline{TS}_u = TS^t_u$ and $N_{u,s}(\overline{\mathbf{A}}_{u,s}) = N_{u,s}(\mathbf{A}^t_{u,s})$, $s \in S$. This process loops until $U_p = \varnothing$, which means that all users' allocations $\overline{\mathbf{A}}_{u,s}, u \in U, s \in S$ are determined.

As shown in Algorithm 3, program MME first calculates the resources remaining in the system after α-TSF allocation and the normalized demand vector for each user. Then, based on whether users have the same normalized demand vector, MME divides U into $K \in N^+$ subsets $U_1 \bigcup U_2 \bigcup \ldots \bigcup U_K = U$, where $\mathbf{d}_{u_1} = \mathbf{d}_{u_2} = \ldots = \mathbf{d}_{u_k}$ for $\{u_1, u_2, \ldots, u_k\} = U_k, \forall U_k \in \{U_1, U_2, \ldots, U_K\}$. MME treats each subset $U_k = \{u_1, u_2, \ldots, u_k\}$ as a group and allocates resources from the group's perspective. The demand vector of each group is $\mathbf{D}_{U_k} = \mathbf{d}_u, u \in U_k$,

Algorithm 3. MME

Program: MME $(S, U, R, \mathbf{C_s}, C_{BW}, \mathbf{D}_u, \mathbf{P}_u, \mathbf{w}, \{N_{u,s}(\overline{\mathbf{A}}_{u,s})\})$
  for $s \in S, r \in R$ **calculate** $C'_{s,r} = C_{s,r}$ *and* C'_{BW}
  for $u \in U$ **calculate** $\mathbf{d}_u = (d_{u,1}, d_{u,2}, \ldots, d_{u,BW})$
  $K \Leftarrow$ Count the number of different $\mathbf{d}_u, u \in U$.
  $U_1 \bigcup U_2 \bigcup \ldots \bigcup U_K = U \Leftarrow$ For $\{u_1, u_2, \ldots, u_k\} = U_k, \forall U_k \in \{U_1, U_2, \ldots, U_K\}$, we have $\mathbf{d}_{u_1} = \mathbf{d}_{u_2} = \ldots = \mathbf{d}_{u_k}$.
  $\mathbf{D}_{U_k} = \mathbf{d}_u = (d_{u,1}, d_{u,2}, \ldots, d_{u,BW}), u \in U_k = \{u_1, u_2, \ldots, u_k\}$
  $\mathbf{P}_{U_k} = (P_{U_k,1}, P_{U_k,2}, \ldots, P_{U_k,m})$
  $P_{U_k,s} = P_{u_1,s} \| P_{u_2,s} \| \ldots \| P_{u_k,s}, \{u_1, u_2, \ldots, u_k\} = U_k, s \in S$

$$\max_{\theta, \{N_{U_k}(\hat{\mathbf{A}}_{U_k})\}} \quad \theta = \min_{r \in R} \frac{\sum_{u \in U} D_{u,r} \cdot N_u(\overline{\mathbf{A}}_u) + \sum_{s \in S} \sum_{U_k=U_1}^{U_K} D_{U_k,r} \cdot N_{U_k,s}(\hat{\mathbf{A}}_{U_k,s})}{C_r}$$

  s.t. $\sum_{U_k=U_1}^{U_K} N_{U_k,s}(\hat{\mathbf{A}}_{U_k,s}) \cdot D_{U_k,r} \cdot P_{U_k,s} \leq C'_{s,r}, s \in S, r \in R_S$
  $\sum_{s \in S} \sum_{U_k=U_1}^{U_K} N_{U_k,s}(\hat{\mathbf{A}}_{U_k,s}) \cdot D_{U_k,BW} \leq C'_{BW}$
  $N_{U_k,s}(\hat{\mathbf{A}}_{U_k,s}) \geq 0, u \in U, s \in S$
  for $U_k \in \{U_1, U_2, \ldots, U_K\}$ **do**
    Program: α-TSF $(S, U_k, R, \{C_{s,r}^{U_k}\}, C_{BW}^{U_k}, \mathbf{D}_u, \mathbf{P}_u, \mathbf{w}, 1)$
    Program: return: $\{N_{u_k,s}(\overline{\mathbf{A}}_{u_k,s}), \overline{TS}_{u_k}\}, u_k \in U_k, s \in S$
    for $u_k \in U_k$ **do**
      Find the user $u (u \in U)$ corresponding to the user u_k.
      $N_{u,s}(\hat{\mathbf{A}}_{u,s}) = N_{u_k,s}(\overline{\mathbf{A}}_{u_k,s})$
      $\hat{TS}_u = \overline{TS}_{u_k}$
return: $\theta, \{N_{u,s}(\hat{\mathbf{A}}_{u,s}), \hat{TS}_u\}, u \in U, s \in S$

and the placement constraint is $\mathbf{P}_{U_k} = (P_{U_k,1}, P_{U_k,2}, \ldots, P_{U_k,m})$. With the goal of maximizing the minimum resource utilization, we can get the allocation for each group. Finally, program α-TSF is used to allocate each group's allocation to users in that group. Here, the procedure α-TSF guarantees that the task share vector of users with the same normalized demand vector is TSF-optimal. This can ensure the fairness among users to the greatest extent.

4 TSF-MME Properties

In this section, we present important and desirable properties that TSF-MME satisfies. Specifically, TSF-MME satisfies soft fairness, soft sharing incentive, Pareto optimality and envy-freeness.

To quantify the fairness of TSF-MME, we use α as the metric that refers to the fairness extent compared with TSF.

Proposition 1 (Soft Fairness). *TSF-MME satisfies soft fairness where*

$$\alpha = min_{u \in U}(TS_u / TS_u^*) \geq \rho.$$

Note that proposition 1 gives the worst-case soft fairness guarantee. Proposition 1 means that TSF-MME can guarantee no less than ρ times fairness relative to TSF, i.e., $TS_u \geq \rho \cdot TS_u^*, \forall u \in U$.

Proof (Proof of Proposition 1.). According to the policy of TSF-MME, we have $TS_u = \overline{TS}_u + \hat{TS}_u$. Combining the formula (10), we have

$$\alpha = \min_{u \in U} \frac{TS_u}{TS_u^*} = \min_{u \in U} \frac{\overline{TS}_u + \hat{TS}_u}{TS_u^*} = \min_{u \in U} \frac{\rho \cdot TS_u^* + \hat{TS}_u}{TS_u^*}$$
$$\geq \frac{\rho \cdot TS_u^*}{TS_u^*} = \rho,$$

where the inequality is directly derived from constraints (12.c) and (12.d).

Sharing incentive is a key property that can provide service guarantee. In our model, sharing incentive means $\sum_{s \in S} N_{u,s}(\mathbf{A}_{u,s}) \geq h_u, u \in U$.

Lemma 1. *TSF in our model satisfies sharing incentive in the presence of different users' weights defined in (4).*

Proposition 2 (Soft Sharing Incentive). *TSF-MME satisfies soft sharing incentive where*

$$N_{u,s}(\mathbf{A}_{u,s}) \geq \rho \cdot h_u, u \in U.$$

Compared TSF, proposition 2 show that TSF-MME can ensure greater or equal to ρ degree of sharing incentive. Similar to proposition 1, the proposition 2 also gives a worst-case soft sharing incentive guarantee.

Proof (Proof of Proposition 2.). According to the design of TSF-MME and the formula (10), we have

$$N_{u,s}(\mathbf{A}_{u,s}) = N_{u,s}(\overline{\mathbf{A}}_{u,s}) + N_{u,s}(\hat{\mathbf{A}}_{u,s}) \geq \rho \cdot N_{u,s}(\mathbf{A}^*_{u,s}),$$

where the inequality is directly derived from the constraint (12.d). Because TSF satisfies sharing incentive, i.e., $N_{u,s}(\mathbf{A}^*_{u,s}) \geq h_u, u \in U$, we have $N_{u,s}(\mathbf{A}_{u,s}) \geq \rho \cdot h_u, u \in U$.

Pareto optimality is a valid efficiency criterion. Pareto optimality means it is impossible to increase the allocation of one user without reducing the allocation of another.

Proposition 3 (Pareto Optimality). *TSF-MME satisfies Pareto optimality.*

Proof (Proof of Proposition 3.). We assume for contradiction that the allocation of TSF-MME is not Pareto optimal. So, for an allocation $\mathbf{A}'$, there at least exists a user u_1 such that $\sum_{s \in S} \mathbf{A}'_{u_1,s} > \sum_{s \in S} \mathbf{A}_{u_1,s}, \exists u_1 \in U$ and $\sum_{s \in S} \mathbf{A}'_{u_2,s} \geq \sum_{s \in S} \mathbf{A}_{u_2,s} (\forall u_2 \in U \setminus u_1)$. Compared with allocation $\mathbf{A}$, the extra allocation of the user u_1 may be allocated in the α-TSF or in the MME.

If more resources are allocated to user u_1 in α-TSF, and the allocation of other users is not lower than the allocation in $\mathbf{A}$. It will lead to $\overline{\mathbf{TS}}' = (\overline{TS}'_1, \overline{TS}'_2, \ldots, \overline{TS}'_n)$ is lexicographically greater than $\overline{\mathbf{TS}} = (\overline{TS}_1, \overline{TS}_2, \ldots, \overline{TS}_n)$. This contradicts the TSF-optimality of $\overline{\mathbf{TS}} = (\overline{TS}_1, \overline{TS}_2, \ldots, \overline{TS}_n)$.

If more resources are allocated to user u_1 in MME compared to $\mathbf{A}$, and the allocation of other users is not lower than the allocation in $\mathbf{A}$. Due to $D_{u,r} > 0$, it will lead to $\theta' > \theta$. This contradicts that θ is the max-min resource utilization among all resources. So far, the desired contradiction has yielded.

Proposition 4 (Envy-Freeness). *TSF-MME satisfies envy-freeness.*

Envy-freeness is the most critical property for fair allocation, and it is also the most intuitive standard to measure the fairness among users. If an allocation is envy-free, there is no user strictly prefers other users' allocations. In our model, envy-freeness can be formulated as

$$\frac{\sum_{s\in S} N_{i,s}(\mathbf{A}_{i,s})}{w_i} \geq \sum_{s\in S} \frac{\min_{r\in R}\{N_{j,s}(\mathbf{A}_{j,s}) \cdot D_{j,r} \cdot P_{i,s}/D_{i,r}\}}{w_j}, \forall i,j \in U.$$

Due to space limitations, we omit the specific proof of Proposition 4.

5 Conclusion

In this paper, we studied the multi-resource allocation problem in mobile edge computing systems and proposed the mechanism TSF-MME to achieve a balance between fairness and efficiency. α-TSF can guarantee no less than α degree of fairness relative to TSF's allocation for all users. MME can improve the efficiency of the system and intuitively reflect the resource utilization of the entire system. For the system consisting of multiple servers, where bandwidth resources are independent of the server and user tasks have deployment constraints, we have presented an algorithm to find the allocation of TSF-MME. In addition, we also proved TSF-MME satisfies soft fairness, soft sharing incentive, Pareto optimality and envy-freeness.

In the future, we will further study the balance between the efficiency and fairness of multi-resource allocation in the cloud-edge collaborative system.

Acknowledgements. This work is supported in part by the National Natural Science Foundation of China [Nos. 12071417, 61762091 and 62062065].

References

1. Poullie, P., Bocek, T., Stiller, B.: A survey of the state-of-the-art in fair multi-resource allocations for data centers. IEEE Trans. Netw. Serv. Manage. **15**(1), 169–183 (2017)
2. Liu, X., Zhang, X., Cui, Q., Li, W.: Implementation of ant colony optimization combined with tabu search for multi-resource fair allocation in heterogeneous cloud computing. In: 2017 IEEE 3rd International Conference on Big Data Security on Cloud (Bigdatasecurity), IEEE International Conference on High Performance and Smart Computing (HPSC), and IEEE International Conference on Intelligent Data and Security (IDS), pp. 196–201 (2017)

3. Li, W., Liu, X., Zhang, X., Zhang, X.: Dynamic fair allocation of multiple resources with bounded number of tasks in cloud computing systems. Multiagent Grid Syst. **11**(4), 245–257 (2015)
4. Liu, X., Zhang, X., Zhang, X., Li, W.: Dynamic fair division of multiple resources with satiable agents in cloud computing systems. In: 2015 IEEE Fifth International Conference on Big Data and Cloud Computing, pp. 131–136 (2015)
5. Ghodsi, A., Zaharia, M., Hindman, B., Konwinski, A., Shenker, S., Stoica, I.: Dominant resource fairness: fair allocation of multiple resource types. In: Proceedings of the 8th USENIX Conference on Networked Systems Design and Implementation, pp. 323–336 (2011)
6. Li, J., Zhang, J., Li, W., Zhang, X.: A fair distribution strategy based on shared fair and time-varying resource demand. J. Comput. Res. Dev. **56**(7), 1534 (2019)
7. Liu, X., Zhang, X., Li, W., Zhang, X.: Discrete interior search algorithm for multi-resource fair allocation in heterogeneous cloud computing systems. In: Huang, D.-S., Bevilacqua, V., Premaratne, P. (eds.) ICIC 2016. LNCS, vol. 9771, pp. 615–626. Springer, Cham (2016). https://doi.org/10.1007/978-3-319-42291-6_61
8. Li, W., Liu, X., Zhang, X., Zhang, X.: A further analysis of the dynamic dominant resource fairness mechanism. In: Xiao, M., Rosamond, F. (eds.) FAW 2017. LNCS, vol. 10336, pp. 163–174. Springer, Cham (2017). https://doi.org/10.1007/978-3-319-59605-1_15
9. Khamse-Ashari, J., Lambadaris, I., Kesidis, G., Urgaonkar, B., Zhao, Y.: An efficient and fair multi-resource allocation mechanism for heterogeneous servers. IEEE Trans. Parallel Distrib. Syst. **29**(12), 2686–2699 (2018)
10. Tang, S., Yu, C., Li, Y.: Fairness-efficiency scheduling for cloud computing with soft fairness guarantees. IEEE Trans. Cloud Comput. (2020)
11. Liu, F., Tang, G., Li, Y., Cai, Z., Zhang, X., Zhou, T.: A survey on edge computing systems and tools. Proc. IEEE **107**(8), 1537–1562 (2019)
12. Joe-Wong, C., Sen, S., Lan, T., Chiang, M.: Multiresource allocation: Fairness–efficiency tradeoffs in a unifying framework. IEEE/ACM Trans. Netw. **21**(6), 1785–1798 (2013)
13. Jiang, S., Wu, J.: Multi-resource allocation in cloud data centers: a trade-off on fairness and efficiency. Concurr. Comput. Pract. Exp. **33**(6), 6061 (2021)
14. Wang, W., Liang, B., Li, B.: On fairness-efficiency tradeoffs for multi-resource packet processing. In: 2013 IEEE 33rd International Conference on Distributed Computing Systems Workshops, pp. 244–249 (2013)
15. Meskar, E., Liang, B.: Fair multi-resource allocation with external resource for mobile edge computing. In: IEEE Conference on Computer Communications Workshops (INFOCOM WKSHPS), pp. 184–189 (2018)
16. Sharma, B., Chudnovsky, V., Hellerstein, J.L., Rifaat, R., Das, C.R.: Modeling and synthesizing task placement constraints in google compute clusters. In: Proceedings of the 2nd ACM Symposium on Cloud Computing, pp. 1–14 (2011)
17. Wang, W., Li, B., Liang, B., Li, J.: Multi-resource fair sharing for datacenter jobs with placement constraints. In: SC 2016: Proceedings of the International Conference for High Performance Computing, Networking, Storage and Analysis, pp. 1003–1014 (2016)
18. Wang, W., Liang, B., Li, B.: Multi-resource fair allocation in heterogeneous cloud computing systems. IEEE Trans. Parallel Distrib. Syst. **26**(10), 2822–2835 (2015)
19. Sadok, H., Campista, M.E.M., Costa, L.H.M.K.: Stateful DRF: considering the past in a multi-resource allocation. IEEE Trans. Comput. **70**(7), 1094–1105 (2021)

20. Li, W., Liu, X., Zhang, X., Zhang, X.: Multi-resource fair allocation with bounded number of tasks in cloud computing systems. In: Du, D., Li, L., Zhu, E., He, K. (eds.) NCTCS 2017. CCIS, vol. 768, pp. 3–17. Springer, Singapore (2017). https://doi.org/10.1007/978-981-10-6893-5_1
21. Ghodsi, A., Zaharia, M., Shenker, S., Stoica, I.: Choosy: max-min fair sharing for datacenter jobs with constraints. In: Proceedings of the 8th ACM European Conference on Computer Systems, pp. 365–378 (2013)
22. Sallam, G., Ji, B.: Joint placement and allocation of VNF nodes with budget and capacity constraints. IEEE/ACM Trans. Netw. **29**(3), 1238–1251 (2021)
23. Zhang, X., Li, J., Li, G., Li, W.: Generalized asset fairness mechanism for multi-resource fair allocation mechanism with two different types of resources. Clust. Comput. **25**, 3389–3403 (2022). https://doi.org/10.1007/s10586-022-03548-9
24. Zhang, X., Xi, L., Li, W., Zhang, X.: Dynamic fair allocation of multi-resources based on shared resource quantity. J. Commun. **37**(7), 151 (2016)
25. Liu, X., Zhang, X., Li, W., Zhang, X.: Swarm optimization algorithms applied to multi-resource fair allocation in heterogeneous cloud computing systems. Computing **99**(12), 1231–1255 (2017)
26. Chakraborty, M., Igarashi, A., Suksompong, W., Zick, Y.: Weighted envy-freeness in indivisible item allocation. ACM Trans. Econ. Comput. **9**(3), 1–39 (2021)
27. Wei, W., Li, B., Liang, B., Li, J.: Towards multi-resource fair allocation with placement constraints. ACM SIGMETRICS Perform. Eval. Rev. **44**(1), 415–416 (2016)

Maximin Share Based Mechanisms for Multi-resource Fair Allocation with Divisible and Indivisible Tasks

Bin Deng(✉) and Weidong Li

School of Mathematics and Statistics, Yunnan University, Kunming 650504, China
dengbin96@126.com

Abstract. Finding a fair and efficient allocation is an important issue in cloud computing systems. In this paper, we propose a maximin share (MMS) based mechanism for the divisible case which satisfies Pareto efficiency, envy-freeness, sharing incentive and group strategy-proofness. We also propose a MMS based mechanism for the indivisible case which satisfies Pareto efficiency, envy-free up to one bundle and sharing incentive.

Keywords: Multi-resource fair allocation · Maximin share · Cloud computing

1 Introduction

Multi-resource fair allocation is a basic problem in cloud computing systems. Ghodsi et al. [5] proposed a well-known multi-resource fair allocation mechanism, called dominance resource fairness (DRF), which is a generalization of max-min fairness. The objective of DRF mechanism is to maximize the users' minimum domination share, which is the maximum share that the user has been allocated of any resource. So far, DRF has been widely used in Fair Scheduler in Hadoop system.

For the divisible case, Ghodsi et al. [5] proved that DRF satisfies Pareto efficiency, envy-freeness, sharing incentive and strategy-proofness. Parkes et al. [18] extended DRF to a more general case where the weighted agents may have zero demands. Li et al. [12] extended DRF to the case where each user has a limited number of divisible tasks. Li et al. [9] extended DRF to the case where the reource demand is time-varying. Kash et al. [6] extended DRF to the dynamic environment. Wang et al. [19] extended DRF to the cloud computing systems with heterogeneous servers. Recently, Zhang et al. [23] proposed a generalized asset fairness mechanism to improve resource utilization. Zhang et al. [16] solve the problem of heterogeneous physical machines resource management, maximizing social welfare. Zhang et al. [25] used machine learning to model the multidimensional resource allocation problem and proposed two algorithms based on logistic regression and linear regression. In addition to general scenarios, some scholars

Z. Cai et al. (Eds.): NCTCS 2022, CCIS 1693, pp. 263–272, 2022.
https://doi.org/10.1007/978-981-19-8152-4_19

have also studied the problem of resource allocation in dynamic environments. To better understand dynamic settings, Kash et al. [6] develop a dynamic model for fair partitioning and provide several desirable properties for dynamic resource allocation mechanisms. In [10], consider a problem that is closer to reality, in which the number of tasks for each user is limited. In this scenario, a generalized dynamic resource fairness mechanism is designed. In [11], a dynamic resource domination mechanism is proposed and further analyzed. Liu et al. [13] considered a generalized version of dynamic resource allocation, where all tasks can be satisfied when allocated, and designed a generalized dynamic resource allocation mechanism.

For the indivisible case, Parkes et al. [18] proposed a DRF based sequential minmax fairness mechanism which satisfies Pareto efficiency, envy-free up to one bundle and sharing incentive. Friedman et al. [4] extended DRF to the cloud computing systems with heterogeneous servers. Zhang et al. [24], in the online resource allocation, the resource allocation problem is transformed into an integer programming model to solve the resource competition problem in the live broadcast service. In [14], due to the gap between the solution obtained by the existing heuristic algorithm and the optimal solution, three population optimization algorithms are proposed to improve resource utilization. In [15], in order to solve the situation of inseparable tasks in the server, a discrete internal search algorithm is proposed to obtain the optimal solution.

In addition to the DRF mechanism and its related mechanisms, there are several other mechanisms that can be substituted. Dolev et al. [3] proposed another probability of fairness, called bottleneck based fairness, which guarantees that each user has the right to obtain its bottleneck resources. Bonald et al. [2] proposed the concept of proportional fairness and showed that in some cases proportional fairness is preferable. Wang et al. [20] propose a mechanism that is both fair and efficient based on the concept of bottleneck sets per device, called bottleneck-aware allocation. In order to deal with the multi-resource allocation problem with placement constraints, Wang et al. [21] proposed a sharing strategy for task sharing fairness. In microeconomics, a commonly used multi-resource fair distribution mechanism for divisible tasks is Competitive Equilibrium from Equal Incomes (CEEI) [17]. Using the concept of CEEI in the Cobb-Douglas utility function, Zahedi et al. [22] proposed a mechanism that satisfies similar properties to the DRF mechanism.

Maxmin share (MMS) fair allocation, proposed in [1], is anther famous topic in resource allocation, where each player's value for his allocation should be at least as high as what he can guarantee by dividing the items into as many bundles as there are players and receiving his least desirable bundle. Assuming additive valuation functions, Kurokawa et al. [7] showed that MMS fair allocation may not exist, and presented an algorithm which can find a 2/3-approximation MMS fair allocation. Recently, Li et al. [8] extended MMS to a more general case where each job is associated with release time, deadline and processing time. To the best of knowledge, there is no result about the strategy-proofness of MMS fair allocation.

In this paper, we present a MMS based mechanism for multi-resource fair allocation with divisible tasks which is group strategy-proofness. We also design a MMS based mechanism for multi-resource fair allocation with indivisible tasks which satisfies the same as sequential minmax fairness mechanism [18]. The rest of the paper is organized as follows. Section 2 presents the related model and some desirable properties. Section 3 introduces the MMS based mechanisms for the divisible case. Section 4 proposes a MMS based mechanisms for the indivisible case. Section 5 draws conclusions and future research directions.

2 Preliminaries

In a cloud computing system, we are given m resources (e.g., CPU, memory, etc.) and n users. The capacities of resources are denoted by a vector $\mathbf{C} = (c_1, \ldots, c_m)^T$ where $c_j > 0$ is the capacity of resource j for $j = 1, 2, \ldots, m$. The demand of each user i for per task is denoted by a vector $\mathbf{D_i} = (d_{i1}, \ldots, d_{im})^T$, where $d_{ij} > 0$ for any i, j.

For convenience, let $[a]$ denote the set $\{1, 2, \ldots, a\}$ for any positive integer a. For each user $i \in [n]$, let $\mathbf{A_i} = (a_{i1}, \ldots, a_{im})^T$ be the resource allocation vector of user i where a_{ij} is the amount of resource i allocated to user j by the system. Let $\mathbf{A} = (\mathbf{A_1}, ..., \mathbf{A_n})$ be the allocation matrix for all users. An allocation $\mathbf{A}$ is feasible if the sum of the allocations of all users for any resource $j \in [m]$ is no more than c_j, i.e.,

$$\sum_{i=1}^{n} a_{ij} \leq c_j, \text{ for each } j \in [m].$$

As in [5,18], the user's utility is the maximum number of tasks she can run by using her allocated resources, i.e.,

$$u_i(\mathbf{A}_i) = \begin{cases} \min_j \frac{a_{ij}}{d_{ij}}, & \text{if task is divisible,} \\ \min_j \lfloor \frac{a_{ij}}{d_{ij}} \rfloor, & \text{if task is indivisible.} \end{cases}$$

Let $\mathcal{A}$ be the set of all feasible allocations. One popular criterion, called maximin share (MMS) fairness, is to compute a feasible allocation in $\mathcal{A}$ such that everyone believes that it (approximately) maximizes the utility in the worst case [1]. Formally, the value of MMS of user i is defined as

$$MMS_i = \max_{\mathbf{A}:\mathbf{A}\in\mathcal{A}} \min_{k:k\in[n]} u_i(\mathbf{A}_k), \text{ for each } i \in [n]. \quad (1)$$

In a cloud computing systems, it is interesting to design a fair allocation mechanism satisfying the following four properties [5,18].

1. Pareto efficiency. It is impossible to increase the number of tasks of a user without reducing the number of tasks of other users. Formally, if there exists a user i satisfying

$$u_i(\mathbf{A}_i) \geq u_i(\mathbf{A}'_i).$$

for any allocation $\mathbf{A}' \in \mathcal{A}$, $\mathbf{A}$ is called Pareto efficiency.

2. Sharing incentive. It ensures that each user's allocation is no worse than evenly allocating all resources. That is, for any user i,

$$u_i(\mathbf{A}_i) \geq u_i(\frac{\mathbf{C}}{n}).$$

3. Envy-freeness. Any user prefers tasks assigned to himself over tasks assigned to other users. That is, for any two users $i, k \in [n]$,

$$u_i(\mathbf{A}_i) \geq u_i(\mathbf{A}_k).$$

4. Group strategy-proofness. No user can schedule more tasks by forming a coalition $\mathcal{C}$ with others to misreports their requirements $\mathbf{D}_i$. Suppose user $i \in \mathcal{C}$ incorrectly reports his requirement $\mathbf{D'}_i$, the returned assignment is $\mathbf{A}'_{\mathrm{i}}$. The number of tasks performed by user i will not increase due to misreported demand, i.e.,

$$u_i(\mathbf{A}_i) \geq u_i(\mathbf{A'}_i).$$

3 The Dividable Case

If the tasks are divisible, the utility of user i under allocation $\mathbf{A}$ is $u_i(\mathbf{A}_i) = \min_j \frac{a_{ij}}{d_{ij}}$.

Theorem 1. *For each user $i \in [n]$, the value of MMS_i of user i is $u_i(\frac{\mathbf{C}}{n})$.*

Proof. On the one hand, we have $MMS_i \geq u_i(\frac{\mathbf{C}}{n})$ by dividing the resources evenly. On the other hand, it is easy to prove that $MMS_i \leq u_i(\frac{\mathbf{C}}{n})$. Therefore, $MMS_i = u_i(\frac{\mathbf{C}}{n})$, that is, the theorem holds.

The MMS based mechanism is to maximize the minimum ratio of the utility of user i to the value of MMS_i. For convenience, let $x_i = u_i(\mathbf{A}_i)$ be the maximum (fractional) number of tasks user i can run by using her allocated resources. Formally, the MMS based mechanism can be formulated as the following linear program (MMS-LP):

$$\begin{aligned} \max \quad & \theta \\ \textit{subject to}: \quad & \\ & \sum_{i=1}^{n} x_i d_{ij} \leq c_j, \qquad \forall j \in [m] \\ & x_i \geq \theta \cdot MMS_i, \qquad \forall i \in [n] \\ & x_i \geq 0 \end{aligned}$$

The first constraint guarantees that the total amount of allocated resources does not exceed the capacity. The second constraint ensures that the utility of each user is no less than $\theta \cdot MMS_i$.

Example 1. Consider a scenario with two users and two types of resources (CPU and memory). The resource requirements of two users are $(1, 0.5)$ and $(0.5, 1)$, and the capacities of two resources are 4 and 8, respectively. By Theorem 1, we obtain $MMS_1 = 2$ and $MMS_2 = 4$. The corresponding MMS-LP is

$$\begin{aligned} max \quad & \theta \\ subject\ to: \quad & \\ & x_1 + 0.5x_2 \leq 4 \\ & 0.5x_1 + x_2 \leq 8 \\ & x_1 \geq 2\theta \\ & x_2 \geq 4\theta \\ & x_1, x_2 \geq 0, \end{aligned}$$

whose optimal value is 1, achieved by setting $x_1 = 2, x_2 = 4$.

For convenience, let $(\mathbf{x}, \theta)$ be an optimal solution for MMS-LP, and $\mathbf{A} = (\mathbf{A}_i, \mathbf{A}_2, \ldots, \mathbf{A}_n)$ be the corresponding allocation where $\mathbf{A}_i = x_i \mathbf{D}_i$.

Theorem 2. *The MMS based mechanism satisfies the Pareto efficiency property.*

Proof. Suppose that $\mathbf{A}$ is not Pareto efficiency, i.e. there is anther solution $(\mathbf{x}', \theta')$ such that $x'_i \geq x_i$ for any $i \in [n]$ and $x'_k > x_k$ for some $k \in [n]$, implying that $\theta' \geq \theta$. We reallocate these resources to construct a new allocation $(\mathbf{x}'', \theta'')$ with $\theta'' = \min_i \frac{x''_i}{MMS_i}$ such that $x''_i > x_i$. Meanwhile, $(\mathbf{x}'', \theta'')$ is a feasible solution of MMS-LP, contradicting the optimality of $(\mathbf{x}, \theta)$. Thus, the theorem holds.

Different from [1,7,8], the optimal value of MMS-LP satisfies the following properties.

Lemma 1. *The optimal value of the MMS-LP is at least 1, i.e. $\theta \geq 1$.*

Proof. Suppose the optimal value of MMS-LP is $\theta < 1$, which means

$$u_i(\frac{\mathbf{C}}{n}) > u_i(\frac{\theta \cdot \mathbf{C}}{n}) = \theta \cdot u_i(\frac{\mathbf{C}}{n}) = \theta \cdot MMS_i = x_i,$$

for any user i, where the last equation can be obtained by a similar proof of Theorem 2. Therefore,

$$c_j \geq \sum_{i=1}^{n} u_i(\frac{\mathbf{C}}{n}) \cdot d_{ij} > \sum_{i=1}^{n} x_i \cdot d_{ij},$$

for any resource j, this contradicts the MMS based mechanism to satisfy the Pareto efficiency.

Theorem 3. *The MMS based mechanism satisfies the sharing incentive property.*

Proof. As Lemma 1, we have $\theta \geq 1$, implying that

$$u_i(\mathbf{A}_i) = x_i \geq \theta \cdot MMS_i \geq MMS_i = u_i(\frac{\mathbf{C}}{n}),$$

where the last equality follows from Theorem 1.

Theorem 4. *The MMS based mechanism satisfies the envy-free property.*

Proof. Suppose that there is a user i envying another user k, which means

$$x_k d_{kj} = a_{kj} > a_{ij} = x_i d_{ij} \geq \theta \cdot MMS_i \cdot d_{ij}$$

for any resource j. Therefore, we have

$$x_k > \theta \cdot MMS_k.$$

As in the proof of Theorem 2, we can find a feasible solution $(\mathbf{x}'', \theta'')$ for MMS-LP with $\theta'' > \theta$, contradicting the optimality of $(\mathbf{x}, \theta)$.

The above theorem also implies that

Theorem 5. *In the optimal solution* $(\mathbf{x}, \theta)$*, for* $i = 1, 2, \ldots, n$*, we have* $x_i = \theta \cdot MMS_i$.

Theorem 6. *The MMS based mechanism satisfies the group strategy-proofness property.*

Proof. Let $U \subseteq [n]$ be the set of users whose true utilities is increased by falsely reporting the demand vector $\mathbf{D}'_U = (\mathbf{D}'_i)_{i \in U}$, where $\mathbf{D}'_i \neq \mathbf{D}_i$ for any user $i \in U$, $(\mathbf{x}', \theta')$ be the corresponding optimal solution for MMS-LP, and $\mathbf{A}' = (\mathbf{A}'_i, \mathbf{A}'_2, \ldots, \mathbf{A}'_n)$ be the corresponding allocation where $\mathbf{A}'_i = x'_i \mathbf{D}'_i$. For each user $i \in U$, since the true utility of is increased, i.e., $u_i(A'_i) > u_i(A_i) = x_i$, we have

$$x'_i \cdot d'_{ij} = a'_{ij} > a_{ij} = x_i \cdot d_{ij}, \forall j \in [m]. \tag{2}$$

Therefore, we can easily prove that the theorem holds by dividing the relationship between θ and θ' into two cases.

4 The Indivisible Case

If the tasks are indivisible, the utility of user i under allocation $\mathbf{A}$ is $u_i(\mathbf{A}_i) = \min_j \lfloor \frac{a_{ij}}{d_{ij}} \rfloor$. In this section, we will design a mechanism for handling indivisible tasks based on the MMS based mechanism. For convenience, let $x_i = u_i(\mathbf{A}_i)$ be the maximum (integer) number of tasks user i can run by using her allocated resources.

Since Pareto efficiency and envy-free are trivially incompatible for the indivisible case, Parkes et al. [18] introduced the notion of **envy-free up to one bundle** (EF1) such that for all $i, k \in [n]$,

$$u_i(\mathbf{A}_i) \geq u_i(\mathbf{A}_k - \mathbf{D}_i),$$

and proved that

Theorem 7. *For the indivisible case, there is no mechanism that satisfies Pareto efficiency, sharing incentive and group strategy-proofness, and is no mechanism that satisfies Pareto efficiency, EF1 and group strategy-proofness.*

Fortunately, Parkes et al. [18] found a mechanism that satisfies Pareto efficiency, sharing incentive, and EF1. We will show that the MMS-based mechanism for the indivisible case also satisfies the three desired properties as mentioned in [18]. If tasks are indivisible, we have

$$MMS_i = u_i(\frac{\mathbf{C}}{n}) = \min_j \lfloor \frac{\frac{c_j}{n}}{d_{ij}} \rfloor.$$

Let $(\mathbf{x}, \theta)$ be an optimal (fractional) solution for MMS-LP defined in the last section. Consider the feasible solution $(\bar{\mathbf{x}}^{(0)}, \theta^{(0)})$, where

$$\bar{x}_i^{(0)} = \lfloor x_i \rfloor \text{ for any user } i, \text{ and } \theta^{(0)} = \min_i \frac{\bar{x}_i^{(0)}}{MMS_i}.$$

For each iteration $t = 1, 2, \ldots$, let $\bar{x}_i^{(t)}$ be the utility of user i at the beginning of the t-th iteration. As the post-greedy method in [18], if $N^{(t)} = \{i \in [n] : d_{ij} + \sum_{i' \in [n]} \bar{x}_{i'}^{(t)} d_{i'j} \leq c_j, \forall j\} \neq \emptyset$, we assign D_k to the user $k \in N^{(t)}$ such that

$$(\max_j \bar{x}_1^{(t)} d_{1j}, \max_j \bar{x}_2^{(t)} d_{2j}, \ldots, \max_j (\bar{x}_k^{(t)} + 1) d_{kj}, \ldots, \max_j \bar{x}_n^{(t)} d_{nj})$$

is lexicographically minimized, and set

$$\bar{x}_i^{(t+1)} = \begin{cases} \bar{x}_k^{(t)} + 1, & \text{if } i = k, \\ \bar{x}_i^{(t)}, & \text{otherwise.} \end{cases}$$

Let $(\bar{\mathbf{x}}, \bar{\theta})$ be the final solution.

Since the remaining resources cannot be allocated to any user in the end, we have

Theorem 8. $(\bar{\mathbf{x}}, \bar{\theta})$ *satisfies the Pareto efficiency property.*

Theorem 9. $(\bar{\mathbf{x}}, \bar{\theta})$ *satisfies the sharing incentive property.*

Proof. For any user i, by the definitions of $\bar{\mathbf{x}}$ and $\bar{\mathbf{x}}^{(0)}$, we have

$$\bar{x}_i \geq \bar{x}_i^{(0)} = \lfloor x_i \rfloor \geq \lfloor \min_j \frac{c_j}{na_{ij}} \rfloor = \min_j \lfloor \frac{c_j}{na_{ij}} \rfloor = u_i(\frac{\mathbf{c}}{n}),$$

implying the theorem holds.

Theorem 10. $(\bar{\mathbf{x}}, \bar{\theta})$ *satisfies the EF1 property.*

Proof. Consider the user $i \in [n]$. When $t = 0$, there exists a resource j such that $\bar{x}_i^{(0)} \cdot d_{ij} = \lfloor x_i \rfloor \cdot d_{ij} \geq x_i \cdot d_{ij} - d_{ij} \geq x_k \cdot d_{kj} - d_{ij} \geq \lfloor x_k \rfloor \cdot d_{kj} - d_{ij} = \bar{x}_k^{(0)} \cdot d_{kj} - d_{ij}$ for any user $k \in [n]$, where the second inequality follows from Theorem 4. It implies that

$$u_i(\bar{x}_i^{(0)} \cdot \mathbf{D}_i) \geq u_i(\bar{x}_k^{(0)} \cdot \mathbf{D}_k - \mathbf{D}_i),$$

for any user $k \in [n]$.

Assume that $u_i(\bar{x}_i^{(t)} \cdot \mathbf{D}_i) \geq u_i(\bar{x}_k^{(t)} \cdot \mathbf{D}_k - \mathbf{D}_i)$ for any user $k \in [n]$ at iteration t. Since at most one user increases the allocation in each iteration, at most one of $\bar{x}_k^{(t+1)}$ and $\bar{x}_i^{(t+1)}$ is changed. If $x_k^{(t+1)} = x_k^{(t)}$, we have

$$u_i(\bar{x}_i^{(t+1)} \cdot \mathbf{D}_i) \geq u_i(\bar{x}_i^{(t)} \cdot \mathbf{D}_i) \geq u_i(\bar{x}_k^{(t)} \cdot \mathbf{D}_k - \mathbf{D}_i) = u_i(\bar{x}_k^{(t+1)} \cdot \mathbf{D}_k - \mathbf{D}_i).$$

If $x_k^{(t+1)} = x_k^{(t)} + 1$, user i does envy any user $i' \neq k$, as $x_{i'}^{(t+1)} = x_{i'}^{(t)}$. If $i \notin N^{(t)}$, there exists a resource j such that $d_{ij} + \sum_{i' \in [n]} \bar{x}_{i'}^{(t)} d_{i'j} > c_j$, which implies that

$$u_i(\bar{x}_i^{(t+1)} \cdot \mathbf{D}_i) \geq u_i(\bar{x}_k^{(t)} \cdot \mathbf{D}_k + \mathbf{D}_k - \mathbf{D}_i) = u_i(\bar{x}_k^{(t+1)} \cdot \mathbf{D}_k - \mathbf{D}_i). \quad (3)$$

If $i \in N^{(t)}$ and user i envies user k, we have

$$(\bar{x}_k^{(t)} + 1) d_{kj} = \bar{x}_k^{(t+1)} d_{kj} > (\bar{x}_i^{(t)} + 1) d_{ij} = (\bar{x}_i^{(t+1)} + 1) d_{ij},$$

for any resource j. It contradicts the lexicographically minimality of k. Therefore, the theorem holds.

In the case of indivisible tasks, we directly assign the feasible solution $(\lfloor x_i \rfloor, \min_i \frac{\lfloor x_i \rfloor}{MMS_i})$ of MMS-LP to each user in the initial state, this step directly shortens the running time in [18], but this is not polynomial time.

5 Conclusion

In this paper, we proposed a MMS based mechanisms for multi-resource fair allocation with divisible tasks, which satisfies the group strategy-proofness property. It is easy to verify that there exists a faster algorithm to find the optimal MMS allocation as in [12,18]. It is interesting to find other MMS based mechanisms satisfying the group strategy-proofness property.

We proposed a MMS based mechanisms for multi-resource fair allocation with indivisible tasks, which is faster than the mechanism in [18]. However, the running time is not polynomial. It is interesting to find a new mechanism for multi-resource fair allocation with indivisible tasks which can be implemented in polynomial time.

Acknowledgements. The work is supported in part by the National Natural Science Foundation of China [No. 12071417].

References

1. Budish, E.: The combinatorial assignment problem: approximate competitive equilibrium from equal incomes. J. Polit. Econ. **119**(6), 1061–1103 (2011)
2. Bonald, T., Roberts, J.: Enhanced cluster computing performance through proportional fairness. Perform. Eval. **79**, 134–145 (2014)
3. Dolev, D., Feitelson, D., Halpern, J., Kupferman, R., Linial, N.: No justified complaints: on fair sharing of multiple resources. In: Proceedings of the 3rd Innovations in Theoretical Computer Science Conference, pp. 68–75. ACM, Massachusetts (2012)
4. Friedman, E., Ghodsi, A., Psomas, C.-A.: Strategyproof allocation of discrete jobs on multiple machines. In: Proceedings of the Fifteenth ACM Conference on Economics and Computation, pp. 529–546. ACM, New York (2014)
5. Ghodsi, A., Zaharia, M., Hindman, B., Konwinski, A., Shenker, S., Stoica, I.: Dominant resource fairness: fair allocation of multiple resource types. In: Proceedings of the 8th USENIX Conference on Networked Systems Design and Implementation, p. 24 (2011)
6. Kash, I., Procaccia, A., Shah, N.: No agent left behind: dynamic fair division of multiple resources. J. Artif. Intell. Res. **51**, 579–603 (2014)
7. Kurokawa, D., Procaccia, A.D., Wang, J.: Fair enough: guaranteeing approximate maximin shares. J. ACM. **65**(2), 1–27 (2018)
8. Li, B., Li, M., Zhang, R.: Fair scheduling for time-dependent resources. Adv. Neural Inf. Process. Syst. **34**, 21744–21756 (2021)
9. Li, J., Zhang, J., Li, W., Zhang, X.: A fair distribution strategy based on shared fair and time-varying resource demand. J. Comput. Res. Dev. **56**(7), 1534–1544 (2019)
10. Li, W., Liu, X., Zhang, X., Zhang, X.: Dynamic fair allocation of multiple resources with bounded number of tasks in cloud computing systems. Multiagent Grid Syst. **11**(4), 245–257 (2015)
11. Li, Weidong, Liu, Xi., Zhang, Xiaolu, Zhang, Xuejie: A further analysis of the dynamic dominant resource fairness mechanism. In: Xiao, Mingyu, Rosamond, Frances (eds.) FAW 2017. LNCS, vol. 10336, pp. 163–174. Springer, Cham (2017). https://doi.org/10.1007/978-3-319-59605-1_15
12. Li, Weidong, Liu, Xi., Zhang, Xiaolu, Zhang, Xuejie: Multi-resource fair allocation with bounded number of tasks in cloud computing systems. In: Du, Dingzhu, Li, Lian, Zhu, En., He, Kun (eds.) NCTCS 2017. CCIS, vol. 768, pp. 3–17. Springer, Singapore (2017). https://doi.org/10.1007/978-981-10-6893-5_1
13. Liu, X., Zhang, X., Zhang, X., Li, W.: Dynamic fair division of multiple resources with satiable agents in cloud computing systems. In: IEEE Fifth International Conference on Big Data and Cloud Computing, pp. 131–136. IEEE, Dalian (2015)
14. Liu, X., Zhang, X., Li, W., Zhang, X.: Swarm optimization algorithms applied to multi-resource fair allocation in heterogeneous cloud computing systems. Computing **99**(12), 1231–1255 (2017)
15. Liu, Xi., Zhang, Xiaolu, Li, Weidong, Zhang, Xuejie: Discrete interior search algorithm for multi-resource fair allocation in heterogeneous cloud computing systems. In: Huang, De-Shuang., Bevilacqua, Vitoantonio, Premaratne, Prashan (eds.) ICIC 2016. LNCS, vol. 9771, pp. 615–626. Springer, Cham (2016). https://doi.org/10.1007/978-3-319-42291-6_61
16. Liu, X., Li, W., Zhang, X.: Strategy-proof mechanism for provisioning and allocation virtual machines in heterogeneous clouds. IEEE Trans. Parallel Distrib. Syst. **29**(7), 1650–1663 (2017)

17. Moulin, H.: REF: Fair Division and Collective Welfare. MIT press, London (2004)
18. Parkes, D., Procaccia, A., Shah, N.: Beyond dominant resource fairness: extensions, limitations, and indivisibilities. ACM Trans. Econ. Comput. **3**(1), 1–22 (2015)
19. Wang, W., Liang, B., Li, B.: Multi-resource fair allocation in heterogeneous cloud computing systems. IEEE Trans. Parallel Distrib. Syst. **26**(10), 2822–2835 (2015)
20. Wang, H., Varman, P.: Balancing fairness and efficiency in tiered storage systems with bottleneck-aware allocation. In: 12th USENIX Conference on File and Storage Technologies, pp. 229–242 (2014)
21. Wang, W., Li, B., Liang, B., Li, J.: Towards multi-resource fair allocation with placement constraints. In: Proceedings of the 2016 ACM SIGMETRICS International Conference on Measurement and Modeling of Computer Science, pp. 415–416. ACM, Antibes Juan-les-Pins (2016)
22. Zahedi, S., Le, B.: REF: resource elasticity fairness with sharing incentives for multiprocessors. ACM SIGPLAN Not. **49**(4), 145–160 (2014)
23. Zhang, Xuejie, Li, Jie, Li, Guibing, Li, Weidong: Generalized asset fairness mechanism for multi-resource fair allocation mechanism with two different types of resources. Cluster Comput. **25**, 3389–3403 (2022). https://doi.org/10.1007/s10586-022-03548-9
24. Zhang, J., Chi, L., Xie, N., Yang, X., Zhang, X., Li, W.: Strategy-proof mechanism for online resource allocation in cloud and edge collaboration. Computing **104**(2), 383–412 (2022)
25. Zhang, J., Xie, N., Zhang, X., Yue, K., Li, W., Kumar, D.: Machine learning based resource allocation of cloud computing in auction. Comput. Mater. Continua **56**(1), 123–135 (2018)

Author Index

Printed in the United States
by Baker & Taylor Publisher Services